WRITING
for the
MEDIA

in Southern Africa

WRITING
for the
MEDIA
in Southern Africa

3RD EDITION

FRANÇOIS NEL

OXFORD
UNIVERSITY PRESS

OXFORD
UNIVERSITY PRESS

Great Clarendon Street, Oxford OX2 6DP

Oxford University Press is a department of the University of Oxford.
It furthers the University's objective of excellence in research, scholarship,
and education by publishing worldwide in

Oxford New York

Auckland Cape Town Dar es Salaam Hong Kong Karachi
Kuala Lumpur Madrid Melbourne Mexico City Nairobi
New Delhi Shanghai Taipei Toronto

with offices in
Argentina Austria Brazil Chile Czech Republic France Greece
Guatemala Hungary Italy Japan Poland Portugal Singapore
South Korea Switzerland Thailand Turkey Ukraine Vietnam

Oxford is a registered trade mark of Oxford University Press
in the UK and in certain other countries

Published in South Africa
by Oxford University Press Southern Africa, Cape Town

Writing for the Media in Southern Africa third edition
ISBN 0 19 578414 6

© Oxford University Press Southern Africa 2001 ·

The moral rights of the author have been asserted
Database right Oxford University Press (maker)

Previously published by International Thomson Publishing
Southern Africa (Pty) Ltd
Second edition by Oxford University Press SA 1998
Third edition 2005

Commissioning editor: Bryony Branch
Editor: Reinette van Rooyen
Proofreader: Marisa Montemarano
Designer: Christopher Davis
Cover design by: Christopher Davis
Cover illustration by: Karen Alschläger
Illustrators: Rassie Erasmus, Bronwen Lusted
Indexer: Jeanne Cope

Published by Oxford University Press Southern Africa
PO Box 12119, N1 City, 7463, Cape Town, South Africa

Set in 10.5 pt on 13 pt Minion by Christopher Davis
Reproduction by The Image Bureau
Cover reproduction by Castle Graphics
Imagesetting by Castle Graphics
Printed and bound by ABC Press, Cape Town

Contents

Foreword

"I want to be part of the South African growing communication industry which needs [the] right people with [the] right qualifications. I have[a] passion for [the] media and think I have a lot to offer in the industry. I want to be in the industry to explore my talents in as many ways as possible. I am also fascinated by the industry itself."

The young, aspirant journalist I'm quoting would be far more specific about why he wants to be a journalist if he had some practical experience or, and perhaps in addition to that vital experiential period, had read *Writing for the Media*. If he had listed *Writing for the Media* on his application form as a book he had recently read or been assigned in class I would feel a little more confident he knew what he was letting himself in for in applying for an entry position in the newsroom. Perhaps we would also be able to have a discussion on the role of the media that goes deeper than "to inform, entertain and educate".

Another more jaded part of me wishes that some news editors and news managers would also pick up a copy of *Writing for the Media* and, casually flipping through its pages, be reminded of what the media is all about. Maybe they could even be jogged into doing something new and better in chasing the story. Lifelong learning should be more than a skills development jargon phrase from the Department of Education and more part of our lives, however pressured they may be in the deadline world of media.

One of the things I believe we should be doing as a nation is finding ways to improve everyone's knowledge of how the media functions, what it really is and why it is important for democracy. *Writing for the Media* explores this connection. In addition, despite the specific reference to *writing* in the title, *Writing for the Media* is about all aspects of media: news gathering, accuracy, ethics and audiences. It is a quality addition to the pitifully small group of South African media textbooks local trainers and practitioners currently have to draw on.

The media is global. As independent media in a fragile and evolving democracy we struggle with the pressures inherent in our own South African situation, and we argue over how to define a good journalist and what the minimum standards for competency should be. Yet, we need to keep our eyes open for best practices and good ideas from elsewhere. Author François Nel's experience of working and teaching in and outside of South Africa is evident. He approaches the media from a South African perspective but avoids parochialism.

At the same time, this edition also attempts to expand our ability to communicate media concepts interculturally. And, as good journalism should be, it is also filled with "real" stories from a variety of different sources as well as the accounts of "real experts" – a sure-hook for the television generation.

I hope this new edition makes its way into the hands of every "wannabe", every media department, and every public library in South Africa. It will make a great contribution to the survival and development of quality in South African journalism and media.

Paddi Clay, Head of Programme, Johnnic Pearson Journalism Training, Johnnic Communications

Preface

When South Africa's print, broadcast and online media editors were asked in 2002 about the abilities of junior reporters, there was consensus: too many were not adequately equipped for their jobs.

Yes, there was a need for journalists and would-be journalists to hone their basic reporting and language skills. But, the editors said, there were other gaps, too. Many younger journalists (the South African National Editors Forum-commissioned study focused on those with three to five years of experience) lacked an adequate understanding of media ethics and media law. They lacked conceptual skills. They lacked life skills.

Key amongst the solutions, editors later agreed, was education and training. There needed to be more learning, certainly. But this also needed to be different in many ways. Educators needed to consider the challenges of life, work and the role of the media in an increasingly complex and competitive environment influenced, amongst others, by political shifts, globalisation, digitisation and changes in media ownership.

It is with the findings of that report in mind – as well the many discussions I had while participating in related events before and afterward – that I set to work on the third edition of this text.

To my generous and talented contributors – Mzilikazi wa Afrika, Les Aupiais, Elizabeth Barratt, Denis Beckett, Mike Behr, Prof Guy Berger, Marcus Brewster, Matthew Buckland, Paddi Clay, Marilyn de Villiers, Alex Eliseev, Jennie Fourie, Harold Gess, Sue Hillyard, Sandeep Junnarkar, Prof Francis Kasoma, Ernst Kotzé, Steve Smith, Rory McCarthy, Charles Mogale, Gilbert Mokwatedi, Lize Odendal, Franz Krüger, Prof Lizette Rabe, Truia Ralph, Elmari Rautenbach, Prof Helge Rønning, Kerry Swift, Jonathan Shapiro, Herman Wasserman, Stephen Wrottesley, Andrea Weiss – and the other students, writers, editors and educators whose questions, advice and work have guided me, thank you. Special thanks, too, to Pierre Antoine. And to the editorial team at Oxford University Press.

Readers will find supporting material – Web links, interviews with leading journalists and more – at http://www.forthemedia.net. There is also the opportunity to give feedback by either completing a short questionnaire or sending an e-mail to forthemedia@iafrica.com.

François Nel

Why the media matters

Introduction

When researchers began comparing studies of the world's oldest civilisations, they discovered a fascinating thing. From the inhabitants of ancient Greece to the remote societies in Outer Mongolia, people shared the same appetite for news. "The first questions Mongols put to each other when they meet is invariably the same," an anthropologist noted in 1921. They ask: "'What's new?' And [then] each of [them] begins to pour out his whole supply of the news" (Maiskii, 1921). Even the same basic definition of what constitutes news remained constant over time. "Humans have exchanged a similar mix of news ... throughout history and across cultures," wrote media historian Mitchell Stephens (1997:27). In fact, they even looked for similar qualities in the messengers they picked to gather and deliver the news: they singled out those who could run swiftly over the next horizon, accurately gather the information, and compellingly retell it (Kovach and Rosensthiel, 2001:9).

How can these consistencies be explained? The answer, scholars have concluded, is that **news** fulfils a basic human instinct – the need to know what is happening beyond our own direct experience (Molotch and Lester, 1974). Being aware of events we cannot witness ourselves gives us a sense of security, control, and confidence (Kovach and Rosensthiel, 2001:9).

When the flow of news is hindered, historian Mitchell Stephens points out, "a darkness falls" and "we grow anxious. Our hut, apartment, village or city becomes a 'sorry' place" (1997:12). The world becomes, as it were, too quiet. We feel alone. South Africa's anti-apartheid hero Nelson Mandela knows that feeling all too well. For much of the 27 years

KEY CONCEPTS

News in society; information gatekeeper; the role of the press in a democracy; media freedom; gatekeeping; journalism in the Internet age; responsible journalism.

Definition

What is the origin of the word "news"?

The original sense of **news** [Zu. izindaba / Xh. iindaba / Afr. nuus*] was "new things"; this is long obsolete. Since the 15th century it has been used to mean "tidings, the report of recent events, new occurrences as a subject or report or talk."

The adjective **new** goes back to Old English. Source: http://www.askoxford.com

he spent in jail, he and his comrades were locked up on Robben Island, cut off from the outside world. He recalled how he yearned for news during those long years behind bars. "Newspapers were more valuable to political prisoners than gold or diamonds, more hungered for than food or tobacco; they were the most precious contraband on Robben Island," he wrote in his autobiography (1994:492). "We were not allowed any news at all, and we craved it."

Stephens calls that craving "a hunger for awareness" (1997:12).

We need news to live our lives. It helps us to distinguish between threats and opportunities, enemies and friends. News helps us orientate ourselves, and it helps us connect with others. If the mass media are the system that societies generate to supply this news, then journalism is its lifeblood. That is why the character of the news and the quality of the journalism are important: they influence our thoughts, our experiences, our cultures. It certainly is a powerful position to be in. And those who want to write for the media – from inside a newsroom as a journalist, or from the outside as a publicist or source – should recognise that power and be aware of their responsibilities.

*Zulu, Xhosa and Afrikaans translations of some key terms have been included primarily to provide "handles" to help those for whom English is not a first language to grasp the concepts. The alternatives provided are not intended to be direct translations. Also, where no common alternatives to English-language journalism jargon are available, translations have been omitted. Practical considerations have meant that we have not been able to include translations in other official South African languages.

LEARNING GOALS

At the end of this chapter, you should be able to:

1 Discuss the assumptions we make about the mass media.
2 Understand the basic role of news in society.
3 Recognise the importance of free media in a modern democracy.
4 Identify the key knowledge and skills needed to be a responsible journalist.

EXERCISE *Mass media in your life*

When it comes to the media, we are typically mass consumers. What about you? Complete the brief questionnaire below. Then, as you read this introductory chapter (and the others that follow), think about how you use the mass media – what, why, and how often. But also think about how the media influences your life, and what your contribution will be to the experiences of others when you write for the media.

Media form	Minutes spent per day	Types of use (Information, social interaction, entertainment, etc.)
Popular books (excluding textbooks)		
Textbooks		
Magazines		
Newspapers		
Cinema		
Radio		
Recording industry products (music CDs, MP3, etc.)		
Television		
Computer information services (CD-ROMs, Internet, etc.)		
TOTAL TIME		

How do you compare? A 2004 study by the French company, Eurodata TV, based on statistics from 72 countries or regions, 2.5 billion viewers and more than 600 channels, showed that that the average television viewing time worldwide is three hours and 39 minutes per person, per day (Indian-television.com, 2004). Among the nations surveyed, the Japanese remain the world's top TV watchers, with a viewing time of four hours and 29 minutes, just ahead of the United States, where the average person spent four hours and 25 minutes in front of the box. In South Africa, the only African country researched, the TV viewing time was two hours and 59 minutes (Anon, 2004).

These results are not too dissimilar to research done by Statistics South Africa in 2001, which showed urban men and women spend almost two and half hours per day reading books, magazines and newspapers, as well as listening to the radio and watching television or videos. Adults between the ages of 20–39 spent about 35 minutes a day "doing nothing", while those aged 40–59 spent 49 minutes each day idling (Chobokane and Budlender, 2002/04).

Are there certain media you seldom or never use? Do you avoid certain media by choice, or is it because access is costly, in terms of time or money? What are the personal and political implications of your answer?

What are some of the assumptions made about the mass media?

The mass media are pervasive, particularly in urban life. Every morning millions of people wake up to the radio. Political candidates spend most of their campaigns and many thousands, even millions, of rands on advertising to woo voters. Modern economies depend on advertising to create mass markets. It is not surprising, then, that every aspect of the media industry – from regulation, ownership, production, distribution to the staffing and the content – is considered to be of public interest. The reason for this, as media scholar Denis McQuail has pointed out (1994:1), is that there are several basic assumptions about the media:

A power resource

The media has the potential to influence, control and stimulate progress and change in society. Can you imagine trying to conduct a national election without relying on the mass media to inform voters of the event, the process and the policies of the participants? Or spreading awareness of the dangers of driving without a seatbelt?

An arena for important events

The media remain the stage where national and international matters are played out. When FIFA, the world soccer governing body, announced the host nation for the 2010 Soccer World Cup, millions of soccer enthusiasts around the globe were glued to their radios, televisions and **Internet**-connected computer screens. As FIFA president Sepp Blatter stepped up to the podium in Geneva, Switzerland, and announced, "The 2010 World Cup will be organised by South Africa," crowds simultaneously reacted from Cape Town to Cairo, and beyond.

Just as it has the potential to place matters at the centre of debate, the media can also ignore issues, or emphasise others that could steer debate in particular directions.

Definition

Internet. A complex web of thousands of academic, government, commercial, and private computer sites that are linked through telephone lines. First created in the 1960s when the US government saw the need for an emergency communication system, the Internet was popularised with the introduction of the graphic World Wide Web interface in 1994.

A major source of definitions

Punk. Goth. Grunge. Hip-hop. Just walk around the streets of any major city in South Africa and you're likely to encounter devotees of some – if not all – of these trends. A concert tour to the UK by the US band, the Ramones, was credited for igniting the punk scene in London in the late 1970s. But what fuelled the upsurge of punk music in Durban, a city largely cut off from the world behind the barriers of apartheid, if not the media? Now when bands such as Limp Bizkit tour South Africa, their concerts are packed with fans that look the part (baseball caps worn backwards, arms festooned with tattoos) and who can mouth the lyrics

("If I say f*** three more times, that's 46 f***s in this f****ed-up rhyme").

Other definitions of identities and social realities provided by the media are more subtle. But whatever the case, it is agreed that the media is a place where the changing cultures and values of society are being displayed, constructed and communicated.

A platform to fame – and disgrace

The media is where instant heroes and villains are made. Think of the reality television programmes such as *Big Brother*, which have turned scores of ordinary people around the world into celebrities. On the other hand, intense and widespread media coverage of the corruption charges against politicians Tony Yengeni and Allan Boesak has ensured that these once-admired men remain on the periphery of public life.

A yardstick for deciding what is normal

Quick, complete this sentence: "The most beautiful person in the world is …"

So, did you pick actresses Halle Berry or Charlize Theron? Or perhaps you fancy footballer David Beckham, hip-hop musician Andre 3000, or actor Brad Pitt? It would not be too surprising if you chose any of these celebrities; all of whom have appeared on *People* magazine's annual "50 Most Beautiful People in the World" list.

It is commonly accepted that media are the source of an ordered and public meaning system, which provides benchmarks for what is **normal** (and what is "beautiful"). The media also make comparisons and draw attention to deviations from the public version of normality.

A focal point for our free time

The media are the single largest focus of leisure-time activity and means of entertainment. South Africans, for example, have said that watching television or a video is their favourite way to spend their time relaxing – and they spend more time on that than any single other activity, other than sleeping and working (Chobokoane and Budlender, 2002:04).

A key role in politics – democratic and undemocratic, national and international

"A critical, independent and investigative press is the lifeblood of any democracy," said South Africa's first democratically-elected President Nelson Mandela, echoing the sentiments of the country's Bill of Rights. "It is only a free press that can temper the appetite of any government to amass power at the expense of the citizens." By contrast, the leader of neighbouring Zimbabwe, Robert Mugabe, went to great lengths to stifle critical media voices. He approved tough anti-press laws empowering the government to close down newspapers, restrict access to government documents and imprison journalists for publishing falsehoods. And he has used them. (Also see p. 339 in Chapter 13.)

What is the role of the media in a democratic society?

On 25 July 2000 President Thabo Mbeki stepped up to the podium to accept the Pretoria Press Club's Newsmaker of the Year Award. Receiving an award, the President said, is always nice. "But," he added, "much more than Thabo Mbeki stands before you tonight, I accept this award, indeed, on behalf of all South Africans who are struggling to create a new and just society. It is their efforts which no doubt led me to catch your eye in 1999 as a newsmaker. And it is their efforts, which will ensure that this country grows in strength, setbacks notwithstanding, and takes its place where it belongs in the world." The efforts of the media, the President said, could play an important part in transforming the society in which we live.

KEY CONCEPTS

Why are news media sometimes referred to as *the* press [Zu. ezamaphephandaba / Xh. amaphephandaba / Afr. pers]?

The word *press* is sometimes used to refer to news journalists and their products (including the electronic news media, such as radio, television and online publications) to distinguish them from other, more entertainment-oriented mass media and those who work for such types of mass media. For that reason, reporters for *ThisDay* newspaper may be called "the press", while it is unlikely that the term would be used to refer to writers for *House and Leisure* magazine.

That's right, most media practitioners and scholars would say, the media *can* contribute to social development. They can, as McQuail summarised (1994:86), disseminate technical know-how, and promote

KEY CONCEPTS

Gatekeeper (of information) [Zu. umlindimasango / Xh. umhluzi-zindaba / Afr. hekwag]: A term developed in the 1950s to describe people who control the flow of information. A newspaper editor, who selects some stories and discards others, acts as a gatekeeper. On the other hand, public relations practitioners, who often control the flow of information from news sources, are also gatekeepers. Can you think of other information gatekeepers?

consumer demand. The media can also encourage individual change and mobility. And, of course, they can help spread democracy by supporting the electoral process.

The media as gatekeepers

But answering the question "How should they go about fulfilling this role?" is much trickier – and raises further questions. Shouldn't the media organisations themselves (and, by extension, the journalists and editors) be free to define their own role? But what about the audiences without whom all efforts would be in vain? What about the rights of media owners and investors? Wouldn't it also be reasonable to give a say to advertisers on whose revenues the survival of most media depends? What about civil society groups, such as religious organisations, who aim to safeguard the moral welfare of the community? And what part should the government play through legislation and political pressure? After all, are they not ultimately responsible for the general well-being of the public?

It is clear, then, that in their role as mass communicators, the media are, as it were, mediators or gatekeepers between, on the one hand, the would-be "advocates" in society with messages to send (such as President Mbeki) and, on the other hand, the public seeking to fulfil their information and communication needs. Of course, not all of these demands and pressures are constraining. Sometimes, the various forces balance each other out, such as when employee unions challenge pres-

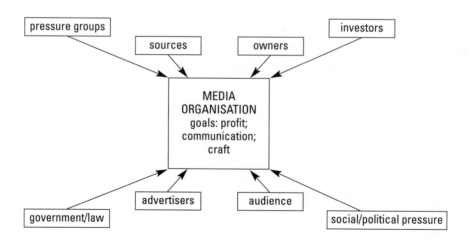

Figure 1 The media organisation operating in a field of social forces. *Source: McQuail, D. and Windahl, S. 1993. Communication models for the study of mass communication. New York: Longman, p. 161.*

sures from investors. At other times, the effects of some pressure groups on media organisations can be very liberating. For example, in South Africa and other **democracies** (some) government policies typically protect the freedom of the media. Whatever the results, balancing these often competing and sometime overlapping pressures is clearly a challenge. Perhaps pressure is a measure of relevance, suggests McQuail (1994:191): "Lack of external pressure would probably indicate social marginality, or insignificance". If no one is talking about the media – and criticising them – then they are probably not doing their jobs well.

If the freedom of the press and other media is typically protected in the legal framework of democratic states, should there not be some consensus on what role they should play? Probably, but even scholars don't have simple, clear-cut suggestions, says Prof Helge Rønning of the Department of Media and Communication at the University of Oslo in Finland. "When we talk about what constitutes a democracy, most of us would mention that one of the cornerstones of a democratic society is the existence of free media. It is therefore remarkable that the role of the media has been treated relatively scantily in democratic theory," he told a forum of editors and trainers who were grappling with how to tackle the challenges of transforming the South African media following the demise of apartheid (2000).

Rønning also pointed out that amongst those who have contributed to the debate is Graham Murdock (1992), who has identified the implications of the media for the democratic process by making references to the different dimensions of what constitutes citizenship. Murdock identifies three important ways in which the communication media serve in the development of citizens' rights:

Firstly, in order for people to be able to exercise their full rights as citizens, they must have access to information on what their rights are. They will also need advice on how they are to pursue these rights effectively. In effect, the media are expected to be a **specialist advisor**.

Secondly, citizens must have access to the broadest possible range of information, interpretation and debate on areas that involve public political choices. Not only should citizens be able to hear a wide range of media voices – but the media should be their **loudspeaker**, allowing them to talk back. Yes, they should be able to be critical. But more than that, they should also have the opportunity to propose alternative models for development. And they should be able to base these proposals on knowledge of events in the local, national and international scene.

And, thirdly, people must be able to recognise themselves and their aspirations, their cultures and lifestyles, in the range of representations on offer in the media. In this respect, the media should act as a **mirror**. Audiences should also be able to contribute to developing and expanding the images that are reflected.

Definition

Democracy. [Zu. ukubusa ngentando yeningi / Xh. ulawulo ngentando yabantu / Afr. demokrasie] 1. a government by the whole population, usu. though elected representatives. a. state so governed. 2. classless and tolerant society. [Greek *demotratia* rule of the people]

Definition

A **weblog**, or **blog**, is a frequently updated website consisting of dated entries arranged in reverse chronological order so the most recent post appears first. Typically, weblogs are published by individuals and their style is personal and informal. Weblogs first appeared in the mid-1990s, becoming popular as simple and free publishing tools became available towards the turn of the century. Since anybody with a net connection can publish their own weblog, there is great variety in the quality, content, and ambition of weblogs, and a weblog may have anywhere from a handful to tens of thousands of daily readers (Walker, 2003). Visit the Globe of Blogs at http://www.globeofblogs. com/ and BlogAfrica at http://allafrica.com/afdb/ blogs/ for listings of Africa-related weblogs.

Media freedom and the law

How relevant are laws protecting media freedom at the beginning of the twenty-first century?

Information is so plentiful, and often freely available on the Internet. Do citizens need the media to supply information about their rights, or to amplify their voices in the public domain? Perhaps entrenching the rights of the press and other media in a country's constitution is an arte-fact of a more restricted and technologically poorer era? Certainly, as Nel (2003), Kovach and Rosensthiel (2001:23) and others have pointed out, the notion of the press as a gatekeeper – deciding what information the public should know and what it should not – no longer strictly defines journalism's role. If SABC News decides not to broadcast some-thing, at least one of the countless talk radio hosts or websites will. There are many examples. The most gripping account of the Iraq con-flict came from a web diarist known as the Baghdad Blogger. "It was the great irony of the war," wrote Rory McCarthy (2003), a correspondent for the *Guardian* newspaper. "While the world's leading newspapers and television networks poured millions of pounds into their coverage of the war in Iraq, it was the Internet musings of a witty young Iraqi living

---

E**X**ERCISE *Freedom of information and expression as a basic human right*

On 10 December 1948, the General Assembly of the United Nations adopted and proclaimed the Universal Declaration of Human Rights. **Article 19** reads: "Everyone has the right to freedom of opinion and expression; this right includes freedom to hold opinions without interference and to seek, receive and impart information and ideas through any media and regardless of frontiers." These sentiments are derived from the First Amendment of the constitution of the United States, which reads: "Congress shall make no law respecting an establishment of religion, or prohibiting the free exercise thereof; or abridging the freedom of speech, or of the press; or the right of the people peaceably to assemble, and to petition the government for a redress of grievances."

These sentiments have now become entrenched in the legal frameworks of newer democratic soci-eties, such as South Africa where Chapter 2 of the Constitution of the Republic of South Africa (Act 108 of 1996) outlines the Bill of Rights, which expresses the right to freedom of expression as:

16. (1) Everyone has the right to freedom of expres-sion, which includes:
a. freedom of the press and other media;
b. freedom to receive or impart information or ideas;
c. freedom of artistic creativity; and
d. academic freedom and freedom of scientific research.

16. (2) The right in subsection (1) does not extend to
a. propaganda for war;
b. incitement of imminent violence; or
c. advocacy of hatred that is based on race, ethnic-ity, gender or religion, and that constitutes incite-ment to cause harm.

The full text of the Constitution is available at http://www.gov.za/constitution/1996/96cons.htm Also see the organisation, Article 19, named after the section, at http://www.article19.org. The group works worldwide to combat censorship by promot-ing freedom of expression and access to official information.

in a two-storey house in a Baghdad suburb that scooped them all to deliver the most compelling description of life during the war." See p. 16 for more on the Baghdad Blogger.

When South African President Thabo Mbeki felt he was not able to get his message across to the public via the media, he scaled down his press briefings and decided instead to publish a weekly "Letter from the President" on the website of his political party, the African National Congress.

"This rise of the Internet and the coming of broadband, however, do not mean, as some have suggested, that the concept of applying judgement to the news – of trying to decide what people need and want to know to self-govern – is obsolete. They make the need all the greater," say authors Bill Kovach and Tom Rosensthiel (2001:24). To support this view, they refer to comments by John Seeley Brown, formerly the director of Xerox Parc, a highly-regarded think tank in America's Silicon Valley. Seeley Brown suggests that rather than rendering the public service notion of journalism outdated, technology has instead changed how journalists fulfil it. "What we need in the new economy and the new communications culture is sense making," he says (ibid). "We have a desperate need to get some stable points in an increasingly crazy world." This means that journalists need "the ability to look at things from multiple points of view and the ability to get to the core of matters" (ibid).

New journalists may not have primary control of deciding what the public should or should not know. Instead, their role is to help audiences make sense of it. "This does not mean simply adding interpretation or analysis to news reporting," say Kovach and Rosensthiel (ibid). "The first task of the new journalist/sense maker, rather, is to verify what information is reliable and then order it so people can grasp it efficiently."

In an era when almost anyone can be a reporter or commentator on the Web "you move to a two-way journalism," Seeley Brown suggests (ibid). The journalist becomes a "forum leader", or a mediator rather than an expert subscriber. The audience become not consumers, but "pro-sumers," a hybrid of consumer and producer.

If citizens have a problem with the news, they know whom to e-mail to correct the record (newspapers increasingly print e-mail addresses and websites including authors' names in hypertext, making it simple to contact writers, editors, and publishers). The interaction of the audience becomes an integral part of the story as it evolves. A column by Guy Berger for *The Media Online* in 2004 is a good example. Some of those named in the piece, titled "Canned journalism", had points to pursue and promptly sent e-mails to Berger, who ended up including those, along

---

See "pro-sumers" in action
Follow links to Guy Berger's column for *The Media Online* at http://www.themedia.co.za. The original piece, titled "Canned journalism: When media vleis meets paparazzi reporting," was published on 23 March 2004, and the follow-up, titled "Media make their X for 10," appeared on 15 April 2004. Berger is head of Journalism and Media Studies at Rhodes University and a key member of the South African National Editors Forum (Sanef).

with his responses, in the following edition of his column.

This kind of high-tech interaction is a journalism that resembles conversation, much like the original journalism occurring in the city squares of ancient Greece and elsewhere. "Seen in this light, journalism's function is not fundamentally changed by the digital age," say Kovach and Rosensthiel (2001:25). "The techniques may be different, but the underlying principles are the same. The journalist is first engaged in verification." It is that commitment to truth-telling that, in my view, separates a journalist from other types of media writing, such as advertising copywriters or film scriptwriters.

One theme runs throughout the discussion about the media's role: alternatives. To fulfil their function in a democracy, the media are responsible for providing a wide range of accurate information that offers alternative perspectives. In practice, then, this implies that audiences (citizens, if you will) be served by various media owners, who deliver diverse media products that are produced by a diverse group of competent media workers, drawing on reliable and diverse sources, while giving voice to diverse points of view. Only then will citizens have the freedom of information that is their right.

What does it take to be a responsible journalist?

In the early 19th century, the term *journalist* [Zu. intatheli / Xh. intatheli / Afr. joernalis] simply meant someone who kept a journal or who wrote for journals, such as Charles Dickens in his early career, but has come to mean a writer or editor who creates articles or reports as a profession for broadcast or publication in mass media such as newspapers, television, radio, magazines, documentary film and the Internet. Regardless of medium, the term journalist now carries a connotation or expectation of professionalism in reporting, with consideration for truth and ethics.

Arguably, then, the most important distinction between journalists and other media writers is, as we have noted, a commitment to serve the public good above all. This, as we'll discuss at greater length later in this book, is more complex than it may seem at first. For now, though, it is important to note the intent. And much like a doctor needs extensive training and frequent updating of her knowledge to fulfil her aspiration to save lives, a journalist needs more than good intentions to make good on a commitment to truth-telling. She needs knowledge and skills. Core amongst them is the ability to systematically gather, analyse and communicate information, which is the focus of the rest of this book. So, if writing **responsibly** for the media is what you want to do, read on.

Definition

Responsible [Zu.–nesibopho / Xh. –thembelikele(yo) / Afr. verantwoordelik]
1. (often foll. by *to, for*) liable to be called to account (to a person or for a thing).
2. morally accountable for one's actions; capable of rational conduct. 3. of good credit, position, or repute; respectable; evidently trustworthy. 4. (often foll. by *for*) being the primary cause.
5. involving responsibility.

What are key challenges for new journalists? US researchers asked newsroom supervisors and journalism educators how important they thought each of the following areas were in preparing people to enter journalism (Medsger, 1996:25). While the two different groups may have slightly different priorities, there is general consensus on what key skills are – the ability to systematically gather, critically analyse, and communicate information clearly and accurately.

Ranking by newsroom supervisors	Importance	Knowledge and skills required for a career in journalism	Ranking by journalism educators	Importance
1	98%	Basic news gathering skills	2	95%
2	97%	Clear writing skills	2	95%
3	96%	Understanding that accuracy and truthfulness are essential in journalism	4	92%
4	95%	Interviewing skills	5	89%
4	95%	Interviewing skills	5	89%
5	94%	Analysing information and ideas	1	96%
6	85%	Ability to organise complex stories with clarity and grace	10	78%
7	82%	Writing on deadline	10	78%
8	79%	Ready to enter the profession as competent beginning journalist	8	83%
9	78%	Well-informed about current events	8	83%
10	77%	Commitment to First Amendment values	6	85%
10	77%	Ability to recognise holes in coverage	12	76%
12	76%	Ability to develop story ideas on their own	15	68%
13	73%	Awareness of the responsibility to provide information people need to be informed citizens	7	84%
14	72%	Ability to converse effectively with sources from a wide variety of backgrounds	13	73%
15	67%	Enthusiastic commitment to journalism	14	70%
16	67%	Developing and covering a beat	19	53%
17	58%	Awareness that a journalist needs to be sensitive	17	61%
17	55%	Using computers as research and communication tools	14	70%
19	51%	Introduction to use of photos, design and graphics in storytelling	18	55%
20	49%	Experience in using government access laws	21	50%
21	48%	Knowledge of press law	16	66%
23	31%	Well-informed about changes taking place in journalism	19	53%
24	15%	Knowledge of the history and evolution of (US) journalism	22	36%
	15%	Familiar with contemporary critiques of journalism	23	35%

*In 1791, the Constitution of the United States was amended to include a Bill of Rights. The first of these amendments was to guarantee, amongst others, that Congress would not make any laws limiting the freedom of speech, or of the press. These sentiments are echoed in Chapter 2 of the Constitution of the Republic of South Africa.

In this chapter, you learned that:

- Sharing news has been an important part of societies throughout history and across cultures and that it fills our hunger for awareness.
- The mass media – especially television – are pervasive in the lives of people in modern societies.
- Scholars have devised models to help explain the mass media.
- The media's powerful role in society is typically protected by the laws of democratic states.
- The advent of new information and communication technologies – particularly the Internet – has reduced the media's traditional gatekeeping function considerably and provided a platform for a wide range of independent voices.
- Journalism's key role in a digital age is not only to provide information, but to verify the facts and help audiences make sense of what is going on.
- A commitment to truth-telling is what distinguishes journalism from other forms of media writing.
- Being a responsible journalist means mastering the knowledge and skills required to do the job – and being dedicated to the best interest of the public.

Putting your learning to work

ACTIVITY The role of writing in media careers

Writing well is an important skill for media workers. But how much of a typical day's work involves writing? Approach someone who works in the area of the media that you hope to enter and ask to discuss a normal day's work. Then write a brief report on the role of writing in that person's job.

How do you pick a media person? Your instructor may be able to help you, but you can also continue on your own:

- For journalists, check local newspapers and magazines for the bylines of people who write about subjects that particularly interest you. Do the same when watching television news or listening to the radio.
- If you are interested in advertising, check with the advertising manager at a local radio station or newspaper. Also, check the Yellow Pages or the Internet for advertising agencies.
- If you are keen on a career in public relations, enquire at large companies, hospitals, colleges or large government agencies for the name of a public relations practitioner.

Most media workers are accommodating when students ask about their work. Usually, arranging a time to meet a person should not be a problem. Follow these steps:

- Call the media person at work.
- Introduce yourself as a student in a media studies course.
- Explain that you would like to visit the media person at work and discuss the role of writing in the mass media. You may want to say that you are interested in how much of a typical day is spent writing, what form the finished work takes, and how writing fits into the product that organisation produces.
- Explain that you will be writing a report for class on what you learn.
- Say that you would be interested in what the person writes in the course of a typical day.
- Stress that your visit will require no more than 15 minutes (and stick to that).
- If the person agrees, set a time to get together.
- Be sure to coordinate with your classmates so that more than one student doesn't call the same person.

The Baghdad Blogger: 'Salam's Story'

The most gripping account of the first weeks of the Iraq conflict in 2002 came from a web diarist known as the Baghdad Blogger. But no one knew his identity – or even if he existed. Apart from a select group of trusted friends, they still don't. Outside the country, many didn't even believe that the man who wrote under the [pen] name Salam Pax truly existed. It was the great irony of the war. While the world's leading newspapers and television networks poured millions of pounds into their coverage of the war in Iraq, it was the Internet musings of a witty young Iraqi living in a two-storey house in a Baghdad suburb that scooped them all to deliver the most compelling description of life during the war.

As with so much in Iraq, it was never meant to be like this. In June 2002, Salam (this much of his name, at least, is real) was a recently graduated architect, aged 29, living at home with his parents and brother in Baghdad. His best friend was Raed, 25, a Palestinian-Jordanian he had met while studying architecture, who was taking a master's degree in Jordan. Raed was at best an infrequent e-mail correspondent and so Salam started writing up his news from home on a weblog, a site on the Internet where he could post his scribblings as often as he liked for his friend to read. He called it: Where is Raed?

No one else bothered to look at it. "The first two months were just: that girl got married, I had the flu, he had I don't know what. Stupid stuff," says Salam. "I never thought there would be this much of a fuss about the whole thing."

Soon, however, he began to search out other "bloggers" posting on the Internet. Few were writing in English from the Arab world, and those that did wrote in heavily religious overtones. That was enough to encourage Salam to put his head above the parapet and one day he identified himself on a bloggers' website as an Iraqi. "I was saying, 'Come on, look, the Arabs here: sex, alcohol, belly dancers, TV shows, where are they?' All you saw was people talking about God and Allah. There was nothing about what was happening here."

As he wrote in more detail, he began to touch more often on the unspoken hardships of life in Iraq under the paranoid regime of Saddam Hussein. He could hardly have taken a greater risk if he had tried. More than 200 000 people went missing under Saddam, many for far lesser crimes than the open criticism of the regime that Salam voiced in his writings. Now that the regime has fallen, human rights workers are tripping over mass graves in Iraq every few days as they trawl through the legacy of 23 years of unimaginable brutality and persecution.

Like all Iraqis, Salam was familiar with the dangers. At least four of his relatives had gone missing. In the past year, for no apparent reason, one of his friends was summarily executed, shot in the head as he sat in his car, and two others were arrested; one was later freed and another, a close friend, has never returned.

Not only had Salam criticised the regime, he had written openly about the fact that he is gay. It was a frank admission in a repressive dictatorship and one that, even in the new, post-war Iraq, which at heart is still a conservative, Islamic society, represents a significant risk. And so he continues to guard his identity. "I am not going to be the first one to carry the flag. I hide behind computer screens," he says.

This is an edited version of a story by Roy McCarthy for The Guardian. *Read the complete story at: http://www.guardian.co.uk/Iraq/Story/0,2763,966819,00.html. Used with permission.*

Salam Pax's weblog "Where's Raed?" is available at: http://dear_raed.blogspot.com/. Though power and telephone lines went out in Baghdad ten days into the war, Pax continued to document his experiences, which have been published as a book: Pax, S. 2003. Salam Pax: The Baghdad Blog, London: The Guardian.

What do you think Salam Pax's story, which shows the inability of gatekeepers in the media and outside to control the flow of information, means for journalists, public relations people, media regulators – and audiences?

Bibliography

Ancn. 2004. The worldwide consumption of television increased by 15 minutes in 2003. [Online] Barcelona 2004, an international summit of broadcasting regulatory authorities made up of broadcasters, producers, viewers and industry experts. Available at: http://www.audiovisualcat.net/forumbcn2004/eng/news/news_150404.htm [Accessed: 30 May 2004]

Chobokoane, N. and Budlender, D. 2002/04. Activities over time: further analysis of the time use survey. [Online] Statistics South Africa. Available at: http://www.statssa.gov.za/publications/TechPaperActivitiesTime/TechPaperActivitiesTime.pdf [Accessed: 24 May 2004]

Kovach, B. and Rosensthiel, T. 2001. *The elements of journalism; what newspeople should know and the public should expect.* New York: Crown.

Maiskii, I. 1921. Sovremennaia Mongoliia. In Stephens, M. 1997. *A history of news.* Fort Worth: Harcourt Brace. p. 9.

Mandela, N. 1994. *Long walk to freedom.* London: Abacus.

McCarthy, R. 2003. Salam's story. [Online] London: *The Guardian.* 30 May 2003. Available at: http://www.guardian.co.uk/Iraq/Story/0,2763,966819,00.html [Accessed: 27 May 2004] Used with permission.

McQuail, D. 1987. *Mass Communication theory: an introduction.* 2nd ed. London: Sage.

McQuail, D. 1994. *Mass Communication theory: an introduction.* 3rd ed. London: Sage.

McQuail, D. and Windahl, S. 1993. *Communication models for the study of mass communication.* New York: Longman.

Medsger, B. 1996. Wings of change; challenges confronting journalism education. Arlington, V.A.: Freedom Forum.

Molotch, H. and Lester, M. 1974. News as purposive behaviour: on the strategic use of routine events, accidents and scandals. *American Sociological Review,* 39 (February 1974): 101-112.

Murdock, G. 1992. Citizens, consumers and public culture. In Skovmand, M. and Schroder, K.C. (eds), 1992. *Media cultures – reappraising transitional media.* London: Routledge.

Nel, F. 2003. Power – who has it, who should get it? *Rhodes University Journalism Review,* 22: 14-16, Summer 2003.

Pope Paul II, 2000. *Authentic Christians and excellent journalists.* [Online] Address to media professionals on 4 June 2000. Vatican. Available at: http://www.ewtn.com/library/PAPALDOC/JJP2JOUR.HTM [Accessed: 20 May 2004]

Rønning, H. 2000. The role of media in a democracy. Training for media transformation: a colloquium for South African journalists, media trainers and media scholars. October 2000. Johannesburg: South African National Editors Forum.

United Nations. 1948. Universal Declaration of Human Rights. [Online]. Available at: http://www.un.org/Overview/rights.html [Accessed: 20 May 2004]

Stephens, M. 1997. *A history of news.* Fort Worth, Tx: Harcourt Brace.

Walker, J. 2003. [Online]. Final version of weblog definition. Jill/txt (Jill Walker's weblog). Available at: http://huminf.uib.no/~jill/ June 28, 2003. [Accessed: 27 May 2004]

2 Inside the newsroom

Introduction

When the call comes, Susan Purén knows she has to move fast if she wants to make the TV documentary on the effects of post-traumatic stress disorder. She has spent months tracking down China Keitetsi, a Ugandan child soldier who had fled to South Africa, but eventually found her way to Denmark. And Purén had waited even longer for her to agree to speak on camera. Then one day, she told a magazine journalist, the phone rang: "Susan, it's China. Do you still want to do the story?" She does. As soon as it can be arranged, she heads to Copenhagen to film a documentary for MNet's flagship magazine programme *Carte Blanche*. Purén's first question to the young woman, who as a nine-year-old had been enlisted to help fight in the Ugandan National Resistance Army, is this: "How many people have you killed in your life?". The reply: "I try to believe it was not me who killed them, but the gun…"

KEY CONCEPTS

Mass media characteristics; audience segmentation and niches; the role of news sources; key positions in the newsroom; the news production process; the importance of deadlines.

"We staked out the property – fully walled off and guarded by a security official – for about 30 minutes before we were spotted," recalls Santosh Beharie, the investigations editor of the *Sowetan Sunday World*. That's when he and photographer Peter Mogaki stepped out and confronted the three men who, as it turned out, were responsible for illegally storing about 50 tons of medical waste, including human tissue. "One never knows what to expect when doing investigations," says Beharie. "It could be both dangerous and exciting."

Although he has a reserved seat in the front row of the *Fairlady* SA Fashion Awards, publicist Marcus Brewster is standing at the back. "One of the golden rules of PR is always sit near the exit," he quips. Brewster is taking notes as the winners' names are called. In a few moments he leaves the hall, discreetly whipping out his cell phone to make a call. Back at the offices of Marcus Brewster Publicity, an account team is on standby to work up a news release and start issuing it through the early hours of the morning. By the time the last party guest has left the gala event, Brewster will have a disc of pictures taken at the awards dinner and fashion show which will be downloaded to his offices so that they can send them to newspapers around the country. Many will make front-page news.

Photojournalist Sue Hillyard is back at Cape Town's Groote Schuur Hospital Emergency Room talking to the nurses, doctors and volunteer staff she has come to know well. It's Saturday night and it's likely to get bloody. It doesn't take long. Soon she's clicking away as another patient is wheeled in. This one still has a knife impaled in his skull. Later, after her film is developed, Hillyard sits down to review her notes and to write captions for the photographic essay, which will run in a magazine.

Purén, Beharie, Mogaki, Brewster and Hillyard all work for different media organisations. While they may not all fit everyone's definition of a journalist, they have much in common. They share the ability to ask probing questions, to absorb and understand complicated background information, and to retell it accurately in clear, simple terms to varied audiences. But if writing for the media is what you want to do, then a key step is to understand how the mass media are defined – and how they typically function.

HOT LINK

You can watch an excerpt from the documentary "China, War Child", which earned the Purén the CNN African Journalist of the Year award, on the *Carte Blanche* Interactive website: http://www.mnet.co.za/CarteBlanche/Display/Display.asp?Id=1792

LEARNING GOALS

At the end of this chapter, you should be able to:

1 Define and discuss the typical characteristics of the mass media.
2 Recognise the key role of technological advancement.
3 Understand how a typical newspaper, and its editorial department in particular, is organised.
4 Know what the primary editorial positions entail.
5 Describe how copy flows through the newsroom.
6 Be familiar with the activities during a typical day in life of a newspaper.

Definition

Media is a plural for the singular noun *medium*. In this book, we will typically use *media* as a short form of the term *mass communication media*.

Towards a definition of mass media

What is a mass medium? The media are considered the "message vehicles" or channels that allow information to circulate and communication to happen. But while the telephone – the channel China Keitetsi used to send her message to Susan Purén – is a medium that is widely used, it is not typically considered a *mass medium*. Instead, books, magazines, newspapers, radio, films, television, and even some Internet sites, movie screens and billboards are considered to be the primary mass media. Researchers (Price, 1997:139) have identified that these mass communication channels or media have a number of things in common: large scale of operation; high levels of industrial activity; formal, centralised organisation; institutional values and practices; mediation of authority; a "standardised" product directed to a mass audience; and the possibility of simultaneous reception of messages by audiences.

Let's look at each one of these media characteristics a little closer.

Large-scale operation

Yes, size matters. We can measure the size – or scale – of media operations in several ways. We could, for example, talk about the large number of media products. South Africa's mass media include over 1 000 newspapers, magazines and specialist publications, hundreds of movie screens, more than 100 radio stations and five television channels (besides the array of channels available via satellite), and scores of Internet news sites.

Scale could also refer to the number of people involved in producing and distributing each product. Or it could refer to the huge amount of information that is processed to turn out each edition. It could also refer to the fact that mass media products typically take a great deal of effort to produce. For example, by the time *Carte Blanche* celebrated their 15th anniversary in September 2003, they had: travelled 3.6 million kilometres, visited 50 countries, interviewed 15 000 people, shot 6.5 million metres of footage, done 2 080 stories, and won 80 awards. Including the anchors and presenters who are the "faces" on the weekly show, there are about 200 people on the *Carte Blanche* team that make that happen.

Increasingly, major media products are part of giant conglomerates; they are a subsidiary or business among a group of businesses under one owner. *Carte Blanche*, for example, is broadcast by the pay TV channel MNet, which is owned in part by Naspers, Africa's largest media company which has extensive operations in over 50 countries on the continent, as well as in Asia and the Mediterranean. Known as Africa's largest media conglomerate, Naspers manages revenues greater than the total annual budgets of many of the countries in which it operates. In fact, its operations are larger than the combined economies of

Swaziland and Mozambique, and just slightly smaller than that of Namibia.

Formal, centralised organisation

The management structure of a modern media organisation is as complex as any other contemporary business. But there are some important differences. Compare, for example, the job of a manager of a motor car manufacturing plant with that of an editor in charge of producing a daily newspaper. A measure of quality in the motorcar factory is that each unit – each car – is made exactly to specifications and that each is identical. By contrast, if a newspaper contained exactly the same content each day, the editor

Figure 2.1 The organisational structure of Naspers, which has media interests in more than 50 countries worldwide.

would be fired. Quality for a newspaper refers to the variety, appropriateness and depth of the reporting, the sparkle of the writing and accuracy of the editing, as well as the impact and appropriateness of the photography. To achieve this on tight deadlines, newsrooms typically have standardised processes that provide a framework for everyone involved – and that is typically achieved by a formal, centralised organisation (see Figure 2.2).

A "standardised" product directed to a mass audience

"Anyone who has ever heard a street seller exhorting passers-by to buy the 'Argie' will know that the *Cape Argus* brand has been burnt into the consciousness of the Western Cape community," writes editor Ivan Flynn in a letter on the company's website (2004). "In fact, the 'Argie' is up there with the other attractions of Cape Town such as the Waterfront and Table Mountain."

Published continuously since 1857, the *Cape Argus* is the country's oldest surviving newspaper, and describes itself as "a family-orientated daily on-day newspaper with a strong community identity, aimed at the needs of readers in Cape Town." In reality, though, the paper doesn't aim to satisfy *all* readers in Cape Town; instead, its contents are calculated to appeal to a very specific group or, as Flynn says, its "target market" – "middle to upper income readers" (Flynn, 2004). That's because most media organisations are commercial enterprises. And what do they value?

They value **profits**. Most large media organsations are answerable to shareholders, who expect to make a profit from their investments.

This also means that they value **advertising**. All media industries,

HOT LINK

The All Media and Products Survey (Amps) is one of the reports produced by the South African Advertising Research Foundation. You can find out more about the organisation's activities and see highlights from their reports at: http://www.saarf.co.za

including the SABC which gets money from TV licences as well, depend on advertising to a large extent to stay in business. A daily newspaper, for example, usually carries between 30 and 60 per cent advertising. As a journalism professor once said, "Every story is printed on the back of an advertisement."

Media houses value **audience spending power**. South Africa's media owners greatly value research, such as the All Media and Products Survey (Amps), which tells them, amongst other things, how much the audience of a particular mass medium earns. They use this type of information to segment audiences and determine their "target market", as Flynn and his colleagues have done. Advertisers are eager to reach the people who have the most money to spend and that is why most media products are directed at the richer segment of our society.

So, each weekday when the calls of "Argie" go out, the editors and advertisers hope readers from these socio-economic groups will stop and buy a copy.

Institutionalised values and practices

Producing millions of pages of copy for over 165 newspaper and magazine titles with weekly circulation of over 13.5 million copies, as well as 53 online sites, takes significant coordination. That's the challenge for managers and editors of Independent News & Media, the international media group that owns the lion's share of South Africa's daily English-language newspapers. To make it happen, the corporation has a controversial strategy of standardising its newsroom policies and practices. They call it the "concertinaed newsroom". They have, for example, taken the localised business sections of daily newspapers, like *The Mercury*, the *Cape Times* and *The Star*, and created one new section, the *Business Report*. This policy of "concertina-ing" newsroom operations has meant that the editorial operations of the former rival newspapers, *Cape Times* and *Cape Argus*, are now on opposite sides of the same open newsroom and share many of the same resources, such as administration and distribution. "We have single, efficient newsrooms all around the world, and we don't make any apologies for being commercial," said Gavin O'Reilly, the global media conglomerate's chief operating officer, in his first in-depth interview for a South African audience (Bloom, 2004). "People with a vested self-interest may not like this reality, but we need to find more efficient ways of putting newspapers together."

Mediation of authority

Napoleon Bonaparte, the legendary military commander who rose to become Emperor of France, is quoted as saying, "Four hostile newspapers are more to be feared than a thousand bayonets." Perhaps that is as it should be. Nelson Mandela, for one, would likely agree. "It is only the free press," he has said, "that can temper the appetite of any government to amass power at the expense of the citizen" (Cryws-Williams, 1997:64). Libertarians would say that the media allows society to keep a check on other powerful groups, such as the corporations, political parties, and religious groups, too. An old journalism adage sums it up this way: the media should keep the powerful accountable and give voice to the voiceless.

The possibility of simultaneous reception of messages by audiences

The ability to get the same message out to a large group of people at the same time gives the media a central role in society. How else would one alert all the people in a country to an imminent threat? But it is the ability of the mass media, principally television, to reach out to audiences across national boundaries that led Canadian scholar Marshall McLuhan (1962) to say that world was being transformed into a "global village." McLuhan first went public with that view in the early 1960s. A few years later, he predicted the global village would shrink even further as people were connected via an "an electronic circuitry system". Certainly, he had a point about television and the Internet. But older media have caught up, too. Electronic networks allow *Time* magazine to print copies of its four regional editions – Asia, Canada, Europe, and the Pacific – at different locations around the globe to ensure that readers from Washington to Tokyo, and Paris to Pretoria, get copies of the weekly news magazine on time. Books, too, have been revolutionised. Think of the queues that form around the world when a new volume of Harry Potter's adventures are published – and released simultaneously worldwide.

▮▮▮ LINK

Extracts of interviews with Marshall McLuhan are available on the Canadian Broadcasting Corporation archive website: http://archives.cbc.ca/IDD-1-74-342/people/mcluhan/

KEY DATES IN THE DEVELOPMENT OF THE MASS MEDIA

1440s Primal event	Johannes Gutenberg devises movable metal type, permitting mass production of printed material.
1445 Books	Johannes Gutenberg prints the first of his Bibles using movable type.
1650 Newspapers	The first newspaper is distributed in Leipzig, Germany.
1800	South Africa's first newspaper, the *Cape Town Gazette and African Advertiser*, appears on 16 August. By order of the Governor of the Cape Colony, no political news is printed.
1824	The private newspaper, the *SA Commercial Advertiser*, published by George Grieg. John Fairbairn and Thomas Pringle are the editors.
1837	*Umshumayeli Wendaba*, the first black African language (Xhosa) newspaper is published by Methodist missionaries.
1876	*Die Afrikaanse Patriot*, the first Afrikaans-language, or as it was called, Cape Dutch, newspaper appears with Rev S.J. du Toit of Paarl as the editor. It folds in 1904.
1884	*Imvo Zabantsundu*, the first black-owned newspaper, appears under editor John Tengo Jabavu.
1877 Recording	Thomas Edison introduces the phonograph, which could record and play back sound.
1888 Movies	William Dickson devises the motion picture camera.
1895	The first movie – the kinetoscope – in South Africa is introduced in Johannesburg.
1895 Radio	Guglielmo Marconi transmits the first message by radio wave.
1923	The first South African radio broadcasts are made from Johannesburg by the SA Railways on December 18.
1927 Television	Philo Farnsworth invents the tube that picked up moving images for live transmission.
1929	The British Association demonstrates television in Johannesburg and Cape Town, but regular television broadcasts are not made until 1976.
1969 Internet	The US Defense Department establishes the computer network that became the Internet.
1991 World Wide Web	Hypertext Markup Language (HTML) written; helps create the World Wide Web. The following year text-based browsers are introduced, but it is not until 1993, when the graphic interface Mosaic, forerunner to Netscape, is introduced that the Web mushrooms.
1994	The *Mail&Guardian Online* becomes the first Internet-based news publication in Africa.
2002	On the Web, creators of online journals, or "web logs," now "blog on."

The role of information technology

Technological change has been a constant factor in the evolution of the mass media. As far back as 2000 years before the birth of Christ, Mediterranean civilisations used technology to create a system of movable type pressing signs into clay. Carvings in stone and hand printing on thin paper made from papyrus plants are further historical remnants of attempts to communicate. In about 1041, the Chinese printer Pi Sheng printed books using movable type made of hundred of clay blocks bearing Chinese characters. That printing technique was introduced to Europe when the Venetian adventurer Marco Polo returned from his travels in China in 1295. However, the development of movable metal type in the Western world by the German Johannes Gutenberg in the 15th century paved the way for the expansion of a print culture. Gutenberg first carved wood so the letter stood out in relief on the blocks that could be rearranged into different words; then, he inked the blocks so multiple copies of documents could be made. The wood blocks made fuzzy letters, but Gutenberg's assistant, Peter Schoffer, soon realised that metal could be used instead of wood to produce a cleaner type. He used this method to print the English Bible in 1455.

HOT LINK

The British Library in London safeguards some of the world's most famous books and manuscripts, including the *Diamond Sutra*, the world's earliest dated printed document, produced in China in the eighth century, and the *Gutenberg Bible*, the first major book printed in Europe from movable type. You can view these at: http://www.bl.uk/about/treasures.html

As new technologies are created, so new options develop for communicators to create and distribute their messages. Technology such as the steam engine and the rotary press made possible early mass media, such as newspapers. Next, new technology, like radio transmitters (early 1900s) and television cameras, allowed the development of broadcast media. More recently, new information technology (IT), especially the microchip used in computers, has given rise to new media, like the Internet, high definition television, satellite information systems, cable television and videotext.

Of course, technology has not only brought about new media options. It has also had significant impact on the processes and content of older ones. James Carey has suggested that the invention of the telegraph and the development of news wire services in the mid-nineteenth century was decisive in the development of a specific form of presenting news – a form which has been equated with the professional value of objectivity (Carey, 1989). The appearance of portable cameras at the end of the 19th century heightened the intrusiveness of the press into private lives and led directly to the notion of a zone of personal privacy in which the press could not intrude (Warren and Brandeis, 1890). Film news reels, radio and, of course, television (as McLuhan and others

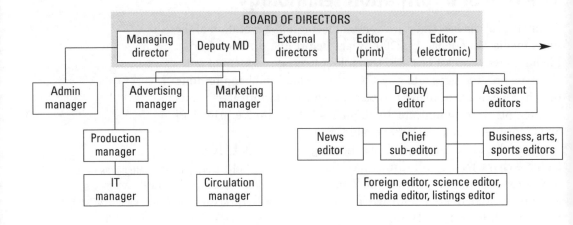

Figure 2.2 *Management structure of the M&G Media Ltd.*

have noted) changed the way journalists gathered and presented news as well as the way the public viewed and understood ongoing events.

However, the interplay between journalism and technology has never been more dramatic than with the emergence of the Internet as a widespread medium of communication in the 1990s. At the beginning of the decade, few journalists and fewer still affiliated with mainstream, mainline media had even heard of the Internet. By 1994, journalists on the leading edge were predicting that the Internet would fundamentally change the way their colleagues would go about doing their work (Reddick and King, 1994). By 1997, the Internet was an integral part of the practice and presentation of journalism. But the Internet has not only emerged as a new tool for research and reporting news and a new medium of publication; it has made it possible to **converge** voice, data and video. As a result, distinct media forms, such as newspapers, often blend or overlap function with newer media, as has occurred when newspaper content can be read online, or a film crew may shoot a story to produce for television, or for broadcast on radio and the Internet.

HOT LINK

The *Mail&Guardian Online* was the first Internet-based news publication in Africa. Visit the site at: http://www.mg.co.za and follow the "M&G History" link at the bottom of the page to find out how one of the world's pioneers in online publishing got started.

HOT LINK

More on media convergence [Zu. Ukudidiyelwa kwezindaba / Xh. Ukuhlangabezana / Afr. mediakon-vergensie]. Henry Jenkins, director of the Comparative Media Studies Program at the Massachusetts Institute of Technology, offers a basic overview of different kinds of convergences – technological, economic, aesthetic, organic, and global – which are redefining our media environment. Read his piece titled "Convergence? I Diverge," at http://web. mit.edu/21fms/www/faculty/ henry3/converge.pdf. It's a good starting point for understanding and researching more on this theme.

Key newsroom staff

There are exceptions, but in all newsrooms someone has to gather and write the news, someone has to check the copy for clarity, someone has to evaluate the stories and pick the best ones and someone has to process the news accordingly. There are, therefore, enough similarities to make some observations about key personnel and their functions.

Editor [Zu. Umhleli/Xh. Umhleli/Afr. Redakteur]

Also known as the editor-in-chief at some newspapers, the editor is responsible for overall policy and management of the newspaper. He does not deal with day-to-day operations in the news department and, unless you begin work as a reporter at a weekly or small daily newspaper (or create real trouble), you will probably have little contact with the editor. The editor's influence is exerted through those who report directly to him, namely the deputy editors and assistant editors.

Editorial-page editor [Zu. Ikhasi lomhleli / Afr. Eindredakteur: redaksioneel]

This person is responsible for producing the editorial page: writing the daily editorial column – which is seen as the official position of the newspaper – as well as editing the letters-to-the-editor section and political columns.

News editor [Zu. Umhleli wezindaba / Afr. Nuusredakteur]

The news editor supervises the reporters who gather local news. He or she directs the newsdesk, which is the hub of the newsroom (local news is the primary news product of most newspapers). The editors of special sections such as entertainment, arts, property, sports or business all liaise with the news editor, who also usually supervises the chief photographer or, in the case of some large newspapers, works with the photographic editor.

Sub-editor [Zu, Isekela lomhleli / Afr. Eindredakteur]

Sub-editors (usually called copy editors in North America) work on the copy desk, where the final editing of stories is done, pages are designed and headlines are written. Often referred to as subs, these are the specialists who polish the stories. They check verifiable facts, including the spelling of names and addresses, watch for legal infringements, write headlines and lay out pages. The person in charge is typically called the chief sub-editor, or chief sub.

Some newspapers, such as the *Cape Argus*, have a single-page editor who helps the chief sub design and lay out all the newspaper's news pages. Across town at *Die Burger* the chief sub sends stories to individual page subs who have control over designing certain pages, as well as polishing the stories and writing the headlines.

Whatever the brief, the copy desk plays an important role in producing the newspaper. It is charged with enforcing deadlines so the newspaper is produced on time. Although deadlines affect everyone in the newsroom, you will have little contact with the sub-editors unless they have questions about something you have written. Even then, the questions may be channelled through the news editor.

Copytaster [Zu. Umkhethi wezindaba/ Afr. Kopieproeër]

Most newspapers use a large percentage of stories (often referred to as "wire copy") provided by news agencies such as Reuters, Associated Press (AP), or the South African Press Association (SAPA). These agencies have a network of reporters who report the news for their agency which in turn sends stories directly to the newsrooms of subscribing media. It is the job of the copytasters to wade through the hundreds of stories, tasting, if you will, which ones are suitable for their publications.

Photographer [Zu. Umuntu othatha izithombe/ Xh. Umntu (sic) ofotayo/Afr. Fotograaf]

The new designation – photojournalists – seems a more precise description for the work of camera-toting newsroom staff. Photographs play a vital part in attracting readers and enhancing the written story or copy. *Newsweek* (24 May 1993:60-61) ran a promotional advertisement highlighting the role of photojournalists under the headline "Every week our readers *see* the news" [their emphasis]. The double-page spread shows work by three of the magazine's award-winning photographers and proclaims: "Their pictures involve our readers in the immediacy of the moment, bringing drama and emotion to each news story" (ibid). Often pictures are used independently with a simple caption (called "stand alones"). Photographers, reporting to a chief photographer, are usually under the authority of the news editor.

Cartoonist [Zu. Umdwebi wekhathuni/Xh. Umzobi wemifanekiso ehlekisayo/Afr. Spotprenttekenaar]

Cartoonists have long had a prime place on newspapers' editorial pages. "The task of the cartoonist is to be insulting to everyone, criticise mercilessly – but equally," wrote cartoonist Dov Fedler in the *Rhodes*

University Journalism Review (June 1991:24). Jonathan Shapiro, aka Zapiro, says "Editorial cartoonists usually report to the editorial page editor or to the editor directly."

Jonathan Shapiro on shooting sacred cows

Jonathan Shapiro spends his days poking fun at the powerful and famous. Arguably South Africa's best-known syndicated political cartoonist, Shapiro was one of several international cartoonists invited to the World Economic Forum in Davos in January 2004 to discuss how political cartoonists could contribute to society. He spoke to Newsweek's Arlene Getz (2004) about his work and the responses it has drawn. This extract is used with permission.

Newsweek: What's your role as a political cartoonist?

Jonathan Shapiro, aka Zapiro: It's to be a person who's able to shoot little arrows into sacred cows and knock politicians off their pedestals, to look

out for hypocrisy, advocate for all sorts of things from social justice to peace. Primarily I'm a social commentator rather than someone who's out to get the belly laugh. The belly laugh is one tool that you can use for that purpose.

Many of your cartoons are vehemently anti-George W. Bush. Do you have any qualms about taking on someone as powerful as the U.S. president?

Doing that is so easy. What's much harder is taking on people in your own community. In my case, being Jewish and taking on the Jewish community of South Africa [through anti-Ariel Sharon cartoons] and their unquestioning support of Israel is a much harder thing to do. Taking on people from the [anti-apartheid] struggle I was part of, who are now in positions of power, and who may be doing

things I don't agree with, is much harder to do. Taking on Bush is easy by comparison.

The old apartheid regime arrested and jailed you. Were you afraid then?

I was afraid. On one occasion in 1987 the security police came looking for me because of a drawing that I'd published. Luckily I wasn't there, and I [then] went into hiding. Later, when I was least expecting it – I was actually preparing to go on a scholarship to study in the United States – they actually did get me. They came round on their usual 3 am visit and detained me without trial. They kept me in solitary [confinement] for five days and then another six days in prison. Of course I never knew how long it was going to be. I was also arrested a number of times. So yes, those were times when I did feel afraid for myself and other members of my family as well.

Are you ever afraid now, under the African National Congress's post-apartheid government?

Certainly I've never felt threatened in that kind of way. There are certain people within the new government who have a slightly disturbing tendency toward authoritarianism, but there are so many checks and balances that in that way their noises are just noises. Certainly in cartooning I'm given huge free rein at the moment. I'm able to publish things that would be very hard to publish in mainstream newspapers in many countries of the world.

What's more important for a cartoonist? A sense of humor or a sense of the absurd?

That's an interesting question. I would think a sense of the absurd is more important for a political cartoonist, because that could define things like a sense of hypocrisy or a sense of the things one has to be skeptical about. Occasionally you can be very funny about it as well.

Used with permission

Graphic designer [Zu. Umdwebi / Xh. Igcisa lokuzoba / Afr. Grafiese ontwerper]

Another type of journalist is gaining a place in publications: the graphic artist or designer. The journalism school at the University of Missouri (which claims to be the oldest journalism school in the world) has created a programme for graphic journalists who are trained to report a story, the way writers do, and return to their computers and create their story in images. Industrial editors, such as Petro van Bosch at Sanlam, have also seen the value of graphics and use graphics extensively in their publications. Graphic artists, like reporters, are usually directly responsible to the news editor.

Reporter [Zu. Umbiki / Xh. Umcholi-ndaba / Afr. Verslaggewer]

When I started my first newspaper job at a bureau of the Pulitzer Prize-winning daily *Charlotte Observer* in North Carolina, US. Dan Huntley was the oldest reporter in the newsroom. Armfuls of accolades for his work and nudges from the paper's management were not enough to move Huntley up the corporate ladder. He tried a stint as a news editor once, but asked to return to his beat. "I don't want to be so far removed from the action," Huntley explained. The thrill of hunting down a tip, interviewing sources and telling a story well was the only job Huntley ever wanted to do. Positions such as sub-editor, news editor, assistant-editor or even editor held no appeal for him.

Understanding what reporters like Huntley do and how they do it is what we will focus on next, starting with looking at how reporters are organised to get the job done.

Categories of news staff writers

To fill a daily newspaper – which easily prints as many words as a novel – or broadcast news show takes considerable planning and organisation. Generally, news staff writers are organised into four primary categories: beat reporters, general-assignment reporters, special-assignment reporters and correspondents.

Beat reporter

The criteria editors generally use to organise their reporters are: **location** and **topic**. A reporter located at a bureau may have to cover everything from police affairs to country fairs. As a beat reporter, you usually know how to plan your day, at least at the beginning. A steady routine is the basis of beat reporting. Each day a court reporter, for example, checks the court roll, attends trials of interest and makes routine stops with the court staff. One day your routine may yield little more than a businessman convicted of assaulting a rival, on other days you might witness a serial killer confessing to his crimes.

At a typical major newspaper, editors usually assign reporters to beats, or specific areas of responsibility, such as the following:

- Police stations, jails, fire departments and hospitals.
- The courts.
- City council (headquarters for city legislative and executive officials), national government and opposition groups.
- Schools, colleges, universities, as well as affiliated groups and unions.
- Civic, fraternal and professional organisations.
- Health associations, such as HIV/Aids, heart, cancer, mental health, alcohol and drug counselling. Also youth organisations and welfare agencies.
- Local, national and international sports teams and organisations.
- Businesses and markets.
- Other media and entertainment and options such as cinemas, radio and television stations. Also, performance spaces and groups (symphony, drama, dance, cabaret), as well as promoters of national and international music groups.

- Tourism groups, convention centres, hotels, airlines and other firms engaged in accommodating meetings and visitors.
- Various special interest news sources, such as technology, ships and shipping, mines and mining, agriculture, fishing, environmental groups.

General-assignment reporter

In contrast to the beat reporter, general-assignment reporters seldom know what to expect when they walk into the office. The news editor often calls on the general-assignment reporter, at a moment's notice, to write about or cover whatever comes up. You learn to live by your wits and, like a Boy Scout, you are expected always to be prepared.

Special-assignment reporter

On special assignment, the task at hand is the most predictable. You know where you will be and what you will be doing. Some large papers create departments or earmark a few reporters to take on special assignments and report back with in-depth stories.

Correspondent

A regular contributor reporting from a distant location is called a correspondent, or foreign correspondent. Such reporters, who are rarely permanently employed by the media house, may also be referred to as "stringers".

Other departments in the news organisation

Like any business, newspapers are profit-making institutions. However, they traditionally differ from conventional businesses in one significant way – the clearer separation between departments. The news department gathers and reports news, even though some of the news may conflict with the interests of the advertising department. The business and advertising departments are relatively independent of the news-gathering operation, ideally at least.

Advertising

Most of a newspaper's revenue is generated by the advertising department. Some magazines, such as *Cosmopolitan*, devote as much as three-quarters of their pages to advertising. At a newspaper, the advertising section is usually divided according to the two major forms of advertising: display and classified sections. Classifieds (often called "smalls") account for the largest chunk of advertising, while display ads (which typically have eye-catching visuals and catchy slogans) are the most prominent. For those journalists who feel themselves superior to the advertising staff, think of the truism mentioned above: "Every story is printed on the back of an ad." Meaning: without advertising, which accounts for the bulk of the income of most media, there would be no way journalists could do their work.

Promotions

This section, which is related but also distinct from the advertising function of the paper, is charged with promoting the media product to its audience and advertisers through activities, such as special events. Projects coordinated by the promotions department may include competitions, concerts, and the like.

> **When editorial and advertising interests collide**
> The South African edition of the health magazine *Shape* announced in May 2004 that it would not run ads for diet pills after 68% of readers indicated in a survey that they believed it was unethical for the magazine to publish such ads. "We have always been ambivalent about diet products," said *Shape* editor Heather Parker (Moodie, 2004). "There are a lot of charlatans out there. But then there are also legitimate ones. Then, when the majority of readers said they thought it was problematic, we decided to put our readers first." The decision affected the bottom line, Parker said, but she believed many advertisers appreciated the magazine spelling out its position in what has long been a grey area.

Circulation

The job of getting the newspapers in the readers' hands belongs to the circulation department. Revenue from copy sales is the second leading source of income. Circulation is also an important factor in setting advertising rates. The general rule is: the higher the circulation, the more advertisers pay to advertise in a publication.

Administration

From a reporter's point of view, this department's most important function is handling the payroll, benefits and insurance. The business or administration department also handles billing, accounts and related functions.

Production

This is where the creative work of the reporters, photographers and editor is translated onto the page. With the advent of desktop publishing technology, most newspapers now compose pages in the newsroom/subsroom. The production departments then manage the reprographics, which is material used to prepare the film, or plates, for the printing press.

How copy flows through the newsroom

It is inevitable. The telephone rings and on the other end is an irate reader. The reporter's side of the conversation is likely to go something like this:

"Yes, sir, I understand your disappointment with the headline, but I did not write it.

"Mmmm. Yes, but I did not choose to place the story about your new hotel next to the one about the national housing crisis.

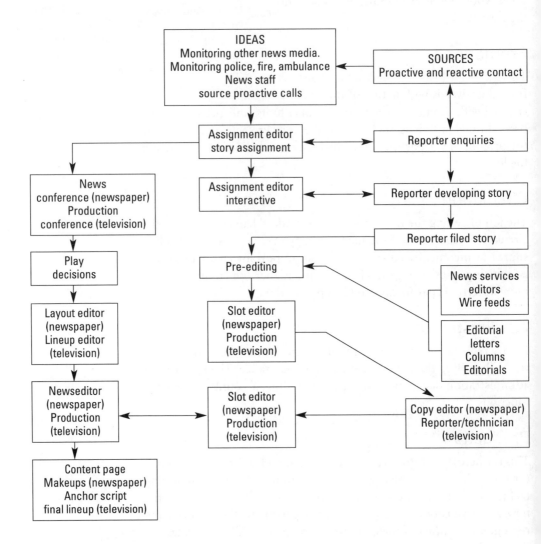

Figure 2.3 *The news production process. Source: Ericson, R.V., Baranak, P.M. and Chan, J.B.L. 1987. Visualizing Deviance. Toronto: University of Toronto Press in McQuail, D. and Windahl, S. 1993. Communication models for the study of mass communication. New York: Longman, p. 179.*

"Yes, sir, I noticed that your name was spelled incorrectly in the caption, but ... yes, Mr Nakasa, I did not write it.

"Yes, yes, Mr Nakasa, I know my byline is on the story – but I am only the reporter ..."

Understanding how a story evolves and moves through the newsroom before finally landing up in the readers' hands is essential.

The labels and arrows make the chart largely self-explanatory but the following points should be noted:

Sources are both proactive and reactive. "News," as Sigal (1973) noted, "is not what happens, but what someone says has happened or will happen. Reporters are seldom in a position to witness events firsthand. They have to rely on the accounts of others." While the amounts differ, a range of studies have shown that typically the vast majority of news stories are not originated by the journalists and reports. News stories come, in the main, from formal sources. Proactive sources are those who contact the newsroom with information or ideas for stories. Sometimes that is simply a telephone call or a **news release**, which is what Marcus Brewster issued on behalf of his client *Fairlady* magazine (see p.18). On other occasions, a proactive source, such as a politician, may call a news conference. Reactive sources are those who only respond to requests for information by the media, such as the men Santosh Beharie and Peter Mogaki confronted during their investigation.

Proactive ideas for content would involve some initiative on the part of the reporters or editors, and this is described as enterprise reporting. For example, no one suggested to freelance photojournalist Sue Hillyard that she document the trauma ward at Groote Schuur Hospital (see p.19). She came up with the idea and made the arrangements herself. Only when the work was finished did she approach a magazine editor to publish it. Being enterprising means making things happen yourself.

Assignment [Xh. Ukwabelo / Zu. ukwabela / Afr. opdrag] refers to the key act of allocating reporters and photographers to established or enterprising story possibilities.

Conferences of editorial staff about how news "plays" in the layout (newspaper) and line-up (television) is an important part in the sequence of news selection. It is at these conferences that the different stories are weighed up and decisions are made about their respective merits.

Some content is usually readily available for use and with control of the organisation (new agency stories, letters, editorials, syndicated columns, cartoons, etc.)

In general, we see a continous sequence from initial content supply, through selection decisions and then to format, makeup, design and

Definition

A **news release** or **press release** [Zu. isaziso sezindaba / Xh. isaziso / Afr. persverklaring] is a formal printed announcement or notice by an organisation about its activities that is written in the form of a news article and given to the media to generate or encourage publicity. When appropriate, photopgraphs, video and audio clips, and other graphic materials are sent out along with written statements.

presentation decisions, where technical criteria are sometimes more important than editorial ones.

The influence of deadlines on news content is unmistakable. All media production is always working to deadlines. In television and radio, schedules are set up to create the material that is booked into the programming slots. Deadlines need to be met or there will be nothing to broadcast. Newspapers have to be "put to bed" (which is how finishing the work is described) by a certain time or they will not be printed in time to be collected by trucks to get to the shops or vendors in time to be sold. Internet news sites have more flexible deadlines, as they are updated continuously.

So, you may think, it makes sense to have deadlines otherwise the media wouldn't be able to operate. Of course, you are right. We should also be aware that meeting a deadline may influence how well a story is researched or who is quoted. Or, as one of my editors used to say: "It's not the best stories that get into the paper, it's the best ones available at deadline. So, get writing!" That is exactly what we will concentrate on next.

In this chapter you learned that

- The characteristics of the mass media include:
  - large scale of operation;
  - high levels of industrial activity;
  - formal, centralised organisation;
  - institutional values and practices;
  - mediation of authority;
  - a "standardised" product directed to a mass audience;
  - the possibility of simultaneous reception of messages by audiences.
- Technological development has had a major role to play in the development of the mass media.

While the mass media, by definition, aims to reach a large or "mass" audience, these target audiences are segmented by interest, income, age and other characteristics. Many media target very specific audiences, referred to as "niches".

Sources of news, whether proactive or reactive, play a key role in setting the news agenda.

Typically media products are the result of the combined efforts of a great many people, who all have very specific roles and responsibilities. While most media products rely on advertising for their economic well-being, traditionally the editorial and advertising departments operate independently.

The news production process is an intricate cycle kept in motion by deadlines.

Understanding additional key terms

Advertorial [Zu. I-athikhili esiyisikhangiso /Afr. promosie-artikel]: Paid for advertising which is presented in the form of a story.

CD-Rom: Stands for Compact Disk-Read Only Memory.

Community radio [Zu. Umsakazo womphakathi / Xh. isikhululo sikanomathotholo soluntu / Af. gemeenskapsradio]: Ownership of South African radio stations can be divided into three categories: public (all SABC stations); private (such as Radio 702 and KFM); and community (such as Radio Helderberg). Community radio stations are non-profit stations which have limited frequency transmitters and focus on community interests. "Community", in this instance, can be defined as a group of people in a select geographical location (for example, Radio CFlat, which broadcasts in the Cape Flats area around Cape Town) or people with a special interest (such as the Muslim station Radio 786, and Fine Music Radio, which airs classical and jazz music. The Independent Broadcasting Authority, which issues all licences and monitors broadcasting in South Africa, has given the go-ahead to about 80 such stations around the country. According to the All Race Radio Diary for the period May/June 1996, 1 309 000 people listen to community radio.

Copy [Zu. Ikhophi / Afr. kopie]: Text written to support an advertisement or the written material used in journalism.

Copy writer [Zu. Umbhali wezikhangiso / Xh. umbhali onelungelo elilelakhe lokushicilela nokuthengisa umsebenzi wakhe / Afr. kopieskrywer]: Abbreviation for Advertising Copy Writer, who writes advertisements.

Cover, verb [Zu. Ukubika ngodaba / Xh. ukusasaza / Afr. dek]: To report on something, as in: "Mzilikazi, please cover the opening of Parliament on Monday."

Cover story, noun [Zu. Udaba olusekhaveni / Xh. ibali eliqulathe okuthile / Afr. voorbladstorie): A story which refers to the cover illustration of a magazine. The cover of the 30 April 2004 edition of the *Financial Mail* featured photographs of Maria Ramos, Wendy Luhabe and Hixonia Nyasulu above the cover headline or coverline "SA's 20 most powerful women in business". The cover story, titled "A fair option: representation of women in business", ran on pages 20–28.

DTP (Desktop Publishing): The computer technology which allows one to write and design publications on a computer, thereby replacing the need for manual production studios.

Editorial, noun [Zu. Udaba lohleli / Xh. okuphathelele kuhlelo / Afr. hoofartikel]: 1. An unsigned article or essay, often very brief, appearing on an editorial or opinion page, usually expressing the views of the management of the paper. 2. **Editorial**, noun [Zu. Umbono womhleli / Xh. inqaku lomhleli / Afr. redaksioneel]: can also be used to describe the content of a publication other than the advertisements.

Editorialise, verb [Zu.Ukuveza umbono ngokuthize / Xh. ukuhlela / Afr. kommentaar lewer): To give your own opinion about an activity.

File [Zu. Isihlabo / Xh. ifayili / Afr. instuur/roep]: Sending (by telephone wire/fibre optic/satellite) or calling in a story.

Freelancer [Zu. Ukusebenza ngokungagcwele / Xh. sebenza njenge / Afr. medewerker/vryskut]: A part-time contributor who sends in stories or photographs. Sports desks, for example, use local freelancers (also sometimes called stringers) in peak seasons.

General assignment [Zu. Ukwethula noma yiluphi udaba / Xh. umsebenzi omiselweyo jikelele / Afr. algemene nuusdekking]: Availability to cover any topic.

Internet: The global "network of networks" which offers information to anyone who has a computer, modem and appropriate software.

Jargon [Zu. Ulimi oluhambisana nomsebenzi othile / Xh. intetho exutywe namagama antsonkothileyo asetyenziswa nabantu bomsebenzi othile / Afr.vaktaal]: Terms with strict definitions within a subject discipline (e.g. journalism or media studies, in this case).

Mass media [Zu. Ezesakazelwa uwonkewonke / Xh. amaphepha-ndaba / Afr. massamedia]: Non-personal mediums which reach large audiences.

Media [Zu. Ezokusakaza izindaba / Xh. izinto zokusasaza iindaba / Afr. media]: The plural of medium; channels used for communication; also used as a short form of mass media.

Multi-media: New mediums which are created as the result of combining several mediums.

News hole [Zu. Isikhala sezindaba / Xh. isithuba ekunokubhalwa kuso iindaba emva kokuba kubhalwe isibhengezo seentengiso / Afr. nuusgat]: Space available for news stories in an issue after advertising space is allocated.

Newsprint [Zu. Iphepha lokushicilela iphephandaba / Xh. iphepha loshicilelo lwamaphepha / Afr. koerantpapier]: Paper used for newspapers (cheaper, poorer-grade paper).

News agency [Zu. Igatsha lezindaba / Xh. iziko leendaba / Afr. nuusagentskap): A company which employs a network of reporters to write stories that are sent directly into the newsrooms of subscribing media. Before the advent of computers these stories were sent via telegraph wires, from there the use of the term "wire services" and "wire copy". Reuters, Associated Press (AP) and South African Press Association (SAPA) are the most popular ones used in South Africa.

Public relations [Zu. Umxhumanisi / Xh. igosa lonxibelelwano / Afr. skakelwese]: According to the Public Relations Institute of Southern Africa (Prisa), PR is the deliberate, planned and sustained effort to establish and maintain mutual understanding between an organisation and its various publics – both internal and external.

Subs' desk [Zu. Ihhovisi elihlela izindaba/ Afr. subkantoor]: Where material is edited, headlines added, and the newspaper content prepared for printing.

Sub-editor [Zu. Isekela lomhleli / Xh. isekela lomhleli / Afr. subredakteur/eindredakteur]: The person who edits, rewrites copy and puts on headlines.

URL: Universal Resource Locator, which is essentially the address where you can find people and companies on the Internet.

Putting your learning to work

ACTIVITY 1 How does the newsroom work in practice?

Divide your class into groups of 10 or so and arrange a visit to a local newspaper, magazine, radio station or television studio. Larger media, such as daily newspapers and SABC radio stations, have public relations officers who regularly schedule tours. It is best to set up the tour several weeks, if not months, in advance.

- Study how the staff in each department is organised and scheduled.
- Draw up charts that show the organisational hierarchy and the flow of work through the organisation.
- Discuss your experience with the rest of the class. Tip: To make the most of the tour, prepare a list of 10 questions and forward it to the person who will be taking you around. It will likely help them to be aware of what you want from the experience – and help you to get the information you require.

ACTIVITY 2 Is the world really a "global village"?

Marshall McLuhan's point was, in part, that television would make the remote seem close. Events from throughout the world would appear with electronic vividness, as if they were happening just down the street from the viewer's home. With the globe shrunk, diverse peoples could become a cohesive community, or a "tribe" as he liked to say. Scan today's news headlines and ask yourself: "Has this really happened?" Veteran television and newspaper journalist Philip Seib doesn't think so. "Of course, the technology may work perfectly, but the sociology isn't that simple," he wrote in *Going live: getting the news right in the real-time world* (2002:14) "Distant happenings might become more comprehensible thanks to television [and other global media], but they still remain foreign, literally and figuratively. The audience takes note of the many wars and disasters (and, occasionally, less depressing happenings) that constitute news, but viewers' emotional and intellectual connections to the people directly affected by these events usually remain tenuous. After all, television is confined to a glass box. No matter how gruesome the scenes on the screen may be, no blood will spill onto the carpet ... The global village can be visited and abandoned at will."

What do you think? Does the global reach of the mass media make the world more cohesive, as McLuhan suggested, or do the media simply inform us of just how different we all are?

HOT LINKS

1 The Media History Project site provides an extensive overview of the development of the mass media: http://www.mediahistory.umn.edu/indextext/WarDrums.html

2 The Government Communication and Information Service provides a useful directory of media contacts in South Africa under the following headings:
- South African Electronic Media (National and Commercial Radio and TV Stations)
- South African Newspapers and Magazines
- Community Radio Stations
- Community and Regional Newspapers
- Foreign Media in South Africa
- Freelance Journalists in South Africa

You can view this directory online at: http://www.gcis.gov.za/gcis/directory.jsp?dir=11

A Day in the Life of an Afternoon Newspaper *by Andrea Weiss*

The Cape Argus *is the country's oldest surviving newspaper and one of the last true afternoon or "on-day" newspapers, and because of this has some fairly punishing deadlines. Over the years, pressure has mounted to get the newspaper out earlier and earlier in the day so that it can be distributed in good time. As traffic congestion has grown, so have our distribution problems. Compounding this has been the proliferation of electronic media which can effectively have a story out almost instantaneously while we have a very short "live" period in the mornings. Essentially, this means that we have to think differently about the news we produce and create newspapers that give greater emphasis to backgrounders and explanations. The challenge is to keep our newspaper fresh and interesting. These impediments notwithstanding, working on an afternoon paper is probably one of the most exhilarating, exciting jobs a journalist can do.*

So here goes:

04:30 – First in is the chief sub-editor to do a national and international copytaste. What this means is that she has to check the copy coming through on our wire services to compile a diary of all the latest and most pertinent stories for the day's paper. This entails reading and evaluating the material on the wires, and comparing it to the morning newspapers to ensure that there is no duplication.

05:00 or thereabouts – News editor, sports editor and picture editor come in to compile their own diaries. The picture editor has to print out copies of the pictures available for first edition. The news editor has to compile a diary of all the local overnight copy, also after reading and evaluating stories, as well as seeing what the *Cape Times* and *Die Burger* have done overnight.

06:00 – First news conference takes place with the editorial executive team deciding what goes on the news pages. Important decisions that get made at this meeting are what the front page picture and lead story are going to be, as well as lead stories and pictures for the first six to eight pages of the newspaper. The other pages will have been prepared the day before. In the meantime, the assistant news editor and backdesk editor come in to start editing copy for first edition.

06:45 – Poster and leader conference takes place directly after the other meeting. While the news editor and chief sub go off to get the show on the road, the editor, his deputy and political editor decide what the leader article should be about (and who gets to write it), and they design four or five posters which will go on street lamps to advertise the paper.

Between 06:45 and 08:45 – Intense production period for first edition, during which time all the stories of the day have to be edited by the newsdesk, sent through to the sub-editors and re-edited with headlines put on them. This happens after the layout subs have designed their pages and assigned the stories to down-table subs (the people who line edit the copy). The final person to pass a story is the revise sub. Different layout subs have responsibility for different pages – with the last page to go being page 1. In the meantime, the news editor and picture editor have to get reporters and photographers (some of whom come in on an early shift at 07:30) to get stories to match any overnight material or to cover breaking stories. Their deadline is about 08:30. An example would be the taxi/bus conflict where drivers were being shot at during the morning commute. It is imperative that these stories get into the first edition. While this is happening, the leader is being written by the editor or a nominee.

08:45 – Newsdesk deadline for the last story – generally the front page lead.

09:30 – Offscreen deadline when all material must be ready to go to pre-press for printing.

Also at 09:30, the news editor convenes a meeting of reporters (most of whom come in at 09:00) to discuss news priorities and stories for the day. This is an important element for creating the next day's paper.

10:30 – Early page conference takes place to

decide on what feature material will appear in the next day's pages. The pages that are affected by this are news feature pages (a bit further back in the newspaper), Life pages and oped [short for "opinion and editorial"].

These pages are prepared and laid out the day before publication. The people who attend this conference are the editor or his deputy, the picture desk, the subs desk and the back desk editor (who has responsibility for the Life pages). Here, an eye for good feature material is required, as well as a sharp news sense.

10:30 onwards – The feature pages are edited and laid out. In the meantime, the news desk is in the process of making sure that the news machine is cranked up and working on materials for both on-day and the following day. This requires making judgments about what should go into the final edition (deadline 12.30) and what should be held over for the next day.

11:30 – Planning conference for the next day's paper. This conference takes in the people who were there for the 06:00 meeting, but also the *Tonight* department, letters page and features pages. During the morning, staff have been working on *Tonight* and letters, and these products are discussed at the meeting. An important element is the discussion on the next day's news pages, including planning for illustrations and graphics and a good lead story. There is a leader article discussion after this meeting as well. Sometimes the leader is written the day before, and sometimes on the day of publication.

12:45 – Deadline for late final updates and final editions from the newsdesk end. Subs have until about 13:30 to get the newspaper offscreen.

13:00 – Night news editor comes in to take up the cudgel for the newsdesk, while the day shift goes off. The news editor tends to linger to deal with other administrative tasks and staff issues. Editors are usually engaged in meetings with other departments in the building for the afternoon.

Reporters spend the afternoon working on stories for the next day and filing to the night news editor, who does an initial edit and diary. Any breaking stories have to be covered by the night team.

14:00 Two reporters come in for the night shift. Photographers also work on a roster basis.

17:00 – The bulk of reporters knock off, depending on what they are working on and what their shift arrangements are. By its nature, news reporting is erratic and reporters are not so much required to work a set shift as to get the job done. Beat reporters tend to have the luxury of managing their time in office hours, while hard-news reporters have to be at the beck and call of the newsdesk.

21:00 – Night news editor goes home after editing copy, watching the evening news on TV and managing the news assignments for the afternoon and evening. Reporters will knock off around 22:00 unless a story requires them to stick around.

Next day – the whole machine cranks up again from 04:30.

• There are times when extraordinary arrangements need to be made. An example is when the big fire was burning in Cape Town, and the news team was effectively called in to work late into the night to produce a paper that covered all aspects of the story (a kind of journalistic carpet bombing which worked very well).

Andrea Weiss was at the Cape Argus *for more than 11 years, covering a variety of beats (health/ metro etc) and hard news. She also had a stint in the subs room, as news editor, and as projects editor.*

Bibliography

Anon. Carte Blanche Interactive. 2004. [Online] Available at: http://www.mnet.co.za/carteblanche/ [Accessed: 29 April 2004]

Anon. About media 24. [Online] Available at: http://www.media24.co.za/eng/community.html. [Accessed: 29 April 2004]

Bloom, K. 2004. The O'Reilly Imperative. [Online] *The Media Online.* 1 May 2004. Johannesburg: Mail & Guardian. Available at: http://www.themedia.co.za/article.aspx?articleid=79989&area=/media_insightcover_stories. [Accessed: 1 June 2004]

Carey, J.W. 1989. *Communication as culture: essays on media and society.* Boston: Unwin Hyman.

Crwys-Williams, J. ed. 1997. *In the words of Nelson Mandela. A little pocket book.* London: Penguin.

Ericson, R.V., Baranak, P.M. and Chan, J.B.L. 1987. Visualizing Deviance. Toronto: University of Toronto Press. In McQuail, D. and Windahl, S. 1993. *Communication models for the study of mass communication.* New York: Longman.

Fedler, D. 1991. Pen sketches: Dov Fedler. *Rhodes University Journalism Review,* Grahamstown: Rhodes. June 1991: 24.

Flynn, I. 2004. Letter from the editor. *Cape Argus* [online] Available at: http://www.capeargus.co.za/index.php?fSectionId=469&fSetId=221 [Acccessed: 4 June 2004]

Getz, A. 2004. Shooting Sacred Cows. *Newsweek Online.* 26 Jan 2004. Available at: http://msnbc.msn.com/id/4066957/ [Accessed: 4 June 2004]

http://link2southafrica.com/newsbulletin/- *ThisDay* in South Africa. http://www.woza.co.za./-Woza News.

McLuhan, M. 1962. *The Gutenberg Galaxy.* London: Routledge & Kegan Paul.

Moodie, G. 2004. Diet pill ads get chop in women's magazines. *Sunday Times* [online]. 25 April 2004. Available at: http://www.sundaytimes.co.za/2004/04/25/news/news22.asp [Accessed: 4 June 2004]

Price, S. 1997. *The complete A-Z media and communication handbook.* London: Hodder & Stoughton.

Reddick, R. and King, E. 1994. *The online journalist.* Dallas, TX: Harcourt Brace.

Seib, P. 2002. *Going live: getting the news right in the real-time world.* Landham, MD: Rowman & Littlefield.

Sigal, L.V. 1973. *Reporters and officials: the organization and politics of newsmaking.* Lexington, MA: Heath.

South African Advertising Research Foundation. 2004. Adults most popular TV programmes, Week 15: Mon 05/04/2004 – Sun 11/04/2004 [Online] Available at: www.saarf.co.za. [Accessed:29 April 2004]

Warren, S.D. and Brandeis, L.D. 1890. The right to privacy. *Harvard Law Review* (4:193) 1890. In King, E. 1997. The impact of the Internet on journalism: introduction. *Electronic Journal of Communication* [Online] (7:2) Available at: http://www.cios.org/www/ejc/v7n297.htm [Accessed: 4 June 2004]

3

Exploring the nature of news

Introduction

A newspaper, says *The Star* editor Moegsien Williams, is a bit like a Madeira loaf. And just like a baker, staff on the newspaper need a recipe. Throwing in the ingredients at random, says Williams, simply won't work. "We must make sure we know what they eat, otherwise we won't be able to produce the perfect Madeira loaf the next morning" (1996:23). Readers' preferences guide the publication, but the publication should also guide the readers. "We need to provoke them, we need sometimes to make them angry, sometimes make them cheer with us, sometimes we need to titillate them." It is not always easy to see how reporters and editors (the bakers, if you will) decide which stories, among the scores of options, to use. Mass media all report news, but news reports are quite different. Many reports focus on events, but not all events constitute news. People feature in many stories, but not all people are newsworthy.

Often we do not agree with the choices. Sensational, we say. Depressing. Boring. Biased. American Senator Adlai Stevenson, who helped found the United Nations, held this theory: "Newspaper editors are men who separate the wheat from the chaff, and then print the chaff" (Bates, 1989:57).

Whatever the case, in order to work in the mass media – or with the media – it is vital to understand how to identify news.

KEY CONCEPTS

News values; bias; objectivity; fairness; spin; agenda-setting; truth-telling.

Towards a definition of news

Here's how an online news site headlines the top stories:

"Crashed bus driver hands himself over to cops"
"Zimbabwe secretly imports maize"
"Ooh la la! Gaily married in France"

These were the top stories on IOL (Independent Online) at 18:30 on 4 June 2004. So, how did a bus driver from KwaZulu-Natal, 400 000 tons of maize stored in silos in Zimbabwe, a shopkeeper and a nurse from the suburb of Begles in the south-western city of Bordeaux in France get to share the same platform on a news site based in Cape Town? Curious audiences often wonder on what basis news is selected and presented. Journalists, on the other hand, are often unable to express clearly on what basis these decisions are made. Admittedly, news judgement cannot be as neatly analysed as a scientist can break down the components of water, or H_2O into two parts hydrogen and one part oxygen. Still, we will try to formulate a definition, but only once we have examined some of the key factors that impact on journalists' news judgements – and once we've examined some of the other biases.

Independent Online draws its content from the Independent group's 14 daily and weekly newspaper titles, as well as news agencies.

"Even at its most presumptous, the news does not claim to be timeless or universal," writes Jack Fuller, a Pulitzer Prize-winning journalist and lawyer who heads the Tribune Publishing Company in Chicago. "It represents at most a provisional kind of truth, the best that can be said" (1996:7). "By its very nature, the news industry is about selection and omission, picking and discarding. And there are three fundamantal **biases** that influence those choices: immediacy; interest for a given community; and significance (ibid).

Definition

Bias [Zu. Ukuchema / Xh. ukuthambekisela bucala / Afr. partydigheid] is an inclination for or against a thing or a person.

The bias of *immediacy* [Zu. Ukuchema okwenzela imanje / ukwenzeka kwangoku / Xh./ Afr. onmiddellikheid]

The basic element of news is clear from the root word new. "News" comes from the Greek *neos*, the Latin *novus* (and from later versions of the same), the German *neu* and the Middle English *newe*. A story may be many things – well researched, finely crafted, cleverly composed – but if the information is not new to the audience, it is not considered news. "This leads journalists to emphasise the recent event or the recently dis-covered fact at the expense of that which occurred before or had already been known," Fuller points out (ibid). "The bias of immediacy is the rule."

The bias of *audience interest* [Zu. Ukuchema okwenzela abalaleli /Xh. ba nomdla / Afr. gehoorbelangstelling]

Decisions about the newsworthiness of an event is usually biased towards the perceived interests of the audience. That, in part, explains several criticisms of the press, including the emphasis on the negative and the indifference towards some events. The medium's audience pro-file guides editors and journalists in deciding which items are newswor-thy, and also what approach to take with the story. Walter Lippman described the press as a searchlight that restlessly prowls across expans-es, never staying on any feature for very long (1922:229). "Actually," says Fuller, "human curiosity is the seachlight. We journalists just go where it points" (1996:8).

Related to this is the reality that news has **commercial value**. It can be bought and sold. On one level news is, quite simply, a product. Many starry-eyed reporters, and even some editors, are uncomfortable with the idea that, except for government-controlled outlets, the media are first and foremost a business. It's been that way pretty much from the start, going back to public squares of ancient Rome.

In 59 BC Julius Caesar ordered the daily acts of the senate (*Acta Senatus*) and the people (*Acta Populi*) to be written up and posted in prominent places in the city's forum, which was the centre of public life. It wasn't long before an enterprising Roman named Chrestus saw a business opportunity. He started collecting a wider range of informa-tion – from news about bumper crops to the burning of witches at the stake – and selling his newssheets on the local markets. "In this sense he became one of the first journalists (from the Latin: *diurnarius*, diary writer)," notes Pedro Diederichs in his account of the history of the press (1993:7). In the Middle Ages, news was spread in Europe by mes-sengers who would recite stories to those willing to pay a coin, an Italian gazetta. The commercial nature of the industry is highlighted in the titles of many South African newspapers, past and present: *The Cape Town Gazette and African Advertiser, South African Commercial Advertiser, Kokstad Advertiser & East Griqualand Gazette* and *Graaff-Reinet Advertiser*. The point is this: readers buy media products because, like bread and socks, they want them. And editors – and advertisers – aim to give readers what they want.

The bias of *significance* [Zu. Ukuchema okwen-zela ingqondo / Xh intsingiselo / Afr betekenis]

While media aim to satisfy the information needs of a particular audience, to suggest that the role of the media is just to deliver information is too limiting. It ties us to the low-value aspects of what we do. Anybody can recite the headline news that most people consider sufficient. And everybody, including the telephone company and the post office, can deliver an advertising message. Editor Reid Ashe, a former Nieman Fellow at Harvard University, makes an important point about the difference between something that is important and something that is valuable: Things that are plentiful, like air and water, are cheap, even though they are vitally important. But if something is scarce, like caviar or diamonds, it is highly valued despite its limited usefulness (1992:7). So, if not information, what does the media offer that is valuable enough for us to to take time out of our day, or money out of our pockets? The answer is an age-old one: meaningful social interaction. News is not just about important information, it is also about stories that help bring us together. News helps us relate to our neighbours, helps foster a sense of community, helps bring the political process, i.e. national politics and corporate politics, within the reach of the individual and the control of the electorate. The significance of news is that it helps orientate us within a community of humans, and not just a system of institutions.

For that reason, news is biased towards information that has **conversational value**. It is not just information about events, it is often about information that is talked about. *Miami Herald*'s Pulitzer Prize-winning crime reporter Edna Buchanan calls it the "My God! Martha" factor. She imagines a couple sitting at the breakfast table and, as the man scans the morning paper, he turns to his wife and says, "My God! Martha, did you read this?" (1987:275). Much of what we consider news – the birth of triplets, the winners of the soccer derby, the latest fashions on the catwalks of Paris – has little or no direct effect on our lives, but it is informative and helps us to socialise, to lean over the breakfast table and speak to our Martha.

Definition

News values [Zu Indlela yokukhetha izindaba / Afr nuuswaardes]: The criteria used by editors to select and prioritise news stories.

Traditional factors that influence news selection

Scholarship about **news values** has endured relatively uncritically since Galtung and Ruge (1965) identified nine factors that increase the likelihood of an event being selected as news. These are: timespan, intensity or threshold value, clarity/lack of ambiguity, cultural proximity or relevance, consonance, unexpectedness, continuity, composition, and sociocultural values. To this we will add: conflict, "visualness", and emotion. Let's look at each of these in turn:

1   Timespan [Zu. isikhathi / Xh. ixesha / Afr. tydsverloop]

An event is also more likely to be noticed if its occurrence fits the time schedule of the medium concerned. For instance, daily newspapers report on what happened today, or since the previous edition. On the other hand, weekly newspapers typically prefer more complex events that take several days to develop. This would explain, in part, that on Friday, 28 May 2004, the lead photograph on the front page of the national daily paper *ThisDay* was of a group of seven high-school girls who had been with President Thabo Mbeki as part of the "Take a girl child to work" day campaign, while the national weekly *Mail & Guardian* led with a photograph of armed men under the headline: "Genocide in the desert – special report from Sudan."

Of course, the advent of 24-hour news television and radio and the introduction of live coverage or "real-time" reporting has heightened the relevance of this point. News comes not as a summary of what has happened; instead the audiences experience it – seeing it unfold. By contrast, some events are too slow in developing, however important, to be really "newsworthy" for the mass media. The process of medical research, for example, is seldom covered outside of announcements of successes or "breakthroughs".

2   Intensity, or threshold value [Zu. ubukhulu / Xh. ubushushu / Afr. intensiteit]

An event is more likely to noticed if it is of great magnitude, or if its normal level of significance suddenly increases so as to attract particular notice. During the time leading up to traditional holiday seasons – Easter and Christmas – news about the traffic-related accidents and deaths often feature prominently in the news. At other times of the year, the issue becomes less topical and the amount of space and time devoted to stories about the issue decreases significantly. Unless, of course, a large number of people are injured or killed in a specific incident.

3 Clarity, or lack of ambiguity [Zu. ukucaca / Xh. ukucaca / Afr. duidelikheid]

The less the significance of an event is in doubt, the more likely it is to be suitable for news treatment. Changes to government policy, for example, might go unreported until the significance of the move is explained to the media. Even so, the criticism often comes that, particularly during election times, journalists emphasise the personality of politicians, rather than report on their ideologies and proposals.

4 Cultural proximity, or relevance [Zu. ukuhambelana / Xh. ngokunxulumene nenkcubeko / Afr. relevansie]

Most events become more newsworthy the closer the action occurs to the audience. Usually, the same event is bigger news if it happens in your town than if it occurs 1 000 or even 10 kilometres away. For the people of Hermanus, on the Cape south coast, the investigation into the cause of a fire which caused R1.24 million damage to a downtown building made front-page news in the *Hermanus Times*, while it received scant mention in the Cape Town city newspapers 100 kilometres away.

Proximity doesn't only refer to geography. The closer the event to the culture and interests of the intended audience, the more likely selection becomes. For instance, on the same Sunday, 6 June 2004, three national newspapers all included sports-related stories on their front pages. But each was quite different:

- *City Press*, which is billed as "the people's paper", led with "Downs poach Chiefs' Baloyi", a story about the soccer star Brian Baloyi quitting Kaiser Chiefs after 14 seasons to join rival Sundowns.
- *Rapport*, the Afrikaans newpaper with the slogan *"ons praat jou taal"* (we speak your language), featured a story about the sport minister's comments about the possible end to race quotas for sports teams.
- In the *Sunday Independent*, which describes itself as "South Africa's quality Sunday newspaper", the lead story was about discontent amongst the nation's top rugby players under the headline: "Fed-up Boks get ready to strike".

Linked to the idea of proximity is the concept of consequence. When the audience will be affected, how the audience will be affected and to what degree the audience will be affected often determine the news value of an item. Increases in the cost of caviar may be ignored by the mass media, but a dramatic rise in the price of bread and milk, which will affect most people, will probably make headlines.

5 Consonance [Zu.-fanelane, -vumelene / Xh. uvumelwano / Afr. konsonansie]

By this is meant that an event which conforms to certain established expections or preconceptions is more likely to be selected than one which does not conform to expectations. For instance, there are some parts of the world where conflict is expected, some activities are inherently dangerous, or where some people are expected to conform to stereotypes.

6 Unexpectedness [Zu. -ukungalindeleki / Xh –ngalindelekanga / Afr. onverwagsheid]

Much of modern journalism is the search for the unusual. Or, as Mitchell Stephens says, "Our news is very much about those events that manage to distinguish themselves from the clip-clop of ordinary experience" (1997:26). A snake biting a man is not news. But, as a *Sunday Times* article illustrates, when farm worker Eddie Mkhize, 54, bit and battered to death a three-and-a-half-metre python which tried to bite him, the story made page three of the giant national weekly (Anon, 1992:3). ("I have to thank God and my strong teeth for saving my life," Mr Mkhize was reported as saying afterwards.)

Another aspect of this factor is scarcity. Typically, rainstorms don't make news, except after a drought.

7 Continuity [Zu. ukuqhubeka / Xh. ukuqhubeka / Afr. aaneenlopendheid]

Once an event has been defined as newsworthy, there will be some momentum to the continued noticing of the event or related incidents. For example, once it's been announced that a politician is under investigation for fraud, readers will want to know more. Will the charges stick? What next? The story will continue (at least for a while) until the focus of attention shifts again.

8 Composition [Zu. ukwakheka / Xh.ukwakhiwa / Afr. komposisie]

These were the headlines in an edition of *The Star* in Johannesburg:
- "Road deaths top 200 and it's not over yet"
- "Zairian rebels push ahead before talks"
- "Can-hurling hooligans mar show in the Karoo"
- "Zion Christian pilgrimage draws 3 million"
- "Three die in shootouts between police and armed robbers"
- "Contestants let their hair down"
- "Who's who in the zoo on April 1"
- "Skies not expected to clear until Thursday"

For its eight front-page stories, the editors selected five hard news items and three soft news stories (including one about staff at the Johannesburg Zoo who were bracing themselves for pranksters who call the zoo on 1 April asking for Mr Oliphant, Mr G Raffe or Mr Lyon. The previous year more than 2 300 such calls were received. "The April Fools' Day calls overload the switchboard, making incoming and outgoing calls difficult, besides driving our receptionist to distraction," a zoo spokesperson said.). Four of the stories originated in Gauteng, one each in Oudtshoorn, Moria (outside Polokwane), Goma (Zaire) and Moscow.

Three images were also used. The largest was of a little wide-eyed girl leaning over a bench; underneath, the caption read: "Bleak future ... a girl attends an Easter mass at one of Kinshasa's Catholic churches yesterday. The political situation in Zaire remains uncertain ahead of peace talks that could begin this week in South Africa." The other two, smaller, images were of singer Miriam Makeba holding cans that had been hurled at her during a performance at the Klein Karoo Nasionale Kunstefees in Oudtshoorn, and of two women in Moscow with hair down to their ankles. The three images were supplied by Reuters and Agence France Presse news agencies, and a staff photographer, respectively.

Editors usually strive for a variety in tone and topic, and news events are selected and presented according to their place in a balanced whole (newspaper or newscast) and some events are consequently selected on the grounds of contrast (such as the one about the long-haired Muscovites).

9 Sociocultural values [Zu. isimo sokuhlalisana kwabantu / Xh. xabisa / Afr. waardes]

Sociocultural values of the receiving audience, or the gatekeepers, will influence choice, over and above the news factors described. For example, you're not likely to see too many in-depth stories about classical music concerts in a mass market daily newspaper such as the *Sowetan*, while SAfm, the SABC's English-language public service radio station, regularly updates listeners on the activities of symphony orchestras.

For similar reasons, we see greater coverage of the events in nations that are perceived to be elite, such as the US, and people that are considered elite, such as wealthy business people, politicians, sports and film stars, and the like.

Additional factors in news selection

While Galtung and Roge's scholarship has been proved over time, their typology can be expanded to include the following factors:

Definition

Sociocultural This term refers to the perspective that looks for the courses of social behaviour in the influences of larger social groups.

10 Conflict [Zu. udweshu / Xh. imbambano / Afr. konflik]

Conflict is the struggle between opposing forces and that is not necessarily negative. From the front page (with reports of corporate takeovers and politicians challenging each other) to the back page (with tales from the soccer field and the boxing ring), it is clear that conflict makes news.

11 "Visualness", or visual appeal [Zu. ukubukeka / Xh. ngokubonakalayo; Af visualiteit]

Visual appeal is important in news publications and, especially, in television news (and obviously unimportant in radio, where sound is key). These media favour stories that are supported by strong pictures, whether of dramatic scenes from a sports field, or of "Biblical"-looking disasters. In the *The Star* news package mentioned above, the image of the little girl gave the story about the Zairean conflict greater prominence than any of the local stories, which either had no pictures or, as in the case of the Oudtshoorn hooligans, a less striking image.

One of the first questions an editor will typically ask is, "What pictures do we have to go with this story?" Strong pictures will often determine whether an image appears on the front page or leads a television news bulletin, and the lack of visuals may push an otherwise significant story to the back of the publication or towards the end of the broadcast.

12 Emotion [Zu. umuno wenhliziyo / Xh.uluvo / Afr. emosie]

Related to visualness is the news factor of emotion. "The suggestion here is that the more an event exhibits an emotional subtext," explains McGregor (2002:4), "the more likely it will be selected." A news event has heightened emotion when it involves common news elements such as tragedy, human interest dilemmas, survivors, victims, children and animals. Think here of the stories of a tearful rugby captain after a championship game, or the forlorn images of people with Aids. In these so-called "tear-jerker" stories, emotion is the key factor in their selection and display.

Hypotheses about how these factors work together to influence newsworthiness

Galtung and Ruge had three hypotheses about how these factors work together to determine the newsworthiness of an event. The first of these is *additivity*, which suggests that the more news factors are associated with a given event, the more likely it is to become "news". Secondly, there is a *complementary* hypothesis, which is that if an event is low on one factor, it may compensate by being higher on some other factor.

That would explain, for example, why a particularly arresting photograph might appear on the front page of a newspaper despite being low on other news factors. Thirdly, there is an *exclusion* hypothesis, according to which an event low on all factors will not become news.

While the study of news factors is useful in helping us understand how certain stories end up being selected amongst all the options, it doesn't help us fully answer a key question: Shouldn't the media be **objective**?

Objectivity and truth-telling in journalism

When South African Broadcasting Corporation newsman Calvin Thusago was hauled from his car and stabbed to death in April 1993, journalists, politicians and community leaders were unanimous in their plea: media workers must be protected. Some of the reasons offered, however, were surprisingly naive.

One media union representative argued that journalists should be protected because they are non-partisan and act merely as channels of information, relaying facts to the public. That journalists relay facts is true enough, but that this process occurs objectively, is not.

The idea that the media should be objective is actually rather new. Early newspapers and magazines were filled with **propaganda** and upfront about it. They reflected the ideologies of a particular political party, or the opinions and aspirations of the single owner – and readers bought them, knowing full well what they would find. In fact, audiences expected a particular slant.

Journalistic objectivity has only been a discussion point since the early 20th century. The reasons offered for this have been varied. Some have suggested that objectivity was merely a ploy by profit-hungry publishers who, concerned that certain advertisers would only support publications that reflected a particular ideology, forced editors to be less obviously biased in order to reach wider audiences (and advertisers) across the political and ideological spectrum. But most scholars (Rosen, 1993) suggest that the claim of objectivity by journalists has been a way of countering interference. In order to counteract meddling by publishers and advertisers, journalists have declared that they needed to tell their story objectively. When politicians and other powerful voices in society complained about the way news was reported, editors and journalists retorted that they were merely telling things the way they were; they were being objective.

But what is actually meant by journalistic objectivity? Westerstahl (1983) divides objectivity into "factualness" and "impartiality". By factualness he means a form of reporting dealing with statements that can be checked against other sources, and which are then presented without

Definition

Objective [Zu. Okungangamelwe yimicabango / Xh. ubukho / Afr. objektief] is defined as not influenced by personal feeling or opinions in considering and representing facts.

Propaganda [Zu. Ukusakaza inkolelo ethize / Afr. propaganda] is the "deliberate and systematic attempt" to shape perception, understanding and behaviour "to achieve a response that furthers the desired interest of the propagandist" (Jowett and O'Donnel, 1986). The term *propaganda* finds its origins in the Roman Catholic church, which set up a congregation of cardinals to spread or propagate its religious doctrines in foreign lands.

comment. Impartiality is an attitude adopted by reporters. Each of these two categories can be further divided, factualness into "truth" and "relevance", and impartiality into "balance" and "neutrality". Let's look at each in more detail.

"Factualness" in journalism

On a philosophical level, truth is about knowing. In the Middle Ages, for instance, monks held that there actually was a hierachy of truth. At the highest level were messages that told us about the fate of the universe, such as whether or not heaven and hell existed. Next came moral truth, which taught us how to live. This was following by allegorical or symbolic truth, which taught the moral of stories. Finally, at the bottom, the least important, was the literal truth or facts, which the theorists said was usually empty of meaning and irrelevant (Kovach and Rosensthiel, 2001:39).

But journalists tend to look at truth practically rather than philosophically. For that reason the first element of truth for the media is accuracy. When the 19th century New York publisher Joseph Pulitzer made "Accuracy! Accuracy!! Accuracy!!!" his motto, he meant the small things: names, ages, addresses (Emery, 1962:374). Like other press barons of his day, he may have committed his share of sins again the larger truths, says Fuller (1997:11). "Nonetheless, his emphatic insistance upon the smaller ones demonstrated a great deal of practical wisdom: Get the little things wrong and readers won't trust you to get the big things right."

Whatever else truth is, it is certainly about getting the details right. Even that is not always as easy as it seems. Should a person be referred to by their given name or the name recorded on their birth certificate? Should a person's death be described as Aids-related, or in terms of the opportunistic condition that was the more immediate cause of his demise?

Journalism's shame is how often it fails to live up to Pulitzer's standard even in respect to the most routine details. Ed Linington, the South African Press Ombudsman, says that the single largest motive for readers' complaints to his office is inaccuracy (2004). There are many reasons for errors: carelessness, mishearing, misunderstanding, mischief. Readers of news do not care about the reasons, just as a

▓HOT LINKS

Mad at the media?
Complaints about articles in the press and other publications are dealt with by the Press Ombudsman, who can be contacted at: Press Ombudsman of South Africa, PO Box 47221, Parklands, 2121 / Tel: (011) 788 4837/29 / Fax: (011) 788 4990/ E-mail: ombudsman@ceg.co.za

Concerns about television and radio programmes can be directed to the Broadcasting Complaints Commission of South Africa (BCCSA), which was set up by the National Association of Broadcasters of Southern Africa in 1993 to adjudicate and mediate complaints against a broadcaster who has signed its Code of Conduct. Visit their website for more details: http://www.bccsa.co.za/

The Advertising Standards Authority of South Africa (ASA), an independent body set up and paid for by the marketing communications industry, regulates advertising in the public interest through a system of self-regulation. Find out more by visiting http://www.asasa.org.za/index.html

diner at a restaurant doesn't care about why there is a fly in her soup. Errors are the journalist's responsibility, whatever the cause.

Impartiality in journalism

We have seen that throughout the process of selecting news, editors and reporters make choices: Which topic is newsworthy? Who are the most appropriate sources? How should the information be arranged in the story? Where and when in the paper or broadcast will the story be placed? How, where and at what cost should the media be distributed? And, how will the audience respond?

It is indisputable that the answers to these questions are influenced by time, money and (of primary importance to this discussion) the reporters' perspectives. Like everyone else, reporters are moulded by their societies, education and exposure – even by their state of mind. News choices are ultimately made by subjective editors who base their decisions, by and large, on subjective interpretations of facts and hearsay provided to them by journalists.

Does this imply that journalists should simply brush aside any effort to keep their personal perspectives in check? No. On the contrary, media workers should acknowledge their own biases and, if their goal is to serve a wide audience, actively work to be balanced and neutral, or fair.

Fairness in selecting stories should prompt sports editors, for example, to feature woman athletes as prominently and frequently as their male counterparts.

Fairness in reporting makes it conceivable that a Jewish reporter can, for example, write an impartial story about conflict between Israelis and Palestinians by approaching a range of reliable sources and presenting a balanced account of the event and its significance to all involved.

Fairness in writing stories means that events are placed in context and age, and that ethnicity, religion, and sexual orientation are not pointlessly emphasised, reinforcing false stereotypes.

Fairness in **playing** stories means a union newsletter would display a story of a corporation's management training programme as prominently as a report on wage negotiations.

Fairness in responding to their readers makes it necessary for newspapers and television stations to display corrections to stories as boldly as the original, faulty report.

Agenda-setting by the media

Discussions about the truth-telling in the media often become very heated, because all parties typically agree on this: the media are powerful. This power is not because the media can necessarily dictate to their audiences what to think (or how to act), but because the media can influence

> *News is "the first rough draft of history"*
>
> PHILIP GRAHAM, FORMER PUBLISHER OF THE *WASHINGTON POST*

Definition

Play [Zu. Ukubonisa, senbeza nga- / Xh. –bonisa, ukusebenzisa / Afr. vertoon, gebruik]: The way a news story is used in the paper or on television, such as where it appears (or is dis*play*ed) and how much space or time is allocated to it.

KEY CONCEPTS

Agenda [Zu. Uhlelo lomsebenzi / Xh. iagenda / Afr. agenda]: An agenda is a list of items to be discussed at a meeting, usually drawn up by the person chairing the meeting, who has the power to arrange them in the order of importance. Terms such as "hidden agenda" or "agenda-setting" in relation to news suggest editors and journalists have the power to decide which items are the news of the day (Branston and Stafford, 1996:134). Read more about agenda-setting (and other media theories) by visiting the Communication, Cultural and Media Studies Infobase site at: http://www.cultsock.ndirect.co.uk/MUHome/cshtml/media/agsetmec.html

what people think (and talk) about. That is called the power of "agenda-setting".

Story selection and play are important because a radio or television station, newspaper, house journal or magazine can set the agenda of issues which we find ourselves thinking about. You might think it is great that there are photographs of scantily-clad women on page three of the *Sun*. Or, you might feel that images that portray women as sex objects are demeaning at best and have no place in a responsible newspaper. Whatever your view on the issue, the point is that you would not be thinking about it if it had not featured in the media. Bernard Cohen first articulated the media's agenda-setting role in *The Press and Foreign Policy* (1963:13):

The press is significantly more than a purveyor of information and opinion. It may not be successful much of the time in telling people what to think, but it is stunningly successful in telling its readers what to think about. And it follows from this that the world looks different to different people depending not only on their personal interests, but also on the map that is drawn for them by the writers and editors, and publishers of the papers they read. The editor may believe he is only printing things that people want to read, but he is thereby putting a claim on their attention, powerfully determining what they will be thinking about, and talking about, until the next wave laps their shore.

EXERCISE *Who has the power?*

The media might have the power to set the agenda for what audiences think about. Have you thought about who sets the media's agenda?

Towards a collective truth

It is unrealistic to assume that any news item, even accurately reported and fairly presented, can equal the reality it presumes to describe. "News – even the best-written – never comes close to equalling or approximating reality," says John Merrill, professor and director of the Louisiana State University's School of Journalism (1984:82). For example, an hour-long show which takes four politicians from opposition parties, touches up their faces with make-up, sits them in a make-believe lounge and questions them about a complex issue, such as economic development strategies, cannot lay claim to having objectively discussed the issue. The best that can be said is that for 60 minutes the show provided a fair platform for a variety of specific voices to discuss a few aspects of the issue.

While news reports should be accurate and fair, they cannot be complete. In a court of law, for example, legal experts have the time and space to collect all the data available and spend days or months pouring over each detail. They then make their case over days, sometimes years. Then a judge mulls thoughtfully over all the information before finally reaching a verdict – and even then, time has shown, some judgements have been incorrect. The news business, on the other hand, doesn't have the luxury of time. And that's the way it should be. News programmes and publications provide running updates and commentaries of events, often as they unfold. Today, money is missing. Tomorrow, someone is suspected. Eventually, charges are filed. Then, the case goes to court. Each day during the trial more details unfold. Each day the news media report what they know at the time. In important and complex cases, there are subsequent contributions on the editorial pages, the talk shows, in the letters to the editor, from the callers to radio shows, on the Internet chat sites – the full range of public and private conversation. A free press ensures that all these contributions, diverse and differing, which allow us to see the event in context, move towards an understanding of the truth of the matter.

Authors Kovach and Rosensthiel explain it this way: "The practical truth is an [unfixed] thing which, like learning, grows as a stalagmite in a cave, drop by drop over time" (2001:47).

The truth here, in other words, is a complicated and sometimes contradictory phenomenon, but seen as a process rather than instance, journalism can get at it. "It attempts to get at the truth in a confused world by stripping information first of any attachment to **misinformation**, **disinformation**, or self-promoting information and then letting the community react, and the sorting-out process ensue. The search for truth becomes a conversation" (ibid).

Only when journalists become aware of the limits of their work and, in turn, discuss these openly with their audiences and sources, will demands for the impossible – the objective news report – cease. And, maybe then those in power will fully appreciate how vital it is to safeguard and support a free and diverse press.

Definition

Misinformation, disinformation The distinction between *misinformation* and *disinformation* has to do with motive. Misinformation is wrong or inaccurate information, while disinformation is information that is intended to mislead. In the former the facts are incorrect; in the latter the facts are deliberately presented or "spun" in such a manner that the audience is misled.

Definition

What is **spin**? In politics, "spin" has come to refer to *the spin* or twist put on a fact, detail, statement, or story which gives it a different look or perspective. "Spin" refers to viewing something in a particular way. If we spin something, our *spins* give the content a particular point of view, perspective, or ideology. We may, for example, *spin* it to give it a positive view in our favour by twisting the facts or statements so that they look more favourable to us. Or we spin something so that it looks more negative for those opposing us. Others have described spin very simply: it is twisting the truth.

EXERCISE Who's spinning whom?

Public relations people are sometimes referred to as "**spin** doctors". But think about this: journalists and editors discuss ways on what angle or a slant to take on a particular story. Is that any different?

Categories of news

Hard news. Soft news. Breaking news. Enterprising news. Journalists use these terms and others to describe different categories of news. Here is a quick overview of the main ones:

Hard news [Zu. Izindaba ezinohlonze / Afr. harde nuus]

Authors Leonard Teel and Ron Taylor have this to say about the hard news report: "To solidify its place at the heart of the newspaper scheme of things, editors have given its content macho names, such as hard news, to distinguish it from sissy soft news ... to give that we-were-there quality" (1988:169).

There can be little argument, however, that whatever the origin of the term, the hard news story is the foundation on which all other newswriting is based. And news editors usually value this type of story above all others.

The term "hard news", say authors Alfred Lorenz and John Vivian (1996:15), applies to event-based stories, such as the opening of parliament or the sinking of a ship, and to depth coverage, which involves stories that explore issues. To that definition, one can usually add the element of time.

Breaking news

When three scientists from Pretoria University announced that they'd found the cure for the Acquired Immunodeficiency Syndrome or Aids and asked the South African parliament for funds to help them further their research, reporters from every news agency pounced on the story. Extracts were taken from the scientists' report, their spokesperson and others were interviewed and journalists scrambled to get the story into the next edition and for the evening newscasts.

Examples of breaking news (also sometimes referred to as "spot news") reports include robberies, plane crashes, hijackings, fires and election results. Details of the announced cure for Aids, for example, was breaking news, but so were the follow-up stories which focused on criticism by the international health community and later the trio's own university which lambasted them for their unorthodox methods.

The characteristics of breaking news stories, say Lorenz and Vivian (1996), are:

- Lead-off sentences (often referred to merely as "leads") are event-based, telling the most significant or interesting development. Other aspects follow.
- With breaking stories, which unravel over time, the latest developments are placed at the top.

- Reporting reacts to events, whether an unexpected occurrence, such as a devastating bush fire, or a scheduled event, such as a news conference.
- Expert sources and witnesses are cited.
- Usually, information for breaking news reports is gathered and written against a deadline.

In-depth news coverage [Zu. Ukwethulwa kwezindaba okujulile / Xh. ukusasazwa kweendaba / Afr. diepteverslaggewing]

Where hard news focuses on events, in-depth coverage (sometimes referred to simply as "depth coverage") is concerned with providing detail and explanation of broad phenomena. In part, it is what the founders of South Africa's first independent newspaper, the *South African Commercial Advertiser*, were referring to when they wrote in the first edition (1824):

> *Tis the privilege of reason to view the scene of life with all its events, not merely in the light of the moment of their actual occurrence may shed upon them, but with the eye of retrospect to what has passed, and of caution for what is to come.*

Investigative journalism [Zu. Ukuloba udaba oluphenyiwe / Xh. umsebenzi wokupapasha iindaba ngokuphanda nzulu / Afr. ondersoekende verslaggewing]

When news reporters try to find information which is of public interest but which someone might be keeping hidden, it is typically referred to as investigative journalism. The *Mail & Guardian*'s Stefaans Brümmer and Sam Sole are amongst the best in the business. Their series on a Nigeria-South Africa oil deal, which government officials implied was to benefit the country, but instead the profits went straight into private pockets, earned them a prestigious Mondi Award. And it also got them lots of criticism from those they exposed. To be an investigative journalist takes skill, tenacity – and a pretty thick skin.

Soft news [Zu. Izindaba ezingatheni / Xh. iindaba zokonwabisa / Afr. sagte nuus]

It would be convenient to say soft news is the opposite of hard news, but the line is not that clear-cut. Some say soft news stories are those whose purpose is more to entertain than to inform (Vivian, 1996:18). However, hard news stories, such as coverage of the first landing on the moon, can be hugely entertaining. Another view is that soft news stories are those stones people want to know, rather than those they feel obligated to know. Then again, the outcome of South Africa's first democratic election on 27 April 1994 was a hard news story which millions of people around the world wanted to know about. Sometimes the terms "human interest" or "features" are used to describe soft news stories. But again, these terms are not the sole domain of soft news.

Perhaps the best way is to look again at the varying time element between the two types of stories. When Prakash Naidoo investigated the state of South Africa's prisons, the *Sunday Independent* (1997:5) devoted an entire page to his reports. At the top of the page was a hard news story under the headline, "The figures reveal the shocking truth about South Africa's crammed prisons", which started this way:

> More than 125 000 prisoners are being held in jails all over South Africa this weekend, at a cost to tax payers of R65,85 a day per inmate.

The time element – "this weekend" – is crucial to the story and would have had to be changed if the story ran the next day or the next week. However, the other three articles would probably be as intriguing if printed in a monthly magazine and, as such, could be considered "soft news". One of them ran under the headline, "The price of survival" and started like this:

> Survival in prison depends on what you can afford and just about anything can be bought as long as you are prepared to pay. But some of the most basic requirements also have to be bought and endemic corruption means that even food rations come only from bribes:
>
> | | |
> |---|---|
> | A small bowl of porridge | R1 |
> | Seven slices of bread | R2 |
> | A small bowl of pap | 50c |
> | Milk for the porridge | 50c |
> | A piece of meat with samp | R4 |

Bright/brite [Zu. Udaba olufushane / Af. stoepie]

A short item, perhaps only a paragraph, that elicits a chuckle or is upbeat in some way.

Changing perspectives on news

We have discussed categories of news as well as the major elements journalists traditionally have used to decide the relative importance of stories competing for space in a newspaper or for time on the air. But recently criteria of news standards, news sources and topics have shifted, and continue to do so.

Changing interests

The bulk of news coverage typically focuses on the Big Four: Politics/government; crime/police/legal; sports; and business/economics/finance. But the range of themes considered newsworthy is changing. Perhaps not too suprisingly, given the impact of HIV and Aids, health has become a prominent news topic. But this goes beyond mere medical issues and also includes fitness and lifestyle issues, such as diet and smoking.

News of Africa at large is also commanding a greater attention in the news. In part, this is because of the role the democratic South Africa plays in regional politics, but it is also because the Internet has allowed greater accessibility to news reports from outside our national boundaries.

With the increase of 24-hour news options – television, radio and the news sites on the Internet – newspapers and magazines also tend to concentrate less on breaking "hard news" than on "softer" news-behind-the-news stories. This might explain greater coverage of themes such as parenting and relationships, real estate and home décor, science and technology, travel, food, and the like.

The interests of audiences are changing and so are their information options – and that is impacting on the agendas of newsrooms.

Changing formats

Many media have accepted the challenge to providing news that grabs readers and allows them to react. The catch phrase is "news you can use". Business sections in newspapers, for example, used to be the sole domain of those with a thorough understanding of economic jargon: "futures markets", "leverage buyouts", "hostile takeovers", and the like. The rest of us had to get help from experts or try to figure things out for ourselves (or not). No longer. New sections on personal finance run in many popular publications, the *Sunday Times* being the prime example. The national weekly's business section includes stories such as how to teach your children about money ("Get your kid to shine his silver spoon"), financial counsel for women who have divorced ("Flying solo should mean regaining control of your cash") and a question-and-answer column, entitled "Rands and sense".

Changing sources

Despite the ideal that the media are to give voice to the voiceless, in selecting sources, journalists have traditionally followed this criterion: the higher the official, the better the quote. But by simply printing statements from official news sources, the media have allowed themselves to be manipulated by community leaders in politics and commerce.

FROM THE NEWSROOM

Prof Lizette Rabe on getting gender right

Prof Lizette Rabe is head of the post-graduate Department of Journalism at the University of Stellenbosch and a key member of the South African National Editors Forum (Sanef). Before she joined academia, she worked as a journalist in various positions, ending her career in media practice as editor of a women's magazine.

1 Why is there a need to emphasise gender-sensitive reporting in our newsrooms?

We live in a male-dominated world; the "male standard" being accepted as "default". It is necessary to re-engineer our thinking in everything we do. It also means we have to re-think the way we practice journalism.

2 How big is the problem?

Journalism was traditionally a male-only profession. Women were only allowed into the "fraternity" in small numbers and over a long period. Standards and practices of how we "do" journalism need to be critically analysed to enable us to become gender sensitive – sensitive towards the female and male population – in order to serve a new world with new standards in a new way.

3 What do you think is the single biggest challenge to overcome in order to address this issue?

We need to overcome our own biases, the stereotypes we have grown up with. This means we have to be constantly alert not to perpetuate stereotypes. However, constant sensitising and conscientising in media newsrooms are not all that is necessary. Media boardrooms also have to be "converted" to an en-gendered mindset.

4 What advice do you have for individual journalists who want to make a difference?

Know what it means to be "en-gendered". Women make up more than 50 per cent of the world population. Several studies have shown that they do not even constitute one-fifth of news sources. As in the slogan of one such study: "Women and men make the news."

5 Can you recommend any other resources?

The South African non-governmental organisation Gender Links' website – http://www.genderlinks.org.za – offers a number of tools to assist journalists, while the Media Monitoring Project – http://www.sn.apc.org/mmp/ – regularly publishes reports on gender coverage in the media.

This practice has also led to the exclusion of other voices, such as those of women. For example, a study by the Media Monitoring Project of gender coverage of the South African national elections in 2004 showed that while women comprise 54% of the population, an average of only 22% of all sources accessed in the media monitored was female.

An important component in the process of defining news values in a democratic society is a healthy respect for the diversity of the audience which, in turn, creates opportunities for their voices to be heard.

Changes in the role of public relations practitioners

Scan the front page of your local newspaper and see if you can spot the influence of public relations practitioners on the type and content of the stories. That report on a new government initiative was probably the result of a statement issued by the minister's spokesperson. And that crime story was likely to have come from the police's media officer. What about interview with the soccer coach? Even if it was initiated by the journalist, the request was probably passed through the media relations person who also made the arrangements.

Public relations practitioners. Media relations people. Spokespersons. Communication officers. Publicists. There are a range of terms used to describe those employed by organisations to manage their relationships with the media and they play a key role in what appears in the news. Recent studies (see Nel, 2002) have shown that journalists' reliance on the efforts of publicists is growing. The reasons for this are varied, but key amongst them are:

1 Economic pressures on editors often result in pressure on newsroom staff to "do more with less". The result is that journalists have to produce more stories, more often. To help them meet relentless deadlines, they rely heavily on prepared statements and images supplied by the publicists who work on behalf of their sources.

2 High turnover of newsroom staff means that a large proportion of working reporters are young and relatively inexperienced. To help them cope with the demands of editors, these rookie journalists often turn to public relations people – many of whom are experienced former journalists – for help.

As a result, the gatekeeping role of the media is weakening, and the power of the publicists – and the organisations that employ them – to set the media's news agenda is growing. Is this bad thing? It depends on whom you ask. Some would argue, yes, the power elites who have the resources to employ publicists are increasingly able to manipulate the news and "spin" stories. Others would argue that greater access by sources contributes to greater diversity. Whatever the view, one thing is certain: thanks to the communication revolution, audiences and activist groups amongst them have greater access to information, and louder voices, and they're using that to hold the media – and by extension their information sources – responsible for what they say.

A definition of news

Considering the factors above, most of us would probably agree with Fuller's definition of news: "News is a report of what a news organisation has recently learned about matters of some significance or interest to the specific community that the organisation serves" (1997:6). This is precise, but perhaps still not quite complete. The definition ignores a crucial party – the audience. Journalists' best efforts are ultimately judged by the audience, and if a news reader glances at a story and says, "This isn't news", then it is not news – at least not for that person.

The French have an old saying, *Plus ça change, plus c'est la même chose*, which translates to: "The more things change, the more they stay the same." That pretty much sums up Mitchell Stephens' view of news. "The basic topics with which ... news accounts have been concerned, and the basic standards by which [we] evaluate newsworthiness, seem to have varied very little. Indeed, the evidence ... points to one conclusion: Humans have exchanged a similar mix of news with a consistency throughout history and across cultures" (1997:27). And what is this definition? "News is, in effect, what is on a society's mind. Has a bill been passed? Has anyone been hurt? Is a star in love? Through the news, groups of people glance at aspects of the world around them. Which of the infinite number of possible news occurences these groups are able to see, and which they choose to look at, will help determine their politics and their philosophy" (ibid).

News, therefore, whatever else it may be, is in the eyes of the beholder: reporters, editors and audiences.

EXERCISE *What do you think news is?*

Write your own definition of news, in about 25 words, based on your personal experience as a consumer of news and your personal sense of mission as an aspiring writer for the media. Discuss your effort with your peers.

In this chapter you learned that:

- News selection decisions are influenced by three fundamental biases of journalism: immediacy, interest for a given community, and significance.
- While the essence of news cannot be measured the way a scientist measures, for example, the component parts of water, scholarship has identified factors that increase the likelihood of an event being selected as news. These are: timespan, intensity or threshold value, clarity/lack of ambiguity, cultural proximity or relevance, consonance, unexpectedness, continuity, composition, sociocultural values, conflict, "visualness" and emotion.
- Truth-telling in journalism is best seen as a process, rather than an event. Each report, along with editorials, letters from readers and talk-show discussions, helps create a more complete picture of an event and its significance. Taken together and seen in context, these help lead us collectively towards the truth.

  Underpinning any effort to provide towards truth is accuracy. Whatever else journalists do, they have to start by getting the observable facts right.

█**HOT**█ LINKS

The Newseum – the world's first interactive museum of news – is online at: http://www.newseum.org. Its stated mission is simple: "To help the public and the news media understand one another better."

Putting your learning to work

ACTIVITY 1 Recognise the elements of a newsworthy story

Among the elements that traditionally make a story newsworthy to a mass audience are:
- timespan
- intensity or threshold value
- clarity/lack of ambiguity
- cultural proximity or relevance
- consonance
- unexpectedness
- continuity
- composition
- sociocultural values
- conflict
- visualness
- emotion

Look at a television news bulletin or front page of a newspaper and see if you can identify the dominant news facts in each story. Discuss your choices with your friends. Do you all agree? What could be possible reasons for disagreement?

Do Galtung and Ruge's hypotheses of how these factors work together help us understand the selection and presentation of stories?

ACTIVITY 2 Checking on the news agenda

Make a note of the day's major news headlines. Think about the extent to which they influence what you and those around you (your colleagues, friends, family) talk about. Jot down your thoughts. A week later, take a look at that day's headlines.
- Do you wonder what happened to stories which, in the first set of head-lines, seemed urgent and important?
- Why did they lose their high status and become less important?
- Does this mean that you and those around you forgot about them – that they went "off the agenda"?

Newshound Denis Beckett on news

Denis Beckett is a veteran print and television journalist and political commentator. He was editor of the Sunday Star *newspaper's "Insight" pages where this piece, "When It's Good, It's Really Bad", first appeared.*

We in the press are supposed to tell people what's happening in the world. That's the theory, anyhow. Of course we're entirely used to people taking swipes at us for not getting it right. Usually they say either that we're too full of Grim Reality and too thin on Light Escapism or they say the opposite, that we waste space on pictures of Claudia Schiffer when we are only telling half of a quarter of what we know about mayhem in Katlehong.

Those are the standard complaints. Once in a while a different one comes up and this week I heard a thought-provoking argument, from my friend Ueli. Namely, that we should not even begin to claim we are reporting "what's happening". We should admit that we are actually in the business of reporting what's happening wrong.

For instance, every day some 90 000 airline flights pass without incident. If we were literally telling people what's happening, we'd have on average 1,7-million stories saying "Successful Trip Completed" for every one story saying "Crash", and news consumers would have an image of airline flight as something remarkably safe and efficient. (Indeed you are statistically safer on an airliner than at your dinner table, where you are unlikely to be in the presence of personnel trained to save you from, for instance, choking on a food particle.) But in fact, of course, when you see a story about an airline, you're almost always seeing a story about a crash.

Or take the annual Easter Road Death Ritual. Year after year, the same crop of recurring headlines. Road Toll Up, Road Toll Rises, Road Toll Fears ... occasionally even Road Toll Drops, but always the toll, never the safe arrivals, never even a mention that in "what's happening" terms the safe arrivals are strictly speaking more newsworthy than the deaths. They go up at a faster rate, as road usage increases.

You could take the argument a long way. What in fact is happening is that maybe a million people go unmugged, unmurdered and unreported in Gauteng each day for every one whose misfortunes hit the headlines. At least as many things are, literally, happening in Switzerland as in Somalia. When did you last see Switzerland in the news?

What's really happening, with overwhelming dominance, is amazing normality – not the grimness and not the escapism either. If gunfire is not the world's chief reality, neither is Claudia Schiffer, and if the press truly told people "what's happening" both the guns and the Claudias would take a distant back seat.

Now you can see that Ueli is not about to get offered a job as a press consultant. If an editor tries to offer his readers Tannie Martha in the kitchen while his competitor is giving them Claudia in a miniskirt, he will rapidly become an ex-editor. Same if he gives them pictures of the mealie crop in Phuthadijaba while his rival splashes casspirs in Katlehong.

That's the trouble with all the "give us good news" demands the people are constantly making of the press. People might think they want good news and say they want good news, but what they actually read is bad news. Bad news is crisp; good news is dull. Bad news is vivid; good news usually means complicated committee resolutions and proceedings. It's not that editors are ghouls; it's that people are more gripped by a snake striking than by a doe grazing.

More than that, bad news is on the whole easy to reach and easy to write. Good news is neither. Pitch up, for example, at a trouble-spot of the "racial tension" variety and one of the first people to greet you will be a photogenic AWB with a gun and a swastika and a big mouth, which he is using to utter quotably disgusting racial insults, whereas the dorp's average white resident ducks as far as he can out of the way of the press (who he thinks are going to shaft him) and if you can finally get a comment out of him at all it is something troubled and moderate, totally unblood-curdling and hard to see surviving the bottleneck struggle for limited news space.

The news media have by no means arrived at the end of history. If we look back now at the newspapers of a century ago, with their front pages devoted to advertisements and their middle pages consisting of huge slabs of leisurely grey small print, we can barely believe that anybody ever read that stuff. A century from now, of course, people will be looking back at today's ways and thinking exactly the same.

The trouble is, we don't know what it is that they,

then, will know better than we know now. But I have a funny feeling that something along the lines of the "what's actually happening" theory might not be a million miles from the mark.

News media, to be true, aren't doing terribly well. Over the last 30 years or thereabouts, while populations and literacy rates have escalated dramatically, the circulation of the news media as a whole has barely increased at all.

Something is amiss, and nobody really knows what it is. There's a key waiting to be found, and it's likely that wherever the key is, it involves a way out of the current diet that presents depression as the main course and artificial relief as the sorbet.

EXERCISE *Is bad news good?*

Why don't you test Beckett's theory? Evaluate the contents of a single newspaper, broadcast or Internet site and list the stories under headings for "bad news" and "good news". Which side has more stories? If you had been the editor and had the power to re-arrange the stories, what would you have done? Why would you have made those choices?

Bibliography and recommended reading

Anon. 1992. Eddie puts the bite on a giant python. *Sunday Times,* September 20, 1992: 3.

Bates, S. 1989. *If no news, send rumors: anecdotes of American journalism.* New York: St Martin's.

Branston, G. and Stafford, R. 1996. *The media student's book.* London: Routledge.

Buchanan, E. 1987. *The corpse had a familiar face: covering Miami, America's toughest crime beat.* New York: Random House, 1987.

Cohen, B.C. 1963. *The press and foreign policy.* Princeton, N.J: Princeton University Press.

De Lange, L., Kruger, T. and Verster, I. 1996. Transformation times. *Stellenbosch Journalism Insight.* University of Stellenbosch.

Diederichs, P. 1993. The fourth estate: a cornerstone of democracy. In De Beer, A.S. (ed). *Mass media for the nineties.* Pretoria: Van Schaik.

Emery, E. 1962. *The press in America,* 2nd ed. Englewood Cliffs, NJ: Prentice Hall.

Jowett, G.S. and O'Donnell, L. 1986. Propaganda and persuasion. In Price, S. 1997. *The complete A-Z media and communication handbook.* London: Hodder & Stoughton.

Fuller, J. 1996. *News values; ideas for an information age.* Chicago: University of Chicago.

Galtung and Ruge, M. Holmboe. 1965. The structure of foreign news: The presentation of the Congo, Cuba and Cyprus crises in four Norwegian newspapers.

Journal of Peace Research, vol. 2, pp. 64–91. Online edition http://www.jstor.org/view/00223433/ap20006/02a00040/0

Kovach, B. and Rosensthiel, T. 2001. *The elements of journalism; what newspeople should know and the public should expect.* New York: Crown.

Linnington, E. 2004. In an interview with Mathatha Tsedu on etv. 2004.

Lippmann, W. 1992. Public opinion. In Fuller, J. 1996. *News values; ideas for an information age.* Chicago: University of Chicago.

Lorenz, A. and Vivian, J. 1996. *News reporting and writing.* Needham Heights, MA.: Allyn & Bacon.

McGregor, J. 2002. Restating news values: contemporary criteria for selecting the news. [Online] Proceeding of 2002 ANZCA conference: communication: reconstructed for the 21st century. Greenmount Beach Resort, Coolangatta. Hosted by Bond University, Queensland.

Merrill, J. 1984. News media, news, objectivity – ontological questions in journalism. *Equid Novi*, 5(2): 79–82.

Nel, F. 2002. Relationships between media organizations and their commercial content providers in a society in transition: a discussion of a South African experience. In proceedings of the European Public Relations Education and Research Association, 9th annual conference. Bled, Slovenia, 6 July 2002.

Rosen, J. 1993. Beyond objectivity. *Niemann Reports.* Winter 1993: 49. Cambridge, MA: Harvard.

Stephens, M. 1997. *A history of news.* Fort Worth, Tx: Harcourt Brace.

Teel, L. and Taylor, R. 1988. *Into the newsroom: an introduction to journalism*, 2nd edition. Chester, Connecticut, The Globe Pequot Press, 1988.

Westerstahl, J.1983. Objective news reporting: general premises. *Communication Research*, 10: 403-424.

4

Reporter's toolbox: a starter kit

Introduction

Writing, it is said, is a craft. In that sense, it's a bit like carpentry. Writers and editors work from a plan and use tools stored on their workbench. The value of the end product depends on the quality of the raw materials, the sharpness of the tools, and the skill with which these have been employed.

KEY CONCEPTS

Enthusiasm, critical thinking, and compassion are essential tools for professional journalists; the common rules of English grammar; taking written notes and recording interviews.

So, before we tackle the task of reporting and writing stories, ask yourself: What tools do I need to do this job? Quick, make a list.

All right. Now, let's see what you came up with. A notebook? Yes, you'll probably need one, as well as a pen to take notes. A tape recorder? Possibly. A cell phone? Most definitely. An Internet-linked computer? That's essential in modern media contexts. And, of course, you'll need certain skills, such as shorthand, typing and knowledge of grammar, to make the most of your tools. Some of what you will require in your reporter's toolbox is, perhaps, less obvious: enthusiasm to explore, the courage to question – and a picture of your mom.

This chapter will cover the most basic tools you'll need and to which you'll be able to add as you continue working through this book.

LEARNING GOALS

At the end of this chapter, you should be able to:

1 Recognise the need for enthusiasm, critical thinking and compassion.
2 Follow some of the most common rules of English grammar.
3 Take fast, accurate notes.

Passion: "Cheque-book enthusiasm"

Philip Graham, the late publisher of the *Washington Post*, described news as "the first rough draft of history" (*Newsweek*, 1963:13). The job of gathering the information and writing that "rough draft" can be exciting, demanding and rewarding for journalists. Of course, much depends on the journalist's attitude.

A key quality for a journalist is the ability to "get interested" in something that minutes before held absolutely no interest.

Trisha Greene, my first editor, used to demand "cheque-book enthusiasm", meaning that reporters should have a bank account full of enthusiasm. Each time you tackle an assignment you need to withdraw some enthusiasm, write a cheque, if you will. I had to write plenty of cheques. Amongst my first assignments were to report on Dental Health Day activities at the local shopping mall, a Parents Without Partners group outing to a local park, and a man charged with "telephone abuse" after he called up the police department and cursed at an officer. If writing for the media is what you want to do, you will need to show the same commitment – and the same enthusiasm – when exploring a range of topics, many of them about things that don't naturally interest you. Veteran reporters Leonard Teel and Ron Taylor (1988:56) think it is essential: "There is no substitute for this sort of blank-cheque enthusiasm: If you don't have it, life gets less exciting when you're suddenly assigned to interview the toothless man on a cross-country trip collecting autographs of celebrities. In fact, if you can't get interested in other people's ideas, you ought to reconsider your choice of career."

> *"You need to be a newshound and have a sense of urgency because the media is dynamic."*
> Matthew Buckland, editor, *Mail & Guardian* Online

Critical thinking

What is that, you ask? Is it the tendency to be contrary, or even negative about things? Or is it the line of thought that many movie critics follow? Is it not the mindset that lets you punch holes in someone else's suggestions? Critical thinking is rarely any of the above; in fact, it is hardly the aggressive approach that the term "critical" might suggest. Instead, as the journalism staff at one university puts it: "Critical thinking is good reasoning; it's good analysis" (UNR, 2004).

Critical thinking relies on your ability to spot the real issues within conflicting points of view – to resist the tug of emotions, and to sense manipulation.

Critical thinking demands an open-mindedness that might cause you to change your opinion once you've seen all the evidence.

All good so far, you say, but why the emphasis now? And why in journalism?

You'll find the answers in newsrooms, says Mohammed Shaikh, former assistant editor of *Die Burger* (2003). There you'll hear news editors and sub-editors constantly complaining about one thing: young journalists who accept everything at face value (especially if a cabinet minister or someone in a high place says so). Too often their stories emphasise who said something, rather than what he or she said. Obvious contradictions in information remain unchallenged. Numbers that don't add up are repeated exactly, or journalists simply say they landed up in a dead end.

"Journalists are in essence storytellers," says Shaikh, "but to tell a story, you must unlock information, dig it out if necessary, and logically piece together a complete picture which can be conveyed to the readers. That's where most young journalists fall short. They foster dreams of big stories and to write a best seller (some day), but have not yet mastered the basic skills of knowing on which doors to knock, which questions to ask, and how to query illogical responses."

The inclination to question is at the core of critical thinking. And that takes courage. You don't only need the nerve to confront those in power, but also the guts to keep positive. Being critical is not the same as being cynical. And it is certainly not the same as being petty or sinister.

Critical thinking, say Michael Scriven and Richard Paul of the National Council for Excellence in Critical Thinking (2004), can be seen as having two parts:

- a set of skills to process and generate information and beliefs, and
- the habit, based on intellectual commitment, of using those skills to guide behaviour.

By contrast, they say, critical thinking is not:

- merely getting and remembering lots of information (because it is about a particular way in which information is gathered and treated)
- the sheer possession of a set of skills (because it involves the continual use of them) and
- the simple use of those skills ("as an exercise") without accepting their results.

Critical thinking varies depending on the motivation underlying it. When the motive is selfish, it is often skillfully used to manipulate ideas to serve one's own, or one's group's, vested

---

Profile of the Critical Thinker
This definition of a critical thinker was passed along to university journalism staff by a colleague. His source was anonymous.
A critical thinker is an individual who:
Reasons his/her way through to a position by considering the evidence available;
Knows what objections are likely to be raised to a position and knows how to examine positions by probing their assumptions and consequences;
Does not allow *vivid information* and *anecdotal evidence* to carry undue weight in his/her reflections;
Realises the effect that emotions and feelings and prejudices may have on his/her thinking;
Is willing to revise his/her position in light of the reasoning of others and of contrary evidence;
Is sensitised to the demands of clarity and is able to detect objectionable vagueness in his/her own thinking and the thinking of others;
Remains unimpressed by the sheer force of someone's rhetoric and conviction when these masquerade as substitutes for reasoning;
Stops to think before arriving at a judgment; is able to say to himself/herself, "Hold on a minute, here. Am I being swept away by the heat of the moment?"
Thinks, judges and acts mindful of the limitations of time and information imposed by the situation.
Source: The Reynolds School of Journalism at the University of Nevada at http://www.unr.edu/unr/journalism/pro.home.html

interests. As such, it is typically intellectually flawed, however practically successful it might be. When rooted in fairmindedness and intellectual integrity, it is typically of a higher order intellectually, though it may be considered "idealism" by those in the habit of using it for selfish purposes.

Critical thinking of any kind is never universal in any individual; everyone is subject to times of undisciplined or irrational thought. Its quality is therefore usually a matter of degree and dependent on, among other things, the quality and depth of experience in a given domain of thinking, or with respect to a particular class of questions. No one is a critical thinker through-and-through, but only to such-and-such a degree, with such-and-such insights and blind spots, subject to such-and-such tendencies towards self-delusion. For this reason, developing the inclination and skills to think critically are life-long pursuits. And that takes courage.

> **HOT LINKS**
>
> Learn more about critical thinking from "Mission Critical", an interactive tutorial, at http://www.sjsu.edu/depts/int and the Reynolds School of Journalism at the University of Nevada at http://www.unr.edu/unr/journalism/pro.home.html

Getting to grips with grammar

Want to skip this section? Before you do, check your ability by completing this short quiz.

EXERCISE *Check your grammar and punctuation*

The following sentences each contain no more than one error. Read each sentence. Circle the error. In the space provided at the end of each sentence, indicate which part of the sentence has the error by noting the number that follows the error.

Example: If the regular season is any indication (1), Kaiser Chiefs should be considered (2) a top challenger (3) for the championship; having downed (4) defending regional champion Spurs twice in the tournament (5) __4__ *(Clauses on either side of a semi-colon should be independent)*

1 The list of candidates (1) being considered as successors (2) to Reserve Bank Governor, Tito Mboweni, have (3) been trimmed (4) to approximately 10 names. _____

2 The computer did not (1) seem to be (2) working today, (3) it kept rejecting the operator's (4) instructions. _____

3 The following afternoon, (1) Wednesday, October 25 a South (2) African Air Force DC-10 (3) put down in the abandoned dirt strip of Cheredzi Airport (4). _____

4 Traditionally expected to be in control of their surroundings, (1) the insecurity of it makes first-year students (2) uncomfortable in their new situation (3). _____

5 Makaba's body (1) will lay in (2) state until services are held (3) at the cathedral (4). _____

6 Hopefully, the council will pass (1) a new noise ordinance (2) before the students return (3) to campus in June. (4) _____

7 Among those who attended the gala fundraising banquest hosted on Robben Island were (1) Bono, the British rock star, (2) Mrs Adele Searll, the Cape Town socialite; (3) Ms Peggy Sue

Khumalo, former Miss South Africa; Mrs Hillary Clinton, a US senator; and Mr Kofi Annan, secretary-general of the United Nations (4). _____

8 She predicted that (1) neither Brazil or (2) Germany would (3) host the Olympics in 2016 (4). _____

9 In its advertising (1), the Steel Company claims that they (2) are in business only (3) to do good (4). _____

10 Bulelani de Lille, head of the (1) People Against Poor Administration (PAPA) (2) ran second in the Oct. 10 (3) race for four vacant student council (4) positions. _____

11 One of every five (1) of the city's residents live (2) in the sort of poverty (3) that drove Erskine Caldwell to march on Parliament (4). _____

12 Three-fourths of the business district (1) in Soweto, Gauteng (2) was destroyed by fire, which raged through (3) the town in 1996 (4). _____

13 Many a girl use to believe (1) that she could acquire (2) practically flawless skin just by eating enough pumpkin.

14 Nkosi says the parade would feature the reigning Mr Gay SA, (1) a marching band will play, (2) drum majorette, (3) and as many floats as possible (4). _____

15 Everyone needs (1) to grab their own gear (2).

What's wrong with the following sentences? Correct each error.

16 Several people, all of them eager to give their opinions and all of them pressing forward to meet the author, who was autographing books for fans in the shopping centre.

17 I like braaivleis and beer, I don't like wine and cheese.

18 Agnes complained, and she had no heat.

19 Being a soccer player, his leg muscles were well developed.

20 The crocodile is hunted for their skin.

This quiz is a modification of the "Grammar Slammer Quiz" developed by Katherine McAdams, an associate professor at the University of Maryland (McAdams and Elliott, 1996:203). See page 83 for the correct answers.

Most journalists (and would-be journalists) think of themselves as language experts. That isn't so, if newsroom managers are to be believed. Here is a short review of some of the most common errors writers of English make.

Subject and verb agreement

Few writers make obvious errors in subject and verb agreement, such as "I is interested in singing" or "The class know it is time to take a break". But many people struggle with the following:

Collective subjects

This can be confusing when the noun appears to be plural – as with scissors, economics, Boy Scouts – but is treated as a singular unit.

> The Boy Scouts is a fine organisation.
> Economics is a difficult subject.
> A pair of scissors is a useful office tool.

- Some, however, have Latinate endings and stay plural, although spoken language tends to make them singular, such as media and alumni. They require plural verbs:

  The media have raised the issue of government accountability.

- Pronouns each, either, neither, anyone and anybody are always singular, regardless of what follows them in a phrase. Take, for example, this sentence:

  Either of the girls is an excellent choice for class captain.

  The phrase "of the girls" does not change the singular number of the true subject of this sentence: the pronoun "either".

Some other examples of correct usage:

Neither has my support.
Either will do.
Each has a terrible problem.
Anyone is allowed to take a break.

- A fraction or percentage of a whole is considered a singular subject:

  A quarter of the cake is finished.
  Seventy-one per cent of the students is successful.

- Compound subjects, in which two or more nouns function as the subject of a sentence, can lead to agreement problems. To solve such problems, substitute a pronoun such as "they" or "it" for the sentence's subject or subjects.

  The students and the lecturer are/is off on a trip. By use of substitution, the subject becomes "they": They are off on a trip.

- When subjects are structured with either/or and neither/nor, use the verb that responds to the subject closest to it, as in the following examples:

  Either the driver or the passengers pay the petrol.
  Either the passengers or the driver pays the petrol.

Correct use of pronouns

Pronouns are the little words – she, he, you, they, I, it – that stand for proper nouns. Look at this sentence:

Media24 is hiring 12 new writers because it is expanding its operations in KwaZulu-Natal.

In this sentence, the word "it" is used to substitute for Media24. Pronouns help us avoid needless repetition in language by doing the work of the larger nouns, which are called antecedents. In the example above, "Media24" is the antecedent for the pronoun "it".

Pronouns must agree with their antecedents, as in the following examples:

Agnes said she (Agnes) would never cut her (Agnes's) hair.
Ethikweni became a model city after it successfully restored the harbour.
Media Studies is a popular subject, and now it prepares students for many careers.

Who and whom

- The word "whom" has almost disappeared from spoken English, so it is not surprising that few of us know how to use it correctly. Even though usage is changing, writers of published material still need to know the rules that govern the distinction between who and whom.
- *Who* is a substitute for subjects referring to he, we, or she or the nominative pronoun (a name).

Who saw the gunman?

The statement "He saw the gunman", as a question becomes "Who saw the gunman?" "Who" is substituted for the subject "he". Relative clauses work the same way when "who" is substituted for a subject. In the sentence "He questioned the man who saw the gunman", "who" substitutes for the subject of the clause "he saw the gunman". This is confusing because the entire clause serves as an object of the verb questioned. But the function of the clause does not change the role of a pronoun. In this sentence, the role of "who" is as the subject of the verb "saw".

- *Whom* is a substitute for objective pronouns such as him, her or them.

To whom did he speak for hours?
He spoke to her for hours.

The statement "He spoke to her for hours", as a question becomes "To whom did you speak for hours?" "Whom" is substituted for "her" as the object of the verb questioned. Substitution works the same way in relative clauses. In the sentence "Hajierah was the one whom he spoke to for hours", "whom" substitutes the object "her" in the clause "He spoke to her for hours". Again, it is the role of the pronoun within its subject-verb structure that determines whether it is the subject or object, and therefore who or whom.

That and which

There is also a fine distinction between "that" and "which". Again, the spoken language no longer follows strict rules, regardless of the subordinate conjunctions, but careful writers need to observe the following guidelines (McAdams and Elliott, 1996:216):

- "That" is a restrictive pronoun, indicating that the information it precedes is essential for correct understanding of the sentence.

   Many Namibians enjoy hobbies that improve their health.

The use of "that" tells us that Namibians prefer a specific kind of activity.

- "Which" precedes non-essential material; therefore, it typically appears with commas (the ones used to set off non-essential information).

   Many Namibians enjoy hobbies, which improve their health.

The use of the word "which" tells us that hobbies improve Namibians' health.

That and which are not interchangeable. As you can see in the examples, the meaning of the sentence is affected when the comma is added in the second sentence and "that" becomes "which". In the first sentence, Namibians like only hobbies that are good for them; in the second sentence, Namibians like hobbies, and hobbies just happen to be good for their health. The second sentence is far more logical.

Modifier placement

- To solve modifier placement problems, place modifying clauses and phrases closest to whatever it is that they modify, as shown in these examples:

   Poor: When running for cover, the man fired three shots at my head.

   Better: The man fired three shots at my head as I was running for cover.

   Poor: We saw a herd of buffalo on the way to our camp.

   Better: On the way to our camp, we saw a herd of buffalo.

   Poor: Swinging from a tree, we saw a baboon.

   Better: We saw a baboon swinging from a tree.

HOT LINKS

Online grammar tips (and more)
Looking for tips on grammar? What about online dictionaries and maps? You'll find these and a great deal more at the Information Literacy site developed by Cape Higher Education Consortium and available online at: http://www.lib.uct.ac.za/infolit/. This one is definitely worth bookmarking on your Internet browser (and if you don't know how to do that, the site has a "Learning the Internet" link, too).

HOT TIP

Make sure that you pay attention to the advice in this section and get yourself a notebook to use when reporting. Approaching your assignments professionally will not only help you write a better story, but it will probably make those you come in contact with treat you with greater respect.

Notebooks

Reporters will write on anything: envelopes, cocktail serviettes, cigarette boxes, backs of cheques and cheque-books. There are even tales of desperate journalists writing on their hands and up their arms.

Even if you're using a digital notebook or electronic tablet, it's wise to keep an old-fashioned paper notebook on hand. Ideally, you should consider choosing a notepad that is convenient for you, but discreet. Many people are nervous when reporters start taking notes on large, obtrusive pads that crinkle when the pages turn.

A good idea is to get a spiral-bound notepad with a hard back that you can comfortably hold with one hand. It makes it easier for you if you have to stand during an interview. Consider numbering and dating your notepads so that you can file them for reference. Remember to write your name, e-mail address and telephone number on the cover; it will increase the chances of getting it back should you leave it somewhere.

Also, avoid putting your notebook on a surface near that cup of coffee (or something stronger) you're drinking. The tales of journalists trying to patch together stories from dripping scraps of ink-stained paper are legendary.

Tips on taking notes

You may have had a fantastic interview, but your efforts are in vain if you have not recorded it in a way you can use. Inexperienced reporters often lose excellent facts and quotes because they do not get the information down fast enough or, in their haste, scribble it so that later even they cannot decipher their handwriting.

Reporters' notepads are covered in strange, sometimes quirky symbols, abbreviations and shortcuts that help them quickly jot down what is said. Because few reporters are trained in secretarial or recording techniques, they usually devise a system that lets them record speedily, accurately and completely – and to go back and retrieve the information with relative ease.

Developing "notehand"

Some of the helpful "notehand" symbols include the following:

atny	attorney	px	police
bk	book	rep	representative
cr	classroom	SA	South African
eg	example	sitn	situation
f	father	sldr	soldier
gg	going	std	standard
hpd	happened	u	you
i.e.	that is	u r	you are
invu	interview	u/stng	understanding
j	judge	wh	what
m	mother	w/	with
nfa	not for attribution	w/o	without
OR	off the record	Xn	Christian
ple	people	y.p.	young people

Also use symbols:

@	at	#	numbers
> <	greater than or less than	;	therefore

Using these shortcuts to taking notes is a little like learning a new language; you will only become fluent with practice.

Tape recorders

More reporters are swapping traditional notebooks for miniature tape recorders. This little gadget has many advantages:

- It provides total accurate recall, which is especially useful when quoting dialogue or extended parts of speech.
- When a reporter is not bent over a notepad, she has greater freedom to observe and react to the interviewee.
- The interview is captured verbatim and disputes with sources over being misquoted can be settled more easily.

But the tape recorder has its disadvantages too:

- The strongest argument against using a tape recorder may be that it is too complete. Instead of returning to the office with selected facts and choice quotes, the reporter has to wade through the entire interview again to transcribe the information. This process steals a scarce commodity: time.

LINKS

Journalists need maths skills to make sense of numbers the way they need language skills to make sense of words. Here are some resources compiled by NewsLab, a non-profit resource centre for television and radio newsrooms, to help you grapple with number-heavy stories: http://www.newslab.org/resources/math.htm

- Some sources feel uncomfortable being taped, while others mumble, rendering the recording unintelligible.
- Technology fails. True, your pen may run out of ink halfway through an interview but it cannot happen without you noticing it in good time, as is the case when the batteries go flat or the tape jams.
- Reporters are not forced to listen as carefully as when they are taking notes. Having said that, I own a small tape recorder and usually have it close at hand. When doing important interviews, I usually ask the source if they mind if I switch on the tape and then I take notes as well. The notes help me focus on what is being said and serves as an index of the taped interview. It is also a backup in case something goes wrong. Back at my computer, I review only the recorded sections I want to double-check and those I want to quote.

Compassion: "Carry a picture of your mom"

Yes, as a journalist you are charged with telling stories that matter to other people. But people matter more. Stories are not ends in themselves; they only have meaning in the context of flesh-and-blood readers and sources. Perhaps this truth might be more real to journalists if they carried a photograph of their mothers with their notebooks and cameras and asked themselves: Am I treating the sources with the care and respect that I would like others to treat my parents, my siblings, my partner or my children? Am I telling stories that I would be proud to show them?

In this chapter, you learned that

- Media workers operate in an increasingly complex environment that demands a wide range of knowledge and skills. For that reason, it is important to recognise that:
  - Following grammar rules is essential for professional communicators.
  - Taking fast, accurate notes requires planning and practice.
  - Professional journalists need to be enthusiastic, critical thinkers, and compassionate.

Understanding key terms

Active voice [Zu. Inkulumo- ngqo / Afr. bedrywende vorm]: Active form of the verb or sentence is preferred in journalism. In the sentence "The man drives the car", the verb is in the active. *See passive voice.*

Diction [Zu. Indlela yokukhuluma / Xh. ingcaciso-mazwi / Afr. woordkeuse]: Style or manner of speaking or writing; choice of words, which should consider the language skills of the readers.

Metaphor [Zu. Isingathekiso / Xh. isikweko / Afr. metafoor]: Use of a word or phrase to indicate something different from (though related in some way to) the literal meaning, as in "I'll make him eat his words". Metaphors can contribute to clear and engaging writing, but can also create confusion. Use metaphors with care. *See simile.*

Object [Zu. Umenziwa / Xh. injongo-senzi / Afr. voorwerp]: *grammar.* Noun, noun phrase or noun clause which refers to a person, thing, etc. affected by the action of a verb, or which depends on a preposition, e.g. in "He took the book" and "He took what he wanted", "the book" and "what he wanted" are direct objects. In "I gave him the book", "him" is an indirect object. In "I received the flowers from her", "her" is a prepositional object.

Passive voice [Zu. Inkulumo-mbiko / Afr. lydende vorm]: *grammar.* Passive form of the verb (werkwoord) or sentence. In the sentence, "The car was driven by the man", the phrase "was driven by" is in the passive voice. *See active voice.*

Pretentious [Zu. Amagama akhangayo / Xh. ngokugwagwisayo / Afr. verwaand of aanmatigend]: *adjective.* Claiming (usually without justification) merit or importance. Journalists who use pretentious words or phrases in their writing do little to build good relationships with readers.

Simile [Zu. Isifaniso / Xh. isifaniso / Afr. vergelyking]: Comparison of one thing with another, as in "she has a face *like* a mask". *See metaphor.*

Subject [Zu. Umenzi / Xh. intloko / Afr. onderwerp]: *grammar.* Word(s) in a sentence naming who or what does or undergoes the action stated by the verb, e.g. "the man" in "The man sang a song". *See object.*

Verb [Zu. Isenzo / Xh. isenzi / Afr. werkwoord]: *grammar.* Word or phrase indicating an action, an event or a state, e.g. sing, carry, happen.

Journalists look out! Challenges ahead!

"The need for training journalists has never been greater. As the world becomes increasingly complex, so does the news that we must cover. Journalists today must have a daunting array of knowledge and technical skills at their fingertips to produce even routine stories," according to Winnie Hu of the *New York Times*, whom Connie Molusi of Johnnic Communication quoted in a speech at the South African National Editors Forum's Skills Indaba (2002). More than a hundred editors, media executives, senior journalism trainers, educators and journalists had met to discuss the finding of an audit of reporters' skills which identified key areas that needed attention, including:

- Poor reporting skills
- Lack of concern for accuracy
- Poor writing skills
- Lack of life skills
- Low levels of commitment
- Weak interviewing skills
- Weak legal knowledge
- Lack of sensitivity
- Weak knowledge of ethics
- Poor general, historical and contextual knowledge

Molusi added: "The single biggest challenge facing journalism and the management of newsrooms is accepting that the knowledge, technology and structure for getting the work done has changed, also that the people doing the work are different …

What are these differences and how important are they? The differences are obvious: race, language, ethnic heritage, gender, age, sexual orientation, disability, social class and educational level. These differences also imply differences in religion, attitudes, and values. Everyone is coming from somewhere with a unique, often deeply held set of cultural values, or point of view. These values and points of view influence how people act in the workplace. *The implications of cultural diversity for learning are enormous.*"

- What do you think "implications of cultural diversity" are for your learning as an aspiring media worker?
- What are you going to do to face that challenge – and the others listed above?

Correct answers listed on p. 84

Putting your learning to work

ACTIVITY 1 Correct word usage

Several of the following words are misspelt in a way that a computer spellcheck can't pick up. Circle the misspelt words and write the correct spelling for each in the space provided.*

1 prophecy (to predict) _____
2 principal (of the school) _____
3 stationery (you write on it) _____
4 suite (of clothes) _____
5 blond (beauty queen) _____
6 canvass (to solicit) _____
7 censure (to cut out offensive material from a book) _____
8 confidant (be sure of oneself) _____
9 counsel (advice) _____
10 complement (add to something to make it complete) _____

ACTIVITY 2 Notetaking

Conduct two interviews with the same person. Do the first interview by phone or e-mail. Do the second in person, at the person's home or office. What were the differences? In the responses to the subject? In the information obtained? In the quality of your notes? How do you feel about your ability to take notes? What would you like to improve on? Make a list of principles you would like to follow to improve your notetaking the next time.

Take your notebook and story along to a meeting with three of your peers who were involved in the activity above. Compare notebooks and stories.

- Has the reporter used abbreviations or shorthand?
- Are the notes legible?
- Are the notes complete?
- Do the quotes in the story match the version recounted in the story?
- Did the reporter mark up the notes after the interview, highlighting important sections?
- Have each person say how he or she feels about his or her ability to take notes and what he or she would like to improve on.
- Make a composite list of principles you would like to follow the next time.

HOT LINK

Strunk, J.R., William and White, E.B. 1979. *The Elements of Style.* 3rd ed. London: Macmillan.

This book, which first appeared in 1935, is truly a classic of its kind and has drawn the highest praise. "No book in shorter space, with fewer words, will help any writer more than this persistent little volume," wrote *The Boston Globe.* "Since only two million copies of the first edition sold there must be people out there who have not only never read it but have never even heard of it," wrote the *Virginia Pilot.* "That's terrible."

I agree. This book, a copy of which I acquired in my first year at university, always remains close at hand. Get one.

Bibliography

Buckland, M. 2004. E-mail correspondence with author. 22 July 2004.

McAdams, K.C. and Elliott, J. 1996. *Reaching audiences; a guide to media writing.* Boston: Allyn and Bacon.

Molusi, C. 2002. Speech to the South African National Editors Forum Skills Indaba. Friday, 20 September 2002. Stellenbosch.

Scriven, M. and Paul, R. [no date] *Defining critical thinking.* National Council for

Excellence in Critical Thinking Instruction. [Online] Available at: http://www. criticalthinking.org/University/defining.html [Accessed: 11 September 2004]

Shaikh, M. 2003. *Opleiding moet positiewe hardekoejawels kweek*. Stellenbosch Media Forum, July 2003: 17.

Teel, L. and Taylor, R. 1988. *Into the newsroom: an introduction to journalism*, 2nd ed. Chester, Connecticut: Globe Pequot.

University of Nevada. 2004. A call to reason. [Online] Reynolds School of Journalism at the University of Nevada. Available at: http://www.unr.edu/ journalism/pro.school.crit_think.html [Accessed: 11 September 2004]

Answers to grammar test

1 It is the *list* that *has* been trimmed.

2 Commas may not separate independent clauses.

3 Commas follow all elements in a complete date.

4 The modifying phrase, in its present location, modifies *insecurity* rather than *first-year students*.

5 Use *lie* when no action takes place.

6 Modifying the council with *hopefully* leaves them filled with hope.

7 Semicolons are used to separate punctuated items in a list.

8 Use neither and nor as a matched pair.

9 Use the pronoun *it* to agree with the noun *company*, which is singular.

10 Phrases that rename subjects are nonessential. Comma after (PAPA).

11 *Lives* is the verb that agrees with the subject *one*.

12 Commas follow both elements of a city and province combination that occurs in mid-sentence.

13 The past tense, *used*, is correct usage in this idiom.

14 Including *will play* in this phrase makes for faulty parallelism.

15 *Everyone* is singular; *their* is plural. Right: *Everyone needs to grab his or her own gear.* You can use *he* as a generic substitute for *he* or *she*, but many consider that sexist. We recommend that you alternate between *his* and *her* throughout your document to avoid writing *his* or *her* every time. If that doesn't work for you, simply rewrite the sentence so you don't need to make the choice. The sample sentence could be rewritten as *You need to grab your own gear.* Changing the subject to a plural also works: *Team members need to grab their own gear.*

16 Sentence fragment. Possible solution: *Several people **were** eager to give their opinions and **pressed** forward to meet the author, who was autographing books for fans in the shopping centre.*

17 Comma error. Semicolon or period needed. *I like braaivleis and beer; I don't like wine and cheese.*

18 Co-ordinate conjunction used where a subordinate, such as BECAUSE or THAT is needed. *Agnes complained, **that** she had no heat.*

19 Modifier problem. His leg muscles are not being a soccer player. *Being a soccer player, **he developed** his leg muscles well.*

20 Agreement. ITS skin. *The crocodile is hunted for **its** skin.*

*Because of variations in style, these are the preferred answers to questions 15-20, not the only answers

Deleted: all of them

Deleted: all of them pressing

Deleted: and

Deleted:

Deleted: were

Deleted: their

Deleted: were

Answers to Activity 1

1 *Prophecy* is a noun, meaning a forecast. *Prophesy* is a verb, meaning foretell, predict, forecast.
2 Correct. *Principle* is a rule, truth.
3 Correct. *Stationary* is to remain in one place.
4 Suit of clothes. There are suites of music, furniture and rooms.
5 *Blonde* is the feminine of *blond*.
6 Correct. A canvas is a cloth.
7 A censor is a person who can censor offensive material from a book. To censure is to condemn as wrong, or to disapprove strongly.
8 A confidant is a close friend in whom you can confide. Confident is to be sure of oneself.
9 Correct. Council is an assembly. Counsel is advice. Consul is a person appointed by his government to serve his country abroad.
10 Correct. Compliment is praise. (Can be used as noun or verb.)

5

Getting started: the process of reporting and writing news

A typical day in the life of a newspaper reporter

For Chené Blignaut reporting and writing for the *Cape Argus* begins with the bbbbrrrrrriiiiiingggg of her alarm at 06:00. The rest of the day goes something like this:

KEY CONCEPTS

The process of news reporting; responsible journalists are sensitive to the impact of their coverage; libel is not only a legal matter; journalism stories can be divided into categories according to particular conventions; media houses typically follow a certain style when writing up stories.

- 06:00: Reluctantly get out of bed, gulp down a cup of coffee and get dressed while keeping an eye on the morning TV news.
- 07:00: Start work in the *Cape Argus* newsroom as one of three reporters on early beat. Start reading morning papers and browsing online news sites, while I wait for the news editor to come out of first editorial conference, where lay-out and content of first three pages are decided.
- 07:15: Get first assignment from editor to be completed before first copy deadline at 08:30, normally a follow-up story to an overnight news event or to a story in the morning papers.
- 07:15-07:45: Make phone calls to police, officials, politicians or individuals on home or cellphone numbers.
- 07:45: Start writing up information gathered so far, while waiting for people to return messages. Keep trying numbers of people who were not available earlier. Liaise with news editor about progress, inform him if story will pan out or not, how long it is likely to be and what the main gist of it will be.
- 08:30: Send through completed story to newsdesk in time for first deadline and hang around for it to be checked in case more info is needed. Look at diary on computer to see what other assignments, if any, have been lined up for the day; read other stories in news queue

to get an idea of news for the day and do a Quickwire search on the subject of my beat to see what stories came through on the wire services overnight and which could be followed up.

- 08:45-09:00: Grab breakfast and well-deserved cup of coffee at the canteen, and read rest of papers. Take a smoke break.
- 09:00: If necessary, do follow-up of new info to be added to story in the first edition by making more phone calls and sending it through as an "add" to the original story for the 12:30 deadline.

  Prepare for assignment or interview set up by researching online and from library files, and preparing a list of questions. Liaise with news editor about length and focus of story.

- 10:00-12:00: Liaise with picture desk and go out with photographer after arranging for car with company garage. Do interview or report story and return to office.
- Noon: Inform news editor of progress and change focus or angle of story, if necessary. Gather further information from telephone calls, online or library.
- 12:00-15:00: Write stories for day. Features have to be in by 15:00 for early pages; otherwise, if a news story, it can be in much later.
- Finally, go home when story is finished – and setting up appointments for next day.

LEARNING GOALS

At the end of this chapter, you should be able to:

1 Describe a typical day in the life of a newspaper reporter.
2 Identify some of the main conventions of hard news stories.
3 Organise a story using two of the most simple structures: the inverted pyramid and the champagne glass.
4 Appreciate the need to have a basic knowledge of the legal impact of writing stories.
5 Work through the story-writing process step by step.

The writing process outlined

It is easy to grasp news writing if you imagine how a friend would tell you about a shooting she has just witnessed. Would your friend tell it like this?

"I was walking down the street this afternoon. It's really a nice day outside, actually. Well, I was just coming back from from that new 24-hour convenience store at the petrol station, where I got some orange juice, sandwich bread and a bag of really nice apples. Do you want to try one? Anyway, I was just strolling along minding my own business when,

HOT TIP

Writing right. While the principle of reponsible reporting underpins all the discussions, it is the focus of the discussion in Chapter 11.

suddenly, a car full of guys pulled to the side just ahead of me. One of them leaned out and ...."

It is highly unlikely that your friend, anxious to share the news, would ramble on like that. Instead, she would probably rush up to you and get right to the point: "This boy was just shot in the back by a bunch of guys who were driving down the street!"

When somebody is waving a loaded gun around, even a non-journalist knows instinctively how to report and tell a story. Typically, though, the process involves six steps:

Step 1   Ideas: thinking about news
Step 2   Collect: reporting the story
Step 3   Focus: considering what story to tell
Step 4   Order: planning the story
Step 5   Draft: writing the story
Step 6   Share: discuss your story
Step 7   Polish: revise your story for readers and editors

Step 1 Ideas: thinking about news

Where do ideas come from?

- From life, says journalist and trainer Paddi Clay (see p.140). Your family, friends, neighbours, classmates, co-workers – all the people you meet by accident or design. How are they keeping themselves busy? The conversations you hear intentionally or otherwise. What are they saying? What are they concerned about? The places you find yourself on schedule or because you've wandered. Is the landscape changing? And, on occasion, you'll find yourself in the position to witness a news event (such as a boy being shot at) as it plays out in front of you.
- From publications, broadcasts and online sites. On his first day as a trainee journalist, recalled Steve Wrottesley, the former chief of staff of Independent Newspaper Cape, he got this advice: "You will be jumped on for many things by your news editor. But one thing he [or she] will not jump on you for is reading the newspaper while on the job" (2003:21). If you don't yet have a news-reading habit, start developing one now.
- From sources. Once you've started working as a reporter (or publicist), you'll be in regular contact with people on your beat. Work on building the types of relationships that will make it easy – and obvious – for them to come to you when they've got stories to tell.

Step 2 Collect: reporting the story

A story is only as good as the information, goes the old adage amongst journalists. To begin the search for information, you must answer questions that people are likely to ask. And you need to think about that before setting out. You could start with the stock questions journalists ask, known as the "Five Ws": Who? What? Where? When? Why? That's a good start, but to place the information in context, you will probably have to ask others too: How? How much? Then what?

Or you might want to begin by listing the sources that are likely to provide the information you need. Do you need to speak to the police, the victim's family, the hospital, the school headmaster, coordinators of community crime-fighting initiatives, the neighbours?

Reporting on children and victims of crime has its special challenges. Are you sensitive to the impact of the event, the process of being confronted by reporters, and the effect the resultant publicity will have on all of those involved? In some instances the act of reporting places those highlighted at risk of revenge or being stigmatised. As journalists aiming to serve the public good, we need to consider a simple maxim: Don't victimise the victims.

HOT TIP

The United Nations Children's Fund (abbreviated to UNICEF) has developed some principles to assist journalists as they report on issues affecting children. Amongst these are:

1 The dignity and rights of every child are to be respected in every circumstance.
2 In interviewing and reporting on children, special attention is to be paid to each child's right to privacy and confidentiality, to have their opinions heard, to participate in decisions affecting them and to be protected from harm and retribution, including the potential of harm and retribution.
3 Those closest to the child's situation and best able to assess it are to be consulted about the political, social and cultural ramifications of any reportage.
4 Do not publish a story or an image which might put the child, siblings or peers at risk even when identities are changed, obscured or not used.

The full guide is available at: http://www.unicef.org/media/media_tools.html

The Soul City Institute for Health and Development Communication (SC IHDC), a social change project, also provides a comprehensive guide to reporting on children at: http://www.soulcity.org.za/downloads/Childrens_Rights_Booklet.doc.

Step 3 Focus: considering what story to tell

Whether you've used a notebook or a voice recorder, the first thing to do when you get ready to decide on where to focus your story is to review your notes. Check if they're complete – and check if you can read or hear them. Highlight – either in the margin of your notebook, or by using a marker pen – the information you think is particularly useful to the story.

Once you're confident that you have sufficient information, put down your pen and fold your hands. It's time to think about how to focus the story. Young reporters often skip this step because non-physical activities such as thinking and planning may seem to others much like idling and dreaming. But a good writer knows that much of the writing happens while your fingers are not tap-tapping away at the keyboard. It's time to decide on priorities, keeping in mind the intended audience – and to ask some frank questions:

- What's the point?
- Why does it matter?
- For whose benefit am I telling the story?
- What does it say about life, about the world or about the times we live in?

Definition

News angle [Zu. Umbono ngodaba / Xh. uluvo / Afr. nuuspunt] is used to describe a particular perspective or approach taken to a story. Think of a diamond. It sparkles slightly differently depending on the angles of the light and the viewer. Similarly, a news event can look quite different depending on which angle the writer chooses to focus the spotlight.

"Generals wouldn't go into battle without a plan. Builders wouldn't lay a foundation without a blue-print in hand. Yet, planning news stories, organising information into coherent, appropriate structures, is an overlooked activity for all too many journalists."

WRITING COACH CHIP SCANLAN (2000:89)

Angling for audiences

The perceived needs and interest of the audience influences the story focus or angle. In an advertisement in the *Rhodes University Journalism Review* (1996:33), Natal Newspapers ran the following examples under the pay-off lines: "Because not all people in KwaZulu-Natal have the same perspective; Natal Newspapers – focusing on core readership":

- "28 labourers at a Durban municipal depot were seriously injured yesterday when a gas pipe exploded during cleaning operations" – *Daily News*
- "The price of butane gas and other inflammables has soared in the Durban area following this week's municipal depot explosion which injured 28 people" – *The Mercury*
- "Environmentalists have lashed out at the lack of safety measures which could have prevented the gas explosion and injury to 28 workers at a municipal depot this week" – *Sunday Tribune*
- "The Phoenix Muslim fathers have launched a special fund to help the victims of this week's crippling gas explosion at a Durban municipal depot" – *Post*
- "Durban restaurant owners, who rely on gas for their cordon bleu cooking, are boiling over the municipality's delay in repairing the gas supply damaged in a serious explosion this week" – *The Saturday Paper*

Rephrasing the questions for the incident above would go like this:

- What is the point of telling a story about an unknown boy being shot?
- Why does the shooting of one boy matter?
- Who will benefit from reading a story about a boy being shot?
- What does the shooting of a boy tell us about life, about the world or the times we live in?

Try to answer the questions. They should help you focus on what the themes of the story are, what the story is really about.

Step 4 Order: planning the story

The problem: You now know what the story is about. But do you know where to put everything? How to order the information?

The solution: A map or plan. Finding the focus of the story gives you a destination. The story map or plan is the route you take to get there. Some writers create an outline. Others draw a map. Whatever technique you choose, there are some essential questions to ask: Where does the story begin? Where does it end? What belongs in between?

There may be several different ways to travel between your home and your office, but you probably follow the same route most days. Similarly, there are some well-worn ways journalists have to plot getting from the beginning of stories to the end. We will review some of the most basic ones here – and point out some of the shortcomings, too.

The inverted pyramid

The inverted pyramid, which arranges the information after the lead from the most important to least important, is the most commonly used form in news writing. It's often the form readers and editors expect. Readers scan the story for the gist and then either decide to continue reading or skip to the next one. In fact, according to a study by Mario Garcia and Pegie Stark of the Poynter Institute for Media Studies, only 25 per cent of the text in newspapers was being looked at or "processed" (1991:70). Editors scan the story and cut it from the bottom to fit the space available on the page.

CLASSIC INVERTED PYRAMID STRUCTURE
LEAD with a summary of most important
or most provocative information
FACTS – supporting details
QUOTES – sources said
BACKGROUND
Previously
reported
FACTS
Minor
point

The inverted pyramid might a good place to start for beginner writers as it is a simple way of learning the discipline of consciously organising information. But international writing coach Don Fry does not like this system at all. He refers to it as "the idiotic structure of the inverted pyramid" (1993:5). Then he really gets going. "This is the biggest piece of rubbish in American journalism. This is destroying us." And Fry has a convincing argument for his point of view:

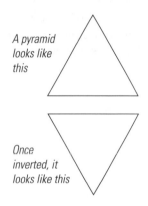

A pyramid looks like this

Once inverted, it looks like this

> *In case anyone is not fresh on the structure of the inverted pyramid, let me remind you. It starts with The Lead! Then we have things that are very important! Followed by things that are Not Important, followed by things that are Boring, followed by BS, and zero. And that's the way you write them.*
>
> *Even worse, you have this template in your mind, so you think like this. What's wrong with the form? The problem with the form is, we have taught our readers who have stuck with us reading these things all these years that we're going to get more boring as we go down. Things are going to get less interesting.*
>
> *So they read like this: "Is he boring yet? No. Is he boring yet? No. Is he boring yet? Yes! Goodbye." Out they go, through the side door.*

Fry says the problem is that we stuff too much information into the lead.

> *The leads aren't simple. You put everything you know in the lead. The reason you like this orgasmic approach is because you don't believe in the reader. You believe that readers don't have any time, that they're dull and stupid and so forth. And, therefore, they kind of sample the sentence up there, and it's your only chance at them. So you put everything you've got up there. The result is dense-packed leads. Nobody can understand the top of the story.*

While there is much criticism of the inverted pyramid structure, I believe it is useful in that it forces the discipline of evaluating information and prioritising it. Once you've mastered this skill, you can move on to more inventive story structures.

EXERCISE *The inverted pyramid*

We have mentioned that the most common structure for news stories is the inverted pyramid.

The term describes story structures that have the most important information at the top. One argument in favour of this form is that readers can quickly find out what the most important key facts of a story are and then decide if they want to continue reading. In fact, research shows that most newspaper audiences are scanners, rather than readers (Adam and Garcia, 1990). They are aware of only 25 per cent of the text, and read just a portion of that. Only about 13 per cent of the stories in the paper are read in any depth – that is, at least half-read. Check this argument against your own reading patterns and ask yourself the following questions:

- There are dozens, sometimes even more than a hundred, different stories in a typical daily newspaper. How many of those do you typically read?
- How many of the stories do you read all the way to the very last word?

The champagne glass

The champagne glass structure, quite simply, adds sparkle to the inverted pyramid with only minimal reorganisation.

ORGANISE THE LEAD SENTENCE ACCORDING TO THE
TRADITIONAL INVERTED PYRAMID METHOD.
THEN BEGIN TO DESCRIBE THE
ACTION IN LOGICAL ORDER.
FIRST THIS HAPPENED
THEN, THAT
THEN
THEN
THEN
THEN
THEN
CLOSE THE STORY WITH A KICK

In the explanation above, the information in the body of the story (the stem of the champagne glass, if you will) is arranged chronologically, the sequence in which the action happened.

17:00	17:02	17:15	22:00	23:00
A boy was shot in the back on his way home from shopping.	A friend called the police.	Police and ambulance arrive.	Hospital spokespeople say the boy has undergone an operation and is recovering.	Police say they received information from neighbours and wish to speak to two of the wounded boy's classmates.

Other stories might best be arranged by grouping areas of action or sources:

At the scene	At the hospital	At the police station	At the boy's school
A boy was shot in the back on his way home from shopping.	The injured boy was taken to hospital by ambulance.	Police say they received information from neighbours and wish to speak to two of the wounded boy's classmates.	The headmaster at the boy's school invited a trauma counsellor to discuss the event with the boy's classmates.
A friend called the police.	Hospital spokespeople say the boy underwent an operation and is recovering.		

Writing the ending

The champagne glass structure suggests that the story is wrapped up with a strong ending, that it closes with a "kick". Often writers use a striking quote from a source. At other times, a strong statement will do. Whatever the approach taken, remember that strong stories have a beginning, middle and end. And if readers keep reading to the final line, they deserve to be rewarded.

Step 5 Draft: writing the story

Now comes the writing. The best advice is to draft at speed, revise at leisure. But getting started isn't always as easy as it may sound. Some editors encourage writers to imagine a specific reader or listener. "Write a letter to your Aunt Janet," they say. Another newsroom favourite is Joe, the average guy. Still, writers are often in turmoil over how to begin or write the lead. Unlike other forms of writing, news writing ordinarily does not allow journalists to build suspense until the last line (like an Agatha Christie mystery) because readers may stop reading at any time.

Journalists don't all agree to what extent the first paragraph should be packed with facts. Some say all the basic details should be there; others argue that they can and should be worked into the first few sentences. Both sides concede that the most important facts should be available to the reader right at the start. And to all, crafting the first lines of a story – the lead-in sentence or paragraph, usually called a lead – has become a high art form.

Types of conventional leads

Hard news leads, softs leads. Many efforts have been made to label different types of leads. This discussion is not intended to add to that confusion. However, conventional hard news stories usually rely on a lead which summarises the action, often in the first paragraph. And that is not a bad idea. Since the inverted pyramid requires that you deal with facts in descending order of importance, the best way to establish what is most important is to summarise at the outset.

Hard news leads. Also called "summary leads" or a "direct lead", a hard news lead is usually 30 words or so – one sentence, maybe two. It summarises the the so-called five Ws (the core details) the story is about – the who, what, where, when and how. In fact, a hard news lead is much like the first sentence your friend blurted out when she wanted to share the news of the shooting incident. "This boy was just shot in the back by a bunch of guys who were driving down the street!" Let's break it down:

- *Who?* a boy
- *What?* shot in the back by a bunch of guys
- *Where?* on the street
- *When?* just a little while ago
- *Why?* not answered
- *How?* not clear, it might have been a handgun, but it could have been a rifle or even a crossbow.

In the same way that your friend would probably follow up the first sentence with more details about what is known (and acknowledge that all details are not available), a hard news lead needs to be backed up with information to support it.

Soft news leads. These are typically short anecdotes, no more than one or two paragraphs followed by a "nut" sentence or paragraph – often shorted to "nut graph" – that summarises the the five Ws of the story. *Sunday Times* reporter Alex Eliseev used a soft lead to tell this story (2004:3):

Anecdotal soft lead of two short paragraphs

> At 10:40 pm last Saturday Brand Pretorius' cell phone beeped. He couldn't have suspected it was the last message he would receive from his girlfriend, Marlé Visagie.

"Nut graph" summarising the key points of the story:

Who: Visagie

What: shot dead by her father

Where: outside her family home in Maggiesdal

Why: Her father mistook her for a car thief.

> "The Lord knows my heart and I love you more than words can describe," the SMS read in Afrikaans. "And by the way … Happy Birthday for tomorrow."
>
> Before sunrise the next day, 19-year-old Visagie would sneak out of the house on her parents' smallholding in Maggiesdal, 3km south-west of Nelspruit in Mpumalanga. She was planning to surprise Pretorius with a birthday present of jeans and track-suit top.
>
> But her father, Rudi "Vleis" Visagie, mistook her for a car thief and shot her dead.

Closing with a kick

Endings create closure – or suggest a follow-up story. For the story on the Visagie shooting, Eliseev chose the former:

> The night after the shooting, Pretorius stayed over at the Visagie house for the first time. He said that when he woke up on the couch the next morning, he had begun routinely typing an SMS to Visagie before realising she would never receive it.
> "I feel empty and lonely," he said. "But it's worth it to wait 60 years to reunite with our promise."

Step 6 Share: discuss your story

HOT TIP

Read Alex Eliseev's account of reporting and writing this story at the end of this chapter.
   More complex story structures are discussed in Chapter 8.

Show someone. Anyone, really. At this stage a writer is usually so involved in the story, he or she often loses perspective. Young writers are often afraid to show their stories to others. Yes, it's difficult to expose yourself so directly to potential criticism. But there is much to gain from getting feedback from someone while you still have the chance to revise your work – rather than to wait until the piece is published for thousands, if not hundreds of thousands, of other people to read. Remember: listen carefully to any comment, even if the person to whom you have shown your story is not a writing expert – or your editor – because their remarks may be very similar to those of your audience who, for the most part, aren't likely to be trained journalists either.

Step 7 Polish: revise your story for readers and editors

The British novelist Dorothy Parker reportedly said, "I can't write five words but that I change seven" (Charlton, 1986:41). Rewriting and rewriting again is common and usually essential for journalists. It is also one of the best arguments for typing directly into a computer. Writing on paper (which means changes are made by erasing, crossing out or drawing lines linking one sentence to the next) or making use of a typewriter (which most often leaves the writer terrified of placing a finger wrong – let alone a word) inhibits writers. Computers, however, allow writers to experiment freely and changes can be made with little effort.

Go back to your story again. Read it aloud. Ask yourself: Does this work? What needs work? Have I answered all the questions as best I can? Have I told the truth as I know it?

Check the details. Have you checked and double-checked the facts? Are all the names and numbers correct? Have you checked your grammar and spelling (Dew knot trussed yore spell chequer two fined awl yore mistakes.)? Does my story conform to the house style of the publication?

Journalists who think that polishing stories is the sole domain of editors and sub-editors are unlikely to have a long career in the field. Not only will careless mistakes irritate the editors, but they are likely to become suspicious of the reporter's ability to do the job. Their reasoning is sound: How can someone who can't even get the names right be trusted to get the other facts right?

The writing process in action

Let's take up the story of the drive-by shooting described at the start of this chapter and see how our reporter – let's say she works for the *Daily News* – goes about getting the story written.

EXERCISE *Recalling the news factory*

Can you identify the traditional news factors (i.e. timespan, relevance, clarity, etc.) in this story? Turn back to Chapter 3 if you are uncertain.

Step 1 Story ideas

Whereas your friend served your need to know, the reporter must serve the readers and ask: What is important to them? Having heard about the incident from a source in the police department, our reporter decides that the *Daily News* readers would care about the shooting of a young man in their area and sets off to collect information.

EXERCISE *Putting together a reporting plan*

How would you go about gathering information? Where would you go? To whom would you speak? What questions would you ask?

Step 2 Collect: reporting the story

When the shooting is over, the reporter has to attempt to piece together the event. Among the questions a reporter would routinely ask are the following:
- Was the shooting fatal?
- Who is the victim?
- Did anyone witness the event?

- Who was the gunman?
- Has the person or people been arrested?
- How did it happen?
- Why did it happen?
- Who reported the shooting?
- When was it reported?
- How long did it take the ambulance to respond?
- What is being done to find the people responsible?

Then there are choices to make about where to find the answers.

EXERCISE *Asking the right questions*

Consider the list of questions our reporter drew up. Would you ask the same questions? Are there other questions that should be asked too? Who would you approach for the answers? Besides speaking to people, where else could our reporter find information?

Step 3 Focus: considering what story to tell

On her way back to the office, our reporter already starts thinking about the story. Which questions remain unanswered? At her desk, she checks her notes, frowns a bit at the sections that have deteriorated into incomprehensible scribbles, and corrects and clarifies the fuzzy bits while the details are still fresh in her mind. She picks out the key facts:

- Who? Steve Smith, 18, a Grade 12 learner at Central High School, who lives at 16 Constitution Street, College Park, with his aunt, Agnes Brice-Featherstone, and uncle, Eddie Brice. Steve had moved in with them five years ago when he left Johannesburg.
- What? Shot in the back with a handgun by a young man who had been expelled from school a few weeks earlier. A neighbour, Eunice Rohan, called the ambulance which took Steve to City Medical Centre; just before deadline, a spokesperson for the hospital said the boy's condition was critical.
- Where? The shooting occurred outside the garage of a house at 21 Constitution Street in the College Park neighbourhood.
- When? About 17:00 Thursday.
- Why? Fellow student, Zakes Khumalo, who had been with Steve for most of the afternoon, said the shooting came after Steve and another student argued and then had a fistfight during the bus ride from school.
- How? The boy Steve had fought later returned in a dark grey Nissan sedan accompanied by three other boys. The gunman got out when

he spotted Steve and his friends sitting on a porch. When the group spotted the boy with the gun, they scattered. Four shots rang out; one hit Steve in the back.

- Then what? Police are continuing their investigation. No arrests have yet been made.

She picks up that she needs to put this incident into perspective. The most basic questions that need answering are: "How much?", or more appropriately in this instance, "How many such shootings have occurred in this neighbourhood this year?" "How does that compare to figures in previous years?" "How does that compare to figures in other areas?" She checks the office statistics, then calls the police spokesperson. The answer: This had been the second shooting in this neighbourhood so far this year, which was the same figure as the previous year.

Step 4 Order: planning the story

All right, our reporter reminds herself, a story needs a beginning, a middle and an end. This event has just happened and the *Daily News* will be amongst the first to report on it, so the story qualifies as hard news. So she settles on a summary lead which will give readers the key facts in the first paragraph. The lead is important, our reporter thinks to herself, but how am I going to organise the rest of the story? She sits down, reviews all her notes and then sketches a quick outline. Keep it simple, our reporter thinks to herself and decides that she'll go through the events chronologically. And the end? She scans her marked-up notes again looking for a strong quote or anecdotes that will draw the story to a close but, since the police are still looking for the gunman, it will also need to suggest that there is more to come.

Step 5 Draft: writing the story

Having decided on a focus and drafted an outline, our reporter is ready to write. Easy, she thinks, and begins to type:

> STEVE Smith, 18, (who) was shot (what) in the back by a vengeful former Central High School student (how).

Not bad, thinks our reporter. She has summed up the main news in only 19 words and she is supposed to hold every lead to under 30 words, if possible. She decides that maybe she can add a time element as well – the when – and rewrites:

> STEVE Smith, 18, (*who*) was shot in the back (*what*) yesterday afternoon (*when*) by a vengeful former Central High School student (*how*).

Just then, the news editor walks by and glances at our reporter's story. "Who is Steve Smith?" she asks, frowning. "That is such a common name, don't you think the victim could be confused with someone else? And how do you know the gunman was vengeful? Keep your own opinions out of the story!"

Our reporter realises she has made several basic mistakes in news writing: she started a story with a name of a person whom few people would recognise and she let an opinion (that the gunman was "vengeful"), which had not been attributed to a source, slip into the story.

Before her next attempt, our reporter decides to review the elements that make a good lead. They are:

- A good lead needs a newsworthy action or result.
- A good lead appeals to a wide readership.
- A good lead gives readers some human interest.
- A good lead gives or foreshadows the key facts.

> **HOT TIP**
>
> While leads are important, experienced writers know the lead is likely to change once the story is written. So, put your notes aside and start writing and consider the advice of journalism teacher Jane Harrigan: "Notes are like Velcro. As you try to skim them, they ensnare you, and pretty soon you can't see the story for the details." Repeat this mantra, she says: "The story is not in my notes, the story is in my head" (Scanlan, 2000:32).

She looks at her lead again. It is okay, she decides, but it's pretty dull. In her head one image keeps coming back: the kids, surprised and terrified, running for cover as a gunman fires at them. If it has grabbed my imagination, she thinks, chances are it will also grab the readers' imagination. Let me see if I can use it. With that, she turns back to the keyboard, types in the dateline "OUR TOWN", and then she is off:

> OUR TOWN (*where*) – A Central High School student (*who*) was shot in the back (*what*) Thursday afternoon (*when*) when a gunman fired four times into a group of terrified youths running for cover (*how*).

"Not bad," says her editor. "You have included some of the most important information in the lead and created some drama by describing the scene. Now support and develop the lead." Our reporter takes up the story and continues to clarify the who, what, where, when, why and how:

> STEVE Smith, 18, of 16 Constitution Street, (*who*) was in a critical condition (*what*) late Thursday (*when*) at City Medical Centre (*where*), a doctor said.
>
> Witnesses say those bullets, fired around 17:00, were the last round in an argument that began on a school bus two hours earlier (*why*).
>
> The gunman and three other young men fled the scene in a dark-grey Nissan sedan, witnesses said. No arrests had been reported Thursday night.

Okay, thinks our reporter, if people stop reading now they will know the key facts of the story. This story's main emphasis is the "how" and "why", neither of which our reporter can answer firsthand. So she organises her story by taking the reader to the scene and describing how she got her information:

> Like dozens of others who live in the modest brick houses in College Park, Maggie Rohan was outside talking to a neighbour, enjoying the sunny spring weather after a day at work. Next door at 21 Constitution St, Steve and some other students sat on the verandah chatting.
>
> "I heard sounds and I thought it was firecrackers," Rohan said. Then, pointing at Zakes Khumalo, she said, "Then he came running and said the boy had been shot."
>
> Zakes, also in Grade 12 at Central High, was with Steve for most of the afternoon. Zakes said he and Steve got on bus No. 42 as usual, when school ended at 13:15. Another young man, Brad Pretorius, who had been expelled from the school weeks before, also sneaked aboard, he said.
>
> During the 30-minute bus ride, Steve and the young man began arguing, Zakes said. At first they traded insults. By the time the bus pulled into the College Park suburb, someone had thrown a punch and a tussle ensued.
>
> Minutes later the bus stopped at a designated stop near 16 Constitution Street, where Steve lives with his aunt, Agnes Brice-Featherstone, and uncle, Eddie Brice.
>
> The boys got off the bus, along with other students who live nearby. Steve and Brad yelled at each other a few more times, before Steve turned towards home. Brice said his nephew came home nursing a bruised hand and said he had been in a fight.
>
> "He said he kicked the boy's butt," Brice said. "The boy had told him that it was not over and that he would be back."
>
> Brice went inside and Steve walked diagonally across the street to the home of George and Tasniem Nichols.
>
> Steve, Zakes, the Nichols' daughter and four other youngsters were sitting on the front porch when the Nissan pulled up at the end of the 5-metre long driveway.
>
> Brad jumped out and pulled out a gun, Zakes said.
>
> "Everyone ran," he said. "We were scared." Four shots rang out.
>
> Steve fell in the carport, a few yards from the rear corner of the house.

Step 6 Share: discuss your story

"Nicely done," says her editor, as she scans the draft of story. "But there are a few very important things we need to discuss:

"You have identified the alleged gunman, Brad Pretorius, even though he has not been charged with a crime. You cannot do that.

What if the witness was mistaken or was lying? We would be incriminating an innocent person, which is not only wrong, it is **libellous**. Our paper would then be open to a lawsuit – and an innocent person will have been traumatised and stigmatised. Take out his name and keep in touch with the police. If he is caught and charged with the crime, we can write another story about that."

"Did you get permission from all those you interviewed to publicly identify these people? I'm concerned that the children in this story might be targeted for revenge attacks, especially since they were eyewitnesses and the gunman is still on the run. Have you spoken to the children and their parents? Have the police given you any advice?

"Also, I want you to double-check the spelling of the names.

"And remember that our **house style** is to use surnames, not first names, for people 18 and older."

"And what about the ending? Look over your notes again. Isn't there something you can use to wrap it up better, a nugget you can use at the end?"

Definition

Libel [Zu. Ukuhlambalaza / Xh –gxeka / Afr. laster] is injury to reputation: Words, pictures or cartoons that expose a person to public hatred, shame, disgrace or ridicule, or induce an ill opinion of a person are libellous. Court actions for civil libel result mainly from news stories that allege crime, fraud, dishonesty, immoral or dishonourable conduct, or stories that defame the subject professionally, causing financial loss either personally or to a business.

Slander is the same thing, only spoken.

EXERCISE *Identify the story form*

Can you recognise the story form our reporter used to organise this report?

Step 7   Polish: revise your story for readers and editors

What could be wrong with Steve Smith? our reporter thinks, as she returns to her desk. But she decides to call the boy's uncle to confirm the spelling anyway. She finds out the actual spelling is: S-t-e-v-a-n S-m-y-t-h-e.

Relieved that the error did not make it into print, she makes the correction and goes back to double-check every fact. Then, she scans her notebook again. That's it! she thinks when she picks up the reflective quote from the victim's uncle. She uses it for her kicker close. The scene rounds off the story. And, in a sense, it rewards the reader for sticking with you all the way.

> Stevan, born in Johannesburg, had been living with Featherstone, who is his mother's sister, since the beginning of 2003. His parents had sent him to Our Town, Brice said, because they thought it was a better environment.
>
> "This was supposed to be his last year," said Brice, taking a deep drag on his menthol cigarette. "I hope he makes it."

Then, our reporter reaches for the phone again. She calls each of the children's parents and then the police. While the gunman is still at large,

Definition

House style Each media organisation (or "media house") typically has conventions about how information is presented. For example, one newspaper might include honorifics (titles), such as Mr, Mrs, Miss and Ms, while others may not. Some publications might give a person's full name on the first reference and then use only the last name for subsequent references, while others might choose to use first names instead. A list of common writing style rules is appended at the back of this text.

the recommendation comes, it would be best not to identify Zakes, one of the eyewitnesses. Her heart sinks. But I did all that work, she thinks. It's such a good story. But she knows that journalism is not just about writing good stories, it is about serving the best interests of society. Who would benefit if the children's names were published? Who would be harmed? She recalls the advice "carry around a picture of your mom" as a reminder that sources are more than just a means to an end. With that, she goes back to the story and starts revising:

OUR TOWN – A Central High School student was shot in the back Thursday afternoon when a gunman fired four times into a group of terrified youths running for cover.

Stevan Smythe, 18, of College Park , was in a critical condition late Thursday at City Medical Centre, a doctor said.

Witnesses say those bullets, fired around 5pm, were the last round in an argument that began on a school bus two hours earlier.

The gunman and three other young men fled the scene in a dark-grey Nissan sedan, witnesses said. No arrests had been reported Thursday night.

Like dozens of others who live in the modest brick houses at College Park, Maggie Rohan was outside talking to a neighbour, enjoying the sunny spring weather after a day at work. Next door Smythe and some other students sat on the verandah chatting.

"I heard sounds and I thought it was firecrackers," Rohan said. Then someone came running and broke the news: "the boy had been shot."

The witness, who cannot be named for fear of reprisal, said Smythe got on bus No. 42 as usual, when school ended at 1.15pm. Another young man, who had been expelled from the school weeks before, also sneaked aboard.

During the 30-minute bus ride, Smythe and the young man began arguing, the witness said. At first they traded insults. By the time the bus pulled into the College Park suburb, someone had thrown a punch and a tussle ensued.

Minutes later the bus stopped at a designated stop near where Smythe lives with his aunt, Agnes Brice-Featherstone, and uncle, Eddie Brice.

The boys got off the bus, along with other students who live in the area. Smythe and the other young man yelled at each other a few more times, before Smythe turned towards home. Brice said his nephew came home nursing a bruised hand and said he had been in a fight.

"He said he kicked the boy's butt," Brice said. "The boy had told him that it was not over and that he would be back."

Brice went inside and Smythe walked to the home of some friends nearby.

Smythe, and other youngsters were sitting on the front porch when the Nissan pulled up at the end of the 5-metre long driveway.

The young man who had fought Smythe earlier jumped out and pulled out a gun, the witness said.

"Everyone ran," the witness said. "We were scared." Four shots rang out.

Smythe fell in the carport, a few metres from the back corner of the house.

Smythe, born in Johannesburg, had been living with Featherstone, his mother's sister, since the beginning of 2003. His parents had sent him to Our Town, Brice said, because they thought it was a better environment.

"This was supposed to be his last year," said Brice, taking a deep drag on his menthol cigarette. "I hope he makes it."

In this chapter, you learnt these lessons:

Lesson 1

A news story is the end result of a process. And if there's something wrong with what's on the page, the likelihood is that the writer skipped or skimped on one of the steps. Some of the most common problems are:

- The story may not be appropriate for the audience (Step 1: News thinking).
- There may not be enough information (Step 2: Collect: reporting the story).
- The notes are illegible (Step 2: Collect: reporting the story).
- The writer hasn't thought about what needs to be said (Step 3: considering what story to tell).
- The information hasn't been logically organised by sketching out an outline or map (Step 4: Order: planning the story).
- The reporter hasn't concentrated on getting the details correct, such as the spelling of names and places. (Step 2: Collect: reporting the story).
- The writer has not respected the conventions, such as the narrator's point of view or the tense, of a particular type of story (Step 5: Draft: writing the story).

Lesson 2

Find answers to the who, what, where, when, why and how. But if they do not add to the story, some points might be omitted (our reporter left out the statistics about shootings in the neighbourhood, because there was nothing out of the ordinary to report).

Lesson 3

Soft news stories often start with anecdotes, while hard news stories typically have leads that summarise the event. Keep summary lead sentences short – generally around 30 words.

Lesson 4

Like films, journalism stories can be divided, and subdivided, into different types or genres, which each has particular conventions. In hard news reports, amongst others, reporters are expected to remain outside of the action. That means the facts are presented without opinion: *Firing a gun is a fact, that it was motivated by vengefulness is an opinion.* Any opinion should be attributed to an appropriate source.

Lesson 5

Reporters need to be sensitive to the needs of audiences and the impact of their actions on their sources. Those who are vulnerable, such as victims of crime and children, may need special consideration. Guidelines are available. If you need to be reminded, take another look at a picture of your mom and ask yourself this: Am I treating all the people in the story the way I would like other reporters to treat her and others I care about?

Lesson 6

Some basic knowledge of law is important. In this instance, it was important to avoid being libellous. Do not name the person alleged to be involved in a story until you have confirmed it with an official source – the gunman in our story had not been positively identified by officials, such as the police, or charged with a crime.

Lesson 7

Remember the mantra: "Accuracy! Accuracy!! Accuracy!!!" Always double-check the facts, starting with the spelling of names.

More key terms

Budget [Zu. Umfunzo / Xh. imfumba yeendaba / Afr. nuuslys]: A list of stories, with priorities indicated, for the day.

Bulletin [Zu. Umbiko / Xh. ibhuletini / Afr. korte/brokkie]: A short item, usually a paragraph, of great importance, usually arriving too late to be developed into a story.

Column [Zu. uluhlu / Xh. umhlathi / Afr. kolom/rubriek]: Standard line width of printed type in a newspaper with a standard depth; an opinion, analysis, or entertaining piece of writing, usually of predetermined length with byline.

Copy [Zu. ikhophi / Xh. ikopi / Afr. kopie]: An article or material prepared for publication or broadcast.

Cover, *verb* [Zu. Bikangodaba / Xh. –xela / Afr. dek]: To report on something, as in: "Neil, please cover the U2 concert on Saturday night."

Cover story, *noun* [Zu. Indaba esekhaveni / Xh. ibali elibhekiselele kumphandle wemagazini / Afr. voorblad-storie]: A story which refers to the cover illustration of a magazine.

Dateline Zu. Isizinda / Xh. indawo asebenza kuyo umsasazi weendaba xa eqokelela iindaba / Afr. datumlyn/pleklyn]: Used to identify the location of the reporter of a story. The term comes from the period before electronic communication when correspondents included the place and date of the report, which could often take days, if not weeks, to reach the newsdesk.

Fluff [Zu. imfucumfucu / Xh. impazamo / Afr. wollerigheid]: Vague and often unimportant copy; poor writing, non-factual writing; also, light, non-serious topic.

Graf [Zu. Isigaba / Xh. umhlathi / Afr. paragraaf]: An abbreviation of (para)*graph*. A peculiarity of newspaper writing which divides stories into short sections, usually one sentence, to keep the reader from being intimidated by long blocks of text.

News peg [Zu. Udaba oluyisikhonkwane / Xh. isikhonkwane / Afr. nuushak]: An idea or event on which a story is hooked or based. Following the accidental shooting of Marlé Visagie, for example, (see p.94) was an editorial asking whether or not the fear of being victims of crime is making South Africans "trigger happy".

Scoop A piece of news made public by a news organisation or by a reporter before its rivals.

Sections [Zu. Isiqephu / Xh. izahluko / Afr. afdelings]: Parts of a newspaper dedicated to one topic, for example, the sports section.

Sidebar Zu. Indaba eyengezayo / Xh. iindaba ezimfutshane ezongezelelweyo ezohluliweyo kwiindaba eziphambili kodwa zishicilelwe kwibhokisi encinane kufuphi neendaba eziphambili / Afr. byvoegsel/kassie]: An additional short news story that is split off from the main story but which is printed alongside it, often in a box.

Slant [Zu. Tsheka / Xh. ukufumana enye imbono / Afr. aanslag]: Direction or emphasis to appeal to a particular audience.

Story [Zu. indaba ezekwayo / Xh. ibali / Afr.storie]: Term used interchangeably with news article or feature.

HOT TIP

The Power of Words. Check out this section of *The Providence Journal* website. You will find examples of good writing and discussions by the writers telling how they handled the stories. Be sure to check the index of writing tips. http://www.projo.com/words/

▓HOT LINK

You'll find most of the information you need to complete this task on the medium's website. Check out the "About Us" (or similar) pages for details on the staff. Typically, advertisers are provided with information about audience and circulation, so you will likely find that information by following the link to "Advertising". Also check out the research provided by the South African Advertising Research Foundation at: http://www.saarf.co.za

Putting your learning to work

ACTIVITY 1 Analyse a mass medium

Choose a radio or television news programme, a newspaper or magazine (electronic or print). Then devise a questionnaire according to which you will analyse the medium. A newspaper could be analysed according to the following criteria:

- Name
- Mass media category
- Editor
- Cost
- Frequency
- Audience profile
- Audience reach/distribution
- Type of information used
- Length of stories
- Type of advertising
- Special features
- Source of the stories (staff writers, newswire services, syndicates, freelancers)
- Deadlines

ACTIVITY 2 Basic story analysis

From several newspapers collect the leads from five different types of stories. Paste each on a sheet of newspaper. Then complete the following:

- List the publication name, section, date, page and headline.
- Describe each story type or genre (news report, feature, analysis, etc.).
- Identify the category of news or "beat" (crime, health, etc).
- Evaluate the approach and perspective of the writers. Do you think it is appropriate?
- Identify the key information in the lead (five Ws). Do you agree with the way the writer has prioritised the information?
- Which traditional news values contributed to the story's newsworthiness? Was there a particular news factor that was likely to have had an overwhelming influence on the journalist's decision to pursue the story? Do you think story received adequate "play" or exposure? Was it overexposed or hyped?

ACTIVITY 3 Writing leads

Notes for story leads are given below.

- List and identify (as "who", "what" and so on) the fact or facts you think deserve the most prominent play in each lead.
- Then write a summary lead for a hard-news story for a daily newspaper and another for a more specialist publication of your choice. Discuss your

efforts with your colleagues and explain why you've chosen to place the emphasis where you have.

a) African Chemical Corp.
   Automotive Products Division
   To lay off 350 hourly-paid workers
   At its plant in Nelson Mandela Metropole
   Plant Manager Robert Plaatjies
   Said layoff to start Friday
   Does not anticipate more layoffs
   Blamed reduced orders from major car manufacturers
   Hopes to call back employees in a month
   Plant employs 2 100 workers
   (Source: Plaatjies)

b) Gauteng Education Department officials
   National Democratic Teachers Union representatives
   To meet at 10:00 tomorrow
   Civic Centre
   Opening meeting in contract negotiations
   Teachers seeking R35 000 minimum salary
   Current minimum is R28 000
   Threaten strike if they don't get it
   Department officials won't comment on demands
   Union represents 3 700 teachers
   Last year's strike lasted two weeks
   (Source: Ms Stephanie du Plessis, union representative)

ACTIVITY 4 Kicker closes

Evaluate 10 endings to stories and try to establish a list of five guidelines for writing successful kicker closes.

- Discuss your recommendations with your peers and create a composite list.

FROM THE NEWSROOM

Alex Eliseev on getting a big story

Born in Moscow, Russia, where he lived until his family's immigration to South Africa in 1991, Alex Eliseev was 21 and still studying for his degree in communications at the University of South Africa when he joined the Sunday Times *as a reporter in March 2004. But even by then he had notched up some solid journalism experience: a year and a half with the* Sandton Chronicle, *a community paper; several articles published in the daily* Citizen *newspaper; a fourth-place finish in the column-writing category of the annual* Sanlam Awards *for Community Press 2003; and part of the team who secured the* Sandton Chronicle's *position as best community newspaper at the* Caxton Excellence Awards *that same year.*

Here he reflects on his experiences reporting his first major story for the Sunday Times, *which ran under the headline, "Tragedy cuts short wedding plans; grief-stricken boyfriend tells how he and Marlé Visagie had already pledged themselves to each other."*

Ironically, on the morning former Springbok rugby player, Rudi Visagie, shot dead his 19-year-old daughter, Marlé, I was driving home from Nelspruit wondering if the production of rose petal jam was the only excitement the town ever saw.

As far as I was concerned, Nelspruit was a one-horse-town – and the horse had died in a freak accident with a 4X4. When the Visagie story rocked every headline in the country on Monday morning, I was stunned.

Everyone was talking about the incident during our weekly diary conference at the office. Since I had just spent the weekend in Nelspruit socialising with locals, I volunteered to return. The daily papers would have already given the story a good week's worth of coverage by the time my piece was to be printed, so I knew it needed a new angle. The excitement of being sent on my first national assignment made me even more determined to find a good one.

At about 6pm on Tuesday, I was given the green light. By 5am the next morning, photographer Thembinkosi Dwayisa and I were on the road. My brief: to profile the Maggiesdal community in Nelspruit, and to get as close to the family as possible.

Luckily, Nelspruit was no Big Apple (although fruit is its main produce). When we arrived, everyone had heard about the shooting and knew where the memorial service was to take place.

We were the first members of the media to arrive at the church, where our request to take photographs inside the church was met with resistance. A compromise was eventually reached. We were permitted to take photos after, but not during, the service. At the memorial service, I met with a close family friend of the Visagies, who was acting as the family's spokesperson. I also took down some numbers, pinned on a notice board, of people involved with the church. We spent the rest of the day visiting the police station and a farmer who lived next door to the Visagies.

My most powerful memory from the trip is of sitting in my hotel room on the first night, too nervous to eat. I could think about nothing but the consequences of returning without a story. I was used to reporting to 60 000 people on community issues, but here I was, out on a story that would reach over three and a half million readers nationwide. The pressure was of a level I had never felt before. I phoned a friend in Jo'burg to calm my mind. I took a short shower. Then I checked my e-mail. Nothing helped. It was 9pm. I picked up the phone and got to work.

It took nearly 40 minutes to convince the Visagie's family friend to meet with me the next morning. She had refused every other paper, but I couldn't take no for an answer. She was my key to getting an interview and I was finally granted an exclusive one, which was to be held at the Visagie's home.

The dedication and persistance I had shown by staying in town and trying various ways of taking the story a step further than the dailies was paying off. It was agreed that I would not interrogate the family about the incident, but rather do a human-interest story about the people involved. After debriefing my editors on the evening of the interview, I was told to track down and interview the girl's boyfriend, Brand Pretorius. The story had taken an unexpected turn.

We returned to our hotel only to discover it had been booked for one night only. As the photographer searched for accommodation, I started making calls. I finally managed to get Brand's number from the same church worker who'd initially refused to allow us to take photographs at the service. Once again, my skills of persuasion were put to the test. I convinced Brand to see us and set out on a 70km journey to meet with him. The interview lasted until 11pm; I was amazed by his strength.

On the morning of the third day, I typed up the story and, despite two hours of computer trouble, sent it off to my editor. The writing was easy because I had already constructed the introduction in my head. The moment Brand showed me the SMS he'd received from Marlé the night before she died, I knew I had my intro. I had also just spent two days with the community and the facts were fresh in my mind.

After working three near 20-hour days, I was exhausted, both physically and emotionally; I had spoken to the father who had accidentally shot and killed his own daughter, as well as the boyfriend who had just lost the girl whom he'd recently made plans to marry. I had functioned on pure adrenaline. Each morning I had woken up with new strength and had worked until I felt ill. But it was worth it. My reward: a page three lead-story.

NOTE: Excerpts from Eliseev's story are on p.94.

Bibliography and recommended reading

Adam, P. and Garcia, M. 1990. *Eyes on the news.* St Petersburg, FL.: Poynter.
Charlton, J. ed. 1986. *The writer's quotation book: a literary companion.* New York, Penguin.
Eliseev, A. 2004. Tragedy cuts short wedding plans; grief-stricken boyfriend tells how he and Marlé Visagie had already pledged themselves to each other. *Sunday Times.* 30 May 2004:3.
Fry, D. 1993. *Ragged Right*, Issue 4, Thomson Newspapers Corporation.
Scanlan, C. 2000. *Reporting and writing: basics for the 21st century.* New York: Oxford.
Wrottesley, S. 2003. Basics first. *Rhodes Journalism Review*, 22:62, September 2003.

6

Identifying story ideas and locating sources

Introduction

Imagine this: "Due to nothing new happening today, the South African Broadcasting Corporation has cancelled tonight's TV news programme. Joanne Joseph will return tomorrow – if something interesting happens."

What about a special musical interlude at 17:00 on Radio 702? Or a newspaper with blank columns, broken only by lively advertisements? This is highly unlikely (except if press censorship returns, that is).

Such scenarios, says sociology professor Gaye Tuchman (1978:17), are plausible only in a system where news judgements are made objectively; a system where, if no item was to meet the clearly-defined criteria, there would be no news for that day.

Cancellations of news reports are unlikely because, in the main, the news media sell news. And they have to find news to fill the spaces between money-producing advertisements, the media's primary source of income. On a Saturday, for example, newspaper journalists have to find more items to fill the spaces between the greater number of advertisements in the thicker Sunday edition. On weekdays, however, thinner newspapers are produced and fewer advertisements and news items are required. For this reason, stories that may have been considered newsworthy on the weekend are now sometimes discarded.

Whatever else a mass medium is – an information service, a voice for the people, a watchdog, an educator, a community builder, an entertainer – it is also a business. And to keep going, it needs news. That's why the most valuable players in the newsroom are those who consistently deliver the goods.

Generating ideas for stories and locating appropriate sources of information are important first steps, and are the focus of this chapter.

LEARNING GOALS

At the end of this chapter, you should be able to:

1 Discuss the characteristics of a news story.
2 Recognise the different applications of the news writing style – reports, features, editorials, columns, sports, and reviews – and the appropriate perspective writers take for each.
3 Demonstrate your ability to use creative techniques to generate story ideas.
4 Know how to go about developing personal sources and gathering information from documents – in person and electronically.

Definition

Remember a **news peg** [Zu. indaba eyisikhonkwane / Xh. isikhonkwane / Afr. nuushak] is an idea or event on which a story is hooked or based: *the news peg for the feature story on how to draw up a personal budget was the annual budget speech by the minister of finance.*

A **news angle** [Zu. umbono ngodaba / Xh. uluvo / Afr. nuuspunt] refers to a specific point of view: *the angle for the story was the extent to which women were represented amongst the candidates for each party.*

What is a news story?

Sure, we've considered the role of news in society. And we have also tried to define news. And, yes, we've looked at the process of reporting and writing news stories, as well as some of the tools you'll need to get the job done. But what exactly is a news story?

Perhaps we should start by looking at what it isn't. "A [news] story … is not simply a random slice of reality," points out journalism trainer and author Gwen Ansell (2002:19). "It has to make a point, answer a question or be organised around a theme if it is to make sense to readers."

Broad themes for news stories are, typically, determined by the aims of each specific medium. The latest trends in home décor, for example, while of primary interest to the readers (and, by extension, the editorial team) at *House & Leisure* magazine, is not the regular theme for the weekly *Financial Mail*. However, the business weekly might include a story about these trends viewed from an economic perspective (or angle), such as the increase in sales at home décor-related businesses.

Dominant news events also influence specific news themes. For example, competitive sports might not be a normal topic for a fashion magazine, but when major tournaments, such as the Soccer World Cup or the Olympics come around, they provide a peg for related stories, such as the wardrobe of football icon David Beckham. Similarly, an accidental shooting might provide a news peg for a radio talk show discussion on gun safety, or a lifestyle magazine feature on coping with tragedy.

General timing also impacts on news themes. Think, for example, of the change of seasons. The advent of summer might dictate themes discussed in a programme on pets, or in a magazine devoted to gardening. The start of the school year might motivate news stories on enrolment trends, features on innovative education methods, an investigation into fees, and a column on the challenges faced by parents.

Of course, journalists and editors ulitmately aim to satisfy the diverse needs of audiences. Why do you turn on the TV, tune into the radio, pick up a newspaper or browse through a magazine? Research has shown that the answers to those questions range from getting information and advice, to simply fending off boredom. (For a complete list see the exercise "What does the media do for you?") It follows then, that writers for the media should ask themselves what they think the audience will get out of reading their piece. Or simply put: "What's the point?"

Definition

The word *genre* comes from the French (and originally Latin) word for "kind" or "class". The term is widely used to describe a type of literature or film marked by certain shared features or conventions. For instance, precise examples of genres might include murder mysteries, western films, sonnets, lyric poetry, epics, tragedies, etc.

Story types or genres

In the previous chapters, we discussed what news is and how it can be described in two broad categories: hard news and soft news. We've also looked at some of the basic tools reporters need to do their job and how those are used in the process of crafting basic news reports. But news is presented in a variety of ways; each draws on different conventions, different **genres**.

Perhaps its easier to first talk about films and theatre shows. When you see a new release billed an "action" film, you expect to see at least one car chase and several tough men matching muscles. A "romance" film is ordinarily about the heartache and ultimate triumph of lovers over adversity. A horror film is expected to send chills down your spine and sweat to your brow.

In much the same way, journalistic endeavour is divided into different categories, each with particular conventions. While we will look closer at some of these later, it is important at this point to note that significant elements of different types of stories are the point of view of the writer and the grammatical tense used.

A reporter is a little like the narrator in a film or play. In a play, for example, a narrator may be off stage, unseen by the audience, using a microphone to relate crucial background information that helps the audience make sense of the action.

Similarly, hard news is presented in a way that the writer's experience – or opinion – is not a part of the action. This also supports the idea that reporters are to be "objective". And that is also why most **news stories are written in the third-person and use the past tense**: *Tshabalala ran into the store and picked up a carton of milk, three packets of jelly beans and a box of rat poison.*

Reporter's Perspective	Outside the action	On the edge of the action	In the action	Focus of the action
Story genres	Hard news reports, features	Features, columns	Features, editorials, reviews	First-person features, columns
Conventions	Typically hard news reports and most features place the writer outside the action – an omniscient or "objective" witness, if you will. When you write in the third person, you generally do so in the past tense: *Xolile ran to the store and picked up a carton of milk, three packets of jelly beans and a box of rat poison.*	In some feature stories and editorial, the narrator steps onto the stage but remains in the wings. Often the third person present tense is used: *They grab their suitcases and hurry to the waiting taxi.*	At times, such as when a reviewer gives an account of his encounter at a movie, his personal experience becomes an important part of the story, although the story is still about the event (in this example, the film or restaurant) not about the writer. These stories are typically in either first-person past tense *(The only thing I enjoyed about that movie was the popcorn)*, or the present tense.	When the narrator's experience is the story, the first-person present or past tense is used: *I look around me, ticket in hand, and realize that I can't identify a single face in the crowd.*

Figure 6.1. The perspective of the writer in relation to the news event impacts on the way the story is told, or the "narrative voice".

Narrators on stage or in films aren't always hidden. Sometimes, they stand at the edge of the stage in front of the curtain. The narrator may also step forward in between scenes to clarify how the action sequences link together. At the end of the play, the narrator may then turn to the audience and draw the story to a close. As we will see, different types of stories provide opportunities for the writer to vary his or her position in relation to the action.

EXERCISE *What does the media do for you?*

Think about the news stories you have recently read, watched or listened to. Pick one you remember and consider what motivated you to pay attention. Now, compare your answer to see if it matches the list of reasons that have been noted by researchers and are listed below. Discuss your observations with your peers – and what they mean for your work as a writer for the media.

Scholars (McQuail 1972, Blumler 1985, et. al.) have noted that audiences use the media to fill the following needs:

• Getting information and advice

• Reducing personal insecurity
• Learning about society and the world
• Finding support for one's own values
• Gaining insight into one's own life
• Experiencing empathy with problems of others
• Having a basis for social contact
• Feeling connected with others
• Escaping from problems and worries
• Gaining entry into an imaginary world
• Filling time
• Experiencing emotional release
• Acquiring a structure for daily routine

News reports [Zu. Imibiko yezindaba / Xh. –xela / Afr. nuusberigte]

A news report is just that: a report. That means reporters are expected to look, listen, question – and to recount the information they found. They are not expected to discuss themselves or how they felt about looking, listening or questioning.

Good reports, however, go beyond the immediate event (called "he-said, she-said journalism"). They include information necessary to place the action in context, like *Cape Times* education reporter Carol Campbell did when reporting on the conflict between the national Minister of Education – a member of the African National Congress – and the Western Cape Minister of Education – a member of the National Party (a provincial government minister is also known as a Member of the Executive Committee or MEC):

Bengu and Olckers are at each others' throats again

This time the war of words between Education Minister Dr Sibusiso Bengu and Western Cape Education MEC Mrs Martha Olckers is over her allegations that he is dodging the blame for "bungling" the cutback in teaching posts.

Bengu has placed an advertisement in today's *Cape Times* to outline his gripe with Olckers, who, he says, is reversing the struggle to achieve equity in South African education (Campbell, 1997:3).

The word "again" in the first sentence reminds readers this is not the first time these two politicians have clashed. And they also know that the quarter-page advertisement, which runs six pages further on in the paper, represents only one side of the story.

There is clearly a difference between putting a story into context and writing yourself into the story. For news editors, the reasoning is simple: a reporter's job is to report news, not to become the news.

"Three levels of reporting can be discerned. At the passive level, reporters report public events and what is said there. At the next level, they seek to explain or interpret what is said. At the third level, they look for evidence behind it. To put it another way, reporting can be general, specialist, or investigative."

DAVID MURPHY, AUTHOR OF *THE STALKER AFFAIR AND THE PRESS* (1991)

Analysis stories [Zu. Indaba ehlaziyayo / Xh. ibali lohlahlelo / Afr. ontledingsartikels]

The analysis story, also called a "think piece", "interpretive story" or "explainer", normally takes up some pressing issue and attempts to make people understand. Not uncommon are headlines such as: "Why I want this: Mining St Lucia is an emotive topic that has the Greens buzzing like flies. But what is the truth? What is best for the country?" Award-winning journalist Denis Beckett (1993:27) analysed the controversial issue of mining the dunes at St Lucia in the "Insight" pages of a Sunday newspaper.

In his story he also illustrates an important aspect of such stories: it is often best to do most of the interpreting yourself since experts tend to speak *expert-ese*, a language foreign to most of your audience. For example:

Earnings from the utilisation of the natural resources at St Lucia, estimated at 0,15% of GDP, would facilitate the exponential decrease in the nation's unemployment.

Beckett decided it would best be explained to his readers in more basic terms, as if he were having a conversation:

"In any story, I'm interested in two things: where does the money come from and where does it go? It's always a major component. Money is always a measure of power and the shift of power."

MARTIN WELZ, FOUNDER OF *NOSEWEEK* AND ARGUABLY ONE OF SOUTH AFRICA'S FINEST INVESTIGATIVE JOURNALISTS (1997)

Is the mining right, then? For sure. It adds 0,15 per cent to the wealth of the nation, and that means 16 500 jobs. Huh? Sounds glib. Of course, it's brief. But at bottom it is unarguable. SA has a R270 billion GDP and 11 million jobs. Add X per cent to the GDP and you add X per cent, give or take, to the jobs.

Beckett's readers can probably all understand that much. "It is not your purpose in the interpretive story to establish that you have learned something," say Leonard Teel and Ron Taylor (1988:170). "It is to help your readers learn something."

Investigative reports [Zu. Imibiko yophenyo / Xh. uphengululo / Afr. ondersoekartikels]

The banner at the top of the website reads: "Welcome to South Africa's unique investigative magazine for inside information on business, the professions, politics, society – anything you weren't supposed to know!" It's the online home of *NoseWeek*, published by Martin Welz, arguably one of South Africa's most courageous journalists. And it sums up what makes investigative journalism different from other types of reporting – it's about news you weren't supposed to know.

Those with money – politicians, business people, and even religious and community groups – come under the spotlight, as this selection of stories from the June 2004 edition shows:

Noseweek takes the maxim of investigative journalism – keep the powerful accountable – seriously. Check out the latest headlines at: http://www.noseweek.co.za

Fishy government deals and empowerment fronts

Look into any major government deal and you'll nearly always find a trust with an empowerment or community upliftment-related name (and suspiciously vaguely defined beneficiaries) on the profitable end of things. Soon it emerges that, despite the caring title, the trust has, in fact, been set up to benefit members of the ANC elite – and, there are more and more reasons to suspect, the coffers of the party itself.

TIPPEX OF THE ICEBERG

There was much that was unusual about the award of a lease at the Hout Bay harbour to the Hout Bay Development Trust. For one thing, it was awarded at a time when the trust was not even in existence. And there were other serious problems. Nothing, however, that a little tippex couldn't take care of.

Hook, line and sinker

The SACF started with high hopes on the part of Hout Bay's impoverished fisher communities. Years later they've still got nothing – in spite of the award of fishing quotas worth millions, ostensibly for their benefit.

A stella performance

Why, we ask ourselves, would Minister of Public Works, Stella Sigcau, disadvantage the state treasury to so massively benefit a private company? Who, or what, is Bluefin Holdings to her?

FROM THE MOUTHS OF BABES

Everyone in Pretoria is keeping mum on what happened after a Sanlam broker came up with a *slim plan* for the Orphan's Fund.

DR JEKYLL OR MR HIGH?

Is surgeon Dr Wynne Lieberthal a caring star of the public health service – or a butcher of innocent victims and a thoroughly bad egg?

NOTES & UPDATES

Maiden: airy tales / Renewable energy: cold water / Volvo: good choice? / Mpumulanga Parks Board: cans justice

Where did that beach go?

The sandman could be making regular visits to the Table Bay coast with his convoy of trucks if a dodgy scheme to extend

Feature articles [Zu. I-athikhili esemqoka / Xh. eyona ndawo ibalulekileyo / Afr. glansbladartikels]

Scribbling notes while ducking bullets or following police sirens isn't everyone's idea of the ideal reporter's life. For those people, there is the feature story.

This does not mean news and features are mutually exclusive. For by magnifying society's eccentricities and styles, feature stories help put the news into context in the same way colour commentary at a sports broadcast supplements the play-by-play.

Also called "human interest" stories or "people news", features usually allow the writer more space: not only more words, but also provide the writer with latitude to experiment with language. Although feature stories seldom

▌HOT TIP

Award-winning investigative journalist (and musician) Mzilikazi wa-Afrika explains why he does what he does on p.199-201.

follow the strict inverted pyramid format, the news peg *(Why is this newsworthy?)* should be clear within the first three or four paragraphs.

Popular feature stories include profiles, service pieces and trend stories. Profiles are in-depth looks at people, organisations and places. Most feature editors like to provide readers with some informational service and regularly provide weekly entertainment listings and "How To" features. The most timely feature stories are those that reflect trends – interests, moods and activities that are moving across the city or country and affecting the lives of your readers.

Some publications encourage writers to become a player in the story and you will find leads like this:

> I'm a fly on the raw-brick walls of VWV Interactive's headquarters at Kyalami and I'm eavesdropping on a brainstorm session.

This article, by features writer Adam Levin, may be appropriate for *Style* magazine (1997:57). But while editors urge journalists to observe the action, many prefer the "flies" to stay on the wall – and not come and sit on the page.

There are exceptions, of course. When the writer's experience itself is newsworthy, then a first-person feature story is warranted. Take Charlene Smith's article for the *Mail & Guardian* entitled: "Rape victims are not statistics … We are people. This is our story." Editors introduced the piece with this summary: "Last week Charlene Smith was raped and left tied up in her own bathroom. But that was just the beginning of her ordeal. By telling the story of that painful night, she hopes to raise awareness of the way rape victims are treated." Here are a few excerpts:

HOT TIP

Read Charlene Smith's article, which earned her a second place in the General News: Print category of the annual CNN African Journalist of the Year Awards, in the *Mail & Guardian* archive at: www.mg.co.za

Every 26 seconds in South Africa a women gets raped. It was my turn last Thursday night. Before I began writing this I took AZT, 3TC and Crixivan. They are anti-retroviral drugs, they will hopefully lessen the potential of my getting Aids from the rapist, assuming, of course, that he is HIV positive. In a country where 1 800 people contract HIV every day, it's a gamble I refuse to take.

But the difficulties I encountered in getting the drug and the treatment I received from medical staff at private hospitals and the district surgeon's office are an indictment against health care policies and the medical profession …

This is about the rape: I came home at 8:30pm. I had met with a French television crew I had given some assistance to. I was tired. My three dogs acted normal. I opened the door, walked in and locked it again. I noticed there were more lights on than I had left on ….

Editorials [Zu. uhla lomhleli / Xh. inqaku lomhleli / Afr. hoofartikels]

On the editorial pages, writers are allowed to be exactly what critics often accuse them of being: biased, subjective, one-sided and opinionated. And this is how it should be.

The editorial pages, which are normally clearly set apart from the news pages, usually carry three types of copy: the unsigned editorial, which reflects the opinion of the editorial board; the editorial column, which has bylines and mug shots identifying the writers; and the letters to the editor, which give readers a chance to be biased, opinionated, one-sided and subjective.

Columns [Zu. uhlu / Xh.umhlathi / Afr. rubrieke]

This is where experienced – and talented – writers get to think aloud about life. Todd Matshikiza, Jeremy Gordin and David Bullard are among the best-known South Africans currently writing feature columns. Such columnists usually deal with human problems, rather than cosmic problems. The tone is sometimes humorous, sometimes sentimental, sometimes gossipy – and almost always personal.

Feature columns are the stuff of which legends and acclaim are made. Todd Matshikiza (the father of the *Mail & Guardian* columnist), for one, deserved it. Matshikiza's elegant columns for *Drum* magazine are some of the best examples of South Africa's "Jazz Age" writers of the 1950s and 1960s. This piece, "Jazzing the blues", appeared in March 1955.

Then said Louisa Emmanuel to Isaac Peterson, "Will you be my turtle dove, or not?" Isaac replied (in the English used in Show biznes), "No I ain't no turtle an' I ain't no durv. So I can't be yo' turtledurv."

Louisa said, "I'm looking for man to sing with me. He must coo as I purr. Coat as I fur. In other words, his voice must match mine."

Says Isaac, "Baby I'se got ze voice. Dunno if I'se got ze match. We'll figure it out. I reckon you'se got ze figure anyhow."

That's how this partnership started.

I was interested in that conversation as I listened through the stage curtain. Louisa was nervous. The lights were on. Bright. Very bright.

Isaac wasn't nervous. Not very. If stage fright got him, Louisa's pretty confident smile would hide his fright. Louisa. One hundred and twenty pounds of vocal dynamite packed into four yards of lace and taffeta ... Or four yards of nylon net and sequins across the chest. Louisa. Pearly white teeth that grace the mouth that lets out the voice that thrills from Johburg [sic] to Rustenburg. Even listening to her speak. I wasn't listening. I was hearing, hearing, hearing ... and hoping she wouldn't stop.

And Isaac. Son of Peterson. Bound by ties of brotherhood to American clothes. Commanded by a little birdie inside him to sing ... sing ... sing to save the sorrows of ten million black voices. You wouldn't know him if you met him at home in Vrededorp. Sits around the corner looking lazy like a lord. Slumps down in a chair like was waiting for some luck. Looks at you with black beady eyes like he's blaming you for it all. And thanks you for his gift of song as if you gave him all.

These two little kids, Louisa Emmanuel (aged twenty), and Isaac Peterson (twenty-three), surprised me once by saying, "We two see things the same way. We met and we're tied hand and foot to the stage. And what showbiz puts together, let no man put us under. We want to stay on the top all the time."

They love a song called "Confess". In fact, it's one of their most famous items. The people say, "We wish those two could fall in love each time they sing 'Confess'". But Louisa and Isaac take love right out of their musical profession. In fact Louisa is "still in mother's care," (as she says) and love will begin to come to her, a little later than now. Meanwhile, Louisa and Isaac are proudly your very own Lord and Lady of Song. They might find time to talk to you between factory hours. Or if you'd like to meet Louisa, her Mom lives with her, and Dad and a fiery dog "Danger", in Vrededorp.

Reprinted with permission from Drum, *March 1955*

Reviews and criticism [Zu. Ukubukeza nokugxeka / Xh. –bhala uncomo-gxeko / Afr. resensies]

These are usually courted and often despised – at least by some. Critics and reviewers basically write editorials about the arts. Some, like Clive Barnes of the *New York Times*, are ruthless. A typical (and legendary) example is his one-word comment review of the play "The Cupboard"; it read: "Bare" (Kessler, 1972:99).

Though the terms "critic" and "reviewer" are often used interchangeably, George Claassen, former professor of journalism at Stellenbosch University, says the differences are worth highlighting (1997):

I think you must make the distinction because of the atrocious state of affairs in review writing in newspapers. Most of the time people not trained in the field of, e.g. literature or movies, get to write on those topics merely because they are journalists at a newspaper and the paper needs someone to write a review. I believe those people are superficial reviewers; maybe we should call them mere critics, writers who do not always motivate and understand why they are criticising.

But what the New York Review of Books *or the* TLS [Times Literary Supplement] *does, is more in the vein of true reviewing. The* NYRoB [New York Review of Books] *calls its reviewers "contributors" but they are all experts in their fields, people with many years of experience. The word "critics" has become sort of derogative, mainly because they are doing exactly that, criticising, often without the proper knowledge to do it.*

Increasingly, newspapers are employing specialists such as author Stephen Gray, who writes on books for the *Mail & Guardian*, and Barry Ronge, film critic for the *Sunday Times*, rather than just tapping someone in the newsroom who merely likes – or hates – films, television, food, visual or performing arts.

Business reports

"At my paper, the *York Daily Record*," says Peter Krouse (1995:8), "there's a city reporter who regards the business section as the newspaper's Siberia. He thinks only bank presidents and chamber-of-commerce muckety-mucks read the business section. And that's only when they're quoted in it."

The reporter Krouse refers to is not alone. For a long time, business reporters were closeted away in special sections of South Africa's newsrooms. Few people seemed to pay attention to the standard of journalism and writing, either because they didn't understand what was being written about, or they didn't care.

But that is certainly changing. "Economic empowerment", "reconstruction and development" and "redistribution of wealth" are some of the phrases that tumble off the lips of ordinary citizens. The business of business – international, national, regional, local and personal – has become the business of all South Africans. And editors and journalists have taken up the challenge of making their reports more thorough and more accessible to ordinary people.

Sports writing

Once when a fellow first-year journalism student complained that reading the newspaper each morning generally depressed her, our lecturer gave this advice: start with the sports. On the sports page, he said, life is ordered. You get to see the score. The winners and losers are clearly defined. And, unlike the front page, there are always winners.

Sports writing is essentially news, features and reviews about sports. Sports offers a reporter all the elements of which good stories are made – triumph, passion, heartbreak, courage, conflict, comedy, pathos, artistry, even love and hate. The latitude given sports journalists is implicit in the common reference to sports writers, instead of sports reporters. Unfortunately, this latitude often gives way to laziness and sports writers, trying to be colourful, frequently spew out clichés instead. Take the lead of this story, "Boks back with a bang" (Van den Berg, 2004:32):

* For an excellent example of sports writing, see the profile of Ashwin Williams by Mike Behr for South African Sports Illustrated on p. 215.

Stripping away months of neglect and despair, the Springboks finally escaped their living nightmare with a powerful and committed start under new coach Jake White.

But it need not be so. Some of the finest, most imaginative writers have been among their ranks, including Paul Gallico, Ernest Hemingway and Tom Wolfe.

As sports become more complex, sports writers increasingly have to move beyond the stadium and locker-room into the boardroom, court-room and even the jail. To understand professional soccer and athletics, sports writers have to know about contracts, sponsorships and antitrust lawsuits. To understand some troubled athletes, sports writers need at least an academic understanding of cocaine, steroids, bribery and assault with a deadly weapon!*

Advertorials

Yes, this term is the hybrid of the words *advertising* and *editorial*. Advertorials are paid-for advertisements written and presented in the style of an editorial or journalistic report. These pseudo news stories should be clearly identified as such; the public is entitled to know when it is reading, listening to or viewing advertorial, because it will regard differently information produced by an advertiser for its own benefit, and information generated by the media in its own right, which is expected to have a level of independence.

Johannesburg's *The Star* newspaper, for one, has formalised this in their code of ethics. Amongst the guidelines in the section titled "Integrity", is this: "Advertising or promotional features should be clear-ly labelled, so as to leave readers in no doubt about the source and nature of the copy" (1999).

Ideas: developing a topic into a story idea

Although at first you will mostly be assigned to work on other people's story ideas, reporters are usually encouraged to be enterprising and come forward with ideas of their own. A topic becomes a story idea when it is clearly defined – it has a news peg, an angle, and appropriate sources. House prices is a topic. The release of a new report could be a news peg. The angle could be what that means for first-time buyers. The sources could include information from Statistics South Africa, proper-ty agents, banks, and would-be home owners.

A story idea becomes an assignment when there is commitment. If an editor approves an idea, the story will be assigned for a certain edition and entered on the budget, or news list, for that edition. That is when deadlines are set.

Generating story ideas is not easy. Certainly some ideas will come to you – the phone rings, a news release arrives, a fire alarm goes off. But others will demand you to be more creative.

Brainstorming

When in doubt, brainstorm. This is one of the most time-tested methods for generating new ideas, so don't skip this step unnecessarily. In order to have a good brainstorming session, clear your agenda for a few minutes. You need to focus your attention to the brainstorming process in order to benefit. If you work with other reporters, suggest a group brainstorming session. The important thing about brainstorming is not to edit your thoughts. Write down everything that occurs to you about the topic, no matter how irrelevant or bizarre. Rain: Thunderstorms. Flooding. Mud. Bad driving. Accidents. Drought. Leaking roofs. Umbrellas. Raincoats ... You get the idea.

The next stage is to make connections between your ideas, and to group them into sub-topics, expanding those that you can explore in more detail. Then see if you can put the groups into some kind of logical order, discarding those that turn out to be inappropriate. In most cases you will find that you have the beginning of an story idea – something that implies a basic point you can explore further and refine into a fully developed article. From the above example, here are a few potential story ideas:

- How much rain is enough?
- How to fix a leaking roof – safely
- What's the latest in waterproof fashion?
- 10 tips for entertaining children on rainy days
- Is there a connection between rainy days and traffic accidents? Suicides?
- Does it rain equally on each day of the week – or is there more rain on weekends?
- How to drive safely during wet weather

You can always take a few minutes out of every day to brainstorm, which can unblock your creative side on those days when inspiration is not working.

░▒▓ TIP

Books on brainstorming
There are several good books on using the brainstorming process to generate ideas for writing, including Tony Buzan's *Use Both Sides of Your Brain* and Gabrielle Lusser Rico's *Writing the Natural Way.*

░▒▓ TIP

Consider the opposites
Think critically; ask questions. When somebody wins an award, the unsuccessful competitors may be disgruntled and have theories of rigged judging. When a company moves offices, there might be a story in discussing the future of the old building. When statistics are released detailing the poor performance of matric students, there is likely to be a story if you can track down a few who have managed to beat the odds.

Mind mapping

Our educational system attempts to teach us to think linearly: step by step from introduction to conclusion. Sometimes it may help to break out of that structure and experiment with free association. Suppose the topic is "health". Logical or linear thinking takes us perhaps to such a pattern:

- HEALTH
- Good
- Factors affecting
- Barriers
- Trends
- Traditional approaches
- State of the nation?
- Cost?

This may be a good start, but this way of thinking is restrictive. Try this mind-mapping exercise: Put a word in the middle of an A4 page and fan out the aspects and associations that come to mind.

You are likely to find that the words and associations work on each other and that soon you will have several directions in which to go.

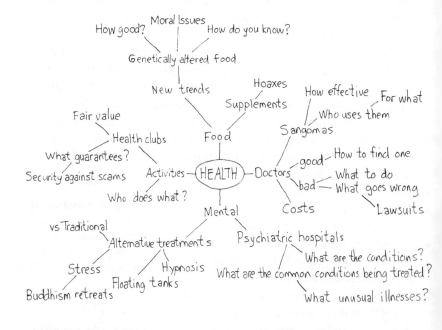

Figure 6.2 Mind mapping recognises that the brain processes information in nonlinear ways.

Pitching your story (or writing a budget line)

Once you've established your story idea, you'll need to convince your editor that it is worth your energy and space in the publication. That process is called pitching. Sometimes, you'll be able to do that face-to-face. At other times, you'll need to pop your editor an (e-mail) note that can be passed along to other decision-makers or discussed at a news conference. A written story pitch is also sometimes called a "budget line", because it becomes an entry on the editor's budget of news stories. Whichever term is used in your context, newsmaking is a colloborative process and you will need to summarise each story idea succinctly and share it with others.

HOT TIP

Anticipate your readers' needs – and responses
Once you've identified the main points of your story, ask yourself some questions about your audience:

Their knowledge
- What do my readers already know?
- What else would my readers need to know to understand the story?

Their attitudes
- What attitude do my readers already have towards this subject?
- Will my story be reinforcing – or challenging – my readers' established views?

Their experience
- With which of the reader's problems or interests might my story coincide?
- What questions is the story likely to provoke?

Adapted from a checklist suggested by journalism trainer and author Gwen Ansell (2002: 23)

Collecting I: reporting information

Reporting is a two-part activity: you need to collect the information; you need to communicate the information. The two activities are fully dependent on each other. Once you know with whom you want to communicate about what topic, you then have to gather the details and formulate the message appropriately.

Collecting information involves observations, interviews, reading and analysis (Scanlan, 2002:66). We will take a look at how information technology can assist reporters. But first, let's consider some of traditional approaches – getting out and keeping your eyes and ears open.

Observing – looking and listening

Keeping your ears open: Journalists often find it hard to leave their work at the office and frequently spend hours regurgitating the day's activities after hours. This is not bad. But be careful not to become one of the reporters (and there are many) who are shunned at social gatherings because they routinely dominate discussions with talk of their own exploits. On the other hand, says Jack Fuller (1996:18), "Good reporters know how to make themselves unobtrusive so that life will go on around them close to the way it would if they were not there." Focus on your next story – and that means listening, at least as much as you speak.

Keep your eyes open: When you see a new building going up, stop to

> *"If ideas are the seeds of stories, then reporting is the fertilizer, the compost of facts, statistics, quotes, interpretations that allows the reporter to produce a factual, complete, clear and accurate story."*
>
> CHRIS SCANLAN (2000:66)

see what it is. When you conduct an interview, report on the details beyond what is said. What does the room look like? What is the person doing with their hands? What are their facial expressions? What were they wearing?

Take this excerpt from a story about New York City police which ran in *Sunday Life* magazine (Perlman, 1997:9):

Bushwick, Leone explains, has historically been a big location for drugs. It has always had a reputation for quality stuff, especially heroin. A lot of kids come across into Brooklyn from Long Island to "score". As we cruise along the quieter streets, Leone points out a pale, wasted-looking woman picking her way furtively along the pavement. "She's looking to buy, maybe do some tricks to pay for it," Leone says.

.... As Leone steps out of the car a young girl who has been hanging out in a doorway taps out a signal on a window close by. "A guy was shot dead in that hallway," Ryan says pointing to a nearby house. "Drug deal gone bad." Then he smiles at an old woman who is making her way home with groceries and a big bunch of flowers. "The majority of people here are decent, hard-working," he says.

Reporting the detail allows your reader to not only know what happened – but to see it too.

Interviewing

Successful stories depend, to a large extent, on the questions asked along with the way. And most of those will be posed to people (personal sources).

Reading

President Thabo Mbeki posed a simple challenge at an All African Editors' conference: "I believe you should answer the question, honestly, whether you yourselves know Africa." Steve Wrottesley decided to investigate. Two geography sections of a questionnaire set by the Journalism Department at the University of Stellenbosch were put to 61 university and technikon students and graduates applying for journalism positions and internships at Independent Newspapers Cape.

In the first section, the applicants were asked to identify the countries in which the following cities would be found: Baghdad, Prague, Antananarivo, Jakarta, Tripoli, Kandahar, Davos, Bujumbura, Manchester, Seoul. In the second section, they were asked to identify the following countries on a map: Ethiopia, the Democratic Republic of Congo, Algeria, Nigeria, Japan, Spain, Saudi Arabia, Afghanistan, Venezuela, and Peru.

The percentage of correct answers: 29% for the first part; 16% for the second. Such results are cause for concern. "How can a journalist relate to famine and starvation in Ethiopia when he identified it on the map as

Spain?" Wrottesley asked. Or how can a reporter understand the attempts to negotiate peace in the Democratic Republic of Congo when, according to one of those tested, it was one of South Africa's neighbours, Zimbabwe?

The good news is that Wrottesley kept on testing the groups of the trainees and found that, after being required to read the newspaper each day, their general knowledge of geography improved dramatically. However, the importance of reading extends beyond merely developing your ability to navigate your way around the world. It helps you to better understand the people and events you encounter along the way.

HOT LINK

Don't have time to read?
If that's your excuse, then perhaps you should work on the speed at which you read. "Speed reading is not magic nor is it a big expensive mystery," says Dennis Doyle of the Glendale Community College in California in the US. "Professional speed-reading classes simply teach a handful of easy techniques that help a person focus his or her attention better. The eye is drawn to motion. Speed-reading techniques put that motion on the page." His guide to self-paced speed-reading methods is available at: http://english.glendale.cc.ca.us/methods.html

Analysing the information

It's not enough to gather lots of information, or even good quality information. You will need to make sense of it, to analyse it. Analysis is simply the process of sorting information by placing it into different categories. Take, for example, a basket of apples. How could you analyse it? Well, you could do that by sorting them according to size – small, medium, large. Or you could sort them by ripeness – green, ripe, rotten. The challenge when analysing information is making sure you use valid criteria, or categories. Some of the categories will be suggested by the story purpose and the angle. For example, information you gather about an election could be analysed according to time: before the election (the campaign), during the election (the vote); after the election (the results).

Remember: A journalist is not simply a recorder of information, the way a stenographer would record the proceedings in a court of law. A journalist is a sense-maker – and that requires engaging a sharp, analytical mind.

"The basic rule is: the more information you discover, the sounder will be your judgements and the more accurate your story."
LEONARD TEEL AND RON TAYLOR (1988:67)

Collecting II: locating appropriate information sources to report

Before you pick up your phone or switch on your computer and spend hours drifting aimlessly through the maze of information available, know what it is you're looking for – and why. You need a reporting plan. It can begin with questions or with sources, or a combination of both (Scanlan, 2002:73).

Developing a reporting plan

News research coach Nora Paul (1994:4) suggests you ask yourself the following questions when you start a reporting plan:

- **Who?**

  Who might have the information I need: a government agency, a newspaper, a report? Who has done this type of research that I might get advice from?

- **What?**

  What information do I already have? What holes do I need to fill in? What is the information I need about: a person, a place, a company, an activity, an event? What kind of information do I need: statistics, sources, background stories? Do I know all the possible angles to the story, or is that what I'm looking for? What kind of story am I writing: a news report, an analysis, a follow-up? What type of sources will be helpful: full-text, citations to articles, or a specific piece of data or opinion?

- **When?**

  When do I need the information? Am I on deadline or do I have some lead time? When did the event I'm researching happen?

- **Where?**

  Where did the person or event I'm researching come from? Where might there have been coverage of the event: newspapers, news broadcasts, trade publications, court proceedings?

- **Why?**

  Why do I need the information: reality-check of a source, looking for a source to talk to? Am I fishing, or is there a specific fact I need?

- **How?**

  How much information do I need; just a few good stories for background, or a full run? How am I going to use the information? How might the information I retrieve be used in the paper? How would the information I find be most usefully presented: extract the highlights, provide full text?

Starting a reporting plan with sources

An alternative approach to developing a reporting plan might be to brainstorm a list of sources you want to reach. One of the story ideas suggested by the brainstorming exercise was this: How much rain is enough? A list of likely sources might be:

- a professor in metereology at a local university
- the national weather bureau
- national rainfall database
- those who depend on the weather for their livelihood: farmers, gardeners, owners of outdoor cafés, umbrella manufacturers.

Whichever technique you choose, remember this: without a plan, a reporter is like a ship without a rudder – going around and around in circles.

Developing personal sources

Face-to-face, on the telephone, by fax or by mail, most of the information used in stories comes from personal sources: people. One of the first challenges of a new reporter is to develop his or her own personal sources. Here are some suggestions on how to do this:

Start your own telephone directory

Use a directory, a notebook or file cards. Whatever system you devise, hold on to every name and number that comes your way. List them so they can easily be retrieved. For example, under "education", you might have the school board, government, unions, colleges, universities and technikons.

Circulate

Get out of the office. Visit the departments on your beat and identify at least one co-operative person in each. Attend functions, sports meets and seminars. Once a month, at least, go to some kind of event you have not attended before.

Be friendly – to everyone

Some new journalists, enthralled at landing a job in this competitive business, consider themselves better than others. The best reporters make friends with street vendors, clerks, bartenders, security guards and prison inmates.

Identify and meet leaders

Make the effort to identify and get to know key people on your beat. Take them to lunch, or plan to meet them at a social occasion. Read widely, including newsletters, brochures, magazines and out-of-town newspapers. Stories are copyrighted, not ideas. Localise and adapt good ideas to suit your medium.

Don't forget the support staff

If the secretaries or personal assistants don't actually do the work for their executives, they often make sure it gets done. Support staff have access to the people, if not most of the information you want. And when you need it most – right before deadline – a secretary can help you reach the boss, whether by slipping into a meeting to deliver a note or by letting you know where she is playing golf.

Definition

To distinguish between types of personal sources, journalists differentiate between **contacts**, **tipsters** and **informants**.

- A contact is an established, usually visible, person who provides information. Some groups and corporations appoint a specific person, referred to as a "spokesperson".
- A tipster often prefers to remain anonymous and may have only partial, unsubstantiated information. A tipster may also direct you to the source.
- An informant gives information not available through regular channels. Informants may want to barter their information; an informant or informer may negotiate with the police, for example, for protection from prosecution.

HOT LINK

The South African Government Online website at
http://www.info.gov.za/ lists national calendars
(schools, parliament, etc.) and also includes details
of conferences and events on the United Nations
calendar.

Watch the calendar

Anniversary dates are a convenient peg for an article. Christmas. New Year. Valentine's Day. Ramadan. Easter. Yom Kippur. These are the obvious ones. But, there are also internationally declared Cancer Day, Women's Day, Pet's Day, Library Day and more. These all make convenient pegs for stories.

Subscribe

Get your name on as many mailing lists as possible. A story about a new invention or a business scam may be waiting in your post box. Of course, you'll need to learn to filter your mailbox – electronic and physical – but if you cut yourself off from newsletters and the like, you might cut yourself off from the next big story, too.

Gathering news with documents

Whether you need to check on someone's past or if you are nosy about cutting-edge news, you're likely to find what you need in a document. Where to find documents – physically and online – and what type of documents you're likely to find is what this section is about.

Libraries

If you want to find a document, chances are it will be in a library. The skill is to know which one. Here is a breakdown of the major types of libraries, as described by research consultant Heather Vallance in *A Beginner's Guide to Research* (1995), and what you can expect to find there:

- Tertiary education libraries offer information on all subjects taught at an educational institution. Although these libraries are the first and most important source of information for students, you can access most library databases online. However, you'll need to get special permission (or pay a joining fee) to get physcial access to the material.
- Public libraries are a source of knowledge and entertainment for communities. Most public libraries carry fiction for general reading, music to listen to, pictures to hang on walls, and non-fiction books on a number of subjects. Public libraries also stock reference books such as dictionaries, encyclopaedias, atlases or biographies.
- Government libraries provide politicians and their aides with the information they need to support policies and the laws they wish to

formulate. Government libraries are found in major city centres where political activity occurs on a regular basis.

- Company libraries are run by some organisations for their staff. These libraries contain specialised information. An engineering company, for example, will buy sources on engineering. Company libraries also store information on the company itself.
- Institutional libraries belong to large research bodies, such as the Human Sciences Research Council in Pretoria.
- Legal depositories are not for studying. They store copies of books and publications either published in a country or written about that country or its activities. Legal depositories are also not lending libraries. A researcher or student must use the sources on the premises. Legal depositories also carry archives, manuscripts and personal collections donated by institutions or individuals. Legal depositories in South Africa are: South African Library, Cape Town; State Library, Pretoria; National Library for the Blind, Grahamstown; Natal Society Library, Pietermaritzburg; Bloemfontein Public Library.
- Newspaper libraries. Some newspapers, such as *Die Burger, Beeld* and *City Press*, have computerised their libraries (sometimes called "morgues"), allowing researchers near-instant access to stories written since 1986 (http://www:naspers.co.za/argiewe/). However, earlier items have to be retrieved manually from files which patient librarians have created by clipping daily stories and pasting them into books. Some newspapers also store their editions on microfiche, miniature photographic negatives of each page which are then viewed through an enlarger. Newspaper libraries commonly are open to the public during restricted hours and provide copies of articles and photographs at a fee. The first online newspaper archive was established by the *Mail & Guardian* and is available at: http://www.mg.co.za.
- There are also a variety of specialised libraries such as those at art galleries, museums, private collections, or societies for the disabled.

Public records

While there has been a significant move to make information easily accessible online, not all documents you'll need are available electronically. Some of the records you might need are:

Birth, marriage, death records

- Contact: Records office, Department of Home Affairs. You'll find details about your local office, as well as downloadable forms, at: http://www.home-affairs.gov.za/

▮▮▮ **LINK**

A useful directory of online library resources in South Africa (and the rest of Sub-Saharan Africa) has been compiled by Stanford University and is available at: http://www-sul.stanford.edu/depts/ssrg/africa/rsalibs.html

- Provide: First and surnames in full and date of birth. Also, information older than 20 years is available in the state archives of each province.
- Cost: A fee is charged.

City directories

Compiled from voters' rolls, these directories provide listings of names and street addresses. Besides giving you information about where the person lives, this will also allow you to track down the neighbours.

Most newsrooms have one, like the *Cape Times Directory*, but you can also get this information by stopping by at your area Deeds Office. http://land.pwv.gov.za/where_to_find_us/deeds.htm.

- Provide: Full name, ID number and date of birth.
- Cost: Documents are viewed free of charge; copies must be paid for.

There are also commercial products that allow you to search property records from your desktop. Amongst these are WinDeed (http://www.windeed.co.za) and Deed Search (http://www.deedsearch.co.za).

Court records

Details of court proceedings, including divorce cases and insolvencies, can be viewed by contacting:

- Clerk of the Court
- Provide: Full names, dates and details of the case (preferably case number).

The Department of Justice and Constitutional Development's website provides a wide range of related information and useful links: http://land.pwv.gov.za/where_to_find_us/deeds.htm

Traffic department records

Should you need the registration information of a vehicle confirmed, you can approach a motor-vehicle registration centre. The vehicle details cannot be given out but any information you have can be confirmed.

- Provide: ID and licence plate number.
- Find details of the traffic departments of South Africa's major cities at:
  Cape Town: http://www.capegateway.gov.za/eng/directories/
  eKurhuleni / East Rand: http://www.ekurhuleni.com/ekurhuleni/index.jsp
  eThekwini / Durban: http://www.durban.gov.za/eThekwini/Services
  Johannesburg: http://www.joburg.org.za/help/drivers_licence.stm
  Tswane / Pretoria: http://www.tshwane.gov.za/

Links to the sites of other cities are available from the SA Cities Network: http://www.sacities.net/.

Also see the: National Transport Information System for statistics on road usage, licensing, and the like: http://www.enatis.com/.

Firearm registration

Firearm licences are issued by police departments. The data, stored on a central computer system in Pretoria, are not available to the public. If you know the address of the person, you may be able to verify at the specific local police station if a person has applied for a gun licence at that station.

The Gun Control Alliance of South Africa keeps useful statistics of gun licensing and crime, and has links to relevant legislation: http://www.gca.org.za/.

Health records and information

The Department of Health can provide a great deal about the nature of illnesses, their scope and impact. If you need information about doctors or medicine, contact the Medicines Control Council: http://www.mccza.com.

For a link to a range of other health organisations – from brain researchers to the Quadriplegic Association – see: http://www.southafrica.co.za/health/organisation.html.

Income tax

Section 4 of the Income Tax Law prohibits the South African Revenue Service from disclosing tax returns. You'll find details about tax legislation and the like at: http://www.sars.gov.za. For questions about the tax system, you are better off contacting a private tax accountant.

Legal newspapers

- The *Government Gazette* provides all details of national legislation, passed or promulgated, relevant to all government departments. You'll find most of what you need at the South African Government Online site: http://www.gov.za.
- *De Rebus* is the official journal of the South African Law Association. It provides current news relating to the profession, establishment of new law firms, law reports and civil procedures, articles concerning national and international legal matters.

  Previous copies of *De Rebus* (the reference section dates back to 1953) can be obtained at the journal's offices in Cape Town. See: http://www.derebus.org.za/.

Politicians

Check the telephone directory for the local contact details of the political parties in your area. A complete list of parliamentarians and other information is available from the Public Education Office at Parliament in Cape Town. See: http://www.parliament.gov.za/.

Prisons

The Department of Correctional Services in your area can provide details of people and sentences. See: http://www-dcs.pwv.gov.za/.

Reference books

On every desk should be the following: a dictionary, a thesaurus (if the computer doesn't have one), a telephone directory and a pocket encyclopaedia. A useful guide to online reference works is available at: http://www.lib.uct.ac.za/infolit/infosources.htm.

Religious institutions

Most established churches have a roll of congregation members and their leaders. Use Ananzi Search Engine: http://www.ananzi.co.za/catalog/SocietyandReligion/Religions/.

Telephone directories

Apart from helping you track down people, telephone directories are helpful when verifying names and addresses. They can also provide ideas for wonderful stories. A look under "B" in Yellow Pages, for example, came up with these interesting jobs:
- Bias binding and waistbands
- Bird breeders
- Biscuit manufacturers
- Blackboard makers
- Blacksmiths (Adams Blacksmiths: Wagon builders, wheelwright, welding, tool smithing and farrier)
- Blasting contractors

You'll find the South African Yellow Pages at: http://www.yellowpages.co.za/sadocs/. A similar database, SA Yellow, is at: http://www.sayellow.com/.

Statistics

Statistics South Africa provides a wide range of official statistics, such as the population census and economic data. Their searchable database is available at: http://www.statssa.gov.za/.

NationMaster is a massive central data source and a handy way to compare nations graphically. The vast compilation of data comes from such sources as the CIA World Factbook, United Nations, World Health Organization, World Bank, World Resources Institute, UNESCO, UNICEF and OECD. You can generate maps and graphs on all kinds of statistics with ease. Available at: http://www.nationmaster.com.

Voters' roll

Details of about elections and statistics on voters are available from the Independent Electoral Commission website: http://www.elections. org.za/.

HOT LINK

Is someone blocking you from getting access to information you need?

The **Promotion of Access to Information Act** provides for the right of access to any information held by the state and any information that is held by another person and that is required for the exercise of protection of any rights. For a plain English version of the Act and help on how to make use of it, see the Open Democracy Advice Centre at: http://www.open-democracy.org.za/.

John Orr interviewed the centre's director, Alison Tilley, for SAfm's "The Law Report". Transcripts of their discussion about the Protected Disclosures Act and the Promotion of Access To Information Act are available at: http://www.opendemocracy.org.za/crimestats/safm.htm.

Zoning and land use

Contact the Zoning Department at the town or city council. The Deeds Office can also provide information.

Computer-assisted journalism (CAJ)

Nora Paul is a librarian. But don't think of a little old lady with wire-rimmed glasses shuffling amongst stacks of dusty books. Paul zips around cyberspace in search of sites and people to assist journalists in finding stories and reporting them – fast. She also teaches journalists how to set up their own databases and to use databases on available online.

If information is the currency of journalism, then Paul is a power broker. She's proved her worth at the *Miami Herald*, the Poynter Institute for Media Studies, and now as director of the Institute for New Media Studies at the University of Minnesota where, amongst other things, she shows others the tricks of the computer-information trade.

"Researching and interviewing, just like writing or doing arithmetic or analysing raw data, can be done without a computer. But by taking advantage of the access to information and people available to you by using a computer, your research and interviewing can have a range and immediacy that is simply impossible without a computer's assistance," says Paul (1994:2).

Paul breaks down Computer-Assisted Journalism into four Rs: Reporting, Research, Reference, and Rendezvous.

- Computer-assisted reporting. Computers can help reporters conduct special examinations through the use of spreadsheet programs for complex calculations, statistical programs for the analysis of large datasets, and database software to build original collections of information.

- Computer-assisted research. "Research, like reporting, requires a special search or investigation," says Paul. "The distinction comes from the sources used by each. Generally, reporting relies on primary sources (firsthand, independent, original), such as interviews, observation or self-conducted analyses." Besides primary sources, research relies on secondary sources (made up of elements derived from something else) as the material being investigated.
- Computer-assisted reference. Reference works, such as dictionaries, encyclopaedias, gazettes, almanacs and glossaries, are available for use on the Internet and through CD-Roms. These virtual reference shelves provide handy and quick access for fact-checking, definitions and spell-checking.
- Computer-assisted rendezvous. The "virtual communities" are places to rendezvous, or meet others. "The ability to hang out, listen in, seek advice and tap into other people's networks of sources is the newest and, perhaps, most exciting aspect of computer-assisted journalism" (Paul, 1994:2).

Each aspect of the four Rs requires different software, skills and knowledge. Some are easier to learn than others. Some are more expensive. Some are used at different stages of journalism. And while all are important to a journalist, this discussion will focus on the four Rs and the Internet.

A vast "network of networks" created by American academics and government researches, the Internet was scarcely available outside of universities and research centres until 1992. No longer. As the Internet has opened to the public, the resources available to journalists have grown. Internet users can send and receive e-mail messages or meet up with others electronically to chat about almost any subject. Most important for reporters and public relations practitioners, they can travel the Internet to explore the new information resources and to communicate with others anywhere around the globe nearly instantaneously.

What you need to get online

This is a brief guide for what you need, what you will find and how you're likely to get it.

To get going, you need a computer, a modem, communications software and access to a telephone service. You will need these to link you through to the network via a host computer to the Internet.

What reporters are finding online is simple: people and recorded information. While bulletin board services (BBS) will provide you with interactive access to the former, databases will provide you with access to the latter.

Database services are electronic libraries of data compiled by newspapers, magazines, libraries and directories. Bulletin boards, on the other hand, are interactive sources for information. You communicate with other people and elicit comment about the information you've found.

Electronic mail

While the Internet has vast resources, one of its primary uses is to act as an enormous electronic post office. People who are signed on to the Internet have e-mail addresses. They can receive e-mail at those addresses or send mail to others with e-mail addresses.

While using e-mail is easy, finding someone's e-mail address often is not. For some useful tips to help you search and find the e-mail address of just about anyone, see About.com's guide at: http://email.about.com/od/addresssearchtip/.

Listservs

If you have a special interest – say, Dalmatian dogs – you're likely to find a group of people who shares your passion. A member who posts a message sends it to everyone else who has subscribed to the listserv by e-mail address. That person will receive all the messages sent by other subscribers.

- TileNet is the guide to lists that use the oldest and most popular programme, Listserv. It is available online at: http://www.tile.net.

News groups

These cover similar areas of interest to the listserv. But unlike the listserv, in which you automatically receive any message posted, you have to go to a newsgroup to read the messages. A comprehensive directory is available at: http://www.cyberfiber.com/.

Telnet

Telnetting connects your computer to a host computer on the Internet. Telnetting works like this: you give the address of a computer on the network to which you want to gain access. Once you have telnetted over to this host computer, the computer you are working on actually becomes a part of the host computer. Once connected, you have the ability to search in the databases, download files or look in the catalogues that are found on the host computer.

Search engines

There is plenty of stuff on the Internet. The trick is finding what you need – quickly. Search engines are the computer "hunting dogs" that help you do it. Google, Lycos, Infoseek, AccuFind and Megellan are examples of search engines. Different search engines are likely to give you different results. If you're looking for information about South Africa, the following search engines and Web directories are a good place to start:

- Aardvark (www.aardvark.co.za) South African and African index.
- Ananzi (www.ananzi.co.za) South African extensive directory of sites, and extra content such as local job info and news.
- SouthAfrica Online (www.southafrica.co.za) Well-lit entrance to the South African Web, comprising a 12 topic directory, along with links to new and cool local sites.

HOT LINK

CyberJournalist.net focuses on how the Internet, media convergence and new technologies are changing journalism. The site offers tips, news and commentary about online journalism, digital storytelling, converged news operations and using the Internet as a reporting tool. Check it out at: http://www.cyber-journalist.net/.

Search Engine Watch provides a guide to the major search engines of the web. Why are these considered to be "major" search engines? Because they are either well-known or well-used. See: http://searchenginewatch.com/links/ article. php/2156221.

Which is the best search engine? The one you learn to use well. You will get help with that from this tutorial on Power Reporting, a site dedicated to providing resources and training in computer-assisted reporting and editing: http://powerreporting.com/altavista. html.

Summary

- Before you look at developing story ideas, you need to factor in the following: the aims of the medium; other dynamics in the news enviroment, such as major news events and the calendar; and the needs of the audience.
- News is presented in a variety of ways: hard news reports, investigative articles, feature stories, columns, reviews, editorials, etc. Each story type draws on different conventions and provides reporters with options to vary the perspective from which they write.
- While events often dictate the stories that are written, there is a range of techniques to develop creative story ideas.
- It is important to devise a reporting plan before you set out to gather information.
- While people typically provide most of the information for news stories, documents and the physical context of the story are also very important sources.

Putting your learning to work

ACTIVITY 1 Recognising sources

Study an in-depth news article in a newspaper and list who you think the sources might have been for the reporter.

- Make a composite list of the sources in class, then invite the reporter concerned to class to discuss the process of identifying the sources, as far as he or she is free to do so.
- Ask the reporter how he or she went about locating the sources. Were there others which would have been preferable?

ACTIVITY 2 Hunting for article ideas

- Take a trip to your local library.
- Scout around – in the databases, on the shelves and notice boards.
- Identify 10 topics you think would be suitable for interesting articles.
- Choose one and apply mind-mapping or another technique to develop a specific story idea.
- Identify a target medium, news peg and angle.
- Plot a reporting plan.
- Write out a story pitch or budget line, which includes:
  - A summary of the story angle, news peg, and details about proposed sources.
  - Name the intended medium and specific section (e.g. *Sunday Times*, sports section) and why you think your proposed story would be appropriate. Also indicate whether or not you have checked to see if a similar story has been published recently.
- Finally, say how long you think the story will be (number of words) and propose some possible illustrations.

FROM THE NEWSROOM

Paddi Clay on asking questions that get stories

Paddi Clay trained at journalism cadet school after completing a B.A. She gained invaluable experience as a "gofer" for the print journals, working on the so-called Information Scandal during the 70s, then moved into radio. She has spent most of her reporting life as a correspondent for foreign networks, covering a wide variety of political and human interest stories in southern Africa. As a manager and trainer she has been responsible for repositioning newsrooms and developing scores of new South African journalists.

Get a life. That's one of the best bits of advice I can give a journalist looking for stories.

Get a life and preserve the tenacious curiosity of the four-year-old you once were. Most stories are found not in the strata of the high and mighty but in daily life, in the small things that are going on all around us, in a slight anomaly in the general experience: the man who begs for books in your suburb when all the others are collecting tins, scrap metal or plastic; the retail store with increasingly empty shelves; a full-page ad placed by an individual politician – all of these could be the start of a really good story.

Good stories emanate from living in, and with, your community. They come from people, not press releases.

Good journalists on the search for stories live full lives, mix with all levels of society, and make a point of meeting different people.

They eavesdrop on conversations. They listen more than they speak. They observe and record. They question even what appears obvious. And they dress appropriately to their task and their subject.

I was once the only journalist to get a scoop interview at a cocktail party being hosted by a head of state for the African National Congress in exile simply because I managed to cobble together an outfit that was more "party guest" than "scruffy journalist".

Unfortunately, the cult of the media personality is damaging journalism. It puts journalists centre stage, it makes us think we are more interesting than our subject matter, and it breeds arrogance.

The whole point of being a journalist is to find out what we and, by extension, our public don't know, and get it to them. But often we censor ourselves before this can happen. We think the question we are about to ask is "too stupid" or the idea we are about to put forward "too bizarre". So, for fear of appearing ignorant, we leave others ignorant.

As the old saying goes there is no such thing as a stupid question – only a stupid answer.

When it comes to interviewing, I have an old-fashioned view. I think courtesy and good manners go a long way to helping you get information. That doesn't mean you cannot be tough. But getting someone's back up is not the best way of getting them to give you something. Leave that type of confrontational interviewing to television presenters.

I believe that reporters must make every effort to keep their own opinions well hidden. No interview subject should know exactly where you are coming from. They will probably be able to make a good guess but there is no benefit to wearing your opinions on your sleeve.

When it comes to story ideas there is one that I still haven't seen realised although I have posed it to scores of journalists in training and working ones.

The question I ask is, "Who decides what is going to be sold by hawkers at the stop streets and intersections of Johannesburg?" What person or business is behind the tons of plastic hangers being thrust at motorists from the roadside?

I still haven't seen the story. And I still don't know the answer.

The answer may not change my world or my perceptions.

But I'm hopeful that an enterprising journalist will one day get me the answer and, in the process, discover a far bigger story. Because the big ones often have small beginnings.

Bibliography and recommended reading

Ansell, G. 2002. *Basic journalism.* Johannesburg: M&G Books.

Anon.1996. Media on the menu. *Rhodes Journalism Review,* December 1996.

Beckett, D. 1993. Why I want this. *Sunday Star,* January 31, 1993.

Campbell, C. 1997. Bengu hits back at 'bungling' claim. *Cape Times,* 28 February 1997:1.

Claassen, G. 1997. E-mail correspondence with author.

Fuller, J. 1996. *News values; ideas for an information age.* Chicago: University of Chicago.

Kessler, F. 1972. Clive Barnes: a man on the aisle. In McDougall, A.K. ed. 1971. *The press.* Princeton, NJ: DowJones, p. 99.

Krouse, P. 1995. Telling tales; business stories should be just that – stories. *The Business Journalist,* February 1995.

Levin, A. 1997. Young, hot and wired. *Style.* February 1997.

Matshikiza, T. 1955. Jazzing the Blues. *Drum* magazine. March 1955.

Murphy, D. 1991. *The stalker affair and the press.* Boston: Unwin Hyman.

Paul, N. 1997. Truth vs money; journalist Martin Welz's costly victory. *Style.* February 1997.

Paul, N. 1994. *Computer-assisted research.* St Petersburg, FL: Poynter.

Perlman, J. 1997. Zero tolerance. *Sunday Life.* March 2, 1997.

Scanlan, C. 2000. *Reporting and writing: basics for the 21st century.* New York: Oxford.

Smith, C. 1999. Rape victims are not statistics … We are people. This is our story. *Mail & Guardian.* 9 to 15 April 1999.

Star, The. 1999. *The Star's code of ethics.* [Online] Available at: http://www.sanef.org.za/ethics_codes/the_star/ [Accessed: 30 June 2004]

Teel, L. and Taylor, R. 1988. *Into the newsroom: an introduction to journalism,* 2nd ed. Chester, Connecticut: Globe Pequot.

Tuchman, G. 1978. *Making news: a study in the construction of reality.* New York: Free Press.

Vallance, H. 1995. *A beginner's guide to research.* Cape Town, B&V Communications.

Van den Berg, C. 2004. Boks back with a bang. *Sunday Times,* 13 June 2004: 32.

Welz, M. 1997. Interview with author.

Wrottesley, S. 2003. Training to unlock the world. *Stellenbosch Media Forum,* 2003: 14-16.

7 Collecting information: interviews

Introduction

Information is the merchandise of journalists. Some data is collected from records, some from observation. But by far the most common way of collecting information for stories is person-to-person conversations: face-to-face, over the telephone, or online.

Still, interviews are tricky – as offbeat journalist PJ O'Rourke noted after meeting Bill Clinton while the former governor was campaigning for the US presidency (1992:2):

On the subject of interviews, I'd like to ask the reader a question. Do you think [former] Governor Bill Clinton was suddenly going to lean across the table and say: "PJ, if I'm elected, taxes will be on steroids, regulatory agencies will spread like sexually transmitted diseases, inflation's going to look like my midsummer opinion poll rating, the stock market will do a cordless bungee jump … ?"

Successful politicians did not get to be successful politicians by being dumb enough to tell reporters the truth. Or tell reporters much of anything.

Then there's the matter of charm. It is the business of successful politicians to have some, and even the most loathsome have enough to last through an average interview. I count myself a hard-bitten newsman – cynical, world-weary, you get the picture – but I have been charmed in my time by [New York] Mayor [Ed] Koch, Imelda Marcos and the Lebanese Shi'ite terrorist leader, Hussein Mussawi.

You start out asking tough questions and before you know it, you find yourself saying, "I loved your last car bomb. It had real style and, dare I say it, wit".

The third and worst problem with political interviews is essential dishonesty of the interviewers. Sometimes this is wilful, but mostly it is uncontrollable, like the action of the aorta …

Exempli gratia, I am a blowed-in-the-glass Republican … I have never voted for a Democrat in my life. Bill Clinton could know the location of the Holy Grail, possess the secrets of the philosopher's stone and have the value of Pi worked out to the last decimal and I'd fudge it.

Interviewing is an imperfect process, that much is clear. Some of the variables (including the interviewer's own biases) can be managed. But it is tough – sometimes impossible – to control the one that matters most: the source. Professional writers work hard to hone their interviewing skills. And there is much to learn: You simultaneously ask questions, evaluate answers, take notes, nudge the source on or redirect them, check your own motives, and gauge the interviewee's reactions. This is not a task for the unprepared.

> *"A reporter who begins an interview without the proper preparation is like a pilot flying without a navigator. Both may make it, but flying blind is not the best way to get there."*
>
> THE MISSOURI GROUP
> (1980:94)

LEARNING GOALS

At the end of this chapter, you should be able to:

1 Prepare for the interview by conducting appropriate research and formulating questions.
2 Recognise the specific challenges of conducting interviews face-to-face, telephonically, and via e-mail.
3 Choose the most appropriate method of recording interviews.
4 Identify ways to ensure that, whatever the motives of the interviewee, the information is accurate.
5 Follow typical journalistic style when citing sources and quoting from interviews.

Preparing for the interview

Winston Churchill said, "Let our advance worrying become advance thinking and planning." That certainly applies in this instance. The success of an interview depends as much on what you do before you pose the first question as it does on the questioning and writing. Once you've worked out your reporting plan (see Chapter 6), you'll need to ask yourself the following:

What is the point of the story?

Before rushing off to contact someone, decide what you aim to achieve. Do you need information for a story, or do you simply need direction to other sources? Do you need new information, or are you checking to confirm facts you got somewhere else? Do you just need a comment, or do you need details of the context (sights, sounds, smells, noises)? Two parties that will influence the answers to these questions are your editor and your audience.

Have you checked with your editor what it is they want from you? This may be trickier than it sounds. "You have to push to be briefed properly," says Gwen Ansell (2002:59). A common newsroom scenario goes something like this:

EDITOR: *Ngema, the FIFA team is arriving at the airport at 3pm today. Book a car and interview them.*

[Instead of merely saying "yes" and rushing off, probe for more details.]

NGEMA: *Sure, is there a specific reason for their visit? Do you have an angle in mind?*

EDITOR: *Yes, they're coming to check on how Soccer World Cup preparations are going. We need to find out if they think we're on track.*

NGEMA: *Anything else?*

EDITOR: *Well, it would be useful to know if they have any concerns, specifically about transport and security, which were flagged as areas for concern.*

NGEMA: *How do think we're going to use the story? Do you want a straight news report, or a feature? How much space do we have? Do you want me to see if a photographer can come along, too?*

EDITOR: *Listen, I've got to get to a meeting. We'll probably run this as a short on page 3, unless something really exceptional comes from it. No, we don't worry about the pics. We'll talk when you get back, OK?*

The important point here is that you need to know what your editor expects from the interview. Then you can ask yourself the next key question: What would my audience want to know if they had a chance to conduct the interview? "Think about who your readers are; put yourself in their shoes," says Ansell (2002:59). "If you're stuck, a quick phone call to a reader you know may help."

What is the deadline?

The urgency of the situation may also be an important consideration. Though sending an e-mail or making a telephone call may be the easiest way to get information on deadline, it is not always the most efficient. If the person you need to contact is not answering their telephone or is not responding to your e-mails, heading out to find them may be the quickest way to get what you want.

What is most appropriate channel to use: face-to-face, telephonic, or e-mail?

If you merely want to confirm a fact, a simple telephone call or e-mail may do the trick. However, if you need man-on-the-street comment ("**vox pops**"), you will probably have to get out of the office – though reporters have used e-mail and random phone calls to good effect. For an in-depth or feature story, you typically need a face-to-face encounter,

Definition

Vox pops is the informal usage of the Latin term *vox populi*, which means "public opinion" or "popular belief". The term is typically used to describe the short comments from "on-the-street" interviews with "ordinary" people.

which gives you chance to collect the colourful details that distinguishes engaging storytelling, as these lead paragraphs by Gus Silber (1992:24) show:

> In a glass cage in the foyer of the Piet Meyer Building, Auckland Park, Johannesburg, a stubble-faced man in stonewashed denims and a Mickey Mouse T-shirt taps out a tattoo on his knees and throws his hands up in the air.
>
> "Hey," shouts Alex Jay, 31, father of two, owner of the spearmint-white Mercedes-Benz convertible gleaming in pole position in the SABC parking lot, "I don't want any more! What's the point? Please! I'm in enough trouble with the taxman as it is."
>
> Alex Jay is talking about money. He's learned his lesson. It can buy you a Mercedes-Benz. It can buy you a holiday in Disneyland. It can buy you a fully-equipped digital recording studio. But it can't buy you Love, Peace and Happiness. So who's complaining?

What background information do I need?

How you research a subject depends on the assignment. If you're covering a spot news story, you may have little (or no) time for research, and will have to rely on your instincts.

For in-depth and feature stories, finding out as much as you can before your interview is imperative. The week before the release of a provocatively-titled film, my editor called me over. She handed me a news release and gave me an assignment: track down and interview the star, a model-turned-actress with links to the community our newspaper served. I had never heard of her, or the film; clearly, I needed to hit the research trail, fast. First, I made a call to the film company to request an advance screening. That would be impossible to arrange before the interview, replied the distribution manager. Did they have a comprehensive publicity pack that could to be faxed to me? Yes, came the reply. At least, I would know the plot of the movie.

Next, I checked the newspaper's electronic library for stories about the woman; since this was a new career move, there were very few. I walked across to the newspaper's fashion editor, whom I knew would be able to fill me in on the woman's modelling career and point her out in some magazine ads. She also gave me a useful tip: the model/actress had attended the same university I had, although she had left a few years before I enrolled. Following a hunch, I telephoned a professor I thought may have taught her. He told me the woman's older sisters had also been to the university. The professor suspected that the young woman's role in a sexy film would raise some eyebrows in her conservative home town. I made a note reminding myself to ask the actress about this.

On the way home, I rented a video of a film in which she had played a small part some six years earlier. I noticed something odd: the fashion editor said the woman's career had taken off after appearing in a TV commercial in which, oozing characteristic Southern charm, she had drawled the line: "Nothing comes between me and my Calvins." Yet in the film, she spoke with a crisp British accent. I know I was on to something. Following the interview, I wrote this short feature:

Andie MacDowell is Southern – she grew up in Gaffney, SC – and she's convinced her newest film is "definitely stuff that especially older Southerners will find uncomfortable".

She's talking about "Sex, Lies and Videotape" which won the Cannes Film Festival's top prize this summer and opens Friday in Charlotte. In it, MacDowell, a 31-year-old actress and model, plays an uptight woman trapped in a disastrous marriage. "Everyone will get something different from it, I think," said MacDowell. What the former Winthrop College student could get is a new-found reputation: that behind the auburn hair and coltish eyes that earn her $500 000 yearly as the "face" for L'Oreal cosmetics is an actress with substance.

Certainly, after MacDowell's first feature-film role – the unplain Jane to Christopher Lambert's Tarzan in "Greystoke: the Legend of Tarzan, Lord of the Apes" – she has something to prove. Director Hugh Hudson cast Mac-Dowell halfway into the project, only to dub out her Southern drawl and dub in Glen Close's crisp British clip – without MacDowell's knowledge.

"I was already doing publicity for them," MacDowell said. "And I called and said, 'When am I supposed to do the looping?' And they said, 'Well, we decided to use a British accent'. So that was that. I was pretty much powerless at that point ...".

A one-question interview

Among journalists a story does the rounds of a reporter assigned to write about legendary comedian Bob Hope's trip to entertain Allied troops stationed near the Iraqi border.

"Absolutely no time for an interview," Hope's manager said. "Please," the reporter pleaded, "just five minutes."

Eventually, after more pleading, the request was granted. But the reporter didn't even get five minutes with the star. Instead, he could walk with Hope from the airport terminal to the plane. He had the time it would take to walk 50 metres. That was it. What do you think the reporter asked Hope? What would you have asked?

After much thought, the reporter came up with this simple question: "Mr Hope, what's your latest joke?" The reporter knew the organisers and other sources could give him other information – such as why Hope was going on the trip, where he would be performing, when he would return, and how the trip had come about. But what joke Hope was going to use to try to lighten the troops' anxiety (albeit briefly) was unique.

Try to get as much information as possible about the subject before you begin an interview. Not only will it allow you to ask more insightful questions, but sources are less likely to fudge answers if they know (or think you know) what is going on. And, of course, it will save you time.

What questions should I ask?

Some editors advise young reporters to brainstorm 10 questions before starting an interview. This is sound advice; it allows the reporter to clarify what he or she is after. Remember, though, interviews seldom go according to plan. You may find after the first question that the rest on your list become irrelevant because your source introduces more important issues. Listen carefully to the responses and let the interview take its natural course.

Face-to-face interviewing tips

Arranging to meet

This may not be as easy as it seems. *Miami Herald* reporter Edna Buchanan tells a story about the time she covered a story of a woman who had been shot in broad daylight, inside a Cuban restaurant (1987:269). The victim had called the newspaper a day earlier, saying that someone was trying to kill her. She was right.

Buchanan greeted the homicide detective at the curb. He could tell her nothing, he said, as he had just arrived. She persisted and followed him until blocked by the yellow tape. The policeman ducked under the tape and stepped into the restaurant. Just then, the telephone rang and the detective picked it up: "Edna, I told you, we just got here, and I don't know anything yet."

Buchanan's advice: "I know it sounds foolish, but often people, uncomfortable at being seen talking to a reporter, will speak more freely over the telephone. It never hurts to remind them that you are out there, waiting. If they know that you never give up, never go away, sometimes they will tell you what you need to know – out of sheer self-defence."

Reporters usually set up interviews by telephone. They simply dial and ask. It is best to identify yourself, to suggest a time and place or even to conduct the interview over the phone immediately if the source is not prepared to see you.

Often, reporters have to work through intermediaries – secretaries or public relations practitioners. In large organisations, the PR department can usually arrange the interview. Be prepared to answer three questions:

- Who are you?
- Whom do you represent?
- What are you writing about?

What if you are freelance? If you are working on an assignment, say so. Don't lie. Don't say you are with a news organisation if you are not on the staff. If you are freelancing on speculation, you have to say that. Even if you hope to sell your story to the *Sunday Times*, you cannot give the impression that you are on the permanent staff of the *Sunday Times*.

Referring to another source can help get an interview. By introducing yourself and adding, "Mr X told me you could probably help me with this", you are, in effect, saying that you have the recommendation of others.

Getting the most from your interview

Before you leave, take a look in the mirror.

Even the best prepared interview can fall apart because of something as petty as your appearance. You would probably frown if your bank manager greeted you in her office wearing shorts – and vice versa.

Most reporters choose to fit in with the environment. As the four University of Missouri journalism professors, known as The Missouri Group, point out: "It is your right to wear your hair however you wish and to wear whatever clothes you want, but it is the source's prerogative to refuse to talk to you" (1980: 97).

Be on time

There is no law that says people should speak to reporters, so respect your source's concession. Consider how long it is going to take to get through traffic, find parking and find the office when you plan your schedule.

Time magazine writer Margaret Carlson was assigned to interview actress Katharine Hepburn, who had recently published her autobiography, *Me: Stories of My Life*. Carlson arrived late. Her story started like this (1992:54):

"How dare you keep me waiting? Are you stupid?" were Hepburn's first words. Not a good beginning. Not good at all. An interview with Katharine Hepburn is not easy under the best of circumstances, even when her publisher has set it up to publicise the paperback release in the US of her best-selling autobiography, *Me: Stories of My Life*. It is going to be awfully hard to ask what she was thinking of carrying on a 27-year affair with the married Spencer Tracy if she keeps her back turned to me the whole time. Apologies are definitely in order.

"I'm sorry I'm late, really I am."

"You are not sorry. You are stupid."

The two women sparred for a few hours and Carlson's story portraying Hepburn as an "arrogant", "overbearing" "bully" ran under the headline, "A bad case of Hepburn".

In letters to the editor a few weeks later, readers aired their opinions of the piece. Some applauded the reporter: "The interview was a fine piece of journalism – really excellent. Give a raise to Carlson," wrote a reader from Helsinki, Finland. Many, like this reader from Denver, Colorado, did not:

I read Margaret Carlson's "interview" with the legendary actress Katharine Hepburn, but found it a total waste of time learning how Hepburn apparently gave poor Carlson heartburn because the reporter was 10 minutes late. If Carlson had taken the time to learn something about the eccentricities of Hepburn beforehand she would not have been late.

On this occasion, Carlson got her interview despite poor time planning. But she might not have been so lucky (and she will probably not be visiting Hepburn again soon).

Time is precious – both your source's and yours. Often the person you most want to interview is precisely the person who has the least amount of time to spend with a reporter. A good policy, when approaching someone for an interview, is to say exactly how much time you would like. It is also good manners.

You are more likely to get an audience with a busy or reluctant source if they think you won't be wasting their time. If you set specific parameters, stick to them. Don't say you want to talk for 10 minutes and then stay for 20. The next time you want to talk to that person, they are unlikely to believe you if you say you will be brief. If your source invites you to stay longer, take up the offer only if there is important information you still need – your time is precious too.

Planning your interview approach

Television presenter Freek Robinson is known as a sharp interviewer. Some say he is cocky, even arrogant. Robinson says he is only doing his job:

> There is apparently an attitude among certain South Africans that a person must have an absolute respect for authority, and that you have to ask questions from your knees ... I don't think that's right. Each one of us, as ordinary citizens, has our own claim on human rights. Obviously a person makes certain concessions if, for example, you are speaking to the president of the country, like giving him more time to answer his questions and interrupting him less. But that does not mean you give him a blank cheque to say in a monologue exactly what he wants. Then it's no longer an interview, but a propaganda session (1993:38).

If anything, Robinson's approach is straightforward. Usually it works, although astute journalists know that getting information depends on more than just asking questions. Rapport – the relationship between the reporter and the source – is crucial to the success of an interview. The relationship is sometimes relaxed, sometimes tense. Some situations may require the gall of a salesman; others, the genuine **sympathy** of a priest. A journalist works between two factors – the public has the right to know most information, yet nobody is legally required to talk to you (Teel and Taylor, 1988:119). Getting what you need requires versatility and plenty of imagination. Here are some possible approaches:

Direct

Introduce yourself and tell the person what you want, as Robinson does.

Be human

Remember, those you interview are more than just means to your journalistic end. Treating people with basic respect is not just decent, it is

Definition

Empathy [Zu. Ukuhawukela / Xh.ukuvelana / Afr. empatie]: The ability to imagine and share another person's feelings, experiences, etc.
Sympathy [Zu. uzwelo / Xh. uvelwano / Afr. simpatie]: The feeling of pity, sorrow or compassion for a person or subject.

also sensible. Convicted mass-murderer Antonie Wessels gave a reporter an exclusive interview because he was the only person who ventured to find out what Wessels was feeling. People in trouble with the law, or otherwise, will often respond to simple manners, for example: "I know there are always two sides to every story. I would like to hear yours."

Maybe one of the most difficult interviews to conduct is one with the family or friends of someone who has just died or who is dying. It is also one of the most common for hard news reporters. My first newspaper job included writing daily obituaries. Every day, I had to call up people, attend funerals and even knock on doors where families and friends were grieving. For a twenty-something rookie, it was tough. But I always recalled some sage advice I'd heard along the way: obituaries often provide people an opportunity, maybe for the last time, to tell the world how much the dead person meant to them. I usually started with identifying myself and expressing my sympathy simply ("I'm sorry to hear of your loss"), and then adding: "We're writing a story about Mr X and I didn't want to go ahead without giving those who knew him best the opportunity to comment."

Wide-eyed

On a routine check of police reports, I ran across an account of a traffic accident caused by a drunk driver. The name looked familiar – that of the elderly local high school vice-principal. I called the school. No, said the secretary, the man was at the courthouse serving on a jury. I called a clerk at the court. No, said the official, the man had called in sick. I knew I had to call the principal. I also knew that a story about the incident, which had put a young woman in hospital, might jeopardise the man's job (a group of parents at the school, calling themselves MADD for Mothers Against Drunk Driving, had recently run a much-publicised "don't drink and drive" campaign in the town).

On the advice of a colleague, I tried this approach: "Hello, Mr X. I am François Nel at the *Observer*. While checking police reports this morning, I came across one with your name on it. Could it possibly have been you?" Then, quite demurely I added, "Tell me, sir, what happened?" The strategy worked and the man gave me his version of the events. (We eventually ran a small story on page three, as I recall. The man went into counselling and joined Alcoholics Anonymous – and kept his job.)

Sit-in

If you really need to see a person and the protectors – secretaries, associates – insist the person is too busy and could not possibly see you today, tell them you will wait. Taking along lunch and a book helps to show you are serious. Although persistence does not always pay off, it is likely to yield greater dividends than no persistence at all.

Head-on

If you glimpse a reluctant source within earshot, make your appeal as quickly and directly as possible: "You have been sentenced to life in prison, Mr Ratheart. Do you think the judgement was fair?"

Planning your questioning technique

Start with broad questions first. **Open-ended** questions are usually less threatening. But don't avoid direct, **closed-ended** questions. At some time you will have to get a straight answer: "So, will you vote for or against Pretoria's bid to become the new seat of Parliament?"

Take care in phrasing your questions. Open-ended questions are less direct and less threatening. A worker may not respond frankly if asked if he likes his supervisor; the question calls for a yes-no response. But an open-ended question, such as "What do you think of Mr Bigwig's managerial style?", is not as confrontational. Open-ended questions are more exploratory and flexible and it is a good idea to use a few when you start your interview.

There are times, however, when the reporter needs to close in on the subject to get specific answers. Instead of asking an accused whether he thinks the charges against him are fair, you simply ask, "Did you forge the cheque?"

Knowing when to put the question depends on the flow of the interview and the chemistry between you and the source. You must make on-the-spot decisions. Above all, listen. If something is unclear, ask. Don't be afraid to push for clarification, especially on technical matters. Once, when interviewing a doctor, I had to stop him and say, "I'm sorry, but you are going way over my head. Let's try this: think of me as your teenage cousin, now explain to me what is *chronic otitis media*."

Do not be afraid to let someone know you are searching blindly. Many interesting details have come from simply asking, "Is there something else you think may help me?"

Definition

Open-ended questions don't demand a specific answer: *Can you please explain what you mean?*

Closed-ended questions require a specific response, yes or no: *Did you take the money?*

HOT TIP

Persistence, privacy and pestering

Yes, as a journalist you are expected to be tenacious in tracking down information in the public interest. But being persistent is not the same as invading someone's privacy, after you've been asked to stop telephoning or e-mailing, or to leave the premises. There's a line between tenacity and intimidation. Don't cross it.

FROM THE NEWSROOM

From author, lecturer and writing coach Foster Winans

A former Wall Street Journal *reporter and columnist, Foster Winans, posted this advice on the Poynter Online discussion board under the headline, "A tip I learned from a master interviewer" (2003):*

At the time I wrote my first book, I was reading a lot of work by John McPhee, the legendary non-fiction writer and author (*Coming Into The Country, Basin and Range*) whose work relies heavily on extensive interviews. He was teaching at Princeton and one of his colleagues there wrote a foreword for a collection of McPhee's magazine pieces. In the foreword, the writer reported that people who John McPhee interviewed would commonly tell their friends afterward that McPhee seemed to be an idiot because he asked the same question several times at different points during the interview. This was deliberate. Each time he asked the question, the answer tended to be slightly different, affording McPhee nuances and facets that he would not otherwise have had and giving him a clearer picture and understanding.

What I took away from that, internalized after all these years, is to care less whether the person I am interviewing thinks I'm smart or informed, and care passionately that I have clearly understood the details of and the meaning behind the answers. That was a long way from the self-involved, self-conscious 19-year-old reporter I had been when I started out in 1968, terrified that the always-older people I was interviewing would not take me seriously, or think me a dope. This knowledge has served me well, over and over again, and I pass it on frequently to the high school and college students I coach in interviewing because I think they need to hear it most. Ask, and ask again, until you feel confident you understand.

Stick to the topic. Don't indulge your source – or yourself – in long, unfocused conversations, unless you think they will pay off at a later stage. Remember: it is your job and you are being paid for your time.

Listen. Always listen closely to what your source is saying and probe when something is unclear. Don't stop listening once the formal interview has ended. That is when some sources loosen up. You are not violating any ethical code if you keep asking questions after you have put your notebook down or switched your recorder off.

Save your interruptions. Give the interviewee a chance to relax before you challenge a point. Occasionally, murmur and chuckle – and keep quiet. A simple *mmmmmm* or a chuckle will let your source know you are listening and encourage them to keep on talking. A pause may do the same, but it can signal more: that the answer was inadequate, that you did not understand or that you are sceptical of what was said.

Keep calm. Keep your cool, grit your teeth, count to 10 or do whatever it takes to maintain a professional attitude.

Keeping control

Few interviewees will give you everything you want to know, clearly and concisely, and nothing more. Therefore, most conversations, if undirected, will touch on this and that and meander over there and beyond. This is just not productive, and it makes wading through your notes and piecing together a story a nightmare. In a note to a young reporter, veteran journalist and former editor of *Sarie* magazine, André Rossouw, gave this advice:

> *I get the impression that you allow people in your interviews to speak as they wish and wander off track, to lose the train of thought. Don't do that. You are the "chairman" of the meeting. If a person is busy with a subject and he/she wanders off, you must immediately interrupt them and take them back to the subject at hand ...play "sheep dog".*

Don't leave without the basics. Never say goodbye before you have the correct spelling of the person's full name, title, company, address and, if possible, age. Even for vox pops, I usually ask for someone's contact details. If you explain that you like to make doubly sure that your facts are correct and may need to call them when you get down to writing the story, few people will refuse.

If you can't get all the basic details you need from the interviewee, get them from his or her colleagues. People love talking to the press if the subject is not themselves.

Finally, of course, always thank your interviewees for their time. It's just good manners.

Telephone interviewing tips

One of the most common gripes heard around newsrooms is that there is never enough time to work on stories. Editors, keeping track of deadlines and budgets, are often seen as tyrants who never stop asking when the next story will be done. Most reporters are expected to write at least one story and sometimes three or four a day. Forced to produce under such pressure, reporters need to plan carefully what information they want from an interview and how best to get it. When pressed for time, reporters may have to make do with getting information by telephone. With the right questions, though, you can still get plenty of details in this way.

One Saturday morning I arrived in the newsroom where an anxious editor told me a teenager had died at a Halloween party the previous evening and they needed a story, fast. The incident had happened at the boy's aunt's house in a town half an hour's drive away and the child's family lived in a city 45 minutes in the other direction. I had no choice but to get the bare-as-bones police report and hit the telephone for the rest. The next day this front-page story ran under the heading, "Teenager strangled at party":

YORK – Mock terror turned to real horror when a 15-year-old Charlotte boy playing a hanged man at a private party was strangled by the noose.

William Anthony "Tony" Odom, a ninth-grader at Garinger High School, was pronounced dead Friday night by York County coroner Jim Chapman amid spider webs and plastic bats decorating the first-floor basement of his aunt Diane Boyd's home.

Shortly before 9pm Tony and several of his friends staged the annual event's grand finale: a haunted house in the unfinished basement of the single-storey home on Mission Road.

Tony crouched inside a free-standing wooden cupboard, intending to fake a hangman scene, said his grandmother, Hattie Carpenter, who was at the party. He was dressed as a pirate wearing black trousers, a red shirt and gold hoop earring. Around his neck was a three-foot nylon ski rope tied into a hangman's knot.

"It was a slip-knot type noose; the more pressure you apply, the tighter it gets," said the coroner.

"One of the kids checked on him before the show began and he was fine, jumping around and waiting for things to begin," Chapman said.

"She didn't hear anything from him and went back to check two to three minutes later and he had slumped over inside the closet.

"Evidently, it was tight enough to cause some problems with his breathing and he either passed out or panicked."

The noose was attached to a bar about 4 feet from the ground, York County sheriff's reports show.

"He would have had to stoop down to show that he was hung," Chapman said. "He could have stood up and loosened the rope; his hands were not restrained."

Odom's 13-year-old cousin found him and ran upstairs to get her mother. Boyd tried to free the noose and had to return upstairs for a kitchen knife before she could cut the boy free. Tony's grandfather, Harvey Carpenter, said he and Boyd tried to revive the boy.

The county 911 dispatcher received a call at 9.36pm, Chapman said. Rescue workers arrived at 9.45pm, but Chapman estimates the boy died between 9 and 9.15pm.

"What was really sad was that the kids thought we were going to be able to revive him, but it was too late. They were scared when we got there, but then they became hysterical," Chapman said.

"It's a real shame. Maxie and Diane (Boyd) go to so much trouble for their kids to have fun at home," said a family friend who asked not to be identified.

"I really felt sorry for the boy's family, but it must have also been really hard for those little kids at the party. I don't think Halloween will ever be the same for them."

Johnson said tests showed the boy had not been drinking.

All the information in this story came from telephone interviews, except for the boy's height which was on the police report.

I called the coroner and deputy coroner, who had both investigated the accident and, after warning them that I was going to be very picky, I started: *When* did you get the call? *What* time did you arrive? *Was* the boy already dead? *What* time did he die? *What* type of house was it? *How* many storeys? *Was* the basement renovated? *How* was it decorated? *Was* the cupboard built-in? *How* big was it? *How* tall was the boy? *What* was he wearing? *How* long was the rope? *How* was it secured? *What* type of rope was it? *What* type of knot was it? *Why* couldn't the boy free himself? *Was* it possible that he had been drinking?

Next, I called the home where the accident happened, but no one would speak to me. I rang up the boy's home where I spoke to both his grandparents. Just before deadline, I called the high school principal to double-check that the boy had been enrolled at his school.

The story closed with three paragraphs from a personal interview with the boy's mother, while she sat on a weight-lifting bench in her son's room. And finally, there were details about the funeral which I got after a call to the funeral home.

E-mail interviewing tips

"E-mail interviews are now like telephone interviews – they have their shortcomings when stacked against the in-person interview format, but they're also a reality for journalists under deadline pressure," said former New York Bureau Chief of CNET News.com Sandeep Junnarkar, now a visiting professor at Indiana University. To make the most of this option for interviewing, he offers these tips (first published on the Poynter Institute for Media Studies website, http://www.poynter.org and used with permission):

Before you pose the questions, consider e-mail etiquette for reporters

- We don't all work for well-known publications like *The New York Times* and *Newsweek*, so remember to introduce yourself and your news organisation, its circulation, and its importance to your community.
- Explain just enough about your story or project to entice the source to participate.
- Make clear how you came across the source's name (someone referred you, etc.).
- Explain how you think their comments can add perspective or insight to your story.
- Provide your telephone number, geographic location, and other relevant contact information.
- Offer to make it a phone interview rather than an e-mail interview.
- Just as you should verify the identity of someone who approaches you via e-mail, the source is uncertain about you. Always give people a chance and enough time to verify your identity.
- Provide links to your previous articles to show that you have covered subjects fairly in the past.
- Stress that you are on deadline. (Be clear about when you need responses by in order to meet your deadline.)
- This is not an e-mail to a colleague, friend, or family member. Use upper and lower case writing, with no abbreviations for common words; full sentences; and correct spelling, punctuation, and grammar.

- Never send questions in an attachment, a Microsoft Word document or other format. People are uncomfortable opening files they receive from strangers lest there be a computer virus or worm attached.

E-mailing the interview questions

- Whether you're conducting a face-to-face, phone, or e-mail interview, do the same rigorous background research to prepare the questions.
- E-mail the questions to at least three sources that have similar backgrounds. Hopefully at least one will respond immediately. (Don't cc the three. Send separate e-mails.)
- Keep questions short, clear, and to the point with just one concept or inquiry per question.
- Start with overview questions – but only a couple. No one feels like typing out long general responses.
- Move on to specific, targeted questions – no more than four or five so you don't overwhelm the source with the request. This is where they find the delete button especially handy.
- Ask questions that get a "yes" or "no" response only to confirm facts or statements.
- Ask for documents, studies, and images relevant to your story. Sources can easily attach and send these to you.
- Request the names of other sources that may be relevant to your story.

Once you e-mai! the questions, what should you do while waiting and how long should you wait for a response?

- If this is a breaking news story, call your sources after an hour or two (or sooner depending on your deadline cycle).
- If this is a feature piece, give them at least 48 hours before sending a second request to the same person.
- Keep looking for other reputable sources you can ask the same questions.
- Brainstorm for questions you might have forgotten to ask.

The response arrives. Now what?

- Don't send the "thank you" note yet.
- Read the responses carefully. Weigh them against the reporting that you have accomplished since sending out the initial e-mail. Are there holes that need to be filled? Are the responses clear? Do you need clarifications?

- Now send out the: "Dear <So-and-so>, thank you for taking the time ... I would appreciate a few clarifications. I want to be sure I understand."
- Request clarifications; politely ask again about questions that went unanswered; slip in the follow-up questions and the new questions you formulated while waiting.

Closing the loop

- Now's the time for the "thank you" note.
- Let the source know that you will send a link or clip of the article when it's available. Then, set up a reminder so you deliver what you promised!
- Build the source's confidence in you: use their responses fairly and in context.

These steps will help you get the most out of e-mail interviews while boosting your credibility in your new sources' eyes, giving you contacts around the country and world to turn to at a moment's notice for future stories.

Guidelines for evaluating sources

Trisha Greene, an editor at the *Charlotte Observer*, had this advice for young reporters: "Don't trust anyone. If your mother tells you she loves you, check it out. Get a second source." That may be overstating the case, but the point is made: the motives of those you interview are not always clear. Some sources are obviously self-serving, as when a politician maligns a rival. Others may be concerned citizens, like the person who calls to report a factory which dumps its refuse in a river. Still others may be revengeful, like the disgruntled employee who, after being fired from his company, called a journalist with information about the corporation's fraudulent business practices.

An interviewee's motives can be complex and varied. A journalist needs to be sure that, whatever the case, the information is accurate. Consider the following:

- Always be wary. Don't take information at face value. Remember a journalist taking notes during an interview is not the same as a secretary taking minutes of a meeting. If someone says something you don't understand, or doesn't ring true – ask them about it.
- Use sources as starting points for stories, but make sure you double- or even triple-check the information.
- Discard information you cannot substantiate.
- Use sources to check facts and accuracy – not to approve your story.

Often, the source of an interview will request to see the final product. Beware. Of course, if you're a public relations practitioner making sure the company president is pleased with the profile you've written about him, that is part of your job. If you're a news reporter, your only obligation is to make sure you have correct information. You should not be in the position where you need to get permission from sources or subjects of stories. Editors may send sensitive stories to the subject of the story for comment – not approval.

- Be careful with confidential or "anonymous" sources. Some sources, in an attempt to manipulate the press or avoid responsibility for what they say, may ask you not to use their name.

Anonymity also invites sources to distort information and take cheap shots at opponents. Don't lead them into temptation. Many publications discourage sources that cannot be named.

There are two concerns: credibility and integrity. Many readers are sceptical when they read such vague attributions as "a man said". They wonder if the source exists, and rightly so. During a social gathering, a newspaper editor acknowledged that when pressed to find a source for information or opinion he thought was valid, he attributed the information to an unnamed person.

He is not alone. But others have been exposed. On September 28, 1980, the *Washington Post* published "Jimmy's World", the story of an eight-year-old heroin addict in Washington DC's black community (Bates, 1989:87–8). The story described how Jimmy's mother looked on as a man injected the boy with heroin: "The needle slides into the boy's soft skin like a straw pushed into the centre of a freshly baked cake". The story was riveting. Riveting enough to earn the reporter, Janet Cooke, a Pulitzer Prize. But when reporters and finally editors tried to confirm Cooke's story, she broke down and confessed: Jimmy did not exist. The incident ended Cooke's career, embarrassed the *Washington Post* and gave more credence to sceptics who tell us not to believe what we read in the papers.

Incidentally, 15 years later Cooke gave her first media interview to discuss the incident. The reporter, Mike Sager, tracked down the once highly paid and highly regarded journalist in Kalamazoo, Michigan, where she was working in a department store for $6.15 an hour. She said, "What I did was horrible; believe me, I think that. But I don't think that in this particular case the punishment fit the crime. I've lost my voice. I've lost half my life. I'm in a situation where cereal has become a viable dinner choice" (Sager, 1996:206).

My rule: Avoid unnamed sources.

If you cannot find someone who will talk on the record, look further. Only in extreme cases – say when a life or the national security is endangered – should you quote someone anonymously. If someone is anxious, read back the quotes you are likely to use. Never use an unnamed source just because you are too timid or lazy to ask the person's name.

When it comes to sources – as in other things – don't create situations where it would be easy for you, or others, to be dishonest.

- Protect your sources. This is not just good advice, it is expected of good reporters. The South African Union of Journalists formalised this directive in item no. vii of their Code of Conduct: "A journalist shall protect confidential sources of information."

    Many people have lost their jobs because they have spoken to reporters. This happens in public and private concerns, and it happens regardless of the truth of the source's information. If information is given to you in confidence, you are honour-bound to keep to the deal. Your source's livelihood – and, in some cases, even his life – may depend on it.

> ▮**HOT** TIP
>
> **Guidelines on confidential briefings and sources**
> The South African National Editors Forum have developed useful guidelines that are available at: http://www.sanef.org.za/ethics_codes/sanef/326000.htm

---

E**X**ERCISE *Use of secret sources*

At the first meeting of the South African National Editors Forum, then President Nelson Mandela and Sanef chairperson Thami Mazwai, editor of *Enterprise* magazine, raised the issue of unnamed sources ("Media on the menu" 1996:7):

Mazwai: *We are currently concerned with Section 205 of the Criminal Procedure Act. Warrants issued under this act and requiring journalists to give evidence in Cape Town recently were withdrawn, but our concern is that the law itself has not been scrapped. We must protect the credibility of the media. Once journalists are subjected to having to disclose their informants, it destroys their credibility. I was a victim of this Section 205 and went to jail for refusing to reveal my sources, as have some of my colleagues. With the advent of democracy, this law should be consigned to the scrap heap ...*

Mandela: *Before you move on, let me say that your concerns with 205 need to be discussed with the Ministers of Justice and of Safety and*

Security present. Now, if a journalist says that a secret source gave information, is this something you in Sanef are proud of? Can it not be abused, where gossip is raised to truth?

- Formulate your own response to the President's question. Discuss your answer with your peers.
- Compare your responses with the comment by Helen Fernand of Gender Links after the Hefer Commission ruled in November 2003 that former *Sunday Times* journalist Ranjeni Munusamy should testify before it about an article she initiated detailing accusations that the National Director of Public Prosecutions, Bulelani Ngcuka, had been a spy for the apartheid regime: http://www.genderlinks.org.za/gemcomm/gemcomm.asp?cid=5.
- It might be interesting to note that Munusamy was suspended from her job and Judge Hefer found that the accusations against Ngcuka were false. The full report is available at: http://www.iss.co.za/CJM/pdf/heferreport.htm.

Notetaking tips

You may have had a fantastic interview, but your efforts are in vain if you have not recorded it in a way you can use. Inexperienced reporters often lose excellent facts and quotes because they do not get the information down fast enough or, in their haste, scribble it so that later even they cannot decipher their own handwriting.

Paper and electronic notepads

Reporters' notepads (paper and electronic ones) are often covered in strange, sometimes quirky symbols, abbreviations and shortcuts that help them quickly jot down what is said. Because few reporters are trained in secretarial or recording techniques they usually devise a system that lets them record speedily, accurately and completely – and to go back and retrieve the information with relative ease.

EXERCISE *Practise your notetaking*

Review the tips on notetaking in Chapter 4 (pp. 78-80) and practise by taking notes during a television or radio interview programme. At the end of the interview, scan your notes and ask yourself: would I be able to write a complete and accurate story based on these notes? If the answer is "no", keep practising.

Tape recorders

Miniature tape recorders are becoming increasingly popular. See Chapter 4, page 79 for a discussion on their advantages and disadvantages.

Cameras

A picture, the old adage goes, is worth a thousand words. If that's true, taking a photograph of a place or situation about which you are reporting will save a lot of time on hand-written notes. Back at your keyboard, you will have a chance to review the visual "notes" and add the details that make great stories.

HOT LINK

Want to learn more about broadcast interviews? The BBC's guide to preparing for interviews for radio, including live studio interviews and vox pops, is available online – and at no cost – at: http://www. bbctraining.com/onlineCourses.asp

Tips on using quotes and citing sources

A basic assumption in journalism is that, unless the reporter is witness to an event or circumstance, the source of information will be cited. Most of the information you gather will be paraphrased. Direct quotes, says writing coach Chip Scanlan, can be used for the following: "For emphasis and authority, to breathe life into a story, when someone says something better than you can paraphrase it" (2002:222).

Style

When quoting people directly (as I have just done), decribe the source fully, include a form of the verb *to say*, and place their exact words in quotation marks: *Bonganie Dube, a 19-year-old student at the University of Tswane, was named Mr Clifton on Sunday. "I'm hot," said Dube.*

In the main, use commas to link quotes with the attribution: He said, "I'm happy." While a colon can be used to introduce direct quotations, reserve this when quoting formal documents and the like: *He said, "Let's sing." Shakespeare wrote: "To be or not to be."*

Punctuation goes before the opening quotation mark and inside the close quotation mark: *Dube said, "I'm hot."*

"I'm hot," Dube said.

When using a document as a source, describe the document fully (do not use academic style and citing). Name the author of the document and preferably use a form of the verb *to write: In a memorandum dated January 10 and addressed to Cabinet ministers, President Thabo Mbeki wrote: "I am looking forward to the challenges of the new year."*

When quoting conversation or dialogue, use separate paragraphs with quotation marks at the start and end of each person's quote:

The judge looked her in the eyes and asked, "How do you plead?"

"I'm innocent," she answered.

In general, try to avoid fragmentary quotes. If a speaker's words are clear and concise, use a full sentence.

If cumbersome language (jargon, technical terms and the like) can be paraphrased fairly, use an indirect construction, reserving quotation marks for sensitive or controversial passages that must be identified as coming from the speaker. *He said that he could not comment on the case because it was **sub judice**.*

Definition

Sub judice is a legal term that means "being studied or decided in a law court at the present time". In South Africa, cases which are sub judice cannot be publicly discussed in the media.

Accuracy

Journalists are expected to keep their biases in check and, for that reason, avoid using synonyms that give the impression that you are judging the speaker. In most instances, the neutral *said* (past tense) or *says* (present continuous tense) is preferable. Consider, for example, how the choice of verb can influence the interpretation of what someone said:

"I am innocent," she maintained.

"I am innocent," she demanded

"I am innocent," she declared.

"I am innocent," she pleaded.

"I am innocent," she alleged.
"I am innocent," she cried.
"I am innocent," she said.

Remember that it is easy to manipulate the meaning of someone's words by changing the context in which it was said. Consider, for example, how the following statement could be manipulated:

Mayor Sally Hadebe: "Perhaps some people think that I'm awful because I don't celebrate Christmas in a traditional manner."

"People think I'm awful," acknowledged Mayor Sally Hadebe.
"I'm awful," confessed Mayor Sally Hadebe.
"I don't celebrate Christmas," admitted Mayor Sally Hadebe.
"I don't celebrate," declared Mayor Sally Hadebe.

The manner of delivery is also part of the context. Reporting a smile or a gesture may be as important as conveying the words themselves: *Ernie Goosen grows pensive at the mention of Mamma Molly's name. "I really loved her," he says looking at the photograph pinned up on the notice board.*

When quoting someone else's words, correct basic errors in grammar and syntax that often go unnoticed in speech, but may appear embarrassing in print. It would typically be acceptable to change "Chicken and steak *is* off the menu," to "Chicken and steak *are* off the menu."

However, do not "clean up" quotes to such an extent that you change the personality of the speaker. Do not, for example, modify "We were just *chilling*" to "We were just *relaxing*."

Use abnormal spelling (such as "gonna" for "going to") only when the usage, dialect or mispronunciation is relevant or helps convey a desired touch in a feature.

Unless it is pertinent to the story, do not try to capture dialect through phonetic spelling: *Ven I hear ze boom, I ran kweeklee.* Not only is this difficult for your readers to decipher, but it could also offend those whose way of speaking is being highlighted. If a speaker's accent is of special interest, describe it, rather than trying to render it phonetically: *Speaking with a distinctly American accent, the South African actress Charlize Theron said …*

Offensive words

A sound basic principle is to refrain from using language that you would not want a child to repeat. Obscenities should be avoided, unless essential to the story and used in direct quotations. Remember, too, that quoting another person does not protect you from being charged with **crimen injuria**.

Definition

Crimen injuria is a term used in South African law meaning an action that injures the dignity of another (e.g. swearing, obscene gesturing, indecent exposure, etc.). A charge can be laid against someone who commits this kind of offence. When describing such a case, always explain the reasons for the charge: *He was charged with crimen injuria for swearing at his secretary.* Do not italicise. (Nel, 2000:36)

House styles differ, but obscene words are usually indicated with either fullstops or asterisks corresponding with the number of characters in the words: f… you, f*** them.

The same method can be used when quoting other insults – racist, homophobic, sexist and the like.

HOT TIP

For guidelines on interviewing children, see Chapter 5, p.89.
    Tips for public relations practitioners on how to work with the media to set up interviews, see Chapter 11, p.280.

Summary

- Interviews are one of the key ways for journalists to gather information. Preparing for interviews includes establishing the exact purpose for the interview, gathering as much information about the interviewee and topic as possible, and brainstorming questions you might ask.
- Depending on the purpose of the interview, the availability of the source and the deadline, journalists typically choose to interview people face-to-face, telephonically, or via e-mail. Each option has its particular advantages and challenges.
- Remember there is no law saying the people – including government officials and celebrities – have an obligation to speak to the press. Being suspicious of your source's motives and the accuracy of the facts is professional. Being unnecessarily confrontational and cynical is not productive.
- Recording interviews accurately is essential if writers for the media are to fulfil their mandate of truth-telling.
- Most media houses have some basic style rules that govern the way sources are cited and quotations are used. Stick to them.

Putting your learning to work

Using quotes accurately

Invite a newsworthy student or alumnus to class for a group interview. Have the lecturer tape-record the session, but use only your notes to write a 250-word report for the student newspaper or alumni journal. Include at least three direct quotes in your piece.

Compare the completed reports in small groups and read the best from each group to the whole class. Complete the following:

- Discuss the various approaches taken to the story (all based on the same information). How does this relate to our earlier discussion about the subjective nature of news?
- Evaluate the quotes with the recorded conversation. Were they accurate? Send the best stories to the intended publications.

Tim Modise on being a proud South African journalist

Arguably one of South Africa's finest media professionals, Tim Modise has been involved in broadcasting since 1980. He hosted his own morning talk programme on SAfm and, from January 2003, has anchored "The Tim Modise Network", simulcast on Talk Radio 702 and 567 Cape Talk. Modise is also a co-presenter for the actuality programme Carte Blanche *on MNet, which he joined in January 2003. He is also the Chairman of the Proudly South African Campaign.*

Amongst his numerous honours is the prestigious 2003 International Jaime Brunet Award for the promotion of human rights, which has previously been awarded to the Dalai Lama. The following is an extract from an interview conducted by Homebrew Films for Men's Health *whose readers voted Modise their media "Man of the Year" in 2004.*

Where did it all start, your career?

I had studied communications briefly at the University of Fort Hare and then the university was closed down at that time. And, coincidentally, Radio 702 was just launched in Ga-rankuwa, which is where I come from, and I joined Radio 702 later in that year. And that's where I started.

What did you set out to do and how did that change over time?

One thing that I always knew I wanted to do was to be in the media. That was very clear to me, but I started off as a controller [for Radio 702] and played music then, and gravitated to news reporting in '85–'86 and went back to music, and back to news and current affairs in the early the early 90s and talk show programmes throughout the nineties until now.

Why current affairs and news?

I supposed that is where the action is really for a country such as South Africa, where we've had the political contest that we've had as a result of apartheid, the push for change, the struggle for change, which by its very nature is a place where you had to exchange ideas. Until 1990 when you

had the unbanning of the liberation movements, the political prisoners and so forth being released, that called for, as far as I was concerned, for more interaction, more discussion on current issues facing our country. And I think we are an evolving society, so there is an even greater need to generate discussion around the issues facing our nation. **Specifically where you are involved, in TV and radio, does that change people's perspective of the world?**

I think it does. For instance, you take stories and issues from other parts of the world. People, through the media of TV and radio, can benchmark themselves as a nation and even as individuals on how they compare with their counterparts from elsewhere in the word. And these things happen in real time, particularly television; it offers you the opportunity to see things around the world in real time. So, in a way, you are part of this diminishing, in terms of space and time, global village. We now experience other parts of the world and situations and events in real time so that makes you part of the global village. And I think people find that useful.

And you think that, on your show in the mornings or the stories you cover on *Carte Blanche*, that you can see change?

Yes, I can see change. An example, is something that happened this morning when we took [broadcast] live the speeches of former President FW de Klerk and former President Nelson Mandela. Immediately, we could get a reaction from our listeners and get a sense of where the mood is in our country. That's the kind of immediacy I think you get. **Your motto in life?**

Do the right thing. Don't worry about being right necessarily. Just do the right thing.

What makes you proud to be a South African?

What makes me proud to be South African at this time is the willingness on the part of so many of us to try something new, to forge a new society, to test values, to be open-minded. I think whether we are aware of it or not, we actually have been encouraged to be more open-minded than we give ourselves credit for. So that makes me proud, because, you know, in the past we were as a people, as a nation, rather, a pariah – and I would say just justifiably so during the apartheid days. But now, under our own steam we are bringing about changes, and in a way building a model of how societies should function, how people should get along. And I'm proud of the fact that ordinary average South Africans, whether they realise it or not, are actually working on this project on a daily basis.

Want to know more about Tim Modise? His favourite music, food, smells? Find the answers to these (and what's under his bed) at: http://www. primerap.co.za/biginterview/

Ever wondered where Modise and other Talk Radio 702 presenters work? Take a virtual tour of a station's studio at: http://www.702.co.za/virtual-tour/studio.asp#. (You can use the arrow keys to change the direction of your view, and use the magnifying glass icon to zoom in and out of the virtual studio).

Bibliography and recommended reading

Ansell, G. 2002. *Basic journalism.* Johannesburg: Mail & Guardian.

Bates, Stephen, 1989. *If no news, send rumors: anecdotes of American journalism.* New York: St Martin's.

Buchanan, E. 1987. *The corpse had a familiar face: covering Miami, America's toughest crime beat.* London: Bodley Head.

Carlson, M. 1992. A bad case of Hepburn. *Time,* June 29, 1992.

Garcia, M.R., and Stark, P. 1991. *Eyes on the news.* St. Petersburg, Fla: The Poynter Institute for Media Studies.

Junnarkar, S. 2003. Step-by-step e-mail interviewing tips. [Online] Poynter Institute for Media Studies. Available at: http://poynteronline.org/content/content_view.asp?id=50462&sid=2 [Accessed: 7 July 2004]

Mazwai, T. 1996. Media on the menu. *Enterprise,* p.7.

McCormick, M.H. 1990. *What they still don't teach you at Harvard Business School.* Transworld International.

O'Rourke, P.J. 1992. Bill Clinton. *Sunday Star Life/People.* 4 October 1992.

Pienaar, R. 1991. Freek Robinson: op die man af. *De Kat.* September 1991.

Sager, M, 1996. Janet's world. *GQ,* June 1996: 200–211.

Scanlan, C. 2000. *Reporting and writing: basics for the 21st century.* New York: Oxford.

Silber, G. 1992. Hot hits and hang ups. *Sunday Times Magazine.* 11 October 1992.

Teel, L. and Taylor, R. 1988. *Into the newsroom: an introduction to journalism,* 2nd ed. Chester, Connecticut: Globe Pequot.

The Missouri Group: Brooks, Brian S. et al. 1980. *News reporting and writing.* New York: St Martin's.

Winans, F. 2003. A tip I learned from a master interviewer. Comment posted on Poynter Online. 27 June 2003 [Online] Available at: http://www. poynter. org/article_feedback/article_feedback_list.asp?user=&id=37661 [Accessed: 4 July 2004]

8 Crafting feature stories

Introduction

Surveying newsrooms of reporters tapping away at their stories, many editors are asking: Where are the writers? The editor who reads this lead has reason to wonder:

KEY CONCEPTS

How feature stories differ from hard-news stories; various types of features; formulas for generating creative story ideas; *The Wall Street Journal* and the Narrative story forms; the qualities of good writing.

Sarajevo's first war crimes tribunal began today when three Serbian men were brought to justice. The international news media flocked to witness the event.

By contrast, the *Guardian* editors who found this account of the same event know that in Maggie O'Kane they have an accomplished writer on their payroll:

The state prosecutors wore their Italian wool overcoats loosely round their shoulders, Mafia style, and there were 18 butts in their ashtray before the court rose for the judge at 10:20 in the morning.

The room was lit with four 1,000 watt bulbs, powered by a generator, and the sound system at the back could have served a modest rock concert. The judge at Sarajevo's first war crimes tribunal made it to the bench by crawling between the tripod legs of a TV camera and past Vioca, the stenographer, who jostled for space to type below the photographer from Reuters. (O'Kane, 1993:10)

Such skilled writing is not available often enough to newspapers, magazines and house journal readers. Too much of what makes it onto the news pages is flat, awkward and downright boring. That need not be. Writing is a craft and the skills you need can be developed and honed.

This chapter looks at some tools to help you construct engaging news and feature stories, too.

LEARNING GOALS

At the end of this chapter, you should be able to:

1 Identify various types of feature stories.
2 Generate creative ideas for feature stories using a range of techniques.
3 Order stories following The Wall Street Journal and the Narrative forms.
4 Incorporate advanced writing techiques when drafting feature stories.

"Good journalists are good storytellers. Good stories are gripping. They have beginnings, middles and ends. They put flesh on the bones of big issues and coax them to life. Good journalists do more than tell you which stories are important, they show you why."

CHARLOTTE BAUER,
FEATURES EDITOR OF
THISDAY NEWSPAPER.

What is a feature story, again?

Veteran Associated Press editor Rene Cappon describes the difference between hard news stories and features this way:

> *The hard news story marches briskly through the whats, whens, wheres, looking neither right nor left, packing in enough details to give readers a clear picture.*
>
> *In features, the immediacy of the event is secondary. The plain ladder of descending news values is replaced by human interest, mood, atmosphere, emotion, irony, humour. Features aim to give readers pleasure and entertainment along with (and, on the fluffier side, sometimes in lieu of) information (Cappon, 1982:100).*

The range of features encompasses the Gourmet column and Orphaned-Dog-of-the-Week report, as well as news enterprise of major significance. The more compelling features supplement the straight news content in timely and topical ways. They illuminate events, offer perspective, explanation and interpretation, record trends, tell people about people.

While feature stories are not easily sorted into neat groups, there are some identifiable categories:

Information features [Zu. ukwazisa / Xh. ukwaziswa / Afr. inligting]

Perhaps the most written, an informative feature does just what its name suggests: it presents information. The latest findings about human cloning. How stress affects our brains. What life is like at a treatment centre for people with Aids. Information features ask the question: "Did you know?" Often, they include figures, graphs, charts, photographs and the like, which help provide the answer.

Interview features [Zu. ukubonana nomuntu nokuxoxa naye / Xh. udliwano-ndlebe / Afr. onderhoud]

Interviews are done for different reasons. The writer may interview a person who is an authority on a subject to obtain information. An interview may be conducted to clarify an issue, or even to find out more about the interviewee, as an individual. So, there are different kinds of interview articles depending on why an interview was conducted. Examples are: an interview piece on somebody who served as a celebrity's bodyguard focusing on her experiences with the celebrity; an interview on the celebrity himself focusing on his latest project.

Personal accounts [Zu. Ulwazi lwento eyakwehlela / Afr. persoonlike weergawes]

Had an unusual experience or achieved something special? Or do you know someone who has? If so, you have the basic ingredient of a personal account feature.

Profile stories [Zu. Udaba olukutshela ngokuthile / Xh. ibali elifutshane ngobomi / Afr. profiel]

Profiles (also referred to as portraits) can be an in-depth look at something or a place, such as a new building or a town. In 2000, for example, the Pulitzer Prize for feature writing went to J.R. Moehringer of the *Los Angeles Times* for his portrait of Gee's Bend, an isolated river community in Alabama where many descendants of slaves live, and how a proposed ferry to the mainland might change it.

More often than not, though, profiles are about a person. While the personal account deals with an achievement or an experience of the subject, the profile focuses on the person himself. The best profile stories leave the reader feeling satisfied: "Ah, now I know what makes 'em tick."

How did Springbok rugby wing Ashwin Willemse get where he is? Where does he want to go from here? Who is he *really*? These are some of the questions that freelancer Mike Behr answered in his portrait of Willemse for *SA Sports Illustrated*. His gripping story was shortlisted for a prestigious Mondi Award. To see why, read extracts from the piece on p. 215. You'll also get to know what makes Willemse tick. And what ticks him off.

GEE'S BEND, Ala.– She hopes the ferry won't come, but if it does, she'll climb aboard. She'll tremble as she steps off the landing, because she can't swim, and she can't forget the many times she's crossed this ugly river only to meet more ugliness on the other side.

But fear has never beaten Mary Lee Bendolph, and no river can stop her. She'll board that ferry, if it comes, because something tells her she must, and because all the people she loves most will board with her, and because if there's one thing she's learned in her difficult life, it's this:

When the time comes to cross your river, you don't ask questions. You cross.

It won't look all that dramatic, just a new ferry taking a 63-year-old great-grandmother and her cousins across a Coca-Cola-colored river. But in this damp cellar of the Deep South, where the river has separated blacks and whites for 180 years, where even the living and the dead are less divided than the black and white towns camped on opposite shores, a new ferry will be like the river itself: more than it looks.

▨HOT LINK

"Crossing Over". That's the simple headline to J.R. Moehringer's portrait of Gee's Bend, Alabama. To that editors at the *Los Angeles Times* added an explanatory paragraph: "After 180 years of separation from their white neighbors, a stoic clan of slave descendants views a ferry as a vessel of hope – and doom." The 10-part story started like this ... *(see newspaper article on the left).*

Read the rest of Moehringer's story in the Pulitzer archive at: http://www.pulitzer.org/year/2000/feature-writing/works/.

Service pieces [Zu. Amasevisi / Xh. uncedo / Afr. diens]

Most newspapers provide an informational service to their readers. There are "What to do" and "Where to go" lists and more. Service pieces are the most obvious answer to readers who say, "We want news we can use," and cover everything from cooking to the correct way to use condoms.

Trend stories [Zu. Inkambiso / Xh. intsingiselo / Afr. tendense]

Readers look to the media to help them make sense of the changes that are taking place in their communities and the world at large. Trend stories help them make connections between series of actions, interests and attitudes that are moving across the city or country and affect their lives. Good trend stories not only point out the trend, but put it into perspective. *USA Today* reporter Stephanie Armour explains it this way: "The breaking-news beat means covering the developments of the day. Writing a trend story requires making the time to step back and ask what it all means" (2000).

FROM THE NEWSROOM

Stephanie Armour on spotting trends

The call came to the newsroom in the late afternoon. A homeless man had been spotted by residents in the suburban neighbourhood of Clive, Iowa. It didn't sound like much of a story.

But under the bridge that Jim Montague called home was a gem of a tale. Yes, he was homeless. He cooked his dinner over an open pit fire and shared his meal – corn stew and stale bread – with raccoons. He had lived on the streets in several cities, he explained, but had grown weary of the traffic, the crime and the noise. And he wasn't the only one. Many homeless people were moving to the suburbs for the same reason as everyone else: it was safer in the 'burbs.

A trend story was born.

Such stories are coming into vogue as newspapers strive to stand out from the competition by giving readers information they can't find somewhere else. The stories engage, challenge, surprise. They show how seemingly random events are part of a broader pattern. And they are a boon to reporters, who can draw on their own beat expertise to craft tales with broad impact and interest.

But spotting trends, proving them, and bringing them to life can require different skills than those used to vigilantly cover a beat. As the workplace reporter for *USA Today*, the bulk of my job involves identifying trends that are changing the way we do our jobs today – the role of technology, the increase in working women, the impact of a drum-tight labor market and others. A breaking-news beat means covering the developments of the day. Writing a trend story requires making the time to step back and ask what it all means.

Read Armour's tips on how to identify trends at: http://www.gannett.com/go/newswatch/2000/july/nw0721-1.htm.

Travelogues [Zu. Ibhukwana ngezokuvakasha / Xh. incwadana ngezotyelelo / Afr. reisdagbook]

To say that travelogues are about destinations is limiting. Yes, many travel features focus on places people take trips to for holidays. They give details of sites to see, cultures to encounter, places to stay, delicacies to sample. But at their best travelogues are at least as much about the journey as the destination. Many literary commentators, such as *The Oxford Book of Travel Stories* editor Particia Craig (1996:ix), have identified the various phases of travel from the Middle Ages on: first there was the journey-as-pilgrimage, then the "Grand Tour" undertaken by the fashionable young gentleman of 17th and 18th century Europe. In contrast, there was also the journey of exploration with dangers and outlandishness very much on the agenda. The traveller-as-student comes equipped with the determination to fathom foreign ways, while the romantic traveller is merely susceptible to the allure of "abroad". As is the traveller, so the travel writing.

▮HOT▮ LINKS

"Too much of a good thing is…" Freelance writer Daniel Radosh's criticism of the trend stories, "The Trendspotting Generation," which was first published in *GQ* (US) magazine in April 1998, is available at: http://www.radosh.net/writing/trends.html

"Travel, with its association with marvels, strangeness, adventure, and so forth, has always proved an irresistible literary subject," says Craig (ibid), "indeed, half the point of going into foreign territory was to write an account of the whole undertaking."

Readers use travel stories to inspire and inform their own trips – or just to escape from the pressures of everyday.

Humorous features [Zu. Amahlaya / Xh. –hlekisa(yo) / Afr. humor]

The main aim is simply to bring a smile to the reader. That's not as straightforward as it might sound. Toeing the line between humorous and humdrum often trips writers up.

Interpretative features [Zu. Ezihlaziyayo / Xh. ukuchaza / Afr. interpreterend]

This kind of feature is a writer's interpretation of or opinion on a topic that may be either controversial or even ordinary but relevant. That is exactly what *ThisDay* newspaper's Aspasia Karras did after a night spent watching muscled fighters pit their skills against each other after being locked in an eight-sided cage. The fighters were allowed to punch, kick and wrestle. The Ultimate Fighting Association, who staged the event, stipulated only three rules: no eye gouging, no tampering with the "crown jewels", and the option to "tap out" if you give up. Karras' article, "White knuckle entertainment", started this way:

"Many people come looking, looking, taking picture ... No good. Some people come, see ... Good!"

Dawa Norbu Sherpa, quoted on the British Guild of Travel Writers website: HTTP://WWW. BGTW.METRONET.CO.UK/ ABOUTUS.ASP.

I have read about the region in the brain where all our basest instincts reside – the hypothalamus. Unusually, its gory workings are hidden by the veneer of day-to-day existence, but occasionally its bloody core is laid bare. I know, I have seen it.

A week ago I drove with what can only be the resolve of the foolhardy to the Carousel Casino to watch a bout of cage fighting. It was a trip to the darker side of the human psyche, and with me came a lot of rather surprising people. I expected the muscle-bound jocks and the bristling presence of the local gangsters. But I also noted respectable, bearded Muslim men, clean-cut financial types, bright-eyed girls, well-groomed women and familiar faces with more than one degree to their names. And, like Professor Lupin in Harry Potter's latest tussle with evil, we all transmogrified into howling beasts baying at the moon for blood. The werewolf, it appears, lies dormant in every neatly packaged accountant and servile storekeeper, waiting for the appropriate circumstances to make its presence felt.

The circumstances involved the payment of a not insubstantial R500 per seat (at a table) and R300 in the stalls, to watch men beat each other up. More than 1 000 people paid up (Karras, 2004).

Karras set out not to report on the event; she left that to her colleagues on the sports desk. She aimed to interpret what it meant. Her conclusion:

... it became increasingly clear that there is a secret language of men. ... Evolutionary social anthropologists are probably entirely *au fait* with these signifiers and there is a probably a strong set of biological determinants to explain them. It has to do with pride, arrogance, swag-ger, a manner of holding oneself, the walk, the pheromones ... I would not be surprised if the male population is, unbeknown to women, busy marking their territory with a secret smell only they pick up ...

Historical features [Zu.izigigaba ezigumlando / Xh. isimo ngokwembali / Afr. geskiedkundig]

This type focuses on a historical event. A re-examination of the battle of Isandlwana. A recollection of the day Nelson Mandela walked free from prison. A piece on the September 11th World Trade Center disaster, such as the one Tom Junod wrote for *Esquire* two years after the event. His starting point was a photograph by Richard Drew; the story, titled "The Falling Man, opened this way:

Do you remember this photograph? In the United States, people have taken pains to banish it from the record of September 11, 2001. The story behind it, though, and the search for the man pictured in it, are our most intimate connection to the horror of that day.

In the picture, he departs from this earth like an arrow. Although he has not chosen his fate, he appears to have, in his last instants of life, embraced it. If he were not falling, he might very well be flying. He appears relaxed, hurtling through the air. He appears comfortable in the grip of unimaginable motion. He does not appear intimidated by gravity's divine suction or by what awaits him. His arms are by his side, only slightly outriggered. His left leg is bent at the knee, almost casually. His white shirt, or jacket, or frock, is billowing free of his black pants. His black high-tops are still on his feet. In all the other pictures, the people who did what he did – who jumped – appear to be struggling against horrific discrepancies of scale. They are made puny by the backdrop of the towers, which loom like colossi, and then by the event itself. Some of them are shirtless; their shoes fly off as they flail and fall; they look confused, as though trying to swim down the side of a mountain. The man in the picture, by contrast, is perfectly vertical, and so is in accord with the lines of the buildings behind him. He splits them, bisects them: Everything to the left of him in the picture is the North Tower; everything to the right, the South. Though oblivious to the geometric balance he has achieved, he is the essential element in the creation of a new flag, a banner composed entirely of steel bars shining in the sun. Some people who look at the picture see stoicism, willpower, a portrait of resignation; others see something else – something discordant and therefore terrible: freedom.

Investigative features [Zu. Ezophenyo / Xh. uphengululo / Afr. ondersoekend]

All stories involve investigation. Those that earn the title of "investigative features" push the boundaries. They seek to uncover those things others want to hide.

FROM THE NEWSROOM

Wanja Njuguna Githinji on investigating domestic violence

Wanja Njuguna Githinji was at the Langata Cemetery in Nairobi, Kenya, attending the funeral of Agnes Wanjiru. Wanjiru had died shortly after midnight some days before. She returned from a vigil to mourn her sister's death and her violent and jobless husband vent his anger on her with an iron bar while their children watched.

"Her story was highlighted as the number of domestic-related deaths had reached an alarming rate, and we in the media had taken it upon ourselves to fight the scourge," says Githinji, a journalist for *The Nation* newspaper in Nairobi.

While Wanjiri's death was horrific, what happens at the young mother's funeral disturbs Wanja even more. One woman leader after another narrates the violence they had to undergo in their own homes before they quit their abusive marriages. "Are these the same women we have all been admiring in the public places who inspire us with the lives they live?" Githinji wonders to herself. "Is this what they hide behind the tough faces?" And with those thoughts in mind, Githinji sets out to speak to these women.

None of them is willing to repeat the same story recounted during the emotionally-charged vigil. Githinji is persistent. Eventually, months later, four high-profile, professional women agree. Their accounts of brutal, repetitive violence – and how they came to break free from those marriages – result in a gripping story entitled "Union Made in Hell". For her efforts, Githinji earned the CNN African Journalist of the Year Award in 2000.

Her investigative feature story started like this:

A tooth knocked out in a fit of anger, a leg broken in a vicious attack, a life snuffed out amid screams of terror in the dead of night.

The all too familiar landscape of domestic violence in Kenya is dotted with tales of woe, with teeming numbers of maimed and destitute victims, with homeless children straying into crime, with wounded hearts crying out in shame.

We're still counting the dead, for there's a victim succumbing to a fatal blow every single day. But even our women role models are not spared by this vice. During the day they smile and beam in bliss before cameras, but at night they are in tears, terrorised and cowed out of their senses by howling and cursing husbands and partners quick to strike a blow.

Now our women leaders are saying no, no, no. Enough is enough of a bad marriage. During the burial last week at Langata Cemetery of Agnes Wanjiru, a victim of violence, the leaders bared their bitter emotions, unfurling reels of repulsive personal experiences about how they flirted with this cruel monster – of violence and other forms of abuse – before they finally ditched him. And they have never looked back. Now they telling other women: kiss a bad marriage goodbye.

Mrs Anne Ng'ang'a, the famous headmistress of Kibera's Olympic Primary School that for years has excelled in the Kenya Certificate of Primary Education, says: "Speaking like that in public was not an easy thing to do; a lot of people have castigated me for it. But I feel the pain of knowing that Agnes could have lived if we, women, were seriously fighting domestic violence. That made me speak out about my bitter past ..."

■HOT TIP

Multiple award-winning investigative journalist Mzilikazi wa Afrika told us what it takes to do what he does. And also why he keeps at it. Read our interview with him on p.199.

Others may identify even more categories of feature stories, such as news supplemental features, seasonal features, entertainment features, how-to features and the like. And some feature articles may fall under one, two or even more categories. For instance, a comic piece on different techniques to find an instant date for Valentine's Day may be considered a practical how-to, a seasonal article, an entertaining piece and a personal account all in one. But most journalists agree: feature stories are challenging – and rewarding – to write.

Revisiting the story-writing process

The advice in earlier chapters on reporting and writing news stories applies to constructing more complex feature stories, too. But because they are not as closely tied to the news of the day, features typically offer writers more time to spend thinking, reporting, planning, crafting, discussing and revising their stories. And more scope to experiment, too.

REVISION: The process of writing and reporting stories

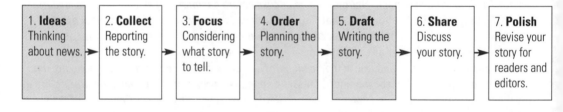

| 1. **Ideas** Thinking about news. | 2. **Collect** Reporting the story. | 3. **Focus** Considering what story to tell. | 4. **Order** Planning the story. | 5. **Draft** Writing the story. | 6. **Share** Discuss your story. | 7. **Polish** Revise your story for readers and editors. |

This chapter will consider in more depth three steps in the writing and reporting process – ideas, ordering stories, and drafting.

Wine. Sometimes, champagne. One glass, maybe two. That, says *Carte Blanche* presenter and former *Sunday Life* editor Les Aupiais, is the oil that gets the cogs in her head turning on those days when she's stumped to come up with an idea for a story. If your budget or your boss doesn't allow you to use spirits to stimulate your muse (and your brain is too tired to brainstorm (see p.124) you could also try these activities to spark creative story ideas for features:

Formulas

There are formula ideas, hundreds of them, that may work for mass audiences. Here are some fill-in-the-blanks formulas that Brendan Hennessy outlines in *Writing Feature Articles: A Practical Guide to Methods and Markets* (1993:57):

- What your ... should tell you about yourself (earlobes, hands, dog, car ...)
- What is the best ...? (diet, education, city, age ...)
- The ... of the future.
- Behind the scenes at ...
- How to ...
- Make the most of your ...
- What makes a ... (successful book, good party ...)
- The world's biggest ...
- The world's smallest ...
- The art of ...
- Why you should ...
- Can ... survive? (universities, handwritten letters ...)
- The truth about ...
- Coping with ... (loneliness, success, claustrophobia ...)
- Recovering from ...

Lists

Some interesting lists can make good stories. The top 10 sangomas in South Africa. The best inn of the world. The oldest barber shop in Bloemfontein.

Read the small stuff

"Watch out for small news stories – ones that are cut back but hint at a behind-the-scenes feature," advises Les Aupiais. "Keep an eye on court cases. Bizarre and interesting things emerge from legal battles." So, pick up that old magazine or newspaper and check out the bits you didn't read the first time around.

Twisting subjects into story ideas

Putting together two subjects can make a story idea. The police by itself is a subject. Story ideas are: the police and drugs; the police and politics, or prostitution, or prisons, or Pretoria, or suicide, or squad cars. What turns a subject into a story idea is an angle, slant or twist. Here are some examples:

▮HOT TIP

The Story Idea Viability Test

To be viable, say Katherine McAdams and Jan Elliott (1996:5), a story idea must pass a five-question test. You must be able to answer "yes" to each of these questions before the reporting begins:

1 Is my topic of interest to my audience? Identify several specific individuals or groups that would want to know about the topic – and make sure that a similar story hasn't recently been published. (If you're not on the staff of a newspaper or magazine, identify a suitable publication for your story.)

2 Is the topic of interest to me? While journalists should be able to "get interest" in a variety of topics, the best writing is only likely to be produced if the writer has an interest in the topic.

3 Is my topic neither too narrow nor too broad? Readers resist topics which are too broad, such as a five-page report about Persian carpets. However, an article about a single Iranian rug may be equally unsatisfying.

4 Are high-quality sources of information on my topic both plentiful and available? Writers owe their audience the best information available. If a story idea requires information that is not available, the writer might do better to change the focus of the story rather than use second-rate or secondhand information.

5 Is my topic of value? No writer wants the audience to glance at a message and respond, "So what?" Thabo Mbeki is not very good at golf – so what? Writing about the a trend amongst politicians to take up the sport would probably attract more readers. Avoid topics that are trivial or of no consequence.

Subject	Story idea
The reasons for rape	Can a rapist talk to his mother?
The police in South Africa today	The South African police: When should they be armed?
English in the schools	Why school leavers can't spell

Creative doodling games

It is best not to try this one in a busy newsroom. Your colleagues are likely to think you've come to the end of your wits. So, find a secluded spot and write down a subject, say "tourism". Then open up the dictionary at random and jot down words which catch your eye. I came up with these words: mug, one, speed, exaggerate, intimate, profound. Then link the words with the subject and let your mind wander:

- tourism-mug: a story about the tourists being mugged
- tourism-one: a profile of tourists that prefer travelling alone
- tourism-speed: mmmm
- tourism-exaggerate: a comparative look at tourism statistics and why some are exaggerated
- tourism-intimate: the growth of sex tourism
- tourism-profound: religious tourism is a staple of Muslim society (many make a pilgrimage to Mecca), but are there other pilgrimages happening?

EXERCISE *Identify your own creative story idea*

Experiment with the various techniques we've discussed and identify three potential stories. Next, apply the Story Idea Viability Test. Then find a story angle using the mind-mapping technique. Next, create a reporting plan which includes likely questions to be asked and accessible sources of information. Once you have checked to see if your target publication hasn't recently run a similar story, write up a short story pitch (or budget line) to sell your idea to the editor.

More ways to order your story

Once you've fleshed out your idea (see p.122), collected the information (see p.125) and established the story focus or angle (see p.130), you need to order your story. You need a story plan.

"When Francis Crick and James Watson discovered the molecular structure of DNA," says *Getaway* magazine editor Don Pinnock

(1996:3), "they provided us with a useful way to describe a good article: 'A complex two-stranded molecule that contains all the information needed to build, control and maintain a living organism.' Remember the picture of that elegant little spiral with bits of essential information suspended in between? Without the spiral you'd have a bag of blobs, and without blobs there'd be, well, nothing of consequence. Think of your article that way. Facts are relatively easy to get. But before you start writing you have to have the spiral or, to change the metaphor, a backbone. It's the *force* of your telling, the underlying *thing* you're trying to say."

Preparing a quick outline can help you organise the facts, but a story is more than the sum of its facts. "Ever since the Industrial Revolution and scientism," says Pinnock, "we have been obsessed by FACTS but, in writing articles, beware of this seduction ... a good story has to have an inner logic, a mental map so the reader knows where he's going and even why he's being sent on this adventure (all women please read 'she')."

Constructing the story's mental map doesn't have to be done formally (although I recommend that you do), but it seldom happens without contemplation. Ask yourself: What is the picture I want to paint? What is the tale I want to tell? Jot down the topics or aspects of the topic you want to cover, then decide in what order to use them.

Earlier, we discussed two of the most common ways to order stories – the inverted pyramid (p. 91) and the champagne glass. Let's consider two more story forms. The first is the so-called the Nut Graf form, also called *The Wall Street Journal* form after the newspaper which is best known for practising it. The second is the Narrative, which is rooted in the traditional way that stories are told.

Don Pinnock on story genes: "Without the spiral you'd have a bag of blobs, and without blobs there'd be, well, nothing of consequence. Think of your article that way."

Learning from *The Wall Street Journal*: the Nut Graf form

It is not a new idea. For centuries, storytellers have used the literary device of focusing on a person as the representative of a group. The tradition continues daily in conversations: "Did you hear that Nonceba's sister, the architect, was retrenched the other day? This recession is really bad. I read that unemployment figures ..."

Telling readers millions of people are starving has little impact until they see the sunken eyes and swollen belly of an infant called Peter. For some readers it is hard to relate to a statistic about 70 per cent of small businesses going under, until they hear about one woman's failed attempt at establishing her own florist shop.

Journalists have often used this technique, but no newspaper has embraced it like the *Wall Street Journal*. It started with Barney Kilgore, who was tired of *today*. He was sick of *yesterday*, too. And, writes journalism scholar Chip Scanlan (2000:16), in 1941 Kilgore had the power to do something about it. "It doesn't have to have happened today to be news," he declared. "If a date is essential, use the exact date." From now on, he decreed, *The Wall Street Journal* would no longer use the words "today" and "yesterday" in the leads of stories. "With that single act, Kilgore, the new managing editor of *The Wall Street Journal*, paved the way for a revolutionary treatment of news," writes Scanlan (ibid). Also known as the news feature, analytical feature and "nut graf" story, this genre's hallmarks include: anecdotal leads that hook the reader, followed by a nut graf that tells the reader what the writer is up to, which then leads to alternating sections that amplify the story thesis and provide balance with evidence that presents a counterthesis.

Applying The Wall Street Journal formula step by step:

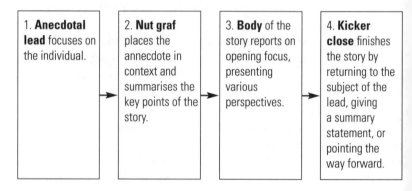

1. **Anecdotal lead** focuses on the individual.

2. **Nut graf** places the annecdote in context and summarises the key points of the story.

3. **Body** of the story reports on opening focus, presenting various perspectives.

4. **Kicker close** finishes the story by returning to the subject of the lead, giving a summary statement, or pointing the way forward.

The Wall Street Journal *form, also called the Nut Graf form, can be broken down into four steps*

This approach works as well for local stories as it does for the national and international stories covered by *The Wall Street Journal.* Daily, its front-page reports put a literary spotlight on the individuals involved in an issue or institution. Consider this *Journal* story Susan B. Glasser contributed to a feature package titled, "Armenia: a new crisis in confidence" (2004:A3). The headline, "Steady exodus is latest chapter of loss," was supported by a sub-headline, "Depopulation of post-soviet country calls society's future into question":

HOT TIP

Here's Chip Scanlan's tip for a quick way to produce a nut graf for your next story: "Make up your mind what the story is about and why people should read it – and then type that conclusion in one or two sentences" (2000:171).

[1] First, her son left for Russia. Then a daughter. Then her other daughter. Last fall, her remaining son, daughter-in-law and three grandchildren moved. One by one over the past decade, they fled this village on a barren mountain peak, abandoning the rocky earth where the family has lived for 100 years.

[2] Now it is Atlas Hadjiyan's turn.

[3] She has sold her two cows and no longer tends the vegetable garden that is necessary to survive the brutal winter. In September, she plans to become another reluctant emigrant, leaving the independent homeland Armenians have dreamt of for generations for the uncertain welcome of an icy Russian city a 1,600 kilometres north. "I don't want to leave," she said, 'but this is no place to live."

[3] For the village, whose name means Black Fortress, where there is no running water, no telephones, no paid work and, for much of the winter, no access to the outside world, Ms Hadjiyan's exit will be another quiet disappointment.

[4] For Armenia at large, her impending departure is the latest of a slow-motion crisis of confidence that has left the rugged mountain country hemorrhaging people for nearly all of its short history of independence. No one knows how many have left, but even the most conservative estimates put the total at more than one million Armenians and counting – with a total remaining population of no more than three million and perhaps as little as two million.

[4] The exodus has made Armenia one of the world's fastest disappearing nations. "I call it depopulation," said Gevorg Pogosyan, a sociologist in the capital, Yerevan. "It calls into question whether Armenia is a country with a future. We are a weak society, weakened both politically and economically by this migration."

[5] At the time of independence in 1991, Armenia's mere existence seemed a triumph over tragic history …

[6] But instead of luring home successful Armenians who had made new lives in the West …

[7] With broad support from its public, Armenia fought and won a war with neighboring Azerbaijan over the disputed enclave of Nagorno-Karabakh in the 1990s …

[8] In a country with no significant natural resources, a collapse in Soviet industrial infrastructure and an economy just now showing signs of recovery …

[9] Russian experts have calculated $1billion (E806,000) from migrants in Russia flows home …

[10] The wave of departures, which hit a high of about 200,000 a year during the mid-1990s, has stabilized, but the cumulative effect remains …

[11] "It's a good part of the population that's gone, the economically active part," Mr Pogosyan said …

[12] No one knows just how few Armenians remain. A long-delayed official census …

[13] In an interview, Armenian President Robert Kocharian said

---

Anecdotal lead. This lead focuses on one family, one person who serves to illustrate the experience of the group.

With a vivid image in the readers' minds, the writer moves on to the nut graf

NUT GRAF:
The nut graf has several purposes (Scanlan 2000:161):
- It justifies the story by telling readers why they should care.
- It provides a transition from the lead and explains the lead and its connection to the rest to the story.
- It often tells readers why the story is timely.
- It often includes supporting material (typically statistics and expert opinion) that helps readers see why the story is important.

BODY OF THE STORY:
Following the nut graf are sections that amplify the story's thesis, and provide balance with evidence that presents a counter-thesis.

Counter-thesis [13]

Support for counter-thesis [14]

Criticism of counter-argument, which supports story thesis [15]

Once the situation has been fully explored, the reader is likely to ask, "So, what now?" The remainder of the story contributes towards an answer.

KICKER CLOSE: Unlike the inverted pyramid, in which the importance of the material diminishes as the story concludes, the *Wall Street Journal* form requires a strong finish.
  This story closes by pointing ahead [19] – and offering a glimmer of hope. (Be careful not to confuse a kicker close with a contrived close. And definitely do not revert to the second-person and slap on the over-used line, "And what would you do?" – or some variation of it.)

there isn't "a serious person in Armenia" who would dispute the accuracy of the census, and he said "migration out of Armenia has stopped" as a result of strong economic growth on his watch …
  [14] U.S. Ambassador John Ordway endorsed the official head count, pointing to U.S. technical assistance …
  [15] But the head of the government agency created in 2000 to deal with the migration crisis is less sanguine. "To say that the wave of migration has stopped would be wrong," said Gagik Yeganyan …
  [16] Most migrants were reluctant to leave and might be persuaded to come home if conditions in Armenia improved, Mr Yeganyan said …
  [17] To entice Armenians back, at least those at the upper end of the income scale, manicured lawns and immaculate California-style suburban houses are taking shape on the outskirts of Yerevan…
  [18] The brainchild of a building magnate based in New Jersey, it was originally pitched to successful expatriate Armenians …
  [19] But of the 32 houses already built or in mid construction, at prices starting at $190,000, 65% have been bought by local Armenians … Not a single resident has come from the U.S.
  [20] Arthur Havighorts, the firm's vice president, said the company has modified its pitch. In addition to ownership, it is offering overseas Armenians time share at the rate of $6,000 for 20 years' worth of one-week vacations. "We're very optimistic," he said. In a week in June, he said, the firm found two takers for that deal – "both in California."

Learning from the short story: the Narrative form

Where most hard news stories follow a set pattern, features allow the writer relative freedom. The reporter can choose any approach, be imaginative. This often leads to comparisons between features and fiction. But news reporters and fiction writers are uncomfortable cousins.

Calling a reporter's article "fiction" is likely to get him heated, at the very least. And many fiction writers balk when asked if their plots or characters are fact; many novels even carry an official disclaimer, such as: "The character and situations in this book are entirely imaginary and bear no relation to any real person or actual happening." Indeed, blurring these battle lines has landed writers from both sides in court.

However, some reporters – like Kerry Swift – are candid about the influence of fiction on their work. Here Swift, a Johannesburg-based writer, discusses how he put together one of his gripping features using the basic tools of fiction – character, settings, themes, conflicts, plots with climaxes and resolutions. Storytellers, Scanlan explains (2000:171), don't give away the story in the first paragraph the way news writers typically do. Instead, they set up a situation, using suspense or the introduction of a compelling character to keep the reader turning pages. Rather than put the least important information at the end, the way an inverted pyramid writer would, the storyteller waits until the end to give the reader a big "pay-off" – a surprise, a twist, a resolution.

This article on vehicle hijacking in South Africa entitled "Bloodhound in the sky" was one of a series of narrative features which gained Swift the unique double of winning both the Siemens and the Transnet Journalism Awards – two of the country's most prestigious writing awards – in the same year (1995). He explained how he went about constructing the story and why:

> *The best stories are always personal testimonies and the best journalism experiential. My approach to feature writing has always been to attack issues from the perspective of the people most intimately involved in the exterior action. This story about truck hijacking in South Africa is a case in point, except I added a new dimension by exploring a few literary techniques along the way.*
>
> *Searching through old newspaper cuttings I found an ideal news peg for a feature on hijacking. It turned on a pilot named John Vinagre whose helicopter charter firm in Germiston, near Johannesburg, had pioneered aerial pursuits of hijacked vehicles. Additionally, he had been shot down during an aerial chase over the black township complex of Tembisa.*
>
> *Potentially it had all the elements to build a racy feature, but the problem was that Vinagre had steadfastly refused interviews on the grounds that media exposure might make him and his family a target of the syndicates masterminding vehicle crime in South Africa.*
>
> *However, the climate had changed. Hijacking had become the central focus of Vinagre's professional life. He was outraged by the rising levels of vehicle crime and the apparent inability of anyone – least of all the police or their political bosses – to stop it. Indeed, a good deal of vehicle crime was the work of renegade cops acting alone or in league with syndicates. Vinagre believed he had an answer to hijacking and some gentle persuasion was enough to convince him to go public with his story.*
>
> *My approach to crafting this feature was to plan two entirely separate stories. The first would be a run-of-the-mill piece one might routinely write – few sparks and mainly formulaic. The second would employ a flashback technique, recreating the events leading up to and including the incident in which Vinagre was shot down in his pursuit helicopter.*
>
> *The challenge was two-fold: how to marry these two stories with their different time frames and tempos, and second, how to craft the flashback story in such a way that readers would get a sense of what*

was going on in Vinagre's head as his aircraft was shot from the sky.

The interviewing was done as a whole, but the two stories were written separately as planned, so that each would have consistency and a logical flow. The first was reasonably straightforward, although I wrote it so that it could break to accommodate the second story as a series of flashback inserts at set stations through the piece.

The second – the flashback story – was far more challenging. This piece demanded a considerable amount of inner detail, which meant digging out the information piece by painstaking piece and my subject was reticent and self-effacing, which made the interview phase difficult. Additionally, although I knew what I was trying to do technically, it was difficult to explain writing technique to the subject.

Technically, the flashback piece was awkward. My intention was to shift point-of-view through the story so that the piece would start and end with an omniscient narrator but would climax with the pilot's own stream of consciousness as his aircraft was shot down. I wanted to transport the reader inside Vinagre's head to experience what he was thinking as the chopper went down.

This required going over every detail of the flashback story with Vinagre after it was written to ensure its authenticity and that the outer and inner dialogue were accurate.

The flashback piece also had to be written with the first story in mind. I knew where the various stations in the first story were and I had to write the second so that it would comfortably arrive and break at those stations.

I wrote it so that as each part of the flashback story unfolded, it would end leaving the reader hanging in mid-air – hopefully anxious to return to the action. I was trying to replicate the old thriller-writing formula where the action moves along on different levels and the writer shifts from one to the other at the most tantalising moments. Serial drama writers have perfected this technique for radio and I thought it could be adapted successfully to feature writing.

The greatest constraint in all this, however, was time. On the one hand, I had four hours' interviewing time with the subject, while on the other, the deadline for the story left just two days to complete the entire job. The writing took the best part of both.

Bloodhound in the sky

It's 6.30 am on April 5, 1994, and South Africa is waking to the prospect of a general election that will either usher in a new democratic future or plunge the country into a debilitating civil war.

Like most South Africans, John Vinagre and his wife Antonieta are concerned about the outcome. They are discussing the upcoming election as they drive to work and take the turnoff into Rand Airport outside Germiston. They park their grey Nissan Patrol in the covered carpark outside the hangers belonging to Capital Air where John is managing director and Antonieta his capable administrator.

As John opens the security gate to Capital Air's reception area, the phone is already ringing. Antonieta glances at her watch. It is 6.45 am. The call, from Bokomo Bakeries in Clayville, north east of Johannesburg, is to report that one of the company's 8-ton Hinos has been hijacked in the Tembisa area. Bokomo is one of John Vinagre's clients and they want him to mount an immediate search for the hijacked truck.

Just a normal day at Capital Air, muses John wryly as he prepares for another aerial pursuit in the crisp Highveld dawn.

In this opening sequence of the flashback story, the reader is presented with an omniscient narrator writing in the present tense for immediacy. The idea here is to put the piece into historical context, but also to emphasise the tense and uncertain atmosphere prevailing in South Africa at the time when these events took place. This opening sequence is immediately followed by the start of the second story, which is a biographical and chronological piece, on John Vinagre running parallel to the action events in the flashback story.

At age 49 and with 18 000 flying hours to his name, John Vinagre is one of South Africa's most experienced chopper pilots. Yet this nuggety Portuguese immigrant, who fled his native Mozambique in 1975 when Frelimo nationalised the family business in Lourenço Marques, taking 14 helicopters along with it, is no ordinary "flyboy". He also has a fair share of diesel mixed with the avgas coursing through those veins. Indeed, John has come a long way with the road transport industry, so much so that he has made it his professional home.

The opening of the biographical piece introduces the reader to the main character and begins to develop his profile. At the same time it provides some background character information.

We meet in the early morning in his well-appointed offices attached to the Capital Air hangers at Germiston's Rand Airport. On the walls are the inevitable posters of helicopters in various locations, including a montage of photographs from a popular local television series called "Skattejag", featuring Scott Scott, Melanie Walker and, of course, John Vinagre who flew choppers into impossible and exotic locations for this televised aerial treasure hunt for almost a decade.

It's 7.30 am and Vinagre has just flown in. He's formal and remote at first. Like most operational pilots, he's a man of few words. Perhaps it's also because this is the first interview he's ever given.

The reticence is not so much a question of modesty, it's just that he's in a line of work which shuns publicity. Media exposure could mean retaliation from the crime syndicates proliferating in post-apartheid South Africa and John Vinagre is nothing if not a careful man.

It was Vinagre, flying "chickenhawk" patrols for Lombard's Transport, who developed the highly successful aerial deterrence against fuel theft back in the early eighties.

This section is setting the interviewee up for the reader. It provides a brief psychological profile of the man, again from the perspective of an omniscient narrator.

Continuing to develop the subject's profile, this completes the first section of the biographical story. The writer now steps across the station to enter the other train ... it's back to the action flashback story.

Subsequently, as operational managing director of Capital Air flying choppers out of Rand Airport in Germiston, he has become South Africa's ace aerial anti-hijacker – the top-gun bloodhound in the sky for numerous fleet operators who regularly fall victim to the highwaymen feeding like leeches off the nation's trucking arteries.

It is a mark of the man that his experience of the crime wave washing over South Africa has made him more determined than ever to make a difference. "We either beat this thing back or it will destroy us," he says and he means it. Like Henry V facing overwhelming odds on the green fields of France, this is one enormously determined guy. Indeed, John Vinagre has turned his job into a one-man crusade against hijacking and he wields his aerial sword with the resolve of a latter-day St George confronting the dragon. Having lost his business in Mozambique to a rapacious state, he is not about to sit back and watch other people lose theirs to a theft of a different nature.

The flashback story gathers pace as we go airborne with John Vinagre. Dialogue enters the piece for the first time. As far as point-of-view goes, we still have an omniscient narrator who is quite prepared to enter the piece to editorialise, namely "There'll always be a hunter ..."

He sprints out to the Bell Jet Ranger, registration ZS HWU, straps himself into the chopper and starts the rotors.

In the back of his mind is a nagging concern that contrary to normal procedures in all anti-hijack flights, this time he has no weapons on board. Putting the thought aside, he completes a rapid pre-flight check and radios the tower.

"Rand Tower, this is Hotel, Whisky, Uniform. Hijack response."

"Clear for take-off Hotel, Whisky, Uniform," comes the immediate reply – air traffic control at Rand has long got used to the urgent scramble calls from Capital Air. "Call in on Jan Smuts once you're airborne," says the voice through the ether, adding sardonically "and happy hunting!"

John eases the Jet Ranger gently off the helipad, drops the nose towards the adjoining road and heads out over Germiston Lake at speed. He notices blurred images of early morning rowers through the mist rising off the lake below, and watches a flock of wild ducks dash for the safety of a reed-bed as the chopper cuts through the clear Highveld air. There'll always be a hunter, and the hunted will forever be running ...

This is an important section of the biographical piece because it sketches the background to the hijacking problem and establishes the subject's credentials in the anti-hijacking business. This is by and large straight reportage, no frills, no bells and whistles.

The story of Capital Air's success really goes back to 1979 when John Vinagre persuaded a number of fleet operators in the Germiston area to pool resources and underwrite aerial surveillance flights along the main freight lanes leading from Johannesburg to the coastal port cities.

At that time, operators plying those routes were experiencing a rash of fuel theft from their trucks and suspected their drivers were siphoning fuel off the rigs and selling it along the road. Vinagre was commissioned to check it out.

It turned out that the drivers were responsible for the fuel losses, but not in the way fleet operators suspected. Drivers were stopping along the road to pick up prostitutes parading their wares for passing truckers. Bimbos on board, truckers would then drive to a nearby township and sow their wild oats.

Most of the highway hookers, however, were in league with petty thieves and while they and their driver "Johns" were flailing about in flagrante delicto, their trucks were being deflowered in a different way. As the old saying goes, nothing for nothing in this life.

"They were mainly after diesel but occasionally they stole from the load as well," says Vinagre. "In most cases, however, the drivers continued on their way without even knowing they had been robbed."

To combat these losses, he came up with the simple idea of aerial monitoring along the main trucking lanes. As he puts it: "The idea was to check on trucks at random by landing the choppers on the side of the road and flagging down drivers. These on-the-road checks meant we could inspect trucks for fuel and load tampering at will. Drivers were never sure when we would drop from the sky and check their rigs. At first I took the transport managers along so the drivers knew it was kosher, but after a while I did it alone.

"The drivers soon got to know me and the mere sight of me or the chopper was sufficient to keep the trucks rolling and the drivers' pants on. It was so effective as a deterrent that soon we were able to stop the patrols altogether."

At 7.30 am, ZS HWU lands at Bokomo headquarters in Clayville and collects three "suits" who join John Vinagre in the hunt for the hijacked Hino. Frederick Miles is Bokomo's financial manager, Otto Weinreibe is from the company's vehicle support section, and Kobus Carstens is transport manager.

With the chopper's rotors still turning, Otto and Kobus climb into the back and strap in while Fred climbs into the co-pilot's seat. They're all fired up, eager for the chase. Three minutes later, ZS HWU is airborne.

Banking steeply to starboard over Midrand, which spreads like an industrial rash across the Highveld, the chopper heads south for Tembisa township, its electronic receiver scanning for audio signals from a hidden transmitter on board the hijacked truck.

John Vinagre contacts Jan Smuts tower requesting clearance for an aerial search of the Tembisa area and Gwen, the traffic controller on duty at Smuts that morning, instructs him to stay below 6 300 ft and clear of Zero3 left, the international airfield's main runway.

The chopper is on a flight path that will take it directly over Tembisa at 1 000 ft at a ground speed of 120 km/h. The four men can communicate with each other but besides John's greeting and a few desultory remarks, there is no time for small talk. Otto Weinreibe repeats the Hino's registration number over the intercom and the four men settle into silence as the chopper starts its first sweep over the township.

Smoke from thousands of wood and coal fires in Tembisa and

There's a lot happening in the passage. It's all short, sharp, staccato writing as the action moves ahead. Things move at speed during the chase and up to the time when the chopper is hit. But then the tempo slows down dramatically as we begin to enter the pilot's thoughts. We are approaching the moment when the writer attempts to change point-of-view and climb inside the subject's head...

neighbouring Ivory Park squatter camp still lingers like fine mist over the township as ZS HWU begins its search.

They fly an east-west grid across the township without success. As is normal procedure, a half hour into the search, John radios his wife back at Capital Air on their private frequency giving his location and reporting no sightings. It's procedural, but in this kind of business a wife needs regular information ...

Switching back to the Smuts frequency, John Vinagre alters course to begin north-south sweeps across the township.

On the third sweep, they spot the missing truck parked among the houses below. The cab has been tilted and a group of people are milling about. Other figures climb from the cab as John takes his aircraft into a tight turn around the stricken vehicle.

From virtual silence, the cockpit is suddenly awash with noise. Everyone is talking at once with Otto shouting as he sees a couple of kids stoning his truck and breaking windows in the cab.

"They're running," shouts a voice through the intercom as the hijackers take off at the sound of the chopper and sprint towards some nearby houses. "The bastards are splitting up. Watch where they go. Don't let the little f***ers escape."

Now it's all expletives and adrenaline as the chopper circles the truck a second time and the occupants feel the rush of the hunt.

That's when John Vinagre hears the gunshots. They resonate ominously through the static of his headset – abnormal sounds in the enveloping yet familiar clamour of the chase. Instinct tells him the chopper's under fire but his mind rejects it. There's no fear. He's measuring the whole thing in his head. But he is also aware of a distinct power loss in the aircraft.

Practised hands instinctively throw the Jet Ranger into a steep dive away from the scene as he tries to evade further ground fire.

"I don't believe it ... they're shooting ..." he shouts into the headset. It's like an afterthought because he knows the chopper's already hit and he's aware that it's going down. That's when the first twinges of fear claw at his chest and his breathing gets tighter.

Time bends and distorts. Seconds stretch as he nurses the crippled ship on. He's aware of voices in his headset and of the growing pressure of someone's feet pushing against the back of his seat ... he levels the chopper out but the engine fails. The chopper's going down ...

Five kilometres to the north west in the Smuts tower, the air traffic controller named Gwen watches ZS HWU disappear off her radar screen.

Again a break in pace as the biographical story unfolds further. It is not accidental that the story begins to creak and grind a bit. I am hoping the reader will be forcing the pace to get back to the action ...

Around 1986, the pattern of vehicle crime changed. For the first time whole trucks began to go missing. "Initially thieves were only after the tyres, batteries and fuel and invariably we would find the vehicle with its load intact simply by flying over the townships. In most cases, the rigs were abandoned by the side of the road. At that time, only about 10 per cent of stolen trucks had their loads tampered with. It was still unsophisticated crime," says Vinagre.

But it didn't stay that way for long. Around 1989 the pattern changed once more. "It was as if someone had flicked a switch. One moment we were finding stolen trucks abandoned in the townships as usual, the next they were nowhere to be found. We spent hours in the air without seeing any trace of stolen vehicles. Something had changed radically in the pattern of truck thefts and the criminals were winning once again."

Once more it was John Vinagre who dreamed up a suitable response. It occurred to him that the Department of Nature Conservation had been successfully using a game-tracking system developed by Professor Gerard van Urk at Potchefstroom University. The system was operated by attaching electronic transmitting devices to the animals which could then be tracked from the air.

"The system had been operated since 1975 but it only had a range of 5 km which was clearly insufficient for our purposes. So I approached Professor Van Urk for help. Not only was he incredibly enthusiastic but over the next few months he developed a number of systems which we put to the test. In all, we put in 30 hours of aerial trials before settling for the system we now use," says Vinagre.

That system, registered under the name Helitrace, consists of an electronic transmitter attached somewhere to the truck which emits an audio signal. Each transmitter makes use of a different frequency which can be tracked from the air over a radius of 80 km in the built-up PWV (Gauteng) area and 120 km in open areas. This allows the helicopter search ship a reasonable degree of latitude to lock onto a hijacked vehicle and to follow at a discreet distance.

Once the vehicle is located from the air, the pursuit chopper calls in the SAPS Hijack Reaction Unit in Isando or Soweto, whose task it is to recover the vehicle, and make arrests on the ground. Alternatively, a private reaction company is called in to recover the vehicle.

I can get it down, thinks John Vinagre as he autorotates the crippled chopper towards an open patch of ground nestled between the tightly concentrated matchbox houses of Tembisa. He doesn't really have much choice – live powerlines to the north and west block any escape.

There's enough space ... I can squeeze it down if I get there on time ... I can do this ... John's concentrated thoughts are interrupted by a woman and child who set off across the open patch, oblivious to the approach of the chopper. John watches their leisurely pace across the dustbowl ... She's big breasted, wearing a colourful floral bandanna and she's scolding the child, half bent over ...

Aborting his descent, he drags the chopper off its crash path. Now he's headed away from the open patch directly towards the houses. He tries to lift the chopper over the fast-approaching toy homes

I open this passage with a cheeky departure in that the writer has literally entered the subject's mind. This shift in point-of-view to stream of consciousness is a literary technique and can have great impact because the reader is transported right into the heart of the action from the perspective of the main protagonist. The passage shifts tempo and point-of-view quite brazenly and breaks off just as the mob is about to descend ...

below. There's not enough speed or altitude and the chopper whistles into the ground between two houses. One of the rotor blades snaps as the aircraft comes to rest on its nose against one of the houses, its tail rotors torn off by the impact as it hits the wall.

Dust mushrooms upwards, a red-brown cloak engulfing the aircraft. With it comes a sickening fear. It is every flyboy's worst nightmare ... fire ... All he can think of is being engulfed in a blanket of orange flame as the rich and intoxicating smell of avgas fills the cockpit.

Fred Miles is already going into shock as John helps him escape from the crippled aircraft. The two passengers in the back are already clear and watching from the nearby road. Fred falls to his knees dragging John down with him. A woman is screaming at them: "Look what you've done to my house, ... look what you've done ..." but there's a far more menacing sound filling his consciousness – gunshots!

Glancing up, John sees Otto and Kobus running towards some nearby houses pursued by a mob. Seeing John and Fred on the ground, however, the mob veers back towards the crash site ... They're shouting and there's only murder in those voices ....

This is the final passage of the biographical piece. The subject ends it in direct speech. I wanted to end it with a warning to the commercial industry from the country's most experienced anti-hijack specialist that unless they act in concert on vehicle crime, their industry could be destroyed. Who better to deliver that wake-up call than the subject of this feature!

John Vinagre has had considerable success with his aerial bloodhound business which now has 1 100 transmitters installed in various fleets, but he points out that there is still a great deal of reluctance among fleet operators to invest in preventative anti-hijack measures.

"We're losing the battle against hijacking by default and, of course, the hijackers are becoming more sophisticated all the time," he says. "What's needed is a concerted effort on all fronts. But, in the short term, I believe the answer to hijacking lies in turning back the clock and reinstating regular aerial patrols along the main trucking routes from Johannesburg to the coast. Monitoring drivers from the sky is the only effective deterrent to this scourge.

"The road transport industry should get together to subsidise day and night aerial patrols of the nation's major highways. These spot checks would have the same deterrent effect on hijackings that they had against theft in the early eighties because most hijackings are unquestionably still the result of driver collusion. Drivers need to know there are bloodhounds in the sky watching them."

Vinagre reckons around R40 000 a month would cover the costs of regular helicopter patrols of the Durban and Cape Town routes in and out of Johannesburg, which are the main playgrounds of the highwaymen.

Taken across the industry, R40 000 is small change, particularly when you realise that hijackers are costing the industry around R11 million a month in replacement costs alone, with hidden costs estimated at between R30 and R40 million a month.

"The only solution to hijacking is for all the players in the trucking industry to combine resources and tackle this problem together. The current ad hoc response by individual operators acting alone against organised crime is a total waste of time," says Vinagre.

... The mob reaches the two unarmed and defenceless men before either has a chance to think of escape. John Vinagre is still bending over his supine colleague when they are attacked. He is stabbed in the back and dragged to one side as the mob begins to beat and kick Fred Miles, now lying in a foetal position on the ground. Grasping hands tear the watch from his arm. Rasping voices shout "Where are your guns, where is your money?" They kick Fred senseless as John tries to protect himself from the mindless wrath of the mob.

> *Otto and Kobus have reached the houses. They run between them until they find a woman at an open door. They beg her for protection and she takes them in, ushering the two terrified men into her bedroom where they climb under her bed and await their fate – breathless and fearful. Their lives are now entirely in the hands of a black stranger as groups of enraged youths scatter through the houses baying for the blood of the two white men ...*

> *... Just as John Vinagre is about to give up hope, a white Cressida backs out of a nearby householder's garage and drives slowly towards the mob which parts as it approaches. There are two men in the car – the driver and a passenger in the back. The back door opens and the passenger shouts at the two battered white men to climb in. Still in shock and badly beaten, Fred Miles nevertheless drags himself into the passenger seat while John drags himself into the back. Before the mob is fully aware of what is happening, the Cressida revs and races away, dust flying from its rear wheels.*

The final passage ends on a high note in that the four men are saved from the mob by members of the black community who clearly show no support for the actions of the mob. I felt it important to end this way because one always runs the danger of racial stereotyping with this type of story. Technically it is straight reportage in the present tense. The omniscient narrator has disappeared.

All four of the men shot down in ZS HWU over Tembisa that morning escaped with their lives. But for the courageous intervention of three black strangers, they would not have made it, that much is abundantly clear.

As for the hijackers, it took Rudie van Olst of the East Rand Murder and Robbery Squad eight months to track them down, but for John Vinagre the hunt goes on ...

Consider the core qualities of good writing when drafting your story

Good writing, according to The Missouri Group journalism professors (1980:251), has five qualities:

- It is clear.
- It is precise.
- It appeals to the senses.
- It has pace appropriate to the action.
- It is tied together with transitions.

Clear writing

A *Cape Times* story under the headline "Judge fingers provocateurs; 'Agents' fuelling unrest – G'stone" began this way:

> JOHANNESBURG – Mr Justice Richard Goldstone yesterday added two new factors to the list of the causes of violence in South Africa, saying political uncertainty and the role of agents provocateurs exacerbated the existing climate of violence (Anon 1, 1993:1).

The writer of that lead added some linguistic uncertainty of his own. Besides, the premise is clearly false. At the time it was hardly original to "finger" thugs and political uncertainty as two factors that worsen the violence in South Africa. The writer (and editors) would have done well to head this advice: Before you type a word, caution the Missouri Group of journalism instructors (1980:253), remind yourself of three simple rules:

1 Rely on simple words and sentences.
2 Use correct grammar.
3 Think clearly.

The writer of "Quick start: the two-minute guide to computer literacy", an article in the *PC Review*, stuck to the rules when he wrote this explanation of computer memory:

> *Memory: Computers actually remember nothing at all; the moment you switch them off their minds die. That's why memory comes in two kinds: active memory known as RAM, which does the thinking, and storage memory which collects those thoughts on a relatively permanent storage medium known as a disk.*

RAM is measured these days in megabytes (a megabyte is roughly equivalent to a million characters). Most computers come with a megabyte RAM installed, but two or four megabytes are needed to run some heavyweight contemporary software (see later) ...

One of the keys to clarifying complex concepts is restraint, knowing how much information is enough. The writer above knew that for his purposes – the article's title is "Quick start: the two minute guide to computer literacy" – a technical definition would be inappropriate. A computer scientist may define a computer floppy disk in this way:

A disk is a flat Mylar plastic circle coated with ferrous-oxide and enclosed in a rigid plastic protective jacket. It is divided into tracks and sectors to facilitate electromagnetic storage and retrieval of data.

Our writer realised a newcomer to computers would read that and still be confused (or more confused), so he described the unfamiliar by relating it to something familiar (ibid:16):

Storage takes place in two places: a floppy disk which looks like a seven single still inside its jacket and a hard disk which looks similar, though you'd never know because it is hidden inside the computer. Both are magnetic media which record data much the same way a tape-cassette records sounds. Both kinds of disks come in different sizes, but on average a floppy disk can store two chapters of a novel and a hard disk can store a couple of novels.

The rules again: rely on simple language to *describe* rather than *define* complex concepts; use correct grammar; think clearly.

Precise writing

Consider this lead of a short *Time* magazine story (Anon 3, 1992:17). The writer aimed to describe how a drop in Tokyo's stock exchange had affected international stock exchanges:

The world's financial markets are so intertwined that when one itches, the others scratch.

Precision in writing means choosing exactly the right word for the job – it's the difference between lightning and lightning bug. A musician must play specific notes at a specific tempo to produce the intended melody; a writer must select the precise word and punctuation to tell an accurate tale. Reporters can make a politician say, claim, argue, announce or point out – but only one is correct.

Writing that appeals to the senses

Scanning lifeless copy, I sometimes get worked up and say to young journalists: "Don't tell me it is dry, show me the cracked mud in the park pond. Don't tell me the man is angry, show me his clenched jaw and the throbbing vein in his temple. I want to see the news, I want to choke on the acrid stench of burning tyres, I want to shudder when the 11-inch hunting knife is carefully drawn across a chest until blood drips."

I owe my understanding of the importance of detail, in part, to Edna Buchanan. "What a reporter needs is detail, detail, detail," insists Buchanan (1987:265). "If a man is shot for playing the same song on the jukebox too many times, I've got to name that tune. Questions unimportant to police often add the colour and detail that make a story human. What movie did they see? What colour was their car? What did they have in their pockets? What were they doing at the precise moment the bomb exploded or the tornado touched down?"

Good writing has details which appeal to the senses: sight, hearing, smell, taste and touch. But a writer must know when a detail makes a story better, rather than just making it wordy. Consider this lead from the *Mail & Guardian*:

The first sentence, although rich with details, provides too much useless information while the second sentence leaves the reader wondering about the significance of 7.08 pm.

As the dying sun filters through the rising smog of evening coal fires, the mood of bustling relaxation is reminiscent of a seaside promenade; kids playing soccer, girls and boys idling in flirtatious banter, women leaning over neighbourhood fences and their men exchanging profundities on street corners. Until 7.08 pm.

Former guerilla commander Michael Malunga says, "Look, they've all gone." And sure enough they have: wiped from view as cleanly as chalk from a blackboard.

Fear is the curfew. Because this is Sebokeng and it is killing time (Beresford, 1993:3).

In this pared-down version, unnecessary details are edited out, the scene is set in the active voice, and the time reference is clarified:

> The dying highveld sun filters through the smog of evening coal fires and the mood is light; kids play soccer, boys and girls banter and flirt, women lean over neighbourhood fences and men chat on street corners. Until 7.08 pm, that is.
> "Look, they've all gone," says former guerilla commander Michael Malunga. Sure enough they have – wiped from view as cleanly as chalk from a blackboard.
> Fear is the curfew. This is Sebokeng and after sundown is killing time.

A good writer knows when detail is appropriate. Every word must count. When space is tight, there is no place for a detail that has no job.

One common means of appealing to the reader's sense of hearing is to include quotes from sources. Fiction writers, in particular, make extensive use of dialogue to let the characters tell the story. Brian Appleyard used this technique in his story in *Sunday Life* magazine about John Wayne Bobbit, who became a celebrity after his wife hacked off his penis with a steak knife. After recovering from reconstructive surgery, Bobbit starred in a porn video, toured the United States with a live show and made plans to launch an album, a movie of his life story and an adult mail-order catalogue. We pick up the story of Bobbitt and his agent in Las Vegas:

> Should John ... carry on down the porn-star route? Aaron [his agent] doesn't think so.
> "I don't think it's best," he explains.
> "It's kind of nice now but it's a crazy thing to happen to him. It's not a good career for a male. The big money in that business is for the women, not the men – 95 per cent of all tapes are bought by men and they want to see the women. Mind you, if he did a gay movie there's huge money, probably seven figures."
> "You tempted, John?" I ask.
> "No."
> "The gay video market is huge," Aaron continues. "It's a known fact that members of the gay community have a lot of money."
> John still looks unimpressed, then he asks me, "Have you ever had sex with a transvestite?"
> "No."
> "Neither have I."
> "Would you try it?"
> "Yeah, I'll try it."
> And so it goes on. John Wayne Bobitt awash in a sea of porn, unrealisable ambition and a steady flow of babes (Appleyard 1995:16).

It worked for Appleyard, but employing extended dialogue is tricky. Consider these pointers:

- Use extended dialogue only when you meet a source who is eminently quotable or when you witness a dramatic scene – and when you have it accurately recorded. Few reporters are skilled enough at note-taking to get down a complete conversation by hand, so I suggest this rule: tape it, or leave it.
- Avoid using dialect. Not onlee is zee dialek deefficult to reed (as this poor attempt at describing a French accent shows), but it often offends the group whose way of talking is being highlighted. If the speaker's accent is of special interest, use it only in the first quote. (There are exceptions to every rule: take another look at Todd Matshikiza's successful use of dialogue on p.119).

Writing with pace

Think film. Now, in your mind's eye, try to recall the latest movie you watched. Can you see how the scenes are knitted together? Consider how the camera moves to capture the action. At times, it zooms in close. Tight. You can see a bloodshot eye, a bead of sweat, a lip a-quiver. Then it stops, pulls back. The actors move across the room and out of view, except for one character who the camera follows as she pulls her coat close, steps through the door, down the stairs, right turn into the street. The camera pauses as the woman strolls away, then it pulls back slowly – you see one building façade, then two, then the whole street comes into view as the woman slowly disappears into the distance.

Cut.

A new scene, new location, new actors. Same film, same story.

In much the same way, a writer may zoom in on a scene, then zoom out and place the facts or anecdote in context. Next, the writer may move to a different location, give voice to different opinions. And, perhaps, much like a narrator in a play, the writer may step in to provide an interpretation, a summary, or a transition to the next scene.

Paragraphs and sentences, as much as words, create a mood. Short sentences convey action and tension, whereas long, drawn-out sentences tend to slow down the reader. But not always. Freelance writer Gus Silber captured the frenetic style of Radio Five's Alex Jay in a 72-word sentence which moves too fast to pause for a full-stop:

EXERCISE *Examine camera technique*

Examine camera technique. (Read the extract from Gus Silber's article carefully (also see p.145), and see if you can notice how he 'filmed' the story through his words, sentences, paragraphs and punctuation.)

> It's the Drive Show on Radio Five, and Alex Jay is back in the hot seat, jabbing digital buttons like a shuttle commander, shifting his gaze from the clock to the television to the computer screen, waving and blowing kisses at people on the other side of the looking-glass, rolling his eyes and tripping over his tongue as a minor pop singer called Prince battles to make himself heard in the background.
>
> Alex Jay is on something. Definitely. It's called air. He lives it, he breathes it, he soars like a kite on it. Four hours a day, five days a week it's the fix that keeps him from going too sane. But when the red light fades and he floats down to earth, Alex Jay knows exactly who and what he is ... (1992:24)

Silber finally puts the brakes on the too-busy-to-quit-now sequence by arranging softer words – "fades" and "floats" – into a plodding sentence. The reader gets a chance to take a breath and learns that, occasionally, Alex Jay does too.

Another factor that contributes to the pace of a story is the construction of the verbs, in particular whether they are in passive voice or **active voice**. If anything, writing news stories is about action – what has happened, is happening and what may happen. Capture the immediacy by writing in the active voice.

Weaving with transitions

These are **word bridges**, which link paragraph to paragraph. They unify the story; they give cohesion and make sense of the story. They act as a road map through the story for the reader. Transitions move the reader not only from paragraph to paragraph but from subject to subject.

Transitions are important because readers are generally curious people, but they are also pretty lazy; they certainly do not want to work too hard to get the facts. Any excuse to stop reading – a lull in the action, an ambiguous detail, and they duck. Transitions keep your readers in the story, giving them no logical place to exit until the end.

They illustrate, present alternatives and summarise. Common transitional words are: but, and, because, nevertheless, that. Also repeat a word as a bridge to a new paragraph. For example:

Definition

Active voice [Zu. Inkulumo-mbiko / Afr. bedrywende vorm] is the form of a verb whose grammatical subject is the person or thing that performs the action, as in: *She was driving the car.* The passive construction of that sentence would be: *The car was being driven by her.*

HOT TIP

Catch passive voice constructions. A good, but not foolproof, way to check for passive voice sentences is to look for the word "by": Hickory, dickory, dock. The clock was run up by the mouse. When editing, I hear a little nagging voice is my head saying: "Bye-bye *by*!" Let it echo in yours, too.

A 22-year-old **man** was jailed yesterday for three years after he was found guilty of armed robbery.

The man told the court he robbed the service station so he could buy drugs.

But the **judge** said the community expected armed robbers to be taken off the streets.

Judge Malcolm Stern said citizens had a right to go about their business without fear of armed robbers and **recent research** showed jail was the best deterrent.

Titled *Barred from Crime*, the **report** to the government examined the experiences of 500 young offenders.

Tips for creating transitions

- **Transitional words**

  A peculiarity of journalism is beginning sentences with conjunctions. Something to which many language purists (like your high school English teacher) would object. Such language purists insist that conjunctions, such as "but", "however", "and", should only be used to link independent clauses in compound sentences. This is not an argument. I am merely remarking that journalists do begin sentences with those little words and others: *nevertheless, however, moreover, therefore*. And the practice is useful. Also used are words of addition (such as, *also* and *secondly*). Words of movement and time, for example: "when", "since" and "while". Words of attribution, like: "according to" and "he said".

- **Repetition**

  Start succeeding sentences or paragraphs with the same word:

  Jon fell in the carport, a few yards from the rear corner of the house.

  Jon, born in Johannesburg, has been living since 2004 with Featherstone, who is his mother's sister.

- **Logic**

  "A question precedes an answer," points out Hiley Ward (1985:179). "Or a national problem precedes its ramifications for the local scene. Your reader can predict expected results once you have set up a logical sequence of statements or questions."

  Listing items using numerals or round dots (bullets) also logically suggests a link.

- **Punctuation**

  Punctuation presents the writer with several options: using a colon will tie a group of sentences or paragraphs together; so will a semicolon.

- **Balance or contrast**

  If, for example, you list a pro, you can use a con as contrast.

Parallels can also be created by referring to the view of one side of the debate, then referring to the other side.

- **Highlighting a theme**
  In this section, I rely on this method: periodically, I weave in references to Gus Silber, which helps tie the discussion together.

In this chapter, you learned that:

- While feature stories are not easily sorted into neat groups, there are some identifiable categories. Amongst them are: Information features, interviews, personal accounts, profiles, service pieces, trend stories, travelogues, humorous features, interpretative features, historical features, and investigative features.
- Besides brainstorming, there are a range of formulas for generating creative ideas for feature stories. To be viable, a story idea should be of interest to your audience and to yourself. It should neither be too narrow nor too broad. Accessible, high-quality information should be available. And, above all, it should be of value.
- Amongst the ways to order feature stories are the *The Wall Street Journal* and the Narrative forms.
- Good writing is clear. It is precise. It appeals to the senses. It has pace appropriate to the action. And it is tied together with transitions.

HOT LINK

How do you learn to tell stories in journalism? Roy Peter Clark, a senior scholar at the Poynter Institute, suggests some excercises that may help: http://www. poynter.org/content/content_view.asp?id=5396

Putting your learning to work

ACTIVITY 1 *Analyse a feature story*

Select a magazine or newspaper feature that you regard as particularly effective. Write the key bibliographic details at the top of the page. Then, after numbering each line in the margin, analyse the article according to the following criteria:

Analysing articles

Type	Is it a trend story, profile, commentary, etc?
Thesis	Describe in one sentence what the story is about.
Purpose	What is the reason for the article? In what way will it be useful to the reader? (Refer to the list in Chapter 6, p.114)
Slant	What is the news peg? What angle did the writer choose?
Story form	Identify the story structure.
Treatment	How does the story unfold? Does the writer describe the interview and use quotes from a single source? Is the piece written as a straightforward report?

Tone	Is it serious and factual, or light and frivolous?
Style	Is the writing clear? Is it precise? Does it appeal to the senses? Is the pace appropriate to the action? And is it tied together with transitions?
	Give examples to support your evaluation.
Illustrations	How is the article illustrated? Photographs? Cartoons? Do the illustrations (if any) complement the copy?

ACTIVITY 2 Demonstrate your ability to craft creative feature stories

You've been handed a reporter's notes with some basic information (see below). The challenge: craft a creative feature story for the Sunday edition of a popular newspaper. To that end, complete the following steps:

– Identify a creative idea for a feature story related to the skydiving accident. Does it pass the Story Viability Test?
– What type of feature story is it (information, service, investigative, profile, etc.)?
– Plot an outline for the piece using one of the story forms discussed in this chapter.
– Prepare a reporting plan (see p.96).
– Write a lead and nut graf for the story, using the information in the notes.
– Write a story pitch or budget line to sell the story to your editor.

- There are 12 000 injuries in skydiving each year – 17 per cent of them permanently disabling the victims. Fourteen people died last year.
- Fifty-five per cent of the injuries are to the spine. Most critics blame poor enforcement of safety procedures.
- Jonathan Levy, 19, a first-year student at the Cape Technikon in Cape Town, has been wheelchair-bound since an accident earlier this year.
- On only his fourth jump, he dislocated his arm while exiting the aeroplane.
- Being unable to pull his main parachute, he opted for his reserve parachute, which had not been packed properly.
- After spiralling severely, Levy collided with powerlines and tumbled to the ground with a broken neck and lower back.
- "I guess I should have been more careful, but I just wasn't paying enough attention when we were prepping for the jump," he said from his hospital bed, two months after the accident.
- Levy studied nature conservation.
- He is an only son and his parents are very distraught.
- They are thinking of taking legal action against the Western Province Skydiving Club, to which their son belonged.

FROM THE NEWSROOM

Mzilikazi wa Afrika

Mzilikazi wa Afrika joined the Sunday Times *as a reporter in 1999 and later formed the paper's multi-award winning investigations unit.*

"Mzilikazi wa Afrika does not live his life according to other people's rules," says his colleague Babalwa Shota. There is plenty evidence for that. Born in Bushbuckridge in the Limpopo Province, Mzilikazi started his journalism career in 1995 as a freelancer for the Witbank News. *A year later he and his brother started the* Mpumalanga Mirror *newspaper. Money was tight. Too tight, in fact. When the paper shut down after a year, he joined the African Eye News Service in Nelspruit. Then it was off to Johannesburg and the* Sunday Times. *In his first year with the giant weekly, he was named 1999* Sunday Times *Journalist of the Year and formed the paper's investigations unit. There has been a steady flow of accolades since – 10 and counting... Amongst them are the 2001 Nat Nakasa for Media Integrity Award and being short-listed for the 2003 Centre for Public Integrity International Investigative Reporting Award in Africa as well as the 2003 Natali Prize for Human Rights Reporting.*

Former President Nelson Mandela has said, "A critical, independent and investigative press is the lifeblood of any democracy." Can you help clarify how this plays out in practice?
An investigative reporter should by all means be independent, critical and cautious. In fact, the whole media industry should be independent and play a very critical role in our society by giving the public news that is not biased or offensive. Investigative reporting is like a public watchdog – whenever government or the private sector is doing something wrong, investigative journalists should expose the rot and inform the public about those who should be held responsible for the mess. We should do that without fear or favour. We should do our reporting with pride. Although we often tell the public something shocking, we are telling them the truth about what is happening around them. The media is not an opposition party but it is the voice, eyes and the platform for the public. There cannot be democracy if there is no

freedom of speech as well as the total independence of the press.

How do you identify stories to investigate?

Any story can be an investigative story but it depends on how a journalist approaches it, and how the journalist puts all the pieces of the puzzle together. For an example, in 1997 while I was a crime reporter for African Eye News Service and based in Nelspruit, I received a police report that a minibus taxi overturned near the Komatipoort border post at about 4 am. All 21 passengers died on the scene. My first questions were: Where did the taxi driver pick up his 21 passengers and where were they going at 4 am? Later, I established that all the passengers were foreign nationals who had just been smuggled into South Africa from neighbouring countries, either Mozambique or Swaziland. What I did was to take down the vehicle registration number, trace its owner and follow his activities for months. When I was convinced that the taxi boss was a modern-day slave trader, I crossed the border to Mozambique where I pretended to be a local who wanted to come to South Africa. Within two days in Mozambique, I was recruited by one of the modern-day slave traders' runners with promises that I would be smuggled to South Africa and that they would also find me a shop. I went through the whole process. After I was smuggled into South Africa, I wrote the story which appeared in the *Sunday Times* on January 24, 1999. The taxi driver is now serving 25 years behind bars. The point: I did not treat the story as just another police accident report; instead, I approached it differently and I came up with a well-researched story. I also won a number of awards for it.

In-depth investigative journalism typically takes a great deal more time and effort than, say, user-friendly stories about personal finance, fitness and technology. What practical and ethical criteria do you use to decide if a story is worth pursuing?

Before pursuing any investigative story, the journalist has to make sure that he or she has *prima facie* [sufficient and obvious] evidence that whatever he or she wants to achieve is out there. Once you are 100 per cent convinced, out of your prelim-inary investigation, that you are on the right direction and that you are not following a hoax tip-off or lead, you start planning your story. How are you going to dig out the dirt? Who are the right people to speak to about the matter? Always remember to speak to people, or sources, from both camps, friends and enemies alike. A good investigative story needs a lot of planning and more reading, researching your subject. A good investigative story needs a lot of patience, too. There are long hours of toiling and meeting strange people in strange places. Another example: I was in a minibus taxi from Johannesburg to Nelspruit in 1999 when I overheard some of the passengers from Mozambique talking about how they "bought" their South African identity documents from Home Affairs at Harrison Street, downtown Johannesburg. When I returned to Johannesburg, I went to the same Home Affairs office where I pretended to be an illegal immigrant and I bought myself an ID book. The same investigation caused the then Home Affairs Director-General Albert Mokoena his job.

What skills do you need when investigating a story?

I always tell myself that being an investigative reporter is like being a clown. While you are interviewing your sources or the people whom you are probing, you have to observe every little thing, calculate their moves, analyse whatever they are doing and how they are doing it, as well as keeping all the information in your memory. If you don't have good eyesight and a very sharp memory, you are not going to make it as an investigative reporter. While doing an investigation, always remember that anything might lead you to the bigger things. Look at the way people dress, the cars they drive (always take down registration numbers to find out who is the real owner/s of the vehicle), the food they eat, the places they visit (after hours or during working hours) and the company they keep.

Any other advice for would-be investigative journalists?

I would advise them that there is no glamour in doing the job. There is lots of sweat, sleepless nights, frustration and tears. In this business, you make lots of enemies and very few friends. Your life will be threatened and those very close to you will go through a rough time, from being bombarded with death threats to being physically intimidated. Life as an investigative journalist is not all "moonlight and roses"; you have to sacrifice a lot of things and have a very close social life. You don't want every Tom, Dick and Harry to know where you would be at a particular time.

For reporters, as well as those close to them, investigative journalism is hard going, even life-threatening. Why then do you keep at it?

Doing investigative journalism is like working for the bomb squad – we all know that it is a dangerous job but someone has to do it because it is for a good cause. An investigative journalist needs to be (a) very disciplined, (b) very careful and cautious, (c) very observant and (d) calculate every single move he or she makes otherwise the journalist or those close to him or her might lose their lives. I am doing this job because I love it. It has taught me to be more disciplined than I was before, more careful than I used to be and not to take anything for granted. In fact, investigative journalism, with all the risks, has moulded me and made me look at life differently. I always tell my friends: if you want people to respect you, you do not need to shoot a raging bull with your gun; instead, hold it by its sharp horns and bring it down to the ground. And it takes not any brave person to do that, but someone with good timing and certain skills. I, like millions other citizens of this country, hate corruption and I

will try by all means necessary to fight it and expose it. I am not doing it for glory, glamour or awards; I am doing it for the love of my country and my people and, above all, out of patriotism. And I am prepared to sacrifice my life for my people and country. People must know that it is better to die for an ideal that will live, than to live an ideal that will die. If something is not worth living for, it is definitely not worth dying for.

FEATURING:
Maxwell Mhlanga
Tshepiso Mpotle
Junior Sokhela
Phuzekhemisi
Esta M

Mzilikazi wa Afrika is best known as a journalist. He's also a musician and he's just released his first CD. Does this mean he's leaving journalism? No, he told a reporter: "I'm here to stay in journalism. The music is a thing I do in my leisure time." Read more at: http://www.suntimes.co.za/2004/05/16/arts/ane09.asp.

Bibliography and Recommended Reading

Anon 1. 1993. Judge fingers provocateurs; 'agents' fuelling unrest – G'stone. *Cape Times*, July 22, 1993.

Anon 2. Quick start; the two minute guide to computer literacy. PC Review in the *Weekly Mail*. June 1992.

Anon 3. 1991. Japan's stock woes batter other markets. *Time*, August 3, 1992.

Armour, S. 2000. Brainstorming, good files help identify trend stories. [Online] Gannett. 21 July 2000. Available at: http://www.gannett.com/go/newswatch/2000/july/nw0721-1.htm [Accessed: 13 July 2004]

Appleyard, B. 1995. Bobbitt: the uncut version. *Sunday Life* magazine, July 9, 1995.

Beresford, D. 1993. Dusk: its countdown to killing hour. *Weekly Mail & Guardian*, July 30 – August 5, 1993.

Buchanan, E. 1987. *The corpse had a familiar face: covering Miami, America's toughest crime beat*. New York, Random House.

Cappon, R.J. 1982. *The word: an Associated Press guide to good newswriting*. New York, Associated Press.

Craig, P. 1996. *The Oxford book of travel stories*. New York: Oxford.

Glasser, S.B. 2004. Steady exodus is latest chapter of loss. *Wall Street Journal*, July 12, 2004: A3.

Hennessy, B. 1993. *Writing feature articles: a practical guide to methods and markets*, 2nd ed. Oxford: Focal Press.

Junod, T. 2003. The falling man. *Esquire*. [Online] September 2003, 140(3). Available at: http://www.esquire.com/features/articles/2003/030903_mfe_falling_1.html [Accessed: 14 July 2004]

Karras, A. 2004. White knuckle entertainment. *ThisDay*, July 13, 2004: 8.

McAdams, K. and Elliott, J. 1996. *Reaching audiences: a guide to media writing*. Boston: Allyn and Bacon.

Missouri Group, The: Brooks, Brian, S. et al., 1980. *News reporting and writing*. New York: St Martin's.

O'Kane, M. 1993. A public trial in Bosnia's sniper season. *Guardian Weekly*, March 19–25, 1993.

Pinnock, D. 1996. The ins and outs of outs and ins: notes on travel writing for *Getaway*. Staff memo, 1996.

Scanlan, C. 2000. *Reporting and writing: basics for the 21st century*. New York: Oxford.

Silber, G. 1992. Hot hits and hang ups. *Sunday Times Magazine*, October 11, 1992.

Ward, H.H. 1985. *Professional newswriting*. New York: Harcourt Brace Jovanovich. British Guild of Travel Writers website: http://www.bgtw.metronet.co.uk/aboutus.asp

Successful freelance writing

Introduction

The good news is that advances in information technology have made it easier to work as a freelance. The other news, according to the South African Freelancers Association (Safrea) website, is this: "More and more skilled professionals have found themselves out of work as companies have tightened their belts. Rather than carry the costs of staff positions, employers are turning to freelancers or contractors to fill their requirements."

That pretty much sums up the situation, agrees Elmari Rautenbach. And she should know. She began her career in magazines as a freelancer and is now the highly-regarded editor of the monthly magazine *Insig* [Afrikaans for *insight*), which is described as "the thinking Afrikaans-speaker's lifestyle magazine." The editorial, advertising and design of this **niche** publication, which reaches about 90 000 readers with each issue, is run by a small team. In fact, a very small team: one part-time and four full-time staff. Yes, Rautenbach tries to write an article for each edition. And the assistant editor and senior journalist do so, too. But writing is only a fraction of their duties. Like many other print and online media in South Africa, *Insig* relies almost entirely on freelance writers for their editorial content. "Probably about 90 per cent," says Rautenbach.

There are certainly many opportunities for freelancers. At one stage, recalls Rautenbach, she was editor of the now-defunct *MagFocus* magazine, book editor for *Insig*, editor of the Afrikaans newspaper supplement *Boekewêreld* [translated as *world of books*], and also worked half-days running the

KEY CONCEPTS

The role of freelancers in the media; the process of getting freelance work accepted and paid for; the key challenges and opportunities for freelancers; the hourglass form of structuring stories.

Definition

Niche [Zu. Isikhundla / Xh. umtyhi / Afr. nis], in this context, is defined media that target a specialised but profitable corner of the audience market.

HOT LINK

South African Freelancers Association: http://www.safrea.org.za

Johannesburg office and arranging book launches for Human & Rousseau publishers – all at the same time. "I almost never slept!" she admits.

Certainly, successful **freelancers** need to have strong journalistic skills. Typically, they have to be flexible enough to apply these in a variety of contexts. They also need a thorough understanding of how the process works. That is the main focus of this chapter.

LEARNING GOALS

At the end of this chapter, you should be able to:

1 Recognise the demands and rewards of freelance writing.
2 Understand the process of getting freelance work published.
3 Be aware of some of the specific challenges freelancers face, as well as where to get assistance.
4 Be familiar with another way to structure feature stories: the hourglass form.

Definition

Freelance [Zu. Ukusebenza okungagcwele / Xh.–sebenza njenge / Afr. vryskut] This medieval term (typically defined as the period from the end of the 5th century to the early 15th century) was originally used to describe soldiers for hire, who often used lances (long wooden shafts with metal tips) in combat – *free + lance*. Today the term is commonly used to describe journalists (and other professionals, such as photographers and editors) who sell their services to different employers without entering into a permanent contract with any of them.

Tips on getting freelance writing published

Newspapers, magazines, corporate publications, advertising agencies, public relations companies, radio stations and television stations all make use of freelancers. But that doesn't mean that it is an easy task.* There are many skilled media workers who try to make a living writing freelance in a very competitive market. Only the good get in. And only the consistent thrive. Following these tips will help you do just that.

1 Deciding on the story idea

Which comes first: the story idea or the target publication? Sometimes you may start with an idea and look for a suitable magazine, newspaper or website. For example, you run into a friend who tells you about a cult in Hout Bay that meets at the beach at full moon. Yes, you think, that could make a good story for *Lifestyle*, the highly-regarded *Sunday Times* supplement. Sometimes the process works the other way round.

* Consider the advice in this chapter and that in Chapter 8 on formulating story ideas, devising reporting plans and structuring stories.

2 Finding a market

The first step is to be sure your story matches the needs of the target medium, not merely in topic and treatment, but also in length and timing. It is no use sending a 1 200-word, humorous first-person piece to *Cosmopolitan*·

HOT LINK

Got writer's block? That's OK, says writing coach Chip Scanlan. Being blocked is part of the process. Read his tips on how to keep the words flowing at: http://poynter.org/column.asp?id=52&aid=60962.

Les Aupiais

Many people harbour the notion that they will try to freelance "on the side" while pursuing other careers. Award-winning editor Les Aupiais tells the story of a surgeon who once told her, "I always wanted to write. Maybe I should try it sometime." Her retort: "I always wanted to do brain surgery, maybe I should try that sometime."

We asked her advice for those who seriously want to make a career of writing for magazines. Her reply:

"Select 10 to 15 magazine journalists, from columnists to investigative writers, and pull apart the way they structure their work, the language they use, the style they have developed. Study the rhythm of their writing and its unique appeal. Writing for magazines is so different from a clinical news reporting style."

"On a practical note, travel whenever you can. Well-travelled magazine writers always have the jump on those who have barely left their home towns."

for their back page. Even if they love the story, it's too long and won't fit onto one page – and that is their formula. Timing is important, too. If you send a profile of a baker who creates elaborate Easter eggs to a magazine in February, your story is likely to be rejected simply because most magazines work on deadlines three months prior to the date of publication.

Rule of thumb: Read – and analyse – at least three copies of the publication from cover to cover before you attempt to write an article for that publication.

3 Approaching an editor

There are two choices: Talk to the editor before you start writing or write the article and send it off to a specific editor (called writing on "spec", for "speculation"). How do you choose? It depends on whether you are an established writer or not. It also depends on the type of story.

- Established writers often get calls from editors commissioning articles. Unknown writers typically have to pitch stories to editors, who will often expect the completed piece before making a decision.
- If you are covering hard news stories, where time is short, you may have to call editors and fish around for a buyer. If you are writing feature articles, you may have time to write a query letter or e-mail a suggestion.

4 Writing queries or story pitches

"Never write a Dear Sir/Madam letter (or e-mail) to an editor," cautions award-winning editor Les Aupiais. Take the trouble to read up about a publication, who works there and the kind of stories they publish. If you are uncertain about to whom to direct the query, make a quick call to the office and ask. "It helps to refer to something specific in your initial letter regarding employment or freelance work," says Aupiais. "It simply shows initiative and a bit of savvy."

Consider these points when writing queries or pitches:

- direct query e-mails (which is the form most editors prefer) to the appropriate person
- include a short synopsis of the article (potential title, topic, slant, the sources of information, suggested length)

- suggest ideas for artwork (illustrations or photographs), if appropriate
- include a date when the piece could be ready
- adding a short summary of your writing background and/or qualifications will also help sell the story and
- don't forget to include your full name (not *nom de plume*) and contact details.

If you are writing without having being commissioned (known as "writing on spec"), do not expect a quick response. "Follow it up with a phone call," suggests Rautenbach. That will give the editor the opportunity to ask any questions about the piece and, if necessary, find out more about you. Also, if you're sending a printed manuscript, you can increase the odds of hearing from the editor by including a stamped, self-addressed postcard with something like this:

Your manuscript, ...,
has been received by the editor
of *The Magazine*.

I.B. Smart

1 Pulitzer Street

Date ....

Signed ....

My Town

Editor ....

007

* If you're sending the manuscript by e-mail, you can set the options to request 'delivery' and 'read' receipts.

Also include a stamped, self-addressed envelope (SASE) for the manuscript, if you want it returned. Send such material by registered mail.

5 Copyright

If your manuscript is accepted, read the conditions of the offer carefully. Typically, publications buy the right to use your work once for a particular publication. Some, however, may purchase the right to resell the work to others. Clarify the copyright for your work upfront, particularly if you intend to reuse the story for another purpose, such as a book or filmscript, or to sell another version of the piece to a publication locally or abroad.

Definition

Copyright [Zu. ilungelo elinikwa ngumthetho embhalweni / Xh. ilungelo lombhali elilelakhe lokushicilela nokuthengisa umsebenzi wakhe / Afr. kopiereg] The right of intellectual property. In South Africa, copyright is regulated by the Copyright Act of 1978. For a straight-forward introduction see this article by attorney Karen Willenberg (2001/2) available on the Script Writer's Association of South Africa website at: http://www. saswa.org.za/article_copyright.htm. Read the full Act at: http://www.legalnet.co.za/cyberlaw/CopyrightAct.htm. Check the Government web-site for recent amendments at: http://www.info.gov.za/acts/index.html.

6 Being edited

Editors usually reserve the right to edit or translate your story. So, don't be surprised when the version of the piece that appears in print is markedly different from the one you submitted.

7 Do not be afraid to talk about money

Some beginning freelancers are so grateful to get published that they forget to ask about the fee. Settle that before the story is published. Afterwards, you have little chance of negotiating. Freelance rates vary widely. Currently, R1,50 to R2,50 a word is considered an acceptable, average fee for magazine articles. Newspapers usually pay less, while advertising and public relations are typically much more lucrative fields.

Some magazines pay on acceptance, while others pay on publication, which may be several months after you've completed the work.

INVOICE

To:Thami Anyone
1234 Her Address
Her City, State, Postal Code
(888) 555 1111
thami@hermail.co.za

From: Your Name
1234 Your Address
Your City, Postal Code
(000) 555 3456
you@yourmail.co.za
Date: (Use the date you're sending the invoice)

Story: Travel feature on cycling safari in Mashatu Game Reserve, 2 000 words @ R2/word	R4 000,00
Photographs: Two images on cycling safari @ R500/image	R1 000,00
Total Due	**R5 000,00**

(add any special instructions, such as "make cheque payable to" or your bank account details)

Thank you,
Your Name

Invoices: "Proof it, mail it and log in when you mailed so you'll know if you're paid promptly or not," advises Wayman. "Simple."

Most publications require an invoice. Veteran freelance writer and coach Anne Wyman points out that when you invoice for your freelance work, you want to include:

■■■■ **LINK**

For some more advice from Anne Wyman about freelance writing, see: http://freelancewrite.about.com/

- The complete contact information for the person/company you're billing.
- Your complete contact information.
- Enough detail so the person you're billing recognises what was done.
- The total.

8 Being rejected

Good stories may be rejected. The story may be right, but not for that magazine. I once wrote a first-person piece and sent it out on spec. It was rejected by two magazine editors who both told me they liked it, but that it didn't quite fit their formula. Two years later, a third editor asked me for something on short notice, so I hauled out the piece again, gave it a little polishing and it was sold.

Do not make enemies with editors. If your work is not accepted, accept it graciously and move on.

Tips on thriving as a freelance writer

"Making money from freelance journalism? Is that some kind of joke?" That is how Arthur Goldstruck responded when his publisher first proposed a title for his handbook for freelancers. At the time, Goldstruck says, "I was making very little money from freelance journalism, and had to make a living from full-time newspaper employment." But that has changed. Goldstruck is now his own boss and you can read extracts from the *South African Freelance Journalist's Handbook* at: http://www.legends.org.za/arthur/howto.htm.

1 Adopt multiple mentors

"Build a support and feedback team," recommends writing coach and freelancer Susanne Alexander (no date). "They help you fight all the self-confidence trashing forces!" She also recommends that you attend writers' workshops and courses, where possible. Read books and magazines about writing of all kinds. But in the end, says Alexander, it is up to you. "Then using your best judgment, without imposing limitations on yourself, try out as much as you can, and keep what works for you. As you grow, be willing to mentor others."

2 Network, network, network!

"Join many different organisations related to writing, journalism, public relations, etc." advises Alexander, "especially those with local meetings (attend them), and keep your membership for at least a year until you determine if it's useful or not. If you can't afford membership dues, at least attend occasional meetings as a guest. Volunteer your time at the meetings and be willing to be an officer when the time comes."

3 Be professional

Use professional tools and methods: computer, e-mail, anti-virus software, high-quality printer, fax machine, 35 mm or digital camera, tape recorder, dictaphone, dictionary, thesaurus, concise query letters, etc. Maintain paper/spreadsheet/database records to track the progress of your queries and articles. Be accessible: have high quality telephones (listed phone number), and professional voicemail. But, above all, says Rautenbach, act professionally. That means meeting the assignment brief exactly – in content, in tone, in length and on time. And if (or when) things don't go to plan, contact your editor soonest. That will help them plan accordingly. And ensure you get work commissioned again.

Freelance writing in action: a case study

Mike Behr is a freelance writer with a string of credits to his name, including being a finalist in the feature-writing category of the annual Mondi Paper Magazine Awards for an interview feature on Springbok rugby player Ashwin Willemse for *South African Sports Illustrated*.

The story structure can be described as a feature variation of the hourglass form. In 1983, Roy Peter Clark began to notice something unusual in his daily newspaper (Scanlan, 2000: 156). Reporters were beginning to combine two forms of writing: the inverted pyramid (see p.91) and the narrative (see p.180). He gave this story structure a distinctive name: the hourglass. Strictly speaking, the hourglass would start with a summary lead, followed by three or four paragraphs that would answer the reader's most pressing questions. Then there's the turn, which is when the reader is alerted that a narrative, usually chronological, is beginning. The narrative section has three basic elements: a beginning, a middle and an end.

The hourglass story form is often adapted for profile features because it allows writers to start with a scene-setting anecdote, followed by a three or four paragraphs that identify the subject of the profile and why that person is newsworthy. Then there's a turn that signals to the reader that the subject's lifestory will be told chronologically. This usually starts with the subject's full names, time and place of birth, and, typically, reference to family (parents and siblings). The rest of the narrative section is straightforward: how did he get from "here" (their childhood) to "there", the occupation, event, achievement (or disgrace) which brought him into the media spotlight? The ending usually looks ahead and answers a simple question: what next?

Next, Behr tells how he went about getting and crafting the story. Later, currrent SASI editor Steve Smith tells why he thinks the end result deserved to be recognised for excellence – and he offers some tips to would-be sports journalists, too.

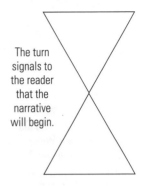

The top provides a summary of the key news points of the story.

The turn signals to the reader that the narrative will begin.

The narrative, typically told chronologically, includes a beginning, a middle and an end.

From the moment he burst onto the international scene, there was always the sense from newspaper interviews that Ashwin Willemse had one hell of a story to tell. But how to get him to open up, that was the challenge.

SA Sports Illustrated editor at the time, Robert Houwing, was in agreement that the only way I was going to have a snowball's chance was to spend time with Willemse.

That might sound a tad obvious. But one of the rather unpalatable realities in magazine publishing these days is the bloody ubiquitous telephone interview. Unless the writer happens to reside in the same town as the subject or the subject just happens to be visiting the writer's home town, it's most likely that the celebrity interview will be conducted on the phone.

It is an indictment of how standards have been allowed to slip. Dangerously so. You can never be certain that you're not talking to an imposter. Nor will you ever be able to tell just how sincere they are being.

Don't get me wrong. The telephone, especially late at night, is often a perfect medium for extracting confessional copy. The instrument should never be underestimated. But it should remain no more than one of the tools in a profiler's arsenal. And it should never replace the one-on-one as the primary source of contact.

So when I heard I would be flying out of town for the Ashwin Willemse assignment, I was not just pleased to be getting away from my desk. I was excited about being able to do the job properly for a change. The cherry on the top was receiving confirmation that I had two days' access to the Bok camp at the height of their World Cup build-up.

When you're freelancing, you dare only move from your desk when the money is good. Like too many of the mainstream magazines, however, SA Sports Illustrated pays a rate that long ago lost touch with the inflation rate.

Fortunately Robert Houwing was an editor who knew how to get

* Kamp Staaldraad
(Afrikaans words, translated literally as Camp Steel-Wire, *idiomatically* Camp Barbed Wire*) was a military-style "boot camp" organised as a "team-building" exercise for the South African national rugby team, the Springboks, during their preparation for the 2003 Rugby World Cup. When the details of the camp came out in the South African media, it ignited a firestorm of protest that quickly consumed much of the upper administrative levels of South African rugby. Read more at:* http://www.therfcc.org/kamp-staaldraad-200877.html.

mileage out of a tight budget. To make the fee a large, worthwhile one, he commissioned a 3 000 word plus profile, which is unheard of in South African publishing where the focus is on catering for short attention spans. Besides making it worth my while, that sort of length would give me all the space I could wish for to develop a story. All I needed now was for Ashwin to spill the beans.

In retrospect, it's amazing that Ashwin ever did. As it happened, my interview with him was scheduled for the week after **Kamp Staaldraad**. It was set up with the then communications manager Mark Keohane who by then had quit in protest over racism in the Bok camp. At the time media relations were in a shambles and it was a miracle that arrangements were not ditched.

When I arrived in Durban, journalists were still trying to get to the bottom of what had gone down at the bosberaad that brought the Boks' World Cup dreams crashing down. Hence I found an understandably suspicious and reticent Ashwin Willemse at the Elangeni Hotel, where the squad was based.

I began with my first interview after lunch on the pool deck, where I sketched what I was hoping to talk about. I had done a fair amount of research and had a list of prepared questions. I knew where I wanted to go.

At the same time I was also mindful of what the legendary Fleet Street feature writer Lynn Barber once said: "Good interviewing is about listening rather than asking questions. Listening for what they don't say as much as what they do, listening for what they say glibly and what they say awkwardly. Listening for the 'charged' bits that touch an emotional nerve. Clever questions in my view are a waste of time. The really clever question is the shortest one that will elicit the longest, most interesting answer."

Following a bit of shadow boxing, Willemse then asked me what I wanted to know. I couldn't believe how easily I had got a foot in the door. My only explanation is that he was relieved that I wasn't there to probe about Staaldraad. And that I showed a genuine interest in where he came from. I also think that there was luck in my timing. I caught Willemse at a moment when he wanted to offload.

I had just over an hour before afternoon practice to win Willemse's trust. I'm not quite sure how I did this. If you think about it, there is no godly reason why a subject should ever do that. Nine times out of 10, he or she has only just met you. And what's more, you're asking questions that they wouldn't normally answer in unfamiliar company!

Hell, if the roles were reversed I know that I never would agree to an interview, let alone treat one like a counselling session. Which is probably why I always start interviews feeling that I'm on a hiding to nothing.

But most times, with enough listening and identification of the subject's feelings (this is critical, especially when it comes to their childhood), a miraculous thing happens. There comes a moment when the subject says to him or herself, "Oh f*** it, here goes ...", or something to that effect. And then off they go, offloading their deepest and darkest ...

It's a moment to cherish. And once it started to happen with Ashwin, I knew that I was halfway home. (For Barber the key to putting a subject in a confessional frame of mind is understanding their childhood. "It's three quarters of the way to understanding them now," she maintains. For me that was especially true of Willemse.)

By the time the Bok winger excused himself for practice 80 minutes later, I had enough material to write a decent story. But I had a feeling there was a lot more to come. And that, under cover of darkness, Willemse might just reveal it. With a firm appointment to hook up in his room after supper, I was confident that the only thing that could derail me now, would be Willemse developing a case of cold feet.

It was touch and go for a while. When I tried to reach Willemse after supper, all I could get was his cell phone voicemail. His room phone just rang and rang. And I was just about to turn away from his room door when he answered it.

But the spade work proved worth it. For the next hour and forty two minutes it was like I was the priest on the other side of the confessional. By the time I walked out of Willemse's room, I knew I had the interview in the bag. And an exclusive one at that.

Of course, you can never be too cocksure of that. As Lyn Barber points out, interviewing is a bit like fishing in that you can come back with a big catch and a grin to match, and then discover down the line, that a colleague landed an even bigger fish. One way of narrowing the odds, is to end every interview with a question like, "Are you about to announce something big in your life that would make me look an idiot for missing? Something in the league of a marriage, a divorce, a new pregnancy or a terminal illness?" But even that is not foolproof.

Following the interview, the most awful part of the feature lies in wait: the transcription. In this instance, over three hours of tape.

Actually, make that memory stick, not tape. Some time back I invested in a Sony digital voice recorder that has become an indispensable interviewing tool. Smaller and lighter than a cell phone, it doesn't intimidate the subject. It also has an awesome storage capacity and brilliant playback quality. Because it's digital, you can download the sound file onto your PC, and then the dedicated software gives your keyboard all the features of a top-flight dictaphone machine.

Transcribing is a pain because it's so damn laborious. And it delays the writing. But for the sake of authenticity, it's something that had to be done, word by word. At the end of the day the effort was worth it, its value being the quality of dialogue I had to work with. (An accurate transcript also comes in handy if your subject ever contests a quote.)

Then came the painstaking process of collating the material. I have yet to meet a subject who relates their life story chronologically. The bastards always flit this way and that, the expectancy being that your base knowledge is at least every bit as good as their mother's.

Once I had everything mapped out on highlighted and notated printouts in front of me – when working with so many words I find it impossible to get perspective even on a 17-inch screen – I set about the writing which, with time and a looming deadline, pretty much took care of itself.

I found that as I wrote, the narrative came easily. As presumptuous as it sounds, and indeed is, I felt I pretty much knew who Ashwin Willemse was. Thankfully he agreed when I later sent him the copy.

A lot of editors abhor this practice. It can cause endless problems if your subject suddenly turns precious, self-conscious or sour. But it can prove invaluable for picking up mistakes, not only of a factual nature, but interpretive ones as well. Writers are not immune to getting the wrong end of the stick. The payoff of this process is when the subject acknowledges they cannot fault your call, especially when you paint a picture that reveals them warts and all. There can be no better compliment.

That said, interviewing is an inexact science. To again quote Barber, a guru when it comes to the interview feature, interviewing is "an attempt to read someone's character in an indecently short space of time."

As I've already said, the key to a good one lies in your style of listening, coupled with a resolve to keep a lid on your own ego. Expressing your opinions always runs the risk of cramping your subject's style.

What's just as vital is curiosity. You have to be really nosey about your subject's life if you want to walk away with copy that writes headlines. That often means going where angels fear to tread.

But perhaps the most essential blessing is a genuine appetite for tolerance. You have to really and truly want to celebrate difference if your goal is a piece that grips the reader's imagination. Like Barber says, "The best interviews – like the best biographies – should sing the strangeness and variety of the human race."

EXERCISE *Can you recognise the hourglass story form?*

Read Behr's story carefully and see if you can identify the three parts: the **top**, which summarises the newsworthiness of the story; the **turn**, signalling to the reader that the **narrative** will begin; the narrative, typically told chronologically, includes a beginning, a middle and an end. Discuss your observations with your peers.

GHETTO DEFENDANT

"You earn respect in this life," says Springbok wing Ashwin Willemse. He's travelled a hard, painful road in search of it. And it nearly killed him …

SASI exclusive by MIKE BEHR

It's 9 pm and Ashwin Willemse's hotel room looks like a bomb has hit it. Clothes and kit are strewn all over the place. Free floor space is at such a premium that I have to use it as stepping stones to pick my way gingerly from the door to a chair on the other side of the room.

So too is fresh air. Before I can jump to any conclusions, Willemse explains that his hastily departing guest – who brushes past me at the door without introducing himself – is to blame for the cigarette smoke haze. Politely apologising for the inconvenience, Willemse opens a window into a relieving breeze.

The Bok flyer, however, takes the rap for the mess on the floor. His excuse is he has just moved rooms and hasn't had time to tidy up. (His World Cup squad roomie, Dale Santon, had been stricken by some sort of bug and Willemse wanted nothing of it.)

I can't help thinking Santon must be relieved to be rid of one seriously untidy bugger. Nor can I help wondering, in the wake of the Cronje-Davids matter, what the outside world would make of this innocent swap if either Santon or Willemse was white.

So what does Willemse think of the racial incident which allegedly tore the Bok camp in two before the tournament? I pop this question at the end of an astonishingly frank and personal interview. But it's the one thing Willemse is not willing to discuss. "I don't want to go there," he declares forthrightly.

Has he experienced any racism since joining the squad? "My personal experience is I've been treated as an equal. No-one has racially abused me or told me to carry bags or sit at the back of the bus."

Although I saw no evidence whatsoever of racial friction at the two Bok practices I watched, lunchtime told a different story. Any outsider walking into the team dining-room would have seen the squad's handful of black players seated together at a half-empty table on one side of the room, while the rest of the squad filled the tables on the other side.

"We just ended up sitting there," explains Willemse. "It's not always like that." Conceding the seating arrangements could be seen as segregated, he claims it's the result of the personal differences you find when any big group of people get together.

"I didn't always think like this," he confesses. "There were times when I thought a player was acting funny because he was racist."

That all changed for Willemse when the squad went into isolation in the bush, post-Cronjegate, for a gruelling four-day bonding session. "We went through a whole lot of stuff as a team which I'm not prepared to discuss. That's when perceptions changed for all the guys in the team. The stuff we did made me rethink that I'm seen as a person and not a black guy. That if Joost or the coach sh*ts on me, it's not because I'm black, but because I've done wrong."

Willemse's comments make interesting reading in the lead-up to the King inquiry into racism in South African rugby. But they're merely an aside to the blood, sweat and tears drama that eventually led to the speedy winger donning the green and gold.

To date the newspapers have depicted his story as a typical "ghetto kid makes good" tale: Caledon-born gangster finds redemption – and cash – in rugby. But the first-ever genuinely in-depth public revelations Ashwin Willemse makes about his troubled past, tell a story far more nuanced, far more profound, than that.

Born on 8 September 1981, Willemse remembers his childhood as a painful, bitter experience. Painful because he grew up never knowing his biological father, bitter because he struggled to come to terms with being poor.

Not dirt poor. As Willemse himself admits, there was always food on the table of the Swartland home that he, his mother and his younger brother shared with his grandmother, his aunt, his uncle and four cousins. But poor enough to always "want".

"You know what it's like being a kid," explains Willemse. "It's difficult to grow up 'without' … seeing other kids around you get what you want but cannot have because there is no money.

"I felt like I missed out on a lot of things. I never watched movies in a cinema. I never went to restaurants. And during school holidays, I worked on the farms or building sites to earn some extra cash because I didn't have pocket money. It was tough. Now and then my mom would have something to give me. She always tried her best to give me what she could. But in the end I just hustled my own way. I am still hustling. I will always be a hustler. I am still doing it to this day. The only difference is I'm in a bigger league."

Whenever Willemse talks about his mother it's in glowing, respectful terms. He's grateful she did her level best to raise him as an honest, God-fearing, conscientious boy. A boy, who by his own account, was good at heart, a decent learner and an excellent sportsman, particularly when it came to rugby and athletics.

But Willemse is also forgiving enough to understand the odds were stacked against a single mom who earned her keep as a hospital cleaner. Stacked not only when it came to meeting his material needs, but especially when it came to meeting the real source of his deprivation: an absent father.

"My mother is a million-dollar woman. I have a lot of respect for her. But sometimes she just didn't know how to cope with raising a boy. She didn't know how to respond to the way I was."

There are boys who cope without fathers. But there are also those who turn self-destructive. Ashwin Willemse was one of the latter. In primary school he began filling his emotional void with petty theft: R2 from his grandmother's purse, cold-drink bottles from people's houses and marbles from the local shop so he and his cousins could play a game most kids take for granted. "I can't remember the first thing I stole. All I know is I stole a lot of stuff."

By the time Willemse hit high school, stealing was as second nature as playing rugby. By Grade 9 he was into housebreaking and by the following year he was a gangster in the making.

"Gang life was always there," he explains. "It was part and parcel of growing up. It was in my face the whole time. There was always the temptation of the good life. Eventually gangsters become role models because they have achieved something."

Career advancement is only half the story. The truth is crime didn't sit easily with Willemse. As he himself admits, he came from a home where "respect and honesty were top of the game". And he had a mother who would have killed him had she got wind of his extra-mural activity.

So although Willemse started stealing to feel better about himself and his place in this world, the more he stole, the worse he felt. He was an addict caught up in a spiral of addiction that provided only fleeting highs.

By the age of 16, Ashwin Willemse felt so bad about himself that he decided to kill himself. His bombshell admission, made deep into the night after hours of gradually cathartic conversation, doesn't come easily. He's never talked about his suicide attempt before.

"I wasn't happy," he reveals. "All that pain and hatred was killing me inside. All that wanting to fit in and feeling like an outsider built up and up until it broke me down. Until I thought, f*ck, this life is not worth living."

An overdose of his grandmother's diabetic tablets – "I took handfuls of the stuff" – put Willemse in hospital for a week, a stay that was anything but cathartic. "Afterwards I couldn't talk about it," says Willemse.

"I've never been a speaker. It's not me to talk about things like that. I grew up learning you don't speak about emotions. I had to be hard ever since I was a small kid. If I spoke, I spoke to myself. If someone f*cked me up, I spoke to myself."

Lying in hospital, Willemse arrived at an awful conclusion. "I was all f*cked up. I didn't know which way to turn. And I know I had this new burden to face up to. At that stage I was Caledon Primary's star rugby player and top athlete. Even though I had f*ck all, it was the only thing I had. And then I went and f*cked it all up because I didn't die. The worst part of suicide was that I didn't die."

Going back to school and facing the shame and humiliation was one of Willemse's toughest times. "I don't wish that on any man. It was the worst thing ever. That's what cracked me up. That's when I thought, f*ck all this, I don't care what anyone thinks."

More angry and bitter than ever before, Willemse hooked up with the notorious Americans gang and plunged headlong into a life of hard crime and drug addiction.

"I started smoking buttons, rocks and dagga. I started living the high life and being a mean motherf***er." (Later, in the only ominous moment of the interview, Willemse claims he's more a gentleman than a mean motherf***er. "I can become a f*cking c*nt. If you're searching for the c*nt in me, you'll find it. But I will always stay a gentleman.") Just how mean he was, he's not prepared to say. "I did a whole lot of sh*t," he says, preferring to leave it up to the reader's imagination rather than provide gratuitous, headline-grabbing detail.

"The worst sh*t you can think of, I've done it. I just went straight to business. If you think of something I would do it. If you think go there, I was first to go."

In much the same way as Willemse is out to turn heads in the green and gold, he was intent on doing the same in the Americans' red, white and blue.

"I did it all just to make a stand," he confesses. "Not to people out there, but to my brothers in the camp. I wanted to show them look, f*ck, I'm down. I'm the man. You earn respect in this life. And I was there to earn respect."

For Willemse, gangsterism was a release. "It was like a vent. A place to get air to breathe. They didn't expect anything from me as a human being. They were like a family, like brothers. I loved them. I found a sense of trust. Being part of the Americans was like having a second home."

It could have so easily ended in a prison cell or a hail of bullets. As Willemse says, he's "looked down the barrel of a gun, been shot at and hit with a gun, and shot people". But throughout his wild and reckless years, Willemse somehow managed to stay safe.

You could attribute this to the values his mother drilled into him as a laaitie, but Willemse, as he frequently does when it comes to his achievements, credits God.

"God was good to me. A lot of my brothers got caught or got killed, but I stayed safe. The Lord guided me. All the time I was doing my sh*t I had this thing in my mind that this life wasn't for me. It might sound like bullsh*t, but I always had this feeling I was doing a job I didn't really want. That's why I never left school or stopped playing rugby. I'd be away for a few months in places like Woodstock and the (Cape) Flats, but I'd always come back to class for a few days.

"The teachers knew. But I was never bad to them. I showed them respect. I never lifted a hand to them. I called them Sir and Miss. And I always passed my exams. I was never stupid. I never failed a standard once. Even when I was doing drugs and gangs."

Willemse's family had their suspicions about his double life. But he managed to dupe them. Until the day his mother caught him in her home as high as a kite. "I checked her face and she was devastated. Seeing what I was doing to her was a turning point. From then on I decided to try live a good life."

Rehabilitation was a gradual process with a few epiphanies along the way, one of them being Craven Week 1999. "It was the first time I'd ever been in a provincial team," he recalls. "And it was an eye-opener. I suddenly realised, f*ck, you can make a living out of this and get self respect and self-esteem. All those things I was getting as a gangster I could get as a rugby player."

On the strength of Willemse's Craven Week performances, then-Boland coach Rudy Joubert invited the promising 18-year-old to join his training camp at the end of 1999. An invitation to join the Boland Academy followed shortly afterwards and Willemse moved away from Caledon and its gangs into Jack Abrahams House in Wellington.

As promising as he was, though, a contract didn't fall into Willemse's lap. "I went through a lot of sh*t at Boland. And it was tough. Often there's wasn't enough money to get home. I had to start hustling again. And I got back into drinking heavily and smoking dagga."

The difference this time round was the hustle. "Rugby was just another hustle: money was why I tried to make teams. And that wasn't easy with all the injuries I was picking up. For the first few years, I was constantly on the injury list. And it started to get to me. I started to feel like a failure. Eventually the constant pain got so bad all I could think of was quitting rugby."

Since donning the green-and-gold, a ball-in-hand Ashwin Willemse has given the constant impression that he never gives up. If you want to know where that comes from you only have to look behind the scenes, first when he made Chester Williams' sevens squad and then when he was called up for under-21 national duty.

Although he excelled under Williams, a persistent groin injury turned sevens into a nightmare. By 2002, the pain got so bad that Willemse was ready to hang up his boots for good. "I played prop because I couldn't run on the wing it was just so sore. I told Chester I was going to quit, but in the end I hung in there because of the money. I was always considering the next contract instead of my physical condition."

In spite of a six-month layoff, Jake White – his eye caught by Willemse's performance for Boland under-21s the previous year – picked the injured winger for his under-21 World Cup squad in 2002. While his teammates trained, the squad's physios worked round the clock to try to get a crippled Willemse up and running again.

A week before the U21 World Cup kick-off, on the last day of the Bok training camp in Hazyview, Willemse could no longer bear the pressure of the gamble. "I didn't want to end up more injured which would have put me out of the running for a Currie Cup contract," he explains.

"And I couldn't handle the thought of making a fool of myself on a World Cup stage." That night a devastated young man pulled out of the Under-21 World Cup in tears.

Back home the next day, Willemse got a call from White who persuaded him to return to the squad and give it his best shot. It echoed the advice of the Willemse family who were telling their son he had nothing to lose.

Talk is cheap when your body isn't on the line. "I have never endured so much pain as a player as I did during that tournament," reveals Willemse. "My first run in six months was against Romania. After that and every other match I had to have physio, not just for my groin, but for my whole body. My hamstrings and tendons felt tight, my shins ached, and my shoulders and back too. My whole body was out of alignment. I got knocks, lammies, every single thing. I never said anything, but it got so bad that the morning before every match, right up to the semis, I wanted to withdraw."

Showing huge courage, Willemse not only helped lift the World Cup, but ended up being one of the tournament's star players, even cracking the nod for the U21 World XV. Anyone else would take a deserved bow, but Willemse tips his hat at his Maker.

"The Lord got me through World Cup. It was just me and Him on that field. If you watched me closely you would have seen me talking a lot on the field. I was just praying all the way and asking Him for His help. I kept repeating this verse I once heard: 'When a man and his God face a mountain, all impossibilities vanish.' I just tried to play like there was no tomorrow and gave it everything I'd got."

Two weeks after World Cup, Sarfu flew Willemse to Johannesburg for surgery to repair a badly torn groin muscle that had deteriorated through incorrect conditioning and overuse.

"After my groin op, it felt as if I had been given a new life," says Willemse, who by now was convinced that his faith and his willpower could move any mountain.

"For the first time in my professional career, I started to enjoy my rugby again, not just because of the money, but also the love of the game. I look forward to practice and going out and enjoying games."

At first Willemse tried too hard on the Super 12 stage. "After 15 minutes on the field I was so *sat* I was almost in a coma," he recalls. "I looked into it more deeply and discovered it was because I was so stressed at wanting to be focused that it was draining me mentally and physically. I had to force myself to relax. Have you checked a sprinter when he sprints and how his cheeks wobble? It's because he is so relaxed. And that's how I decided to play my game."

After a cracking Super 12 for the Cats, all that stood between Ashwin Willemse and his Springbok début was veteran Pieter Rossouw who, as fate would have it, was injured.

He remembers his Bok baptism against Scotland in Durban in June as if it were yesterday. "Some people say I looked so calm, but I had some sh*t nerves that day," he recalls. "Afterwards I wrote that my stomach felt like a spring garden with all these butterflies flying around. (Penning thoughts and feelings on his new laptop alone in his room is how Willemse favours spending free time.)

"It's the first time in my entire life I felt like that. I felt special, but sh*t scared, not of my opponents, but the unknown and the chance I'd f*ck it up. Then the whistle went. People say your first Test is over before you know it. But it wasn't like that for me. I captured every single moment of that match. I didn't want it to end. For me it felt like a never-ending match."

Maintaining his good form, Willemse was one of few Boks to come out of a disastrous Tri-Nations with his reputation intact. A lot of that has to do with ever-growing confidence and a strong work ethic that spurns complacency.

Willemse hopes to be back in Johannesburg with the Cats in 2004, for more than one reason – he finally tracked down his dad this year a few days after scoring two tries in the Cats' victory over the Highlanders at Ellis Park.

The call was an emotionally-charged one. "I had a picture in my mind of how I would react, but when it happens you act differently. He spoke about my games, but I didn't have anything to say. I just cried." Since then father and son have maintained telephonic contact. Shortly before Willemse left for the World Cup, he made arrangements to hook up with his dad on his return. In spite of the past, he wants a relationship with his father.

"It was tough growing up without a father. From about the age of 14, I had a stepfather, but as hard as he tried, he couldn't fill the gap. I went through a lot of emotional pain that's still around today. But I'm not bitter about it. I don't even want to know why my father left. He's got his reasons and I respect them because I have dealt with the situation. Maybe if I wasn't as successful as I am now, I would have a lot of anger. But I don't."

Willemse doesn't want his lessons to go to waste. "I want to inspire young kids when I get back from World Cup. I want to visit schools and let them know that no matter how bad they're feeling there's always hope … that when they're feeling like there's no way out they must sit still and think of it this way: that Ashwin Willemse, who is a Bok today, also went through these emotions. And look where he ended up."

Used with permission

FROM THE NEWSROOM

Steve Smith on tackling sports journalism

After completing his BA (Hons) degree in political studies at UCT, Steve Smith gave up on his dreams of ruling the country and then the world to become a journalist. He was deputy editor of Sports Life *and* SL *magazines, the editor-in-chief of the Tiscali World Online portal, and is now editor of* SA Sports Illustrated *magazine.*

What do you think makes Mike Behr's feature "Ghetto Defender" an excellent example of good sports journalism?

Not only is Mike's feature a good piece of sports journalism, but it's a particularly good piece of sports magazine journalism. Before I tell you why though, it's important to understand the context in which *SA Sports Illustrated* magazine operates ...

We face an interesting dilemma – with the massive amount of sports consumed in this country (four to five dedicated satellite channels, three to five pages in the daily newspapers, plus some well-established and frequently-visited websites), what kind of information can we provide to sports fans that they've not already been exposed to? Add to that the fact that our national teams haven't been performing very well over the last five years means magazines like ours face a unique challenge within sports media.

Fortunately for us, sports fans remain sports fans ... they may become unhappy sports fans, but they don't, for example, become knitting fans.

As a magazine, we need to provide information that adds to the fundamental focus of a sports fan, i.e. watching the game live or on the telly. As opposed to a match report you'd read in the papers, our well-researched and in-depth magazine articles provide background information that equips our readers with in-depth knowledge that gives them a higher appreciation of what they're watching. Simply put – the more you know about a sport, the more you are going to enjoy it.

What the "Ghetto Defender" story also did was help create a real South African sports hero – a pretty rare phenomenon in our country. Members of our national rugby and cricket teams are a fairly two-dimensional bunch who are tightly controlled by their unions. They are scared of saying the wrong thing and, consequently, you rarely get anything more than a predictable soundbyte out of them.

Thanks to Ashwin's courage and Mike's skill as a writer, the story revealed an aspect of the Bok winger no-one knew about. It showed us that heroes aren't necessarily people who win all the time – heroes are also people that fans can identify with. They are people that have tasted defeat but still display their human qualities of courage, resilience, determination, and the ability to overcome adversity.

Are there unique challenges that sports journalists face?

In this country, definitely. As I mentioned earlier, our guys are so scared of saying anything other than the safe soundbyte that it's really hard to get a genuinely interesting story. The juicy comments and insights only come from ex-players who are out of the game. You can't blame the current players; I mean, why should they jeopardise their livelihoods?

The real challenge is dealing with the admin bodies like the UCB [United Cricket Board], SARFU [South African Rugby Football Union] and SAFA [South African Football Association]. They've hardly had impressive track records over the last decade. Taking them to task is the biggest challenge.

What advice do you have for would-be sports journalists?

Be consistent and honest in your writing. And make it clear that a love of SA sport is what drives you. It should be a tough love: one that necessitates you asking tough questions when you need to, but readers should understand that while you may be raising something controversial, it's with a view of seeing an improvement in SA sport.

There's no question that a nation's sporting success has a tremendous impact on social unity. Our rugby World Cup victory in '95 is the perfect example. We need to help rehabilitate SA sport and I believe this means SA sports writers have a very important social responsibility.

EXERCISE *Are you ready to work as a freelancer?*

Are you ready to work from home as a freelance writer? Why don't you take this quiz to double-check: http://freelancewrite.about.com/library/quiz/blworkfromhome.htm.

In this chapter, you learned that:

- Working as a freelance is a viable option – and sometimes a necessity – for media writers.
- Successful freelancers have talent and also understand the process of getting work published.
- Amongst the specific challenges self-employed media specialists face is that they can become isolated and, according to the South African Freelance Association (Safrea), can find themselves at the mercy of unscrupulous employers who pay badly, take a long time to process payments and ignore copyright laws. Knowing how the freelance commissioning and payment process works and networking with others, such as Safrea members, helps balance the scales.
- The hourglass form can be helpful in structuring profile feature stories, amongst others.

Putting your learning to work

ACTIVITY 1 Pitching for freelance work

Choose a local magazine or website that publishes the stories that you like to read. Analyse the publication carefully (see the guide in Chapter 8, p.197) and then see if you can come up with a story idea. (For a reminder of techniques for developing story ideas and reporting plans, see Chapter 8.) Next, write up a story pitch or query letter. Discuss it with your peers and then send it off.

ACTIVITY 2 Writing for publications beyond the borders

The mass media, Canadian scholar and commentator Marshall McLuhan said, has transformed the world into a "global village". For freelance writers that means there are opportunities to sell stories beyond the country's physical borders. A good place to find some of these is in the Writer's Market, which has been decribed as the "bible" of freelance writers. Sign up for a one-month contract which, at the time of writing, cost US$2.99 [about R22] at http://www.writer'smarket.com/ and identify three potential markets for a version of the story used for the basis of your pitch in Activity 1.

HOT LINK

Want to see an example query letter? See: http://freelancewrite.about.com/library/samples/blsamplemag-querylt.htm.

Bibliography

Alexander, S.M. [No date] *Freelance journalism top ten tips ... and then some* [Online] Available at: http://www.claricomm.com/fw_tips.shtml [Accessed: 18 August 2004]

Anon [No date] *Kamp Staaldraad*. The Real Facts Contribution Company. [Online] Available at: http://www.therfcc.org/kamp-staaldraad-200877.html [Accessed: 18 August 2004]

Behr, M. 2003. Ghetto defendant. *South African Sports Illustrated*. December 2003: 30–38.

Willenberg, K. 2001/2. Introduction to copyright. South African Scriptwriters' Association. [Online] Available at: http://www.saswa.org.za/article_copyright.htm [Accessed: 19 August 2004]

10 Editing

Introduction

The typical newspaper editor's job has little to do with editing stories. Instead, much of the editor's energy is spent managing staff, budgets and relationships with key people outside the newsroom. The day-to-day job of getting stories into the newspaper falls to those with composite titles – news editors, business editors, features editors, sports editors, business editors, and the like. They make the bulk of the decisions about which events get covered and who does it. At their best, story editors are coaches.

Once the stories are written and the photographs taken, the material is sent off to the sub-editors (also called *copy editors*) for polishing. Facts are checked. Missing information is questioned. Legal and ethical concerns are raised. Awkward structure is fixed. Spelling and grammar are repaired. Headlines and captions are written. It is a thankless job a lot of the time. There are no Pulitzer Prizes for sub-editing. Like the goalkeeper who only gets attention when he misses a block, sub-editors usually are in the spotlight only when there is a problem with a story, headline or caption.

This is why the best sub-editors are experienced reporters who are well-informed language experts and, as veteran editor Arthur Plotnik suggests, compulsive (1982:1). Of course, there is good compulsiveness and bad compulsiveness. Sub-editors who are compulsive about the wrong things – like holding to favourite rules of usage, whatever the effect on communication – make life unnecessarily tough on reporters.

Good sub-editors are compulsive about serving readers. "Functional or reader-related compulsiveness is the neurotic drive enabling editors to do a full six weeks of work in a four-week cycle, month after month," says Plotnik (1982:2). "It is the built-in alarm, the timebomb system that glows red when there are omissions, delays and errors which, if not corrected, will devastate deadlines and subvert communications."

But leaving the accuracy of a story to the sub-editors alone is (to continue our soccer metaphor) much like holding the goalkeeper responsible for the final score. The best defence against errors is to ensure that they don't creep into your story in the first place. The best way to prevent that from happening is for you to work closely with your assigning editor during the reporting and writing process – and to check your own work closely before passing it along.

LEARNING GOALS

At the end of this chapter, you should be able to:

1 Identify how newsroom coaching can improve your reporting and writing.
2 Guide sub-editing compulsiveness in four areas:
  a Stories.
  b Headlines.
  c Captions.
  d Proofreading.

Coaching writers, polishing stories

Story editing is about more than simply assigning reporters to tasks and fixing stories when they're submitted. At its best, editing is about coaching writers throughout the whole process. The process begins with the idea, or assignment. At the other end is the story draft (see Chapter 5).

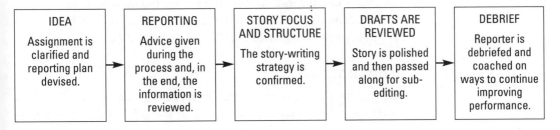

IDEA	REPORTING	STORY FOCUS AND STRUCTURE	DRAFTS ARE REVIEWED	DEBRIEF
Assignment is clarified and reporting plan devised.	Advice given during the process and, in the end, the information is reviewed.	The story-writing strategy is confirmed.	Story is polished and then passed along for sub-editing.	Reporter is debriefed and coached on ways to continue improving performance.

Figure 10.1 "The central job of the editor is to help the writer to produce a better story," says veteran editor and advocate of newsroom coaching, Bruce DeSilva (Grimm, 1998).

Newsroom coaches can look to their sports counterparts for guidance. A soccer coach, for example, stays off the pitch when a game is played. He [or she] is confined to selecting the team and preparing the players.

Before kick-off, he clarifies the game plan for each fixture. Then he sends the team onto the field with a few words of encouragement. During the match, he's on the sidelines, watching. Interventions are limited: a nod; a hand gesture; perhaps some advice is called out. Under-performing and injured players are substituted. At half-time, he meets with the team in private. Questions are asked; the game plan is revised; recommendations are made. The players take a breather, grab a drink and then head out for the final challenge. After the match is over, the coach and players meet to debrief. Performances are reviewed – including those of the opposition. Backs are patted and butts are kicked, as appropriate. Then, the focus moves to the next match.

The finest coaches care about the game, the team, and the individuals. Yes, they confront, cajole and challenge the players. But coaches recognise that the way to get the best performance – and the most effort – from everyone is to inspire them. Intimidating or humiliating players is shortsighted.

The coaching process in the newsroom can work in much the same way.

Pre-game: Before the reporters head out, the editors consider all the imperatives – the newsworthy events, the editorial space, the deadlines, the available staff – and then assign the stories.

"Follow that murder."

"Cover the press conference."

"Let's do something on drugs (or the new mall, the election, the weather)."

What about the drugs, the mall, the weather? Which of all possible angles do we choose? Assigning stories is not simply about shouting out topics, instead, it is about developing ideas (see p.122). That is done through conversation.

Editor and reporter need to talk about the possibilities, and settle on an idea before the investigation begins. For the most part, editors need to ask questions. And listen to the answers. Writing coach Chip Scanlan suggests you start with this one: "How can I help?" (2003).

The first half

During the newsgathering stage, the reporting team are mostly left on their own. They may call in or stop by the editor's desk to offer an update. Perhaps to ask for advice.

Half-time

Once the reporter has gathered much of the information required, it's time to find a focus and plot the story structure. It's time to ask some tough questions (Scanlan, 2002):

1 Why does it matter?
2 What's the point?
3 Why is this story being told?
4 What does it say about life, about the world, about the times we live in?

"Newspaper writing, especially on deadline, is so hectic and complicated – the fact-gathering, the phrase-finding, the inconvenience, the pressure – that it's easy to forget the basics of storytelling," Von Drehle wrote in an essay published in *Best Newspaper Writing 1995* (quoted in Scanlan, 2002). "Namely, what happened, and why does it matter?"

"Reporters in particular need to ask – and answer – those questions before they write their story," says Scanlan. "Again, I think **freewriting** often produces surprising insights and prose that, while not perfect, can be polished. More than once, I've seen reporters scribble answers that surprise their colleagues – and themselves – with their raw eloquence." Sometimes answers are elusive, Scanlan acknowledges, but the questions have to be addressed since those are the questions that readers and viewers bring to the news.

This technique, Scanlan says, is especially useful for reporters struggling to write a nut graf as well as those who are struggling with focus. When they finish answering the four questions, editors should ask them, "What's your story about – in one word?" The critical thinking that went into answering the four questions often brings them to a sharper understanding of their story's theme.

We live in an age awash with information but, argues Jack Fuller in his book *News Values: Ideas for an Information Age*, "readers don't just want random snatches of information flying at them from out of the ether. They want information that hangs together, makes sense, has some degree of order to it. They want knowledge rather than just facts, perhaps even a little wisdom" (1996:227).

Second half

Once the first draft is written, Scanlan (2002) recommends asking the following two questions to drive the revision:
1 What works?
2 What needs work?

His argument: "Underlying the first question is the notion that writers build first upon success that, once identified, can be repeated. Also, because many writers arrive for a story conference exhausted, pessimistic and insecure about the quality of their work (although they may mask it with bravado, indifference or defensiveness), focusing on what works may give them a much-needed confidence booster.

Definition

Freewriting means simply that you write without stopping. It is a way to break the habit of trying to write and edit at the same time. The idea isn't to produce a polished (or even "good") piece of writing, but to simply get in the habit of writing without censoring and editing. In freewriting, says Peter Elbow, the author of *Writing without teachers*, you don't stop to look back to cross out something, to wonder how to spell something, to wonder what word or thought to use, or to think about what you are doing. The only rule of freewriting is this: keep writing (1973).

HOT LINK

"How can I help?" Chip Scanlan of the Poynter Institute says he usually approaches coaching writers by first asking that question, and then listening to the answer. He thinks of it as "The Coaching Way." Read his first-rate advice – and links to tips from other newsroom coaches – at: http://poynteronline.org/column.asp?id=52&aid=33974.

"Even though I ask them what needs work, reporters often frame the second question as 'What doesn't work?' It's a subtle difference but an important one that reflects the need for optimism as the writer enters the revision stage. More important, it allows the reporter, rather than the editor/teacher/coach, to identify elements that need revision. The conference becomes less a battle of wills than collaboration between writer and reader" (2002).

Post-game debrief

Editors can help writers reach deeper levels of understanding about their stories by using a basic journalistic tool: open-ended questions, says Scanlan (2002).(Of course, writers can ask themselves these questions too.)

- **What surprised you about this?**
  "Good writers never lose their sense of wonder," says Scanlan (2002). "This question is designed to help writers cultivate ongoing interest and curiosity."

- **What lesson did you learn from this?**
  "Critical thinking," says Richard Paul of the Center for Critical Thinking and Moral Critique, (quoted in Scanlan 2002), "is thinking about your thinking while you're thinking in order to make your thinking better." This question prompts reporters to think about – and track – their own learning.

- **What do you need to learn next?**
  "Learning to write well is a journey, not a destination," says Scanlan. "This question helps reporters create their own paths for continuing education" (2002).

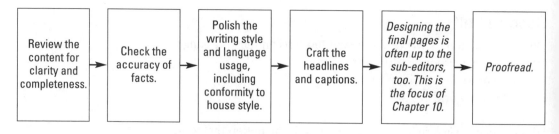

Figure 10.2 Good sub-editors are compulsive about getting the details right.

Sub-editing the content

Begin sub-editing by folding your hands.

Now, read – or at least scan – the whole article. Before you start fiddling, you need to have an idea of what the writer set out to accomplish. If you're the writer, you need to see if all the bits you have been working on hold together as a logical whole. Good grammar, perfect spelling and solid facts are useless if the story doesn't make sense.

When editing a story's content, ask the following questions:

- Focus   What is the point of the story?
- Clarity   Is that point spelt out in the lead or nut graph?
- Information   Is there enough information to back up the point?
- Logic   Is the information arranged in a logical order?
- Balance   Are opinions clearly distinguished from fact? Is more than one side of the argument presented or at least acknowledged?
- Originality   Is the information fresh and the perspective innovative?

Check for accuracy

Accuracy isn't negotiable. It is the foundation on which the trust in the media is built. Without the trust of sources, reporters find it difficult (if not impossible) to access information for stories. Without complete and accurate stories, the media won't win the long-term trust of audiences – and might even face crippling legal action. Without significant audiences, the publication won't attract the circulation and advertising it needs to be viable. If the publication isn't viable, you (and your colleagues) are likely to be without a job.

Of course, newsroom managers typically work hard to secure the well-being of their products. As such, those who put that at risk are typically purged from the system before they bring down the entire operation. So, if you aim to have a long and rewarding career in this field, ensuring that the information in your stories – and those you edit – is accurate is something you cannot ignore.

The *Sunday Times* accuracy check is a good way to make sure you have considered this point thoroughly.

SUNDAY TIMES ACCURACY CHECK	
REPORTER:	
NEWS EDITOR:	
CHECKER:	
SLUG:	
SYNOPSIS OF STORY:	

CHECKLIST

Are all names correct and spelt correctly?	
Are all figures, including percentages, correct?	
Are all dates and ages correct?	
Are the facts correct (Are there two sources)?	
Are quotations correct (check against notebook)?	

CONTENT

Are you satisfied that the story is accurate?	
Are you satisfied that it is angled correctly?	
Are you satisfied that it is fair to all parties?	
Did you contact all parties involved?	
If not, what steps did you take to contact them?	
Are we being fair to the subject?	
Have you put the subject's comments/denial high up in the report, or have you simply added them/it at the bottom of the report?	

LEGALS

What legal problems do you foresee?	
Were you threatened with legal action?	
Does this report need to be checked by lawyers?	
Is this a pending case?	
Is this report based on documents merely filed in court or based on documents referred to in open court?	
Do you have all the necessary documents to back up your report?	

Are they authentic?	
If you are investigating the directors of a company, have you checked the facts with the Registrar of Companies?	
If so, can you produce the documents?	
ADDITIONAL CHECKING	
Do you object to us contacting your source/s for checking?	
Do you object to them receiving a questionnaire?	
DATABASE	
Have you entered all your contacts into the *Sunday Times* database?	
SIGNED:	
REPORTER:	
CHECKER:	
DATE:	

Posted at: http://www.sanef.org.za/ethics_codes/sunday_times/277060.htm

Polish the language

Having adequate information logically arranged is crucial to a good story. But it is not enough. Like spinach, a story is seldom consumed merely for its intrinsic value; it must taste good, too. That is the writer's challenge. Editors' concern with language leads them to consider grammar and spelling, the general conventions of journalistic writing, and the specific conventions of the medium, also referred to as the house style. And, of course, the editors are looking to see if it's a story well told.

███ LINK

Following the law, following your conscience. Stories may be accurate and well-crafted, and may still violate legal and ethical principles. Sub-editors need to flag those, too. For more on these points see Chapter 13.

Editing for language means asking the following questions:

Language use checklist

- Is the information presented in a way that will involve the reader?
- Is the tone of writing appropriate for the intended medium?
- Does the lead draw you into the article?
- Is the lead clear?
- Has the writer used common, concrete words?

"Language provides the medium of conscious life, and those professionally concerned with it ought often to point this out. If language becomes truly unexpressive, we indeed become a mob ..."

RICHARD A. LANHAM IN STYLE: AN ANTI-TEXTBOOK (1974:1)

- Is the writing concise, free from needless words?
- Are the sentences instantly clear, free from confusing constructions?
- Are most of the sentences in the active voice?
- Are the sentences and ideas linked by transitions?
- Has a grammar and spelling check been carried out?
- Does the piece conform to the house style?

Editing for style

Most newspapers, magazines and websites have their own style guides – sets of guidelines telling journalists whether to write *Celsius* or *centigrade, Amabokoboko* or *amaBoko-boko*. Style refers not only to uniformity, but also to clarity. Both aspects are important, and both rely on a solid understanding of the rules of English grammar.

As in fashion, style rules in the media vary greatly – as do editors' support of them. "Some don't think it's important," says Louis Boccardi. "Some agree that basically there should be uniformity for reading ease if nothing else. Still others are prepared to duel over a wayward lower case."

Boccardi's observations are in the foreword to the Associated Press' stylebook which, with the United Press International's stylebook, is the major source of American newspaper style. In the United Kingdom, *The Economist*'s stylebook is one of the yardsticks.

Whatever their opinion of specific points of style, those who care about communicating have at least this in common: George Orwell. His essay "Politics and the English Language" was first published in 1946 and has been widely circulated and quoted ever since. Orwell's six elementary rules are still relevant (Orwell and Angus, 1968):

HOT LINK

Read George Orwell's essay on "Politics and the English Language." It is posted at http://www.resort.com/~prime8/Orwell/patee.html.

1 *Never use a metaphor, simile or other figure of speech that you are used to seeing in print.*
2 *Never use a long word when a short one will do.*
3 *If it is possible to cut a word out, always cut it out.*
4 *Never use the passive where you can use the active.*
5 *Never use a foreign phrase, a scientific word or a jargon word if you can think of an everyday English equivalent.*
6 *Break any of these rules sooner than say anything outright barbarous.*

Some general peculiarities of journalistic writing

The language many newspapers are written in today has its roots in the 1920s, 1930s and 1940s, when newspapers began to standardise the presentation of information to a public that still got most of its news from the press. In those days, newspaper leads worked much as today's television and radio summaries. As American columnist Charles McDowell, who is a leading critic of newspapers' "artificial" prose, points out: "We jab, hit, lambast ... We have peculiar adjective clauses: 'The remarried, 25-year-old mother of three'" (Teel and Taylor, 1988:165).

The traditional newspaper language is much the language of headlines. The news story is a form of abbreviation and contraction of sentences (Teel and Taylor, 1988:166). Here are some of the peculiarities of newspaper writing, including techniques journalists use to make their writing shorter and tighter:

The reporter does not editorialise

A news reporter's job is to report on the action, not take part in it. Consequently, he does not use I, me, my, we, us or our in a news story except when quoting someone. (Certain types of byline stories are exceptions to this rule; see the discussion of 'voice' on p.113.).

- Instead of: The lawyer lost his temper.
  Say: The lawyer threw down his pen.
- Instead of: She is well qualified for the job.
  Say: She is a graduate of the University of Zululand and has 10 years' experience.

Eliminate unnecessary words

Connectives – the word "that" is one of the frequent syntactical interruptions to be avoided.

- Instead of: Cronjé said that he was not a crook.
  Change to: Cronjé said he was not a crook.

Clauses
- Instead of: The man who was driving the car ...
  Change to: The man driving the car ...
  or: The driver ...

Unnecessary articles
- Instead of: The union members attended the meeting.
  Say: Union members attended the meeting.
- Instead of: He returned a part of the money.
  Say: He returned part of the money.*

** Only unnecessary articles
should be avoided. For
example, the article in "He
returned part of the money"
cannot be cut. This also
applies to "a" and "an".*

Lengthy word forms
- Instead of: The union will hold a meeting.
  Say: The union will meet.
- Instead of: The judge arrived at a decision.
  Say: The judge decided.

Adjectives, adverbs, prepositions
- Instead of: The men were completely irrational.
  Say: The men were irrational.
- Instead of: He stepped off of the platform.
  Say: He stepped off the platform.

Phrases
- Instead of: The tests took a period of 10 days.
  Say: The tests took 10 days.

Redundancies
- Instead of: Past experience taught her how to react.
  Say: Experience taught her how to react.

Making a positive out of a negative

Convert negatives to positives? No, we're not suggesting that you convert copy into so-called "good news". Instead, try to figure out a way to say what is, instead of what isn't, suggests Laurie Hertzel of the *Minneapolis Star Tribune* (Hatcher, 2002). Saying what *is* is usually shorter, clearer and more direct. (Obviously, there are times when for various reasons you want to break this rule, as I did above.)

Look for "not" and "wasn't" (or "isn't") or "no" and see if it makes sense to redraft.

- Instead of:"   The movie wasn't engaging and most people didn't stay for the end."   .
  Say: "The movie was dull and people left early."
  or
- Instead of: The City Council vote was not unanimous."
  Say: "The council's vote was divided."

E**X**ERCISE *Making positives out of negatives*

Go through an article and find "negatives," sentences that talk about things that aren't. See if they can be reworded to be positive statements.

Journalese consists of jargon and clichés that are particularly cherished by journalists. Audiences look to the media for new information and fresh perspectives; copy riddled with clichés won't convince them that your efforts will deliver.

Here are some of the prime examples of journalese; the preferred – and often much simpler – words are in parentheses:

Avoid these clichés	Instead use
Burgeoning	Growing
Constructed of	Made of
Conservative estimate	Estimate, opinion, guess
Cutback	Cut
Filled to capacity	Filled
Give consideration to	Consider
Hit by fears that	Fear
In order to	To
In the light of	Because
Left much to be desired	Unsatisfactory
Left people dead/angry/hurt	People are dead/angry/hurt
Major	Big, large
Massive	Big
Meaningful	Real, significant
OKs, okays	approves
Parameters	Limits
Probe	Inquiry

▓HOT LINK

Banished words

For 25 years, Michigan's Lake Superior State College has been issuing annual lists of "Words Banished from the Queen's English for Mis-Use, Over-Use and General Uselessness." If something shows up on the list, chances are you might want to keep it out of your publication. Some banished words from 2004:

- **X** – "Marketers have latched onto this letter to grab the "Generation-X" demographic. X-files, Xtreme, Windows XP and X-Box are all part of this PR-powered phenomenon," said John Casnig of Kingston, Ontario.
- **LOL** and other abbreviated "e-mail speak", including the symbol "@" when used in advertising and elsewhere – Alex G. of Warsaw, Poland, says, "It's everywhere on the net! OMG! u r chattin to sum1 then …lol this and lol that …Get it away!"
- **Shots rang out** – I'm tired of hearing this phrase on the news. Shots don't "ring" unless you are standing too close to the muzzle, and in that case you don't need the reporter telling you about it." Michael Kinney, Rockville, Maryland.

Check out the latest list at: www.lssu.edu/banished .

EXERCISE *Editing for style*

Correct the following sentences, where necessary:
a) She moved to RSA.
b) The deadline was extended from Jan. 15, to 12 Apr.
c) He was described as a Greek God.
d) "let's have a coke," the barman said.
e) They said they would be there at seven p.m., but did not arrive until 8.
f) He rode down Fourth St.
g) "Mister Livingston, I presume"?
h) She is an out of town guest.
i) I love 60's music even more than 80's music.
j) Who wrote Long walk to freedom?

See Appendix C: Style guide on p. 383 for correct answers. Topics covered include: abbreviations, capitalisation, numerals, punctuation, spelling, expletives, and obscenities.

Crafting headlines

The "writing" portion of a sub-editor's job generally consists mainly of headlines and captions. It's no small challenge. The best stories in the world are worthless if no one reads them. The job of "selling" the story falls, in large part, to the headline.

Choosing the right words is a challenge. The headline writer's job is further complicated by design considerations: space, which depends on the number of columns the headline must cover, and the typeface and point size in which it is being written. Sometimes there is only enough space for two or three words to a line, or maybe half a dozen words for headlines that are stacked several column lines deep. Editors must also decide if they want to use all capitals or caps and lowercase.

These are the basic combinations:
- **All caps**

  ANOTHER STUDENT VANISHES FROM BOND CAMPUS

  Tests show that all-caps headlines are difficult to read (Harriss et. al., 1992:448). However, they can be effective when used for single-word or short-phrase headlines like "WE WON" or "DISASTER". These punchy headlines, often referred to as "hammer headlines", are usually packaged with kickers.

- **Caps and lowercase**
  The standard style is to capitalise only the first letter of each word:

  Botswana Under Pressure Over Peacekeeping Role

  Another headline style requires that conjunctions, prepositions and definite and indefinite articles also be in lower case.
- **Down style**
  This is a popular contemporary option, where only the first word and proper names are capitalised:

  Nothing to celebrate on this Heritage Day

"Simplicity" is the buzzword in modern design. For headline writers this means shorter main heads and fewer, if any, secondary headlines. Some newspapers avoid stacked headlines entirely. Most headlines are simply one line and flushed left. This is not just an aesthetic decision. Edmund Arnold, whose *Modern Newspaper Design* is something of a bible in the field, says: "To the best of the knowledge that we have at this time, flush-left setting is the most effective for heads, for it is based on the instinctive pattern when the reading eye moves" (1969).

Here are some of the most common headline designs:
- **Flush left**

  Headline type
  is aligned with the left-hand
  margin of the column

- **Flush right**

  Type is aligned with
  the right-hand edge
  of the column

  The result is a ragged left edge, which can be difficult to read.

- **Centred**

  Often, centred heads
  are arranged in a
  pyramid
  form
- **Drop or stepped lines**

  Two or three lines of approximately the same length
  are arranged with the first line flushed left,
  the last one flushed right and the centre line centred

** **Design** If the publication doesn't have a specific layout and design team, the task of putting together the pages often falls to the sub-editor. For a basic introduction to typography and layout, see Chapter 12.*

- **Hanging indents**

  The first line is flush left
      and the others,
      of equal length,
      are indented at
      the same space

- **Kickers**

      Some headlines are written with secondary headlines
          or kickers above
        The main headline

- **Reverse kickers**

          In these headlines
      the subsidiary line is run below the main headline

Tips for writing better headlines

A headline's job is pretty straightforward: it should let readers know how the story differs from previous stories on similar topics, and arouse their interest anew.

In Cape Town, known as the Cape of Storms, this *Cape Times* headline "Storm lashes Cape" (1993:1) arouses only a sense of déjà vu. And it does little to sell a story which starts this way:

> The storm-bruised Cape Peninsula continued to be lashed by gale force winds and rain that have already claimed the life of a father of two, ripped tiles off roofs, uprooted trees and kept fishing trawlers in the harbour. And the storm, with winds gusting to up 70 knots, is showing no sign of abating.
>
> A weather forecaster at [Cape Town International] Airport said last night that more cold fronts, accompanied by strong winds, are expected today.

Of course, the story has its own problems. Not the least of which is that the lead contains not a single item of information that would have been new to Cape Town readers, experiencing the third day of the storm for themselves; the man had died two days earlier and it is unlikely Capetonians would have needed to read the newspaper to tell them the stormy weather had continued.

The headline "Storm forecast: more ahead" zooms in on the latest information – the news – and summarises the story.

Be careful with cuteness

Magazines, especially, often use puns in their headlines. Consider these examples from the *Sunday Times Lifestyle* magazine (June 13, 2004):

> **Tap Tap dancing; in search of a boxing legend**

(for a story about Tap Tap Makhathini)

> **NOT SARAFINISHED YET**

(for an interview feature on Mbongeni Ngema, creator of the Broadway hit "Sarafina").

> **Graham Greene's purple patch**

(for a story about the acclaimed novelist's flawed attempts at crafting lyrics)

Poor puns are not funny – at best they are irritating, at worst they are insulting, both to the readers and the subjects of the stories.

Don't overstate the story

There is something far worse than an unimaginative or 'punny' headline: a dishonest one.

"Death in the suburbs" might be a technically correct way of summarising a story about a dog's untimely death under a car wheel. But it is an exaggeration. If a reader feels cheated by a headline, she – like any other customer – is likely to think twice before buying the publication again. Rule: do not cry wolf.

Each headline writer develops his own techniques, but there are some general principles. Some of the following are pointed out by Julian Harriss et al. in their book, *The Complete Reporter* (1992:451–2):

- **Headlines should be a complete sentence with the unnecessary words omitted:**
  Poor: Man sustains fatal injury
  Better: Guard killed in gun fight

- If a headline is stacked, each deck must be a full statement and stand alone:

  Poor: HUGE OIL SLICK
              100 MILES LONG
              Reported by
              Navy Ship
  Better: HUGE OIL SLICK
              THREAT TO COAST
              covers 100 miles,
              reports Navy

- Do not repeat a thought or word:

  Poor: THE MAD WORLD OF
              PETROL ECONOMICS
              Petrol pricing confuses consumers
  Better: THE MAD WORLD OF
              PETROL ECONOMICS
              a pricing guide for
              confused consumers

- Include a verb so that the headline does not appear merely as a label. The verb should be in the first line if possible, but a heading should not start with a verb.

  Poor: New highway
  Better: New highway opens
  Poor: Planned food scheme for city's needy
  Better: Food scheme planned for city's needy

- Use the active voice for impact:

  Poor: Strikers warned by Minister
  Better: Minister warns strikers

- Use specific language

  Poor: Youth injured in knife battle
  Better: Youth slashed in knife fight

- Use single quotation marks in headlines:

  Poor: "Heaven help us"
  Better: 'Heaven help us'

- Avoid using acronyms. Brevity is important, but do not compromise clarity. A headline like 'TRC: TLC A.S.A.P' might save space, but few people will understand it. Use only the most common acronyms. Advice: Do not use acronyms that have been in common use for less than a year.

- Words, phrases consisting of nouns and adjective modifiers, prepositional phrases and verb phrases should not be split between lines:

  Poor: Council passes sales tax
              despite protest
  Better: Sales tax passes despite protest

- **Opinion headlines should be attributed or qualified:**
  Poor: Taxes too high on business
  Better: Taxes too high say businessmen

Crafting captions

What is the caption's job? Firstly, a caption needs to help clarify the story being told in the pictures. And, like stories, captions come in a variety of formats and styles. Let's take a look at a standard approach:

overline

main body

credit line

BLIND COURAGE Vukani Simelela, 54, with her twin sons Sipho, left, and Fikele this week in Cape Town. Vukani, who has been blind since she was 30, reached the summit of Table Mountain during a recent expedition with her two sons. (Photo by Eric Malema.)

The various parts of the caption are as follows:
- **The overline (Zu. *Amagama ahehayo* / Afr. *vet koppie*)**
  "Blind Courage". A few bright words to draw the reader's attention and put across the point of the picture. Use verbs in overlines, avoid labels and dull phrases.
- **Main body of caption**
  "Vukani Simelela, 54, with her twin sons Sipho, left, and Fikele ..." When there are more than two people in the picture, identifying one as "left" and the other as "centre" leaves the understanding that the third person is the one on the right. In the example above, Vukani is in the centre of the picture and is obviously the focus of the picture, and there is unlikely to be confusion since she is also the only woman.

  If there are a number of people in a photograph and they are roughly in a line, a convenient way to identify them is "from left", followed by their names. For example: Registering for classes at the Mandela Metropolitan University are, from left, Daniella Arendse, Nonceba Silwana, Luthando Makoliso and Dominique Wolf.

  When there are several rows, continue with the "from left" format, but break down the identification to front, centre and back rows. Start with the front row since readers usually focus there first.

  Occasionally – thanks to inventive photographers – the subjects in a group are roughly in a circle. A helpful way to identify the people is to say "clockwise, beginning at the top with ...". Readers, asked to examine the photograph as they would a clock, usually expect to begin at "12 o'clock".

- **Credit lines**

  "(Photo by Eric Malema.)" Photographers get credit lines the way reporters get bylines. Publications vary in their policy on giving credit and, at some house journals and newspapers, the sources are not credited at all, or only receive credit for exceptional work.

- **Typography and layout (Zu.** *Indlela yokubhala nokuhleleka* **/ Afr.** *tipografie en uitleg***)**

  Many publications choose to set captions in italics, boldface or a font that is different from the body type. Credit lines can be set with the rest of the caption; however, some publications choose to set them in very small type (4 or 6 point) and place them directly below the photograph.

EXERCISE *Classifying captions*

Magazine consultant John Fry (1988:160) has recognised at least eight types of captions:

1 Identifying captions – what you see.
2 Information captions – more about what you see.
3 Teaser captions – to entice readers into the text.
4 Pull-quote captions – what the person says (a variation on teasers).
5 Questioning captions – draw attention to something in the picture.
6 Mood-evoking captions – reflect and enhance the mood of the photograph.
7 Headline, blurb – serves as a caption where none is necessary.
8 Sidebars and short text items – where text surrounds a photo.

Task: Browse through a magazine or newspaper and see if you can identify examples of the different types of captions. What type was used most often? Which was the most effective caption you came across?

Tips for writing better captions

Successful captions match the mood of the story and the image – and they don't repeat obvious information.

Writing captions (sometimes called *cutlines*) is an art. The reason so few journalists master it is because, for the most part, so little time is spent at it (Goldstein, 1992:268). But writing good captions is no mystery. Following a few basic guidelines (listed below), together with a touch of writing flair, can produce readable and informative captions.

Whatever their specific function, all captions have this in common: they aim to supplement and even explain the pictures – they should not repeat obvious information in the photograph.

For a story on Johannesburg fashion designer Nkhensai Manganyi (Rossouw, 2004), *Time* magazine ran a deep-etched photograph of a model showing off the Stoned Cherrie range, as well as a headshot of the designer. The single caption read:

CLOTHES ON THE MOVE: Drawing on the 1950s, Manganyi (inset) is changing the way South African women dress.

Do not restate the obvious ("Model wears clothes by Manganyi") or the like.

- While brevity is essential, captions should not be telegraphic and omit words that are important for smooth reading.
- Tense is important. Captions should be in the present tense even though the publication date may be different from the picture's action. The photograph captured a moment and froze the action.
  Write: King Goodwill Zwelethini tells a crowd at ...
  Not: King Goodwill Zwelethini told a crowd at ...
- People in the pictures should be identified by their full names and some description.
- Subjects should be identified as to their position in the picture, because many readers will probably not know them well enough to recognise them.
- When a story accompanies the photograph, the caption should not repeat lengthy facts from the article: captions are not expected to be a summary, but a supplement. However, readers should not have to read the story before they understand the significance of the photograph; people are more likely to look at a newspaper photograph than to read the copy. Photographs are usually the point of entry into the story, not the reverse.
- The caption's mood should match that of the picture. The overline for the caption for the pictures in the Manganyi package ("Clothes that move") echoed the thesis of the story ("a young designer on the move") as well as the obvious action of the model.

  Similarly, the caption to a tragic photograph should be sober and factual; a picture of a happy scene calls for lighter lines.
- A good rule of thumb is: if a story can be told by a photograph and a caption, it should be – and the article can be cut.

Ten (plus one) tests of a good caption

1   Is it complete?
2   Does it identify, fully and clearly?
3   Does it tell when?
4   Does it tell where?
5   Does it tell what is in the picture?
6   Does it have the names spelt correctly, with the correct names relating to the correct people?
7   Is it specific?
8   Is it easy to read?
9   Have as many adjectives as possible been removed?
10   Does it suggest another picture?

Then there is a last rule never to be violated – Rule No. 11 (the cardinal rule):
Never write a caption without seeing the picture first. (Adapted from Goldstein, 1992:268)

Proofreading

Once the pages have been designed and the layouts are complete, one step in the sub-editing process remains: proofreading. Running a computer spellchecker is not enough. Some editors suggest reading the piece once for sense, a second time for grammar and style concerns and finally reading the lines backwards. This, they claim, is the best way to concentrate on each word and not to get caught up in what is being written.

Instruction to printer	Textual mark (example)	Marginal mark
Delete	point sizes	ℐ
Delete and close up	point seize	ℐ /
Delete and leave space	point/size	#
Leave as printed	point/size	stet
Insert new matter	⟋ size	point ⟋
Change to capital letters	point size	CAPS
Change to small capitals	point size	s.c.
Change to lower case	(POINT)size	lc
Change to bold	point size	bold
Change to italics	point size	italics
Underline	point size	insert rule
Change to roman	{point size}	rom
(Wrong fount) replace by character of correct fount	point size	w.f.
Invert type	pout size	⊙
Replace damaged type	point size	X
Close up	point siz e	◡
Insert space	point size	#
Make space equal	point/sizes/ used	eq #
Space between lines	POINT SIZE ←	2 pt
Reduce space	point / size	less #
Transpose	used\sizes/point	trs
Move to right (left)	⌈point size	⌈

Although most editing is done electronically, final editing of publication proofs may also be done by hand. Using the marks depicted in Figure 10.3 will ensure that your printer understands what you want.

Final check: Before sending the pages to the printers or publishing them online, the writer, story editor, and sub-editor must ask themselves: Would I take money from my pocket and time out of my day to read this article? If the answer is "no", the job is not yet finished.

Instruction to printer	Textual mark (example)	Marginal mark
Indent 1 em (2 em)	⬜ point size	⬜⌃
Take words (or letters) to beginning of following line	The Phoenix⌊and the Turtle	take over
Take words (or letters) to end of preceding line	The Phoenix and⌋the Turtle	take back
Raise (or lower line)	point size	↓
Correct vertical alignment	‖ point size	‖
Figure (or abbreviation) to be spelt out in full	⑫point twelve⦾pt	spell out
Substitute separate letters	phœnix	oe /
Use diphthong (or ligature)	manoeuvre	œ
No fresh paragraph	point of the pen.⌐ ⌊The hair line of the	run on
Begin new paragraph	point of the pen.⌋The hair line of the early	n.p.
Insert punctuation mark indicated	point size⌃	,⌃
Substitute punctuation mark indicated	point size /	⊙/
Insert em (en) rule	point/size	em ⌃
Insert parenthesis or square brackets	⌃point size⌃	( )
Insert hyphen	point⌃size	/-/
Insert single quotes (double quotes, apostrophe)	⌃Phototypesetting⌃	⸜ ⸝
Refer to appropriate authority	⑮ point Helvetica	ⓘ
Substitute superior character	boys⊙girl-friends	⸜
Substitute inferior character	boys⊙girl-friends	⸝

Figure 10.3 Proofreaders use standard marks in the text and in the margin to indicate errors and desired changes.

Definition

Copytaste is to review stories from news agencies, such as the South African Press Association (SAPA), see if they "taste" good enough to be used. Those charged with news-sampling responsibilities are often called copytasters.

In this chapter, you learned that:

- Editors have overall responsibility for managing the newsrooms.
- Effective story editors coach writers before, during and after the process of crafting stories.
- Sub-editors are compulsive about the details of polishing stories: ensuring they're accurate, engaging and conform to ethical and legal imperatives.
- Engaging stories are devoid of journalese – jargon and clichés.
- Conforming to house style is principally about communicating clearly.
- Writing effective headlines and captions is a craft that calls for writing and design skills.
- Proofreading is a meticulous procedure.
- The most effective way to prevent errors being published is to guard against them slipping into the story in the first place.

More key terms

Add [Zu. Enezezela / Xh. -dibanisa / Afr. byvoegsel]: Additional material to be included in the story; a way of numbering pages (second page is FIRST ADD, third page is SECOND ADD).

Sic: Latin word meaning so or thus. It is often used, set in square brackets, in direct quotations to indicate the accuracy of a reported error in speech: *"They is [sic] wicked, man."*

Trim [Zu. ukucwenga / Xh. –ukulungelelanisa / Afr. sny]: Cut back length of a story; a portion that is trimmed.

Update [Zu. Ukwengeza ulwazi olusha / Xh. –hlaziya / Afr. aanpas]: Add more recent facts to a story.

Putting your learning to work

ACTIVITY 1 Compare editing styles

News agencies, such as the South African Press Association (SAPA) and Reuters, supply stories to all major newspapers. Collect the same day's editions of several different newspapers and compare how they treated the same agency story.

- Compare the headlines' content, size and style.
- Have the sub-editors rewritten the lead and other parts of the story? If so, which news value(s) was enhanced?

ACTIVITY 2 Checking readability and human interest

So, you say it's tough to read certain articles? And boring, too? Well, get out your calculators and we'll measure just exactly how tough and how boring.

Research into the readability and human interest-levels of prose goes back to the 1920s. Early work identified various factors – such as sentence length, word length and prepositional phrases – that affect the readability of prose. Dozens of formulas were developed, though only a few are still used. Probably the best-known are those proposed by Dr Rudolph Flesch* in the 1940s.

* *Among the more significant of Flesch's books are* Say What You Mean, The Art of Plain Talk, The Art of Readable Writing *and* How to be Brief: An Index to Simple Writing.

To use Flesch's formula you need 100-word samples of text; get one from a weekly international news magazine, your local newspaper and a text-book.

- Divide the number of words by the number of sentences to get the average sentence length (asl).
- Next count the syllables (that's syl-la-ble) and divide by the number of words to get the average word length (awl).
- Then insert these values into Flesch's formula:
  Reading ease = 206.835 – (84.6 3 awl) – (1.015 3 asl)

Your score should fall between 0 and 100; the higher the score, the easier the material is to read. A score in the 70–80 range is "fairly easy"; a Grade 6 pupil could understand it. Scores below 50 are considered difficult reading. Scores below 30 are generally found in scientific and technical journals.

Note: When counting words, consider contractions and hyphenated words as one word; when counting sentences, count clauses separated by colons and semicolons as separate sentences.

But we know it takes more than short sentences and short words to keep us interested. Flesch figured that out too and came up with a "Human Interest" formula. It's based on the number of personal words per 100 words and number of personal sentences per 100 sentences. Personal words are pronouns and any other words that are either masculine or feminine. Personal sentences are direct quotations, exclamations, questions – questions that address the reader directly. The formula:

Human interest = pw/100 words 3 3.635 + ps/100 sentences 3 0.314

A score below 10 is dull; 20 to 40 is interesting; above 40 is very interesting. So when you wonder if your own writing is on track, get out the calculator!

ACTIVITY 3 *Writing better headlines*

Using any newspaper, magazine or house journal, clip five headlines that violate the rules for headline writing.

- Jot down the problem with each headline and then rework it to correct the errors.

ACTIVITY 4 *Writing better captions*

Select five faulty captions from a publication.

- Note the errors the writer committed, then rewrite each as well as possible.
- What information do you need to complete the caption?

HOT LINK

Freewriting tips for writing coaches. "Freewriting: A Means of Teaching Critical Thinking to College Freshmen," an excellent paper on the uses of freewriting in college English courses, was written by Wendy Major and is available at: http://webster.commnet.edu/grammar/composition/major_freewriting.htm. Her paper contains an extensive bibliography on freewriting and other such techniques.

ACTIVITY 5 Using proofreading symbols

Edit the following news item down to 150 words using proofreading marks:

A strike by 2,500 workers at 3 Da Gama textile plants in the eastern Cape is adding fuel to the call for a National industrial Council in the Textile Industry.

The South African Clother and Textile Workers Union (SACTWU) this week pointed out that there are huge wage discrepancies in the industry and thatt this is gicving some copmanies a unfair edge.

As an example, Sactwu this week showed that worker of a grade at Da Game (spinners who are paid R375 a weak) earn half the wages thier colleagues on the same grade at the Frame clothing Company in KwaZulu Natal (R750 a week).

Employees on strike are demading a R140 a weak increase back dated to January, a ten percent allowance on night shift and a service bonus of 50 cents a wekk for every uyear of service.

Satcwu also claims that Da Gama's Buffalo City plant pays the lowest wages in the country and says the strike has won it new members.

Da Game financial director NIck pietersma acknowledged that the companies employees are 'paid less', yet he added: 'To the best of my knowledge we are thge only tectile company that is making money.'

FROM THE NEWSROOM

Mail & Guardian Online editor Matthew Buckland

Matthew Buckland is the editor of Africa's first news website, the Mail & Guardian Online *(www.mg.co.za). He has been involved in online media from shortly after its inception and has worked in London for the BBC's commercial website division, local portal iafrica.com, MNet's Carte Blanche and Johnnic Publishing. He is a columnist for* The Media *magazine and a contributor to the US journalism site Poynter Online. He graduated from Rhodes University with a Bachelor of Arts in journalism, philosophy and history.*

How does the editing process online differ from that followed in printed publications?

1 *Space.* Because enormous amounts of digital data can be stored quite easily, the online news editor/sub-editor is under less pressure to cut articles. On the other hand, a reader's time is limited, so it is important to have the strong, juicy part of the story near the top and the more mundane details at the bottom. The inverted pyramid structure is crucial for online news articles. When a reader is satisfied with a story, he or she will simply stop reading, even if they are halfway through the piece. But for those who want it (and have the time to read from beginning to end), the longer more in-depth version is there. Dull or irrelevant writing gets cut whether there is space or not.

2 *Interactivity.* The Internet is all about linking. For news editors/sub-editors that means constantly being on the lookout for areas in a story to which they can add links to other sites or related stories within the same news site.

3 *Timelessness.* In the online world time is fluid. There is no such thing as "today" or "yesterday". An online story is "published" each day a

person accesses it. Therefore, it is crucial to be very specific about references to dates. That means "last month", "this week," or "last year" is not used.

4 *Multidisciplined approach.* Most online publications have small teams. At the *Mail & Guardian Online*, we combine the sub-editor and news editor functions. An online sub is expected to copytaste (decide which stories go where on the site), sub-edit, picture edit and occasionally do some reporting, too. We typically require more multiskilling than in print environments. It also means online stories will go through fewer editors and fewer quality assurance processes, so extreme care is necessary.

5 *Solid journalism fundamentals.* Principles of good journalism apply as much to online stories as to print stories: Are there multiple sources? Are the sources and information reliable? What is motivating the sources? Are the facts correct and have they been checked and rechecked? Does the piece represent fair comment?

6 *Global audience.* Online publications don't necessarily only cater for a community in a town, city or one country, but are available to a wide, global audience. That means some publications need to be more explicit and sensitive when explaining regional, parochial concepts or using words of the vernacular. Of course, it really depends on each publication's strategy.

7 *Newsworthiness vs. time.* A lead is determined by two factors: Newsworthiness and time. For online publications that specialise in breaking news, the lead becomes weaker the longer it is up on the site and must make way for more recent news (even if the recent news is not as strong as the current, but older lead). It is not a perfect science and often leads to fierce debates in our newsroom ...

8 *A story is never finished.* We may publish a short version of a story as the news breaks, then go back as the news develops to re-edit the story and to add another angle or a fresh detail. Stories are dynamic.

9 *Break the story up.* People tend to skim and scan copy on the web, so it is often a good idea to break a story up into sub-headings and separate blocks to keep the reader interested.

10 *Explicit headlines.* Online publications want their readers to click on a headline link to read the corresponding story behind that link. The entire story isn't immediately available for the reader to read (unlike in a newspaper), so it's better to make your headline explicit and straightforward rather than something mysterious and overly witty. This doesn't always apply though. My view is that there should always be a mixture of humour and mystery, but with a general tendency towards straightforward headlines.

What advice do you have for reporters and editors considering a career in online journalism?

- The fundamental principles of news gathering and the ethics surrounding journalism for print and online are identical. Make sure you are well-versed in them.
- You don't need to be a programmer, but you need to be computer literate and comfortable with the Internet. Some very basic Internet language is required, but can be taught on the job within a day.
- Online publishing is a relatively new industry and we are making the rules up as we go along. Standards and methods of publishing are often different from publisher to publisher. For example, most companies use custom-made content management systems to publish their websites, unlike the newspaper or magazine industry where most of the players use Quark or similar standard software. That means you need to be willing to adapt and be a problem solver. The Internet is flaky and things often go wrong.
- You need to be multiskilled. And you need to love the news because you will need to cover all aspects of it – copytasting, sub-editing and reporting. Some journalists thrive in this demanding environment because they have a great degree of influence and control; others find it difficult to adapt to so many different tasks.
- Online is a tough industry. There is lots of pressure and budgets are, at the moment, squeezed. It is, however, a dynamic area of journalism, a place of innovation. Be prepared for lots of hard work.

Bibliography

Arnold, E. 1969. *Modern newspaper design*. New York: Harper & Row.

Elbow, P. 1973. *Writing without teachers*. New York: Oxford University Press.

Fry, J. 1988. Eight ways to set words to pictures. *Folio magazine*, March 1988:160.

Fuller, J. 1996. *News values: ideas for an information age*. Chicago: University of Chicago Press.

Goldstein, N. ed. 1992. *The Associated Press stylebook and libel manual*. New York: Addison-Wesley.

Grimm, J. 1998. DeSilva blames lack of knowledge for lack of coaching. [Online] *Detroit Free Press*. November 1998. Available at: http://www.freep.com/job-spage/academy/desilva98.htm [Accessed: 20 July 2004]

Harriss, J., Leiter, K. and Johnson, S. 1992. *The complete reporter*, 6th ed. New York: Macmillan.

Hatcher, J. 2002. The greatest writing tips the world has ever seen. [Online] *Poynter Online*, Dec. 11, 2002. Available at: http://www.poynter.org/content/content_view.asp?id=13061. [Accessed: 20 July 2004]

Lanham, R.A. 1974. *Style: an anti-textbook*. New Haven, Conn: Yale.

Orwell, S. and Angus, I. eds. 1968. *The collected essays, journalism and letters of George Orwell*, Vol. IV. London: Secker & Warburg.

Paul, R. http://www.criticalthinking.org/University/univclass/Defining.html

Plotnik, A. 1982. *The elements of editing: a modern guide for editors and journalists*. London: Collier Macmillan.

Rossouw, H. 2004. Dressed for success. *Time*, June 7/June 14, 2004:72.

Scanlan, C. 2002. Helping writers take charge: five tools for editors. [Online] Poynter Online, 27 Nov. 2002. Available at: http://poynter.org/column.asp?id=52&aid=11369 [Accessed: 22 July 2004]

Scanlan, C. 2003. The coaching way; getting the best from yourself and others. [Online] Poynter Online, 15 May 2003. Available at: http://poynter.org/column.asp?id=52&aid=33974 [Accessed: 22 July 2004]

Strunk, Jr, W. and White, EB. 1979. *The elements of style*, 3rd ed. London: Macmillan.

Teel, L. and Taylor, R. 1988. *Into the newsroom: an introduction to journalism*, 2nd ed. Chester, Connecticut: Globe Pequot.

11

The publicist at work

Introduction

At his desk on the fourth floor of Cape Town's historic Newspaper House, former *Cape Argus* columnist and wine critic David Biggs used to receive piles of mail. Many letters were comments on his daily column, "Tavern of the seas". The majority of envelopes (scores each week, he recalls) contained press releases from organisations hoping to have their people, products and activities mentioned in Biggs's column which reached thousands of readers five days a week.

KEY CONCEPTS

The complex role of the publicist; effective publicity supports organisational strategy and communicates appropriate messages to target audiences; effective news releases meet the requirements of editors, the audience – and the organisation that issues them.

About 90 per cent of those releases – the product of countless hours of work – are trashed after a mere glance. The reason? "I think it's because lots of people when they write press releases probably don't know what makes them work," Biggs says.

Many people go about writing press releases the way some primitive tribe may act if asked to build a television, he says. Using a bit of wire, rope and tree bark, they may be able to make something that closely resembles a TV, but it probably will not function as one because they do not know what makes a TV work. "It's the same with a bad press release or a bad story. It's like a TV set with no works in it," he says.

Biggs is not alone in his criticism of the waves of press releases flowing into newsrooms. A survey of newspaper editors found that the following six factors particularly goaded editors about news releases (Baxter 1981: 30):

- Information that is not localised.
- Information that is not newsworthy.
- Releases containing too much advertising puffery.

- Releases that are too long and cumbersome.
- Releases that arrived too late to be useful.
- Releases that are poorly written.

Media releases remain one of the most basic – and popular – tools at the disposal of publicists for reaching their target audiences. But releases are not the only ones. We shall look at the role of the publicist, how media relations fits into organisational strategy, the range of tactics available to a publicist – and how to avoid the apparent shoddiness with which releases are often planned and executed.

Definition

Public relations is defined by the Institute for Public Relations and Communication Management (Prisa) as "the management, through communication, of perceptions and strategic relationships between an organisation and its internal and external stakeholders" (Prisa, 2003). The task of communicating, therefore, lies at the heart of what public relations practitioners do. Sometimes that will mean getting messages across by speaking to individuals face-to-face, other times that will require meeting with groups, making speeches, creating newsletters and websites and the like. On occasion, it will mean reaching audiences by getting relevant newsworthy information published or broadcast in the mass media. Those who specialise in this area are often called media relations specialists or **publicists**, which is the term we will use in this chapter.

LEARNING GOALS

At the end of this chapter, you should be able to:

1 Understand the role of the publicist.
2 Apply the basics of planning publicity that supports organisational strategy.
3 Identify the opportunities and challenges of publicity.
4 Write news releases for print and broadcast.
5 Be familiar with the protocol and pitfalls of working with journalists.

The role of the publicist

Every day, newsdesks and editors' e-mail inboxes are swamped by a tidal wave of media releases, of which very few are ever published.

Most editors will tell you this is because publicists or media relations practitioners do not know how to write. But there is more to it. The majority of publicists find themselves in the crossfire between the media and their managements or clients and they do not quite know how to balance these relationships in a way that will keep both parties happy. This is no easy task – but it can be achieved.

The key to being a successful public relations journalist, or publicist, lies in a thorough understanding of what is expected of you, by whom.

What does management want and what do the media want?

With a few exceptions, management regards news-desks as a source of free advertising, a vehicle to tell the world just how wonderful the company and its people are – as and when management sees fit.

HOT TIP

For a comprehensive overview of the theory and practice of public relations, see Skinner, J.C. and Von Essen, L.M. 2004. *The Handbook of Public Relations.* 7th ed. Cape Town: Oxford University Press SA.

Management believes that it is the job of the publicist to persuade newspapers, radio stations and television channels to carry glowing reports about the company in a format and language that will sell their image, products and services to their specifications. What is more, management seldom understands why this approach causes problems and often gets upset when the publicist or the media (or both) suggest anything to the contrary. This kind of pressure from the top may explain why many media releases tend to resemble puffy, badly written advertising copy.

News editors, on the other hand, tend to have a completely different view of what they should publish (see Chapter 3 for a complete discussion on news values). Generally speaking, though, the news media consider themselves to be the watchdogs of society who have to protect the community by providing them with relevant information on which they can base the decisions that shape their lives.

In short, management wants free advertising and news editors want cold facts. In view of these apparently opposed points of view, no one can be blamed for assuming that the purposes of management and editors are mutually exclusive and that publicists find themselves backed into a permanently unresolved catch-22 situation. They would be wrong.

Yes, bringing together the expectations of management and news editors is tough. But it can be – and is being – done. If you know what news is and you know what your company's objectives and aspirations are, you can, with some effort, marry the two and write news that will satisfy both parties.

What to tell management and what to tell the media?

"Educate your client," says award-winning journalist and publicity consultant Lize Odendal. "It's more important to educate your client about what you can do and what they can expect of you, than it is to have good media contacts."

What can companies expect from journalists?

The first point to make to a client is that there is a difference between *controlled* and *uncontrolled* media exposure. And the difference is money. If you're paying for it – an advertisement or space for an article (called an *advertorial*) – you can call the shots, within reason. You are likely to get the amount of exposure (time on radio or television, or space in a publication or website) at the time (hour, day or month) and manner (wording and visuals) outlined in the contract.

On the other hand, if you're not paying for it, you don't have a say. If an editor decides to use the information you have sent, she has the right

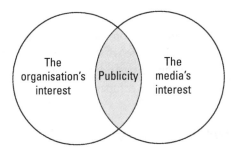

Figure 11.1 Publicists operate where the interests of the organisation and interests of the media overlap.

to edit the material and schedule it as she sees fit (of course, as long as the information remains factually correct).

If an editor keeps giving away space to promotional material – which is the major source of income for most media – the medium is unlikely to survive for too long.

What can companies expect from achieving media exposure?

Credibility

That is the major reason why publicists doggedly pursue editorial coverage for their clients. If a journalist writes an article about Zanzibar and mentions the wonderful experience of staying at the Ras Nungwe Beach Resort, the reader is likely to believe the information far more readily than an advertisement for the resort which claims "We are wonderful".

Cost saving

Besides providing clients with highly useful media exposure, publicists can also save the client money. In August 2004, a full-page, colour advertisement in *Drum* magazine cost R24 500 plus VAT. A 30-second radio spot between 06:00 and 09:00 on Radio Metro would cost R4 500 plus VAT. The rate for a 30-second advertisement during the 19:00-19:30 SABC3 news programme would set the client back R25 500 plus VAT. It is clear that paid-for media exposure can cut down a client's promotional budget significantly.

What can journalists expect from publicists?

Media relations is, ideally, a two-way street. Publicists send information to the media about events and issues they feel would be newsworthy and, when necessary, they field queries

▓▓▓ LINK

Check out case studies of early publicity campaigns and other details in the history of public relations (from an American point of view) at the Museum of Public Relations on-line at: http://www.prmuseum.com. The PRHistory.com site is at: http://www.prhistory.com.

from the media for information about the organisation and its activities. There are, of course, limits to what a journalist can expect from a public relations person or publicist. And generally the line is drawn at information which would harm the company.

Planning publicity

Publicists often work with surprises. The organisation's staff announce a strike. A staff member wins a national award. A new board member is appointed. However, there are usually long-term projects which allow – and require – publicists to create a strategy to guide their activities.

Strategies are usually created to promote a particular event, like the publicity strategy the Gordons Bay Chamber of Commerce created when business leaders in the coastal town decided to start up an "Anchors & Antiques Festival" (see p.283). But publicity can also be used strategically when a company wants to address less tangible behaviours which could affect its business. The financial services giant Old Mutual, for example, used various promotional methods, including publicity, to combat two environmental factors which they identified could affect their business: low numeracy skills in South Africa and the rising incidence of infection with HIV, the virus which leads to the killer disease AIDS.

Whatever the application, the basic steps to create a media strategy remain the same:

- Know the company.
- Know the key stakeholders.
- Know the media.
- Know the objectives and key messages.

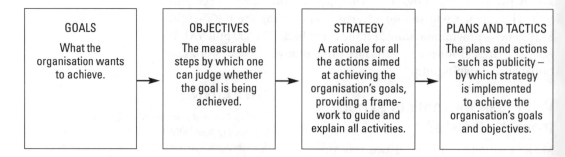

Figure 11.2 Publicists should align their media efforts with the overall aims of the organisation (Adapted from Steyn and Puth, 2000:31).

- Know which communication method to use.
- Know the timescales and deadlines.
- Know the available resources – budgets as well as staff.
- Know how media efforts will be evaluated to measure its success.

Know the company

For a publicist to be able to translate the communication objectives of an organisation or client into news, she must have an intimate knowledge of the organisation's goals, the image it wants to project and events taking place in the organisation. To be worthwhile, publicity efforts have to support the organisation's overall aims.

Know the audience

The next step is to determine the audience you want to reach. Astute publicists know that it is useless to direct their efforts at a faceless, unidentified mass flippantly referred to as "the general public". The first step here is to find out who the organisation's stakeholders are. *Stakeholders* (from the word *stockholder*) is a term used to describe those people who have a stake or an interest in the company's activites.

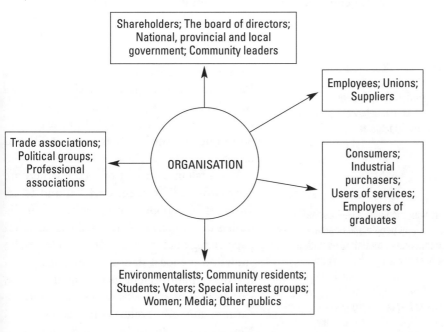

Figure 11.3 Organisations have to maintain linkages with a variety of stakeholders to reach their objectives successfully (Source: Steyn and Puth, 2000:66).

Customers or clients are only one stakeholder group. Others, typically, include employees, unions, community organisations, government, investors and the media.

Once you know the various groups with whom the organisation has links, the next step is to figure out which media would be best suited to reach them. These questions will help provide you with the answers:

- Are the stakeholders male or female?
- How old are they?
- What are their levels of literacy and education?
- Where do they live?
- What do they think and believe?
- What interests them?
- Which publications do they read?
- To which radio stations do they listen?
- Which television channels do they watch?
- Which websites do they visit?

Know the key media

Once you've determined which stakeholder groups are relevant to your orgnisation, you need to determine specifically which media to target in order to reach them. If, for example, you are working for a publicly-traded company, such as the communications giant Telkom, amongst the stakeholder groups will be investors, financial analysts, brokers and the financial press. For those stakeholders, your target media would then include: wire services, such as Reuters; business magazines, such as *Financial Mail*; and business pages of newspapers, such as *Business Day*; business desks at television and radio stations, such as Summit TV and SAfm.

Don't fall into the trap of thinking there are only two media categories: local and large. *Local*, as you might expect, refers to media outlets in your city or region – the local newspaper, a regional magazine or two, a few radio shows on the local station stations. *Large*, on the other hand, refers to the media outlets such as the *Sowetan*, *Huisgenoot* magazine, the *Carte Blanche* television show and News24.com. The reality is that while local and large might be important target media, they are not the only ones. The best media

HOT LINK

The South African Advertising Research Foundation's *All Media and Products Survey* provides valuable information for public relations practitioners and other business strategists on the behaviour of South Africans. See the summary findings at: http://www.saarf.co.za.

HOT LINK

Need help drawing up your media list? Guides that catalogue the media, contact people and deadlines are useful ways of identifying potential news outlets. Preview some of the best-known guides in South African online: *Brewer's Almanac*, now published by Interactive Marketing Services (IMS), at: http://www.brewers.co.za; the *Media List* is at: http://www.medialist.co.za; and the South African Rates and Data (Sarad) guide is at: http://www.sarad.co.za. For international media outlets, see the ABYZ News Links site at: http://www.abyznewslinks.com.

opportunities might well be the dozens of the smaller-scale papers, magazines, newsletters, community radio stations, satelite television channels (such as the business-focused Summit TV), and special-interest websites that may be more effective in getting your message to the appropriate people than a story in the large media might.

Remember: it is important that you check out each medium yourself so that you know precisely what type of news each editor is looking for.

Know the key messages

With the background information about the organisation, the stake-holders and the media, you can then consider the specific objectives of each publicity effort. Quite simply: what do you want to achieve? The answer to that question should form the goal of the publicity campaign. The objectives are the measurable steps which will lead to the realisation of the goal.

An easy formula (Tucker et. al., 1994:25) for developing objectives is:
- *Start with the word "to", followed by an accomplishment verb.*
- *Specify a single behaviour to be accomplished with each publicity effort.*
- *Specify a target date for accomplishment.*

For example, each quarter Telkom needs to inform stakeholders (which include, but are not limited to, its shareholders) of its financial results. Of course, some quarters the results may be positive, at other times business may not be going as well. Each time, the publicist must sit down with the key members of management and determine what the overall objective of the communication efforts will be.

Once the objectives have been established, they need to be translated into messages. The message is not the same as the facts. The facts might be, for example, that Telkom has done very well over the last quarter. But in anticipation of queries by consumer groups, the publicity message might be: "Telkom's on-going business success is the result of effective and efficient management and not because of high telephone call tariffs."

The American Institute of Wine & Food's behavioural objective, to generate public endorsements by the nation's health leadership that all foods – in moderation – fit into a healthy diet, had three priority messages (Tucker et. al., 1994:30):
- *Restrictive food regimes fail to improve the dietary behaviour of most Americans.*
- *Taste is the number one motivation for making food selections.*
- *There are no good or bad foods. Low- and high-fat foods can be balanced over several days to meet dietary recommendations.*

Publicists should be able to articulate the message they want to convey in one simple sentence. If you can't do that, then how can you expect the audience to get the point?

Know which communication methods to use

Once the publicist knows what needs to be said, to whom and for what reason, the next step is identify the best way to say it – the best tactic. For example, the publicist for a new hotel may invite specific journalists to tour the facility and interview the general manager and other staff. Other media may only receive press packs with news releases, photographs and the like. We'll take a look at these options more closely later in this chapter.

Know the timescale and deadlines

Setting out who will do what by when – and keeping track of the work – is a useful way of making sure all the work is on track. The essential elements of an action plan are:

- Step-by-step tasks leading to the completion of each tactic.
- Individuals responsible for each task.
- Targeted deadline dates.

ACTION STEPS	Target media	Responsible person	Target starting date	Target completion date	Actual completion date	Remarks (e.g. opportunities or problems; key contacts discovered)

Figure 11.4 Detailed action plans allow publicists to keep track of the different media activities.

Know your budget

Publicity activities are likely to cost significantly less than advertising (one rule of thumb is that public relations activities should come in at 10 per cent of the organisation's total advertising and promotional budget). Estimates of cost are made for *out-of-pocket expenses* and *time*. Photographs, printing, postage, telephone and travel costs are all out-of-pocket expenses. But the budget is not complete if it does not detail the professional and administrative support time required.

Hourly rates can be determined for professional time by adding an individual's compensation and overhead expenses (office space, equipment, supplies). Publicity agencies add a percentage for profit.

Know how to evaluate your efforts

The only way to know if all the effort has been effective, is to monitor and evaluate the outcomes. Press cuttings, statistics and achievements can also be circulated to key people (management, investors, etc.).

Ongoing monitoring and evaluation will typically include:

Extent of the coverage. Number of press releases issued and take-up rates (these can be broken down by media (eg local, national and trade press, broadcast media etc). That is where media monitoring companies, such as Newsclip, can help. Such agencies track publications, television and radio coverage for mention of a company or person. But gathering raw data is only the beginning.

Type of coverage. Cuttings can be analysed by how effective you have been in getting your key messages across or by how positive, negative or neutral the coverage has been. Some questions to be asked are:

- Depth of mention – How many times was the company mentioned in a story?
- Type of media – In which media (publications, radio, television, websites) did the stories appear?
- Region covered by media – In which area did the stories appear?
- Byline – Who covered the story? (The assumption being that a story by a well-known journalist would be considered more valuable than one by an unknown reporter.)
- Images – Were photographs or other graphics used to illustrate the story?
- Source of stories – Did the stories originate with the publicist, the journalist, or someone else?

Financial value of the coverage. Many clients want to determine the value of the media exposure in monetary terms. Typically, this is done by measuring the size of the article (publications) or time (broadcast media) and calculating what it would have cost to place an equivalent advertisement. For example, the makers of Louise Vuitton luggage could compare a three-page feature on the history of the luxury goods brand which appeared in Condé Nast's *House & Garden* magazine in September 2004 with the publication's advertising rate which, at the time, was R28 500 for a full-colour page. Placing a three-page advertisement would have cost them 3 x R28 500 = R85 500.

Often, these Ad Value Equivalencies (AVEs) are then multiplied by factors between 1 and 6, depending on the perceived value of the story and media audience. Let's assume *House & Garden's* target audience is exactly whom the luxury-goods company wants to reach and that the "PR value" factor was felt to be three (3), the final calculation would then be: R85 500 x 3 = R256 500.

▓HO T LINK

Not everyone agrees with the use of AVEs and so-called "PR values". Amongst the critics is the Commission on Public Relations Measurement and Evaluation, an initiative of the Institute for Public Relations, the only independent foundation in the public relations field. "Calulating AVEs is not a problem in itself," says Bruce Jeffries-Fox in an article for the Commission (2003:3). "Its problems stem from what it is called and how it is used." He points out that calling it an "advertising equivalent" strongly suggests that a news story of a particular size has equal impact to an advertisement of the same size. At this stage, at least, there is no factual basis for this assumption. "That is," says Jeffries-Fox, "there has been no research to confirm whether this is true." Read the rest of Jeffries-Fox's argument – and check out the other valuable reports and publications by the Commission – at: http://www.institute-forpr.com/measurement_and_evaluation.phtml.

▓HO T LINK

The Association of Media Evaluation Companies (UK) website carries some very useful information about the purpose of media evaluation, how to brief an agency and how to use media evaluation to best effect. The case studies make for interesting reading, too. See: http://www.amec.org.uk.

While it is certainly useful to investigate the extent of media coverage achieved by publicity efforts, placing a specific financial value on the result and the use of AVEs and "PR values" cannot, at this stage, be justified by research.

Publicity tactics

On deciding how best to get their message to the media, publicists have two basic options: get information to the journalists where they are, or get the journalists to collect the information from them. The first option would, typically, include pitching a story to the media by making a telephone call, and sending news releases or complete press packs electronically, by post or by hand-delivery. The latter option usually involves staging some event, such as a launch or news briefing for several journalists at the same time (think of the ones you've seen on the television news or re-enacted in a film or show), or setting up individual tours and interviews. Here are some tips on how to make the most of your efforts.

Press materials

Fact sheets

A good place to start is to develop a short (usually one page long) fact sheet of the specific news event. Begin by gathering the information required to answer the standard questions journalists ask: Who? What? Where? When? Why? How? Now summarise the facts in short parapgraphs with headings. Add the term "Fact Sheet" at the top, followed by a punchy headline and don't forget to include your contact details at the bottom. Fact sheets are helpful to journalists who need quick access to additional material for articles and they will typically form the basis for any further materials, such as news releases, which you will create.

A news release

Although a good journalist will probably write his own report, a well-written news release is a standard way to alert the media to newsworthy stories. If the reporter is pushed for time, he just might use it or, at the very least, it could influence him to use the news angle you prefer. We will take a closer look at writing news releases below.

Hi there

With the deadline for the conversion to EMV (Europay, Mastercard, Visa) smartcard technology drawing closer, Prism has delivered and implemented Thales e-security EMV P3 (Personalisation Preparation Process) software at three of SA's leading banks.

If you need more info please contact me on (011) 804 4900 or e-mail me.

Kind regards
Marilyn

Hi-Tech Security

09 June 2004

PRISM HELPS BANKS ACCELERATE PREPARATIONS FOR EMV ROLLOUT

IN DEALS valued at over R6,4 million, three of South Africa's leading banks have accelerated their preparations for the introduction of payment smart cards with the purchase of sophisticated smart card personalisation applications from JSE listed Prism Holdings.

NOTE TO EDITORS
JSE-listed Prism Holdings Limited is a leader in the field of secure electronic transaction products, solutions and services. The Group has a strong presence in South Africa and an established and expanding footprint across Africa and South-East Asia.

Prism has a proven track record in the delivery of secure electronic payment technologies and end-to-end solutions for the retail, utilities, banking, cellular and petroleum industries. The Group has developed and implemented innovative payment-centric Intellectual Property that bridges the following technologies:

- Chip cards including SIM cards, financial smart cards and telephone cards
- Point-of-Sale frameworks, applications and devices
- OEM transaction modules including PINpads, card readers and self-service terminals
- Transaction security modules and servers
- Payment servers, messaging gateways and value-added-services gateways
- End-to-end secure electronic payment architectures for wired and wireless networks

issued by : Citigate PR +27(0)11 804 4900
for : Prism Holdings +27(0)11 548 1000
www.prism.co.za
contact : Gerhard Claassen, MD, Prism Crypto and OEM Business Unit or Marilyn de Villiers, Citigate PR

Figure 11.5 Communications group Citigate South Africa typically send out news releases as e-mails, which are then re-worked by journalists for their stories.

Pitch letter for coverage

Some publicists develop a simple one-page pitch detailing the Who, What, Where, When, Why and How of a story they feel is newsworthy. The information can then be sent off to alert editors who make news assignments, or pitched to them in a phone call. It's good idea to write out your pitch as a document before you pick up the phone, because an editor's response to a successful telephone pitch is usually, "Let me have some more information." When that request comes, you should be ready to hit the "send" button on your e-mail.

Press packs

There are occasions, such as the launch of new product or a major event such as a festival, when a single news release isn't enough. For such occasions, publicists compile press packs (or media kits) that include relevant background material, visuals and even sound and video clips. Usually, press packs are distributed in a physical (printed)

HOT LINK

For some sound advice on pitching to the media – as well as examples of pitch letters – see the Publicity Insider at: http://www.publicityinsider.com/pitch.asp.

format, but when the organisation's news is of interest to a geographically-dispersed audience, press materials are often made available online, too.

To be effective, press packs must be easy to use and contain the right amount of information. Take care not to overwhelm the journalists and avoid turning your press packs into some kind of lucky dip for journalists by including superfluous back editions of the company house journal and excessive corporate gifts.

In addition to a basic fact sheet and news release, you would typically include some of the following in your press pack, whether it's in print or online:

- **A programme of events**
  If the media kit is issued to back a media conference or function, it is good practice to provide the journalist with a programme so that he or she can plan the day. Journalists are usually strapped for time and may only be able to stay for certain relevant aspects of your programme. For example, at a luncheon at which a speaker will be making a significant announcement, journalists would prefer to be informed of the full programme and times so that they can skip the sections they are not interested in (for example, pre-dinner drinks, welcome, appetisers) and arrive in time for the main speaker.

- **Copies of speeches**
  Most journalists like to follow what the speaker is saying and mark pertinent sections for later use. Copies of speeches also greatly reduce the risk of misquoting.

- **CV and biographies**
  These are often referred to as a "bio" and recount pertinent facts about an individual. Most companies keep a file of bios of all top officers. When writing a straight bio use the inverted pyramid formula (see Chapter 4), with company information preceding personal details.

  Narrative bios are written in a breezier style and will often include comments by colleagues about the person, as well as anecdotes.

  A short, quarter-page curriculum vitae of each speaker is often useful, but be sure to emphasise why the speaker is pertinent to the occasion.

- **Backgrounders**
  Backgrounders, as the name implies, provide background information that helps explain an event or a situation. If a government agency is retrenching workers, the public relations office may put together a set of statistics showing how the costs of operations have risen faster than the income. The backgrounder may also describe the agency's pressing needs and new

HOT LINK

Does your organisation need to make publicity material available to journalists internationally? Setting up an online media office might be one solution. Check out the Online Press Office for British Airways, the world's largest airline company, at: http://www.britishairways.com/press/.

programmes or services which have been implemented to benefit citizens.

"Whatever the topic, a backgrounder provides a look at the past, the present and the future" (Tucker et al., 1994:265). It gives a context for a situation, without making a judgement. Backgrounders are seldom used in their entirety, i.e. they are usually excerpted. While backgrounders are issued to news organisations, they are often also made available to other stakeholders.

- **Visuals**
Fraser Seitel, director of Public Affairs for Chase Manhattan Bank, says: "Visually arresting graphics may mean the difference between finding the item in the next day's paper or in the same day's wastebasket" (Seitel, 1991:223). When appropriate, include graphics or photographs – with captions. One good visual with an extended caption is often more effective than pages of copy.

  For business pages, the pie chart or graph works every time, says publicist Marcus Brewster. Business pages are difficult to illustrate and a good graphic significantly increases the chances the editor will use the information.

  If you are operating on a limited budget – and time permits – send a page with photocopies of available photographs and phone the editors to ask which picture they would like to use.

- **Position paper**
While the backgrounder is free of opinion, the position paper is not. It gives the organisation's point of view on an issue or situation. South Africa's bid for the 2010 Soccer World Cup elicited diverse reactions. A civic group like a ratepayers' association or a major corporate sponsor, such as Standard Bank, may establish an organisational position on the event. Other issues that may require an organisational position paper include issues such as employees with Aids and the environment.

- **Additional information**
Additional information like brochures, house journals and annual reports should only be included when they are relevant and have a direct bearing on the content of the announcement.

Tips on writing effective news releases

Once you are sure you have news and you have picked your audience, as well as a publication or broadcast station that caters for them, you need to focus on presenting the information in the right way.

There is a big difference between writing for readers and writing for listeners. Readers have certain advantages over listeners. For example, a reader can scan material, focus on topics that appear interesting and reread sections that seem unclear. Listeners, on the other hand, get information in a set order and they usually do not get a second chance if they miss something. That is why we need to have a separate discussion on creating news releases for print and broadcast.

Writing for readers

Before a release gets to your readers, it has to get past an editor. Should you send a printed news release, or an e-mail version? Well, that depends. Many journalists prefer electronic versions of news releases because they can easily rework the material for a story. Others who find their e-mail inboxes flooded with spam, still prefer to receive printed material. The only sure way to know is to ask. A simple phone call to the media will usually do the trick.

- A compelling e-mail subject header or headline. The first question a journalist usually asks when picking up a news release is: "Is this information important?" A good headline tells the story in no more than six words and will help convince the journalist to keep reading.
- An introductory paragraph that covers the five Ws: who, what, where, when and why. Remember the journalists are looking for the facts first; if they decide the story is newsworthy, they'll typically rewrite the material to tailor it to their specific requirements. For that reason, the inverted pyramid and champagne forms (discussed in Chapter 4) remain the most effective ways to structure a press release.
- Target your releases carefully and try to give a local angle. The editors of the *Daily Dispatch* in Port Elizabeth would have little use for this release:

DURBAN – Patricia Chivuka has been named a director of the photo lithography and printing company Graphco.

But the same release would almost certainly be used in the *Eastern Province Herald* if amended like this:

DURBAN – Patricia Chivuka, a graduate of the Nelson Mandela Metropolitan University, has been named a director of the photo lithography and printing company Graphco.

- Adding quotes from an authority in your company or outside certainly will add some spice to your release, but be careful: staid quotes filled with jargon and puffery are worse than no quotes at all. "The news release can't be used as the private soapbox of the release writer," says Fraser Seitel. "Rather, the release must appear as a fair and accurate representation of the 'news' that the organisation wishes to convey" (Seitel, 1992:206). Attribute all information and be sure to get permission from the people you mention in the story.

- Add a short paragraph at the end of the release with background information about the organisation, which will help place the news story in context. This paragraph might include a synopsis of the activities of the organisation, how long it has been in business, and any specific achievements. If the news release is about an author's new book or an entertainer, then cover career high-points.
- Make sure, too, that you write your release in a style that suits the publication. The tone of a news release targeting the irreverent men's magazine *FHM* is likely to be quite different from one aimed at *Business Day*.
- Contact information, including an e-mail address for the media contact and website address of the company. Reporters working on deadline will often choose to call a company representative rather than wait for a reply by e-mail. Be sure that in addition to e-mail contact information, a phone number for the press contact is listed. American publicists usually add this information at the top of the first page, below the letterhead. That way, the argument goes, all the contact details are together. A guide from the Institute for Public Relations and Communication Management (Prisa) places these details at the bottom of the release. Whichever format you choose, provide as much contact information as possible: full name of the individual to contact, address, land line and cell phone numbers, fax, e-mail, website address.

  If you are writing the release but cannot adequately field questions from the press on the subject, list the name of the person(s) who can (see the release in Figure 11.5).
- Embargo or release date. Indicate whether the release can be used immediately or if it should be held until a specific date. In a time of instant communication and increased competition, editors frown on embargoes. So, if you need to hold information, wait until the appropriate time to get the release to the editors.

  A release must also be presented in a manner that allows the editor to use it easily.
- Type. Use standard and upper- and lowercase type. Never use all capitals, which is very difficult to read. In e-mails, CAPITALS ARE CONSIDERED RUDE BECAUSE THEY SUGGEST THAT YOU ARE SHOUTING!
- Spacing. Printed news releases should always be typed one-and-a-half or double- spaced on one side only of A4 paper.
- Margins. Margins should always be wide enough for editors to write in them, i.e. about 2,5 cm.
- Paper. Use plain, white paper. Expensive coloured paper with embossing and other embellishments arouse suspicion. Good editors are impressed by the news content and not the extravagant packaging.

- Length. "Screeds and screeds of copy helps no one," says Raymond Joseph, former Cape Town Bureau Chief of the *Sunday Times*. A release should seldom be more than two pages; more than three pages can almost never be justified. Paragraphs should also be short – no more than six lines.
- Slug lines. Slug lines help editors and journalists keep track of different pages of the release as it moves through the editorial process. A story about an art festival might be slugged "art fest" or "festival". Start the second page with the slug, followed with "add 1" to indicate it is the first added page. "Add 2" indicates the second added page.

Some publicists use "page 2" for the second page, and so on, although this is not the convention.

The term "more" should be used at the bottom of pages if there is additional copy. At the end of the final page of the news release write "end".

Slugline
(one word from the headline)

Monday, January 4, 1996

EMBARGO: Thursday, January 7, 1998, 1.30pm

HEADLINE

This is a model news release format preferred by the Public Relations Institute of Southern Africa (PRISA).

Use plain, white paper.

New releases should always be typed one-and-a-half or double spaced on one side only of A4 paper.

Margins should always be wide enough for editors to write in them, i.e. about 2,5 cm.

Use standard and upper- and lowercase type. Never use all capitals, which is very difficult to read.

If your organization has letterhead stationery, use it. Otherwise type the name and address single space at the top.

Embargo dates should be used only when it is vital that the information not be released. For general releases rather write "FOR IMMEDIATE RELEASE".

Should the final paragraph on the page be quite long and continue on the next page, do not split the paragraph, but rather start the new paragraph on the new page.

\more...

Slugline two last

Always indicate with the word "MORE" that at least one more page follows.

The information should be arranged so that the first reader – the editor or journalist – can pick up immediately what the story is about. If you are sending a feature release it may be useful to set a paragraph, which contains the traditional 5Ws and the H of the Inverted Pyramid Form, in a contrasting font at the top of the release. then follow with the soft lead of the feature article.

Few news releases should go beyond two pages, which is the maximum for most printed stories.

At the end of the release, identify the writer and the client.

Ends

ISSUED BY: Nonceba Silwana
Media Liaison Practitioner
The Mass Media Group
21 Jump Street
Sandown
Tel: (011) 434-3344 (o)
(082) 333-0007
Fax: (011) 434-3333

CONTACT: Lennox Mogale
Headline Company
33 Main Street
Newtown
Tel: (011) 555-1212
(083) 717-1234
Fax: (011) 555-1213

Figure 11.6 The news release format preferred by the Insitute for Public Relations and Communication Management.

Writing for listeners

Millions of South Africans get their news from radio and television. Radio is often the primary source of news for teenagers. Many are reluctant to read newspapers and will leave the room when the TV news comes on, but they are unlikely to change stations for the few minutes during which radio news broadcasts are aired.

Getting your company's information broadcast is therefore a good idea, but you should not simply send radio stations the same release you send to the press. Consider this news release:

```
  Cape                          P.O. Box 652, Cape Town 8000
  Kaapse                        Posbus 652, Kaapstad 8000
  Technikon
                                Longmarket Street Cape Town 8001
                                Langmarkstraat Kaapstad 8001
                                Telegrams . TECCOM . Telegramme
Contact:   Willemien Law:       Telex . 5-21666 . Teleks
           460-3257, 8.30am-4.30pm   Telefax (021) 461-7564
           913-3977, after office    Tel.: 461-7564 Main
                     hours            Tel.:460-3911 Zonnebloem



                         START TIME: 10am Oct 14


     MARKETING AWARD FOR CAPE TECHNIKON STUDENT
              (80 words; 30 seconds)

A 23-year-old Capetonian with a flair for computers and a seven-
handicap golf record is the Cape Technikon's Young Marketer of
the Year for 1997. Patrick Hall today received his trophy from
Nasionale Tydskrifte, who sponsor the competition. In December
Hall will compete against winners from other technikons for the
national title. The Technikon's marketing department head Mr Mike
du Plessis said the Young Marketer of the Year Award showed
technikons were doing the job industry wants.

                         -30-


FOR ADDITIONAL INFORMATION ALSO CONTACT:

Mike du Plessis:  Tel (021) 460-3257, 8.30am-4.30pm weekdays
                  (082) 555-1234, after office hours
                  Fax: (021) 460-4321

October 12 1997
```

Figure 11.7 A sample broadcast news release (for radio).

Making the effort to tailor your release specifically to broadcasters' needs will pay off. Once, in response to a release I sent to SABC Radio's Nico de Kock, I received a fax (a rarity for any public relations practitioner) which began like this: "It was indeed a pleasure to receive a news release in true radio style. I could not miss it and had great joy in scheduling it for broadcast."

Format and style directives to consider when preparing releases for broadcast are outlined below.

Format

Your release is written for three audiences:
- The editor, whom you have to convince of its importance.
- The audience, whom you have to inform and, when appropriate, entertain.
- The news reader, for whom the information must be clearly set out.

To accomplish these goals you can apply the basic directives for press releases, with the following exceptions:

Public service announcements

While hard news stories are not likely to be repeated, this type of announcement (e.g. a fundraising walk for the Cancer Society) is likely to be used more than once. For an announcement of a fundraising concert at, for example, 8 pm, July 21, indicate start and stop dates at the top right of the release like this:

> START DATE: July 14
> STOP DATE: 7 pm July 21

Notice that the release is still valid on the day of the activity (which is not the case for print releases) and that it can be used almost until shortly before the event starts – just give the listeners enough time to get there.

Also, send copies of public service announcements to the station's programme manager or the producer of a particular show. Hard news releases are sent to the news editor or to particular journalists.

Length

Keep it very short. Broadcast news items seldom exceed 30 seconds; most are between 10 and 20 seconds long. At an average reading speed of 10 words per four seconds, a release should contain between 25 and 70 words.

Margins

For radio releases set your margins to allow for a 75-character line, which should give you about 10 words per line (when writing in English). This will allow you to calculate the length of your release easily, without counting every word. A 20-second release, for example, will be five lines long.

Word breaks

Never break a word at the end of a line or sentence at the end of a page. This is likely to make the newsreader pause at an unnatural place in the story.

Word count and estimated time

Put the number of words and estimated time under the headline. Your time may be slightly off, but professional newsreaders will know how many words they read per minute.

Visuals

If you are sending out a visual with your release to a television station, set your left margin to allow for a 35-character space. This will allow about five words, or two seconds per line. On the right, include a brief description of the visual.

Style – one central idea

Decide which *single idea* you want to convey to the listener in the few seconds at your disposal and discard all extraneous information. When you listen to something – a conversation, an address or a lecture – which part is likely to stick with you? If you answered "the last bit" you are right. That is why the inverted pyramid formula is not the best approach when writing for listeners.

Unlike readers who have to focus on the copy to get the information, listeners are likely to be doing something else – driving, tanning, getting dressed or fussing in the kitchen. This means that the primary job of your introduction is to draw their attention, to get them to pause and move closer to the radio.

Once you have their attention, you can move into the story. End by clearly stating the single idea you would like them to remember. Consider this example:

> If you've got a thing about creepy crawlies and the thought of stepping on a snake makes you sick, then spare a thought for John Nkoli from Durban.
>
> John's going to be surrounded by snakes ... many of them poisonous ... for up to a fortnight. He's planning to sit crosslegged in a three by four metre tank with more than 40 serpents to keep him company in a bid to break the world record for snake-sitting.

Now, cover the report with a piece of paper and answer the following questions:
- What is the person's name?
- Where does he come from?
- How many snakes will keep him company?

- How big is the tank?
- Why will he be doing it?

Quite likely you had some difficulty finding the answers to the first four questions, but I am sure you remembered straight away the guy was trying to break the world record for snake-sitting.

For a more accurate experiment, simulate a broadcast by reading the report above to a friend and then ask him or her to answer the five questions.

Broadcast writers often express the formula used above like this:
- Tell 'em you're gonna tell 'em.
- Tell 'em you're telling 'em.
- And then tell 'em you've told 'em.

Immediacy

One of the greatest strengths of broadcasting is its immediacy. Capitalise on this attribute by writing in the present or present perfect tense.

Past

In Polokwane, a leading anti-apartheid activist escaped unharmed yesterday after an assassination attempt ...

Present perfect

In Polokwane today, a leading anti-apartheid activist has escaped unharmed following an assassination attempt ...

Present

In Polokwane police are searching for the gunman who fired three shots narrowly missing a leading anti-apartheid activist ...

Punctuation

Remember listeners and viewers cannot see the text. Therefore you should avoid all punctuation except for fullstops and the occasional comma. This will affect the way you structure the information. Consider this statement:

A Zambian government official, said a South African diplomat, was pressuring foreign businessmen to relocate urban factories to rural sites.

If you were listening to it – without seeing the punctuation – the meaning conveyed would be quite different.

> A Zambian government official said a South African diplomat was pressuring foreign businessmen to relocate urban factories to rural sites.

Use simple, declarative sentences

The following sentence is awkward and overdramatic:

> After struggling for three hours to free the mangled body from the shattered truck, firemen said the horrific crash was one of the worst they had seen in their lives.

This would be better:

> Firemen with steel cutters took three hours to free the body from the wreckage. They said it was one of the worst crashes they had ever seen.

Numbers and statistics should be rounded off

Nobody will remember this example of bad luck:

> A Bloemfontein man lost R997 983 in a three-day gambling binge at Sun City.

But stated this way, the point is certainly made:

> A Bloemfontein man lost nearly a million rand during a three-day gambling binge at Sun City.

Attribution should precede a quote

> National Assembly Speaker Baleka Mbete says that no amount of intimidation will convince her to prematurely try and sentence honourable members of parliament ahead of time.

Especially in contentious statements, the attribution cannot – and should not – be held back until the second sentence:

> South African students are a shiftless, lazy bunch of spongers who should be forced to sweep the streets until they find a decent job. So said Dr Ike Know-all at a news conference ...

The first sentence turned a highly debatable assertion into a statement of fact, and the danger is that the audience may miss the attribution that follows (because another driver hoots, the phone is ringing or the kettle is boiling) and identify the opinion with the newsreader.

Careful attribution is crucial where facts asserted are still to be proved. Avoid direct quotes.

Direct quotes often complicate sentences unnecessarily – remember the listener cannot see punctuation marks. It is therefore better to paraphrase.

Pronunciation

If your release contains names or words the newsreader may find difficult to pronounce, add the phonetic symbols in parenthesis. The *Associated Press Broadcast Stylebook* recommends a system based on the familiar principles of English usage with respect to the sounds of vowels and consonants, for example:

Guatanama (Gwhan-tah'-nah-mah)
Feisal (Fy'sal)

Note that the apostrophe is used to show where the accent falls. The following should cover most contingencies:

ah	pronounced like the a in arm
a	pronounced like the a in apple
eh	pronounced like the a in air
ay	pronounced like the a in ace
e	pronounced like the e in bed
ee	pronounced like the ee in feel
i	pronounced like the i in tin
y	pronounced like the i in time
oh	pronounced like the o in go
oo	pronounced like the oo in pool
uh	pronounced like the u in puff
khg	guttural
zh	pronounced like the g in rouge
j	pronounced like the second g in George

The symbol "ow" is sometimes misunderstood, since it can be pronounced as in "how" or as in "tow". Therefore, it may be necessary to specify some pronunciations like this: "Bough (rhymes with how)".

GARDENS PRESERVATION LEAGUE GET NATIONAL GRANT
(70 words; 30 seconds).

Video

Audio

Slide No 1
(Exterior:
Orange House)

Slide No 2
(Interior:
Orange House;
architect
measuring room)

Today national recognition came to the Gardens Preservation League's restoration of the Orange House. The Pretoria-based National Trust for Historic Preservation has awarded an R8 000 grant to the volunteer group. The grant will be used to fund an architect who will prepare restoration plans for the 170-year-old Cape Town house. Following its restoration, the Orange House will be sold to a new owner who will guarantee its future preservation. -30-

Figure 11.8 The layout of a broadcast news release (for television).

Tips on interacting with reporters and editors

A key to successful media relations is to conduct yourself as a professional corporate journalist and to treat the media in the way you would like to be treated. In practical terms: if a reporter asks you for something, get back to him timeously so he can process the information before his deadline. If they use a specific style, write for that style. If you have to translate a release, make sure the translation is correct.

In the past, public relations practitioners were often seen as a hindrance placed in the path of journalists in order to obscure what was really going on in the company. But that is changing. Companies are realising that fair media coverage is an essential part of projecting a credible image. The better you treat the media, the better your chance of putting forward your side of a sticky story. And often, when a reporter needs an opinion on something related to your industry, she will ask you, the publicist, because she knows you are reliable and credible. In the process you will be getting positive exposure for your organisation. There are several pointers that may be helpful to this end.

Once you have picked the media your company needs to use and prepared the information the media can use, the time has come for you to get to know how those media work – and who does the work:

• Who are the people who get things done?
• Who decides what is news and what is not?

- What do they regard as newsworthy?
- Do they have any particular interests (the arts, environment, health issues) or dislikes (the arts, environment, health issues)? What are their style and language preferences?
- What are their deadlines?
- What can you do to make their work as easy as possible?

Directing the release at the right person

Most TV and radio stations have a news director, and all news releases should be addressed to him or her. Newspapers, however, are more complicated since various section editors may be interested in the news you have to offer. The following guidelines may prove helpful.

Releases aimed at a single topic (such as food or sports) should go to that section editor. If the release is of general local interest, the news editor is usually the right person for it. If one reporter covers your organisation all the time, send the release directly to him or her.

Knowing the deadlines

Keep in mind that the deadline schedules of weekly papers differ from those of dailies. Radio journalists have several deadlines each day, while some magazines need information up to three months before publication. Online news sites update their stories throughout the day.

You must know the deadlines in order to get the release delivered on time. The deadline of a weekly published on Thursdays may be as early as Monday.

Veteran journalist and editor Raymond Joseph makes this important point: "It's not the best story and picture that makes the paper. It's the best story and picture available at the moment."

Be careful when inviting daily journalists and magazine writers to the same event. "By the time mags can use a story, the dailies have killed it," says Lize Odendal, an award-winning magazine journalist. "If you have wasted people's time, they can get really resentful. Check this first with the journos [sic] you invite."

Exclusive stories

The media is a competitive business environment and all journalists love scoops. If you have a good relationship with an editor in your target area, you may consider giving him or her an exclusive story. Never lie about giving a scoop, though. You are likely to harm your relationship with an editor who expects to be running an exclusive, which he or she then also sees in a rival publication. Try to come up with new and different angles for each publication. "The challenge for the publicist," says Marcus Brewster, "is to get in everywhere, every time."

Giving the press gifts or freebies

Of course, the issue becomes an ethical one when showing the press common courtesies crosses the line into bribery. "For the most part, I think the media have a deep suspicion of gifts," says Marcus Brewster. "They are highly sensitised to the moral dilemma it places them in. Personally, I think of gifts in the same way as I think about lunching with journalists. If your story is not strong enough to be published, it won't go in, gift or not." Brewster is right. Many media organisations have policies on the matter. The *Sunday Times'* one is straightforward: "WE DO NOT ACCEPT ANYTHING FOR FREE (their emphasis). We pay our own way, and we do not accept gifts, freebies, inducements, special offers, tickets, free trips, and so on that are not available to us as ordinary citizens" (*Sunday Times*, no date).

HOT LINK

Check out the *Sunday Times'* policy on accepting gifts and freebies at: http://www.sanef.org.za/ethics_codes/sunday_times/277048.htm. The International Public Relations Association's "Campaign for Media Transparency" has the goal of reducing the incidence of unethical and sometimes illegal practices in the relationships between public relations professionals and the media. See details of their annual surveys of international practices at: http://www.ipra.org.

HOT LINK

Do you have experts on-hand who are comfortable with media interviews? Consider listing them with a service such as ProfNet, which makes expert sources available to journalists: http://www3.profnet.com.

Tips on pitching for media interviews

Enterprising publicists seek out opportunities to promote their organisation or client either as the focus of an interview or as sources that can provide expert comment on other activities. Universities, for example, usually have on hand a list of academic experts and the areas on which they are able to comment.

If you're seeking to set up an interview with a reporter, being professional means the following:

- First, determine if the person or topic is relevant or newsworthy for that medium.
- If the reporter follows up on the offer, provide: concise background information, adequate time, and a conducive atmosphere in which to conduct the interview. Radio reporters, for example, would rather not do an interview near a noisy air-conditioning unit or buzzing light fixture. Television reporters need a visually pleasing or significant setting. The rule: ask each reporter what he or she requires.
- Be on time and, if the interview takes place in an office, make sure the phone doesn't constantly interrupt the discussion.
- If you are planning to sit in on an interview, know that the reporter is likely to mention it in the story. Ask yourself: Is that the impression I would like to create?

Definition

Spokesperson or **spin doctor**? *Spin* refers to twisting information to suit a particular agenda. Success in this is called "spinning the story," ideally by "putting a positive spin on the story." For example, if a politician was caught swearing at his butcher, a spokesperson could "spin" the story into a tale of the politician "expressing outrage at the corporate middlemen marking up meat prices at the expense of our nation's farmers."

Specialists either at executing spin, or especially at planning it, are often referred to as *spin doctors*. Whatever else it may be, spin doctoring is about the intent to distort information and to deceive the audience, rather than to communicate honestly. In a globally networked environment in which information is readily available and facts easily checked, spinning is typically quickly detected and discredits the source and the organisation they represent. For more on spin doctoring, read PR Watch at: http://www.prwatch.org.

Being approached by the media for information or an interview

If a reporter approaches you for an interview, being professional means paying attention to the following suggestions:

- Be courteous, but find out as much about the intended interview as possible in order to brief your client or company spokesperson thoroughly.
- Act on requests, even if it means you have to decline. Not responding to a reporter's request may end up with the reporter writing exactly that.
- Even if you don't have the information the reporter is looking for, or can't release the information, speak to the reporter. Simply saying, "We're checking out the details and will be happy to let you know what's happening when we know more," will sound much more reasonable in the next day's newspaper. If you promise to get back to the journalist with a statement, make sure you honour your word.
- Avoid saying, "No comment." That phrase is synonymous with "I'm guilty" in the minds of journalists – and of their audiences.
- Recognise the value of media exposure. Politicians and public figures, such as film stars and sports heroes, rely a great deal on publicity to secure their positions in society. But, says former editor of *FHM* magazine editor Neil Bierbaum, many public figures forget that important point:

> *The secret to fame is, whatever you do, make sure it's in front of the camera. Which is what our sportsmen – with their new-found celebrity status – are discovering. A top Springbok rugby player gets paid to play rugby. This takes place in front of a camera. Because his face is so well-known, and presumably because he means something, he gets offered sponsorships. More money. More cameras. Then comes the appearance money – speeches at dinners, promotions at shopping centres, that sort of thing. And all the time cameras.*
>
> *This has led to a small problem: these sportsmen have commission-earning managers who have convinced them that once they become famous, they can begin to charge the cameras for being there. An example: François Pienaar's agent wanted to charge us R12 000 to interview and photograph him. Ever heard of biting the hand that feeds? They are famous because of the cameras, not the other way round (Bierbaum, 1997:10).*

Bierbaum's advice to famous figures – as well as their publicists and agents – is this:

To make the team is to earn a salary from the [rugby] union. The peripherals – the sponsorships, the paid public appearances – those are the bonuses. This doesn't fall to everyone. It falls to the chosen few whom the camera likes. And they should be grateful for that.

Press events

Never call a news conference if a simple news release will do. Journalists are usually strapped for time and resent being called from their offices, getting into their cars, hunting for parking, traipsing off to a room and waiting for someone to read a statement which could just as well have been faxed, e-mailed or hand-delivered.

The only reason to have a news conference is to provide an authority who will respond to journalists' questions about a complex matter or to exhibit something which cannot be satisfactorily displayed in a photograph, such as extensive restorations to a historic site.

Even on such occasions, be sure not to waste time. *Successful Salesmanship* editor Linda Trump notes that many publicists ply the news media with invitations to social occasions and gifts "assuming that journalists simply love the distraction of breakfasts, cocktail parties, tennis matches, and the like" (Trump, 1991:23). Trump recounts the following anecdote:

> *At a recent meeting I attended, a prominent financial editor deliberately arrived late and then interrupted lengthy introductions by stating, "Who cares who I am? Just get to the point and tell us why you dragged us out here in the first place."*

Fussing over minor mistakes

There is one thing that irritates journalists more than making errors and that is having someone point it out to them. Do not pester the media and make a fuss over small mistakes, but do not hesitate to request a correction when a significant error appears in print.

In this chapter, you learned that:

- The role of the publicist is a complex one. It takes special skills to balance the demands of management with the requirement of the media.
- Successful publicity supports organisational strategy and communicates appropriate messages to target audiences – and can be evaluated.
- Effective news releases meet the requirements of editors, the audience – and the organisation that issues them. Publicists need to pay special attention to the content, the format and the ways of distributing the information.
- Professional publicists are competent writers and strategists, have extensive knowledge of the media and a commitment to behaving ethically.

FROM THE PUBLICIST'S DESK

Marcus Brewster

Marcus Brewster has been in publicity and public relations for over 15 years, including a five-year stint in the record industry where he became Group International Promotions Manager for EMI Music. He founded his own company in 1991 and represents clients as diverse as FHM magazine, Louis Vuitton, Virgin Active and Yardley.

1 How can you stay current with an ever-changing and expanding media universe?

By constant application. Keeping up to date is almost a full-time job by itself. If you can't afford to subscribe to magazines and other publications, spend time at a news agent. Spend two to three hours every fortnight checking out the latest issues on the racks. Don't neglect to read the masthead – familiarise yourself with the names of editors and feature writers. With radio and TV, make friends with your remote control. The cyber newsletters like biz-community, MarketingWeb and MediaBytes are also very useful for daily updates on the industry.

2 How important are contacts in media relations?

Critical. Although the technology of PR has changed dramatically in the last decade, the importance of good relationships hasn't. Possibly the most beneficial part of this networking is that it makes the pitching and liaising process so much more pleasant if you know who you're dealing with.

3 What special tips can you offer in dealing with the media?

Know the media. Know the publication, its target market, its formula. Know the editor, both personally and professionally. Know deadlines. Know when to stop pushing and be the first to say thank you.

4 What are the qualities you look for when appointing staff?

Articulateness, initiative, common sense, a passion for media, grooming.

Putting your learning to work

ACTIVITY 1 Evaluating a news release

Refer to the news release from Citigate South Africa (Figure 11.5 on p.265) and answer following questions:

- Who is the target audience for this news release?
- To which news media would you have sent the release?
- Can you identify any electronic media options that the publicists could have used?
- How would you rewrite the release for a suitable radio programme?

ACTIVITY 2 Creating a mini media campaign

Using the facts below, devise the following:

- A media strategy (consider adapting the template for a communication strategy provided by the Economic and Social Research Council).
- A one-page fact sheet.
- News releases for print and broadcast.
- A pitch letter for a media interview.

The Gordons Bay Chamber of Commerce is co-ordinating the first "Anchors & Antiques Festival", 14–15 October, on the Gordons Bay promenade. Gates open at 9 am each day.

Admission: R20, adults; R10 children 6 years and over; 5 years and under, free. Parking is free.

More information: Gordons Bay Chamber of Commerce: 555-000 or info@gordonsbayfestival.co.za.

Programme highlights include:
- A yacht race, organised by the Gordons Bay Yacht Club, will begin at 9 am on 14 October. Details: 212-2222.
- A 5 km fun run and 10 km race will begin at the promenade at 9 am on 15 May. Registration is at 7 am. Details: Gordons Bay Runners 999-007.
- Wandering musicians and magicians from 9 am to 5 pm daily.
- Antique market and food stalls open from 9 am to 5 pm daily.
- The SA Navy support vessel, SAS Outeniqua, will be open for tours at the Gordons Bay Yacht Club from 9 am to 5 pm each day.
- Auction of fine antique furniture, paintings and carpets at 3 pm each day at the Riebeeck Hotel. Proceeds to benefit the Red Cross Children's Hospital.
- "Jazz on the Bay" concert from 7 pm to midnight, 14 October, hosted by Radio Helderberg and featuring international star Prince Kupi. The supporting act is the jazz quartet Tribe. Admission is free. [Further details about the musicians are available from the www.music.org.za website.]

HOT LINK

The Economic and Social Research Council (UK) offers a comprehensive online communications toolkit, which includes a template for devising a communications strategy. While it is designed to assist academic researchers publicise their work, the material can easily be adapted for other purposes, too. Check it out at: http://www.esrc.ac.uk/commstoolkit/intro.asp.

- The Cape Town Opera will perform extracts from George Bizet's "The Pearl Fishers" at 8 pm on 15 May, with a fireworks finale at 10 pm. Admission is free. [Further details about the CTO are available at: www. capetownopera.co.za].

Bibliography

Baxter, B.L. 1981. The news release: an idea whose time has gone? *Public Relations Review*, Spring 1981.

Jeffries-Fox, B. 2003. A discussion of Advertising Values Equivalency (AVE). Institute for Public Relations. [Online] Available at: http://www.instituteforpr. com/pdf/2003_advertising_value_equal.pdf [Accessed: 23 August 2004]

PRISA, 2003. Definition of PR. Institute for Public Relations and Communication Management (Prisa), 13 February 2003. [Online] Available at: http://www.prisa. co.za/index.php?page_id=490&id=196 [Accessed: 26 August 2004]

Seitel, F.P. 1992. *The practice of public relations,* 5th ed. New York: Macmillan.

Steyn, B. and Puth, G. 2000. *Corporate communication strategy.* Johannesburg: Heinemann.

Sunday Times [no date]. Policy on gifts and freebies. [Online] Johannesburg: *Sunday Times.* Available at: http://www.sanef.org.za/ethics_codes/sunday_times/ 277048.htm [Accessed: 24 August 2004]

Trump, L. 1991. PR should sell, not tell. *Rhodes University Journalism Review*, Dec. 1991.

Tucker, K., Derehan, D. and Rainer, D. 1994. *Public relations writing.* London: Prentice Hall.

12 Publication planning and design

Introduction

To begin with, design is not just about how a newspaper, magazine or house journal looks. It's about what the publication is. It's about where it comes from, why and for whom it exists, and to what it aspires. These elements determine how the publication is presented to the world.

Design affects every aspect of a publication and every person in the newsroom – as editor David Hazelhurst explained after one of his publications was revamped (1992:27):

We decided on a total redesign. And by that I don't mean layout – we redesigned our approach to news, the way we wrote stories, the architecture of the stories, the layout, our typography, our use of colour – and we redefined news.

Design wasn't there for designers; colour wasn't there to dazzle; headlines weren't there to be clever; pictures and graphics weren't there merely to be looked at; layout wasn't there to impress layout subs.

Design was there to get people to read the writers. [his emphasis]
The content was paramount – the rest, the candy floss and pizzazz that would get the stories read.

As with people, there are no set theories and rules on how to design perfect publications. But there are guidelines. And they are as important to the writers as they are to those responsible for the graphic elements in the publication, says internationally recognised design expert Jan

White: "Tradition, bad guidance, and miseducation have propelled them [reporter and editors] into that boxed view that splits the team of communicators into two hostile camps: the word people and the visual people," he says.

"How to use design for editing? Start welding the two factions into one team, whose individual members understand how vital their shared efforts are to the success of the product's acceptance by the public" (1992:6).

Our objective, then, is primarily to help "word people" who work as publication editors to work better with the "visual people" – and to get that "welding" started. While we will focus here on the process of planning and designing a corporate publication, the principles can be applied in traditional print media and, to some extent, in an online context, too.

LEARNING GOALS

At the end of this chapter, you should be able to:

1 Plan a corporate publication.
2 Set a design philosophy.
3 Make informed decisions about grids, typography and photographs.
4 Put together a publication for print.

Planning a corporate magazine

It is impossible for management in large, sophisticated organisations to be in close, personal contact with all employees, or for employees to be as closely linked to each other as they are in smaller concerns. Managements of large corporations have come to rely on some form of organised communication programme to make and maintain contact with employees (Pigeon, 1979:63).

Publication editors and trainers Tom Ferreira and Ingrid Staude (1991:9) say:

The success or failure of companies in South Africa will be determined by the people on the shop floor, the people who sweep the streets, the people who dig for gold kilometres underground. The company that manages to keep its staff motivated and happy is on the road to success. This can be achieved only through effective communication. Top management will have to listen to ordinary people, to their needs and expectations. They will have to keep their employees informed of the company's decisions and plans, however demanding this may be. It is the right of all employees, including the general manager, to be informed.

Looking at the big picture

When planning and executing a communications strategy, modern corporate communicators make use of various communication *tactics*. These tools include:

- face-to-face conversations/meetings (which have been proven to be the most effective means of communication)
- meetings and discussion groups
- memoranda
- bulletin boards
- videos
- e-mail
- Inter- and intranet
- newsletters and house journals
- shop-floor radio and industrial theatre

Communication tools are sometimes used separately to communicate a message, but more usually they are used in conjunction with one another in order to achieve the desired result.

One way to look at the interaction between the elements of a communication strategy is to imagine a symphony orchestra. Consider the music score as being the communication strategy or plan, the communication tactics listed above as various instruments and the director as the corporate communicator. Each instrument can create music. But if the instruments follow a well-composed score and the directions of the conductor, they can create beautiful harmony together. Of course, no single instrument can produce the magnificent sounds of an entire orchestra.

It is also true that some "instruments" will be used more often than others. Though the house journal is a popular "instrument" in the internal communication "orchestra", it may sometimes be left out of the "performance". It all depends on the "music" the corporate communicator wants to create.

The role of the house journal

A house journal can be defined as "a publication which does not aim to make a profit, through which an organisation communicates with its internal or external target audiences at least twice a year" (Ferreira and Staude, 1991:6).

But what is the role of the house journal in an organisation? Or what should it be? One of the easiest ways of describing the role of the house journal, is first to explain what it *can't* do and then to look at what it *can* do (in relation to what other communication tools can't do).

What the house journal can't do

- It should not be used as the only communication tool in an organisation. Under no circumstances can it replace face-to-face communication – the most important form of communication in an organisation.
- It cannot rectify internal strife and infrastructure problems in the organisation.
- It cannot communicate upcoming changes to front-line employees. In their book *Communicating Change*, T.J. Larkin and Sandar Larkin say:

> *The company newspaper has absolved managers from the responsibility of designing real communication. Communication that reaches the front line and changes behaviour. To improve communication, consider banning all company newspaper articles informing front-line employees of upcoming changes. This ban would deprive senior managers of the illusion that an article in the company newspaper was communication. It would force them to say aloud which is the case anyway, that there is not communication (1994:117).*

- The house journal cannot improve morale. "Morale is improved by better communication between employees and their supervisors. The effect of the company newspaper is too minuscule to be seriously considered" (Larkin and Larkin, 1994:120).

What can the house journal do?

- The most important thing a house journal can do – and there are still many organisations which do not understand this role fully – is to reinforce messages which have already been communicated to staff. "Companies with the least understanding of employee communication rely exclusively on the company newspaper to communicate changes. Those with greater understanding use printed communication as back-up" (Larkin and Larkin, 1994:120). The authors, quoting research done by General Motors, the giant international automobile company, say: "GM's research was among the first to reveal that communication should come from the supervisor, face-to-face, with issues relevant to the local work area. But even GM cannot wean itself from a dependence on printed publications."
- A house journal can recognise the achievements of its staff, in the workplace and outside of it. This would be, for instance, publishing

photographs and articles about staff who excelled in their work or sport, or are attending one or other convention in recognition for good production. It shows staff that organisations are interested in their success.

- The house journal is also a written form which provides a permanent record. It can form a very important part of the archives of any company and is invaluable for research and follow-up articles.
- A house journal can also contribute to the relationship between management and employees. That, of course, depends on a number of factors. Briefly, theorists have pointed out that amongst the key factors of an organisation's relationship with its stakeholders, such as employees, are: trust, control mutuality and commitment.

Trust, according to researchers (Hon and Grunig, 1999; Huang and Grunig, 2001, et al) can be defined as: Someone's level of confidence in another and the willingness to themselves keep to fair and aboveboard dealings.

Control mutuality is defined as "the degree to which partners agree about which of them should decide relational goals and behavioural routines" (Stafford and Canary, 1991:224). The use of two-way communication can help produce control mutuality in a relationship. For media specialists that means creating ways for the audience to share in content decisions and also to provide avenues for feedback.

Relational commitment has been defined (Hon and Grunig, 1999:14) as "the extent to which one party believes and feels that the relationship is worth spending energy to maintain and promote". Since formalising communication channels is one way of showing commitment to a relationship, a regularly-produced house journal that appears on time can help demonstrate an organisation's devotion to their employees.

The role of the editor

Quite frankly, the one who pays the bills calls the shots. Or as Clampitt et. al. write in *Exploratory Research on Employee Publications* (1986:16): "First, the publication is funded and supported by management. Hence the purpose of the publication must be consistent with the goals and philosophy of the organisation. The responsibility is to the well-being of the organisation first, the audience second and society at large, third." Does this mean staff of that organisation have to be satisfied with boring brainwashing messages from the MD and other managers who are only interested in seeing their own picture in print? Not at all.

Rex Gibson, a former deputy editor of *The Star*, says: "The fact that house journals are, by

HOT LINK

Want to know more about how to evaluate the success of organisational communication? See the research papers by the Institute for Public Relations at: http://www.instituteforpr.com/measurement_and_evaluation.phtml

their nature, small-screen, narrow-focus enterprises should not leave their producers with an inferiority complex. Not every publication can deal with a war or a political revolution. But at the very least, all publications should be professional enough in approach and presentation to make them acceptable, not only to readers but to journalistic craftsmen in other fields" (Ferreira and Staude, 1991:vii). This implies, then, that the editor must have the skills to balance management and staff expectations on both content and presentation. One way of keeping up with the latest developments in the field is through membership of professional organisations, such as the Institute for Public Relations and Communication Management.

Increased emphasis on transparency in organisations means that house-journal editors have had a slightly easier time in introducing more sensitive and controversial issues into their publications, says Truia Ralph, a communications manager at Old Mutual.

On the other hand, Ralph points out, the editor's responsibility is much greater when working with sensitive information. Once the publication is printed and distributed, it can fall into the hands of anybody – including the organisation's rivals. And, believe it or not, house journals are read by competitors as they often contain valuable information not found elsewhere. If articles disclose information which the competitor can use to harm your own company, it means staff will also be affected in the process. This must be considered at all times.

So, how does the editor know where to draw the line? Check the content of every issue with the objectives set out for the publication and also check whether it is in line with the mission of your company.

Tips on planning a new publication

Most publications fail because the editorial team has little or no understanding of exactly what it wants to communicate. Why is the publication necessary? Every successful publication is designed to communicate for a very specific reason. For example:

- A house journal is published primarily to keep employees informed about what is happening in the company.
- A marketing brochure is designed to inform potential clients of the benefits of a product or service in a way that will promote sales.
- A magazine for scuba divers will be designed to keep divers abreast of the latest developments in their sport with regard to diving sites, techniques, equipment, legislation, and so forth.

Setting specific objectives for your publication is the only way to measure if you are doing a good job. These objectives should directly, or indirectly, contribute to the business goals of your organisation.

These objectives should always determine the content of your publication. A good strategy is to revise your objectives from time to time as business goals are continuously being re-evaluated and updated and editors need to go with, and ideally be in advance of, this ebb and flow.

Who is the target audience?

If design is going to render the message acceptable and understandable to the audience, it is essential for the editorial or design team to have a clear picture of their audience. What does your target audience look like? Are they male or female? How old are they? Where do they live? What are their interests? What are their levels of education and literacy? What is their home language? How much do they earn?

A publication aimed at promoting better farming methods among semiliterate subsistence farmers in Limpopo Province will not be designed in the same way as a scientific journal for academic agronomists.

What do they want?

"Research, research, research," says Petro van Bosch, who has edited award-winning publications for the financial services company Sanlam. "In a creative environment or during brainstorming sessions, corporate communicators can so easily be trapped by their own ideas. A beautiful new publication, they think. A totally different look and content. But did they ask their readers if they wanted it? Or better still, did their readers ask for it?" (1997).

The first thing to do is to survey potential readers to find out what kind of information they want, how frequently they would like the publication to appear, and so on. If you can't do that upfront, then do such a survey after the first year and, thereafter, every second year.

How will we achieve our objectives?

For a publication to be successful it is important that the editorial team should understand exactly what it is they need to tell their target audience. In the case of a house journal, for example, this will probably include the following:

- corporate news
- regional or divisional news
- information with regard to promotions and appointments
- insight into corporate philosophy and thinking
- guidelines on how to derive maximum benefit from staff regulations and procedures
- feedback columns, such as readers' letters
- social news
- sports news

What will the publication look like?

If you have an unlimited budget to spend on a publication, the sky is really the limit. You can hire journalists, graphic designers and photographers and buy whatever technology you want. But, unfortunately, this is not usually the case. Before design decisions can be made, the questions raised above and a few others need to be answered. These answers make up a publication profile or publication brief, which is necessary as most publications need to be approved by management and are created by a team, all of whom need a clear understanding of what is going on.

Planning the publication content and integrating the process

- Writers, of course, spend a lot of time writing but they also need to think about how the reader is drawn into the text. Ideally they should spend time thinking about the package as a whole – graphics, photographs and heads, as well as the text itself.
- Editors enter the process at many sections – assignments, content, style judgement, story placement. Along the way they also check accuracy, clarity, and focus and monitor visual support.
- Designers usually come in late in the game. Their task is to integrate all the parallel efforts of writing, photography and graphics into a compelling layout. They should be included from the start.

The WED concept – the integration of Writing, Editing and Design – is to create a graphic awareness at all levels, especially among reporters. The term "WED" comes from the Poynter Institute for Media Studies, where many gurus of our industry – including Don Fry, Mario Garcia and Nora Paul – work. "WED works," says Jan White, "when words and visuals of a story are marked by common meaning and interpretation" (1992:6–8). That means the photographs, colour, typographical selections, and graphics are chosen or created for the meaning they convey, whether that meaning is political, technical or emotional. And it means that the words are precise and a story carefully narrated.

> ##### HOT LINK
> Learn more about how WED works by visiting
> http://www.poynter.org/content_view.asp?id=4553

To marry these disciples, all the relevant parties must "own" the package and be involved from the start.

Planning a network of contributors

It is quite unlikely that you will ever have no news or too little to write about, but it is a good policy to involve as many staff members as possible.

* Note: See the production guide discussed on p.317.

"Art is wonderful.
Craft is admirable.
Design is teachable."

EDWIN TAYLOR, FORMER
DESIGN DIRECTOR OF THE
LONDON *SUNDAY TIMES* AND
EX-MANAGING EDITOR OF *US
NEWS AND WORLD REPORT*

If you work for a large organisation with branches across the country, write a letter to each of the branch managers, asking them to provide you with the name of a person who would be interested in regularly informing you about happenings and photographs of happenings at that particular branch. Try wherever possible to get this function written into that person's job description so that your "reporters" become accountable. Staff who take up this challenge should be rewarded for their efforts.

Once you have the names, you can "educate" these people, telling them exactly what you want from them.

Many house journal editors also run annual competitions for "Best correspondent of the year". If this competition is kept alive during the year, it can have very good results. In a smaller organisation, a similar approach can be taken for the different departments.

Planning the design

Louis Heyneman knows about design. He studied under some of the best designers as a graduate student at the University of Missouri and brought those ideas back home and applied them as associate editor of *De Kat* magazine. He knows that there are no quick answers when it comes to publication design (1993):

Indien daar 'n waterdigte teorie sou bestaan oor hoe 'n koerant of tydskrif visueel daar moet uitsien, wat daarin moet staan, of selfs presies wat daarmee bereik moet word, sou mens dit bloot soos 'n koekresep kon toepas en die resultaat sou volmaakte tydskrifte of koerante wees. *[English translation: If a watertight theory existed on how a newspaper or magazine had to look, what had to appear in it, or exactly what it had to achieve, one would merely have to apply it like a cake recipe and the result would be a perfect magazine or newspaper.]*

Refer to p. 317 for some examples of his critique of modular layout configurations.

Creating a design philosophy

Although there are no foolproof formulas for design, there are some good basic guidelines. Some of the best come from Jan White, whose many books on publication design include *Editing by Design*, *Graphic Design for the Electronic Age* and *Thoughts on Publication Design*.

What's in it for me?

Potential readers are all looking to see if the publication has information they can use. Teaser boxes are the most obvious example of the what's-in-it-for-me factor. So are blurbs or story summaries, fact boxes and boxes that tell the reader the exact location, ticket and booking information (that means prices too!) and contact details of the play that is reviewed or bicycle race that is discussed. This factor is closely linked to the second one.

Speed

Most readers' attention span has been reduced to about 11 minutes – the break between television commercials. Readers want to know what's in it for them – and they want to know fast.

Obviousness

This is the third crucial element. Publications must be designed and edited in a way that makes complex information simple to absorb and understand. "Information turned into visual form can be grasped faster than verbal descriptions or statistics," White says (1992:6). Obviousness translates into the following elements:

- Headline typography that is bold, readable and positioned so that it shows the relative importance of the story.
- Modular page layout (see full discussion below) where stories in horizontal shapes and pictures are arranged on the page so that it is instantly clear what belongs with what, and how long an item is.
- Better cropping of pictures so that it is immediately evident what element of the picture is relevant to the story.
- Colour that is not only decorative, but which helps to organise, highlight and emphasise.

Salesmanship

"Readers aren't really readers," White says. "At least they don't start out as such. First they are lookers. People scan, hop and skip around, pecking here and there, searching for goodies until something catches their attention. Seldom do they start reading at the start of an article. They enter where they damn well feel like entering. Watch how you read yourself ... That's why we must build in as many welcoming doorways as we can. Because, once fascinated, lookers will indeed start to read."

Emotional involvement

This is based on the assumption that we relate better to emotional truth than to intellectual truth. For journalists, that means more pictures and fewer long stories. Describing this factor as "news that touches your life", Hazelhurst said: "We saw no point in running long, important stories that used to feel good but weren't going to be read" (Hazelhurst, 1992:27).

Guidance

Readers want to be able to find their way around the paper easily and distinguish what is most important. Grouping stories under standard headings – for example, local news, international news and sport – and keeping them in the same place in the paper is a start.

Personality

This means that the publication must have a distinctive character. In other words, you have to set design guidelines and largely stick to them so that your reader recognises the look and style of the publication!

Money

Good design has proved to be good business. Three months after the *Mail & Guardian* was redesigned – in response to readers' suggestions – the paper posted record advertising revenues. However, beware: glitzy design alone is not enough to keep readers captivated; they also want the right stories and they want them to be well written. Twenty months after the much acclaimed redesign of the *Sunday Star*, the money-losing paper was closed down. The managing director at the time, David Kovarsky, was quoted as saying: "The regrettable closure demonstrated a lack of direction" (*Cape Times*, Jan. 20, 1994:5).

Using grids

Very few newspapers or magazines are printed as a single mass of text across a single page. To make them more readable they are printed in a column format or according to a pre-determined grid.

A grid allows one to arrange text on a page in an accessible and legible format. As such, choosing a grid involves a major design decision.

A grid also establishes a natural reading rhythm that helps to lead the reader through the publication. Different grids establish different rhythms. Large, one-column or full-page grids slow reading speed down because the reader's eye has to travel a long way across the line length. If you want your reader to ponder over what you are telling him, or make a weighty statement, a wide column grid can be a useful tool.

Narrow grids, on the other hand, make for faster reading. If you want to establish a snappy, businesslike style, narrower columns are very useful. They also work well in short news-snippet sections.

Like the human voice that becomes monotonous if the tone is not varied, a publication that uses only one column width throughout quickly becomes boring to the reader. By mixing column widths you can create a very interesting publication. However, it is essential to ensure that the widths remain compatible with regard to rhythm.

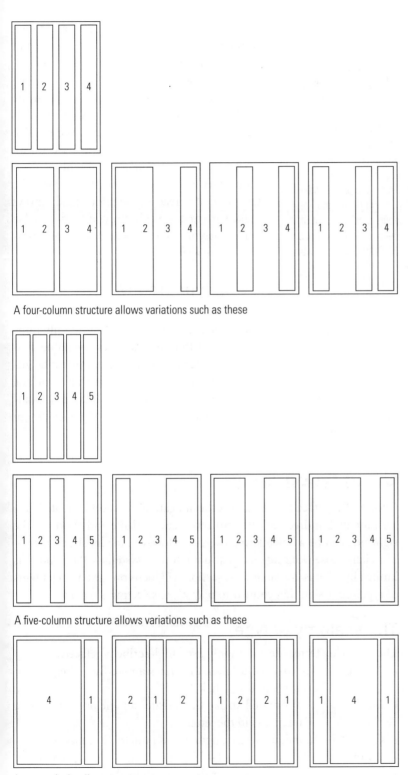

Figure 12.1
Column formats or grids

A four-column structure allows variations such as these

A five-column structure allows variations such as these

A group of miscellaneous page arrangements

▮HOT▮LINK

Eyes on the news. The Poynter Institute for Media Studies published a book, *Eyes on the News*, in 1990, in which it documented a study of newspaper-reading habits. The study used a special camera mounted on the heads of readers that tracked their eye movements as they read a newspaper. The study found that only 25 per cent of the text in newspapers was being looked at or "processed" (Adam and Garcia, 1990:70). Of all the elements processed in newspapers, text was looked at the least, compared with 80 per cent of the artwork, 75 per cent of the photographs, 56 per cent of the headlines, 52 per cent of the advertising, 31 per cent of the news briefs and 29 per cent of the cutlines (1990:70). Of the text that was processed, 30 per cent was news, 23 per cent was features and 19 per cent was sports (1990:70).

Read more about a follow-up study which investigated how readers 'eye' online media at: http://www.poynter.org/content/content_view.asp?id=5675.

If, for example, you are using a basic three-column grid you can also apply variations of it, such as 1 x 6 col, 6 x 6 col, and 9 x 6 col.

When choosing the basic grid, it is important to take into account the language of the publication. Afrikaans text, for example, tends to run considerably longer than the English equivalent. If the column width used for an Afrikaans text is too narrow, it will result in numerous word breaks, thereby making the text difficult to read and to understand. Always make sure that the column width you choose will serve your purposes of design and message to the optimum.

Using typography

Choice of typeface greatly affects the appearance of a document. There are literally hundreds of different typefaces available and choosing the right one can be quite a bewildering exercise. However, for most designers – especially those working on desktop publishing systems – their choice is limited by what is available. This section will focus on the basic elements of typeface design that come into play when selecting a typeface.

Using typography

Choice of typeface greatly affects the appearance of a document. There are literally hundreds of different typefaces available and choosing the right one can be a bewildering exercise. However, for most designers – especially those working on desktop publishing systems – their choice is limited by what is available. This section will focus on the basic elements of typeface design that come into play when selecting a typeface.

The anatomy of type

The following terms are commonly used to describe typefaces.

- Ascender   The part of a letter that rises above the x-height, for example in b, d, f, h, k, l and t.
- Bowl   The rounded stroke that creates an enclosed space in a character, as in the letter b.
- Character   Individual letters, figures and punctuation marks.
- Counter   The space enclosed – fully or partially – within a character.
- Descender   That part of a letter that falls below the baseline.

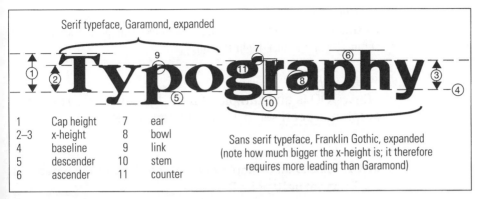

Figure 12.2 Serif and sans serif typefaces

- Families   All the sizes and type styles (i.e. bold, medium, light, italic, condensed, expanded, etc.) of a particular typeface.
- Font   A complete set of characters, i.e. lower- and uppercase characters, figures and punctuation marks.
- Lowercase   Small letters are called lowercase characters.
- Serif   The lines crossing the main strokes of a character (the little feet).
- Stress   The direction of thickening in a curved stroke.
- Uppercase   Capital letters are called "caps" or uppercase characters.
- X-height   The vertical height of a letter, excluding ascenders and descenders.
- Roman   Roman means upright, i.e. not italic.

Understanding fonts

Fonts are divided into several main categories:

- **Serif**
  These typefaces have serifs or little finishing strokes at the end of the stems, arms and tails of characters. It was originally intended that these serifs would separate the letters and stop them from running into each other, thus providing built-in spacing within the typeface.
  Serifs come in several basic varieties, namely full bracket, fine bracket, hairline, wedge and slab:

  Full bracket serif
  PLANTIN is an example of a full-bracket serif face. This paragraph has been set in 10 point Plantin Roman.

  Fine bracket serif
  BEMBO is an example of a fine bracket serif face. This paragraph has been set in 10 point Bembo Roman.

Hairline serif

FENICE is an example of a hairline serif face. This paragraph has been set in 10 point Fenice Light Roman.

Wedge serif

LEAWOOD is an example of a wedge serif face. This paragraph has been set in 10 point Leawood Roman.

Slab serif

ROCKWELL is an example of a slab serif face. This paragraph has been set in 10 point Rockwell.

Examples of more commonly known and widely used serif typefaces include: Times, Garamond, Baskerville and Cheltenham.

TIMES is an example of a serif face. This paragraph has been set in 10 point Times Roman.

GARAMOND is an example of a serif face. This paragraph has been set in 10 point Garamond Roman.

BASKERVILLE is an example of a serif face. This paragraph has been set in 10 point Baskerville Roman.

CHELTENHAM is an example of a serif face. This paragraph has been set in 10 point Cheltenham Light.

- **Square or slab serif**
  These typefaces are also called Egyptian type. They were developed in Britain at the turn of the century (Sutton, 1986:53) not long after the discovery of King Tutankhamun's tomb. At the time the entire country was fascinated by Egyptian culture.
  Examples include Rockwell, Lubalin and American Typewriter.

ROCKWELL is an example of a slab serif face. This paragraph has been set in 10 point Rockwell.

LUBALIN is an example of a slab serif face. This paragraph has been set in 10 point Lubalin Graph Book.

AMERICAN TYPEWRITER is an example of a slab serif face. This paragraph has been set in 10 point American Typewriter Medium.

- **Sans serif**
  Also known as Gothic, these typefaces do not have serifs (*sans* is French for "without") and often have strokes that are the same thickness throughout.
  Examples include Futura, Franklin Gothic, Helvetica and Univers.

  FUTURA is an example of a sans serif face. This paragraph has been set in 10 point Futura Book.

  FRANKLIN GOTHIC is an example of a sans serif face. This paragraph has been set in 10 point Franklin Gothic Roman.

  HELVETICA is an example of a sans serif face. This paragraph has been set in 10 point Helvetica Roman.

  UNIVERS is an example of a sans serif face. This paragraph has been set in 10 point Univers Medium.

- **Text**
  Also known as Blackletter, these faces are likely to remind you of the writing on old newspaper titlepieces and in Bibles. That is not surprising, since the type was introduced by Gutenberg when he printed the first Bible in 1450 and was widely in use until the twentieth century. Recently this type – which is not very legible – has lost popularity.
  An example is Old English.

  Old English is an example of a Blackletter face. This paragraph has been set in Old English.

- **Cursive**
  Also known as script, these typefaces resemble formal handwriting. Most script typefaces are not easily legible and, as a rule, should be used with utmost discretion – if at all. Examples are Palace Script and Brush Script.

  Brush Script is an example of a script face. This paragraph has been set in 12 point Brush Script.

- **Ornamental**
  Also known as novelty typefaces, these come in a great variety. Design expert Tony Sutton gives this advice (1986:54): "Smart editors use [ornamental typefaces] to add impact to feature pages; wise editors don't!"
  Examples include Dom Casual and Technical.

Dom Casual is an example of an ornamental face. This paragraph has been set in 14 point Dom Casual.

Tekton is an example of an ornamental face. This paragraph has been set in 12 point Tekton Normal.

Measuring type and layout

Typography and layout calculations are traditionally done in points and picas.

- **Points**
  Points are small measurements, approximately the size of the mark made by a finely sharpened pencil. Small areas in a publication, such as the height of type and the thickness of rules, are measured in points.

  12 points equal 1 pica.
  72 points equal 1 inch, or 2,2 cm.

- **Picas**
  Often called ems, picas are used to measure larger areas in publications, such as the width and length of columns of type and in sizing photographs.

  6 picas equal 1 inch, or 2,2 cm.

- **Kerning**
  This refers to the space between individual letters. Kerning is usually adjusted to make type fit better into a set space.

- **Leading**
  The space between lines, usually set at 110 per cent of the type size (e.g. leading for 10 pt type will be set at 11 pt).

Tips on typographic communication

"Typographic clarity comes in two flavours: legibility and readability," writes Allan Haley (1992:9). Legibility is the quality that affects the ease with which one letter can be distinguished from another. Readability is the quality that affects the degree of ease with which typography can be read.

The following tips on legibility and readability have been compiled from advice given by design experts such as Haley, Sutton and White.

- **Upper and lower case**
  All-caps type is more difficult to read than upper- and lowercase type. Use all-caps sparingly.

- **Adequate x-height**
  Remember that type measurements include ascenders and descenders. Therefore, two fonts of the same point size may appear very different.

  Type with a large x-height and small ascenders and descenders will appear more substantial than a font of the same point size with a smaller x-height. Type with a smaller x-height and longer ascenders and descenders will appear smaller than a font in which the x-height is larger.

  Rule: Fonts with medium to large x-heights are more readable than fonts with small x-heights and extended ascenders and descenders.
- **Expanded or condensed**
  Normal-width type is more legible than condensed or expanded type.
- **Too big or too small**
  Type sizes of between 10 pt and 19 pt are more legible than smaller or larger sizes.
- **Italics**
  Tony Sutton (1986:58) says: *"Italic type can add contrast and emphasis when used – occasionally – to highlight key paragraphs of long feature items. Be careful, however, for overuse will look like a rash on your page."*
- **Fancy typefaces**
  Ordinary typefaces are more legible and readable than eccentric ones like Zapf Chancery, which has been used here.
- **Reversals and type over pictures**
  Black type on a white background is more legible than reverse type (white type on black background). Colour type and colour paper should be used very conservatively. Follow Edwin Taylor's advice: "Discretion is the better part of colour" (Sutton, 1992:7).
- **Line length**
  Research shows that for a 9 pt typeface the most readable line length is between 11 and 14 picas (Sutton, 1986:56), which gives about 10 English words per line. However, newspapers have conditioned many people to scan slightly smaller columns (approx. 9,5 picas or 4 cm) with ease. Avoid using very narrow columns when designing your publication. Remember: certain typefaces give you a lesser word count per line than others.
- **Justified left or right**
  Justified and flush left/ragged right type are equally legible, provided that the justified type is properly spaced.
- **Leading**
  This term refers to the space between lines of type. Body copy with one or two points of extra leading is more legible than type set solid or excessively leaded.

Titlepiece
Titelhoof

Teaser panel
Prikkelberig

Reverse heading
Omgekeerde opskrif

Initial caps (also called drop caps)
Begin letter

Mugshot
Nabyskoot

Turn line
Stop reël

Body type
Hoofdeeldrukletter

Display type
Vertoondrukletters

Halftone photograph
Raster fotografie

Caption
Onderskrif

Company logo
Maatskappy logo

Deep-etched photo
Afgedekte foto

Lead story
Hoofberig

Serif type
Skreef druklettertipe

Sans serif type
Skreeflose druklettertipe

Rule/border
Randomlyning

Figure 12.3 Knowing the right terms to use when refering to elements of a publication layout will help the "word" people communicate more effectively with the "picture" people.

- **Paragraph indentation**
  Some editors have decided to do away with indentations in favour of a line of white space. Don't! These white lines create what Tony Sutton (1986:56) describes as "horizontal rivers of wasted space".

Using photographs

You are unlikely to cover something quite as momentous as Nelson Mandela's release, but even routine stories and photographs need to be planned. Remember the primary purpose of a photograph is not to fill a hole in your design but to enhance your message. To help you plan your picture to do just that, the following checklist may prove useful.

- **Why?**

Why am I taking this picture? Is it going to be used for a news story or will it be used in a marketing brochure? What am I trying to achieve with the picture? What message am I trying to put across?

- **What?**

What am I taking a picture of – a person, a product or a place?

Think about it. For example, what exactly is your product? What does it mean to your target audience and how do they "see" it? Can you find an angle that will emphasise what they see or what you are trying to say?

Of which place are you taking a picture? A hotel, for example, is not just a building with bedrooms; it is a holiday or a home away from home. How can you convey this with a picture?

What is your organisation and how can you depict that in a photograph?

- **Who?**

Who am I taking a picture of?

The MD – sure. But, who is the MD? In a house journal you may want to depict him as a homely, approachable person. In the annual report you may want to portray him as a competent captain of industry and leader of a team of executives.

Decide which aspects of a person's personality and appearance will convey the desired messages in a picture.

"Who?" will often also determine your approach to the person. If he is a difficult person, plan your approach accordingly and dress accordingly. Don't take the risk of offending your subject in an attempt to show that you are artistic.

"Who?" will also mean having to find suitable models from time to time. As you move around your organisation make a note of who you think would work well in a photograph and keep their names on file. If you use models, however, make sure you get them to sign release forms or you could end up with an unexpected additional expense on your budget.

- **Where?**

Where can you get good photographs in your organisation? As you move around, note interesting locations.

Try looking at the world from a different angle. There is no rule that says you must stand flat on the ground. Why not climb a ladder or a flight of stairs and shoot from above your subject, or get down on your knees – the world looks different and quite exciting from down there! (Have you ever wondered what a child sees? You can relive it!)

"Where?" is also an important point in making sure that you arrive at a shoot. Being in the right place at the right time is part of being professional. Make sure you know where you have to be to take the picture.

Photographer Ulli Michel: "It was the most important picture of my life."

- **When?**

 "When?" is important to consider in your planning. Make sure you know what time on what day you have to take the photographs and get there well in time. "When?" can also refer to the time of day needed to create the right atmosphere. What do your headquarters look like at sunrise or at sunset? The best atmosphere shots do not necessarily happen during office hours. Get to know what your "wheres" look like at different times of the day.

- **How?**

 Once you have gone through the five Ws you should be able to arrive at a pretty good "How?", which should result in a good photograph that enhances your message. Below are a few examples of the types of picture you can take for specific situations.

Type of picture

In addition to layout requirements, and often more important, are editorial demands. It is usually clear from the start that certain types of pictures will be needed to illustrate a particular story. If the story is being photographed anew rather than being assembled from "stock" shots, the photographer can be given a shooting brief.

Definition

Stock pictures are those that are available from photolibraries (internally or externally) and agencies, such as SouthLight Picture-Net which provides photografhs of recent and past news events. Check them out at: http://www. picturenet.co.za. (Registration required but non-registered users can do sample searches.)

Sometimes pictures not contained in the brief may be taken during the shoot, and these may be used on their own merits. Photographs can be classified by the information they convey and the effect they have on developing a story. Not every story will require all these pictures and many photographs will fulfil a combination of several functions.

- **Point pictures**
  Variously called by different magazines, point pictures are the necessary illustrations for points made in the text (hence the name). They are used even if not visually exciting and often appear small.

- **Establishing shots**
  These are photographs that set the scene for certain kinds of story: an overall view of a city, for example, in which a story is set. Such pictures are generally used large and early on in a story.

- **Typical appearance/product shots**
  At some point in many picture stories, whatever is being featured must be shown clearly. If the subject is an invention or a household object, the photo could simply be a routine, "no frills" still-life, but it could equally well be an exciting abstract showing the "image" of the subject rather than the subject itself. Explicitly larger subjects, such as landscapes, broaden the scope further.

- **Key personalities**
  Just as a featured subject must be clearly illustrated, so must personalities who feature prominently in the story. Again, the type of picture will vary considerably according to the approach taken in the story. A formal studio portrait may be most appropriate in some instances, while an "involved" reportage shot may be better in others. Typically, a portrait will be combined with several "candid" shots to give a rounded view – the portrait providing the lead picture.

- **People at work**
  If the activity of a human subject is more important than the personality, it (and not the person) must feature prominently in the picture.

- **Unique images**
  This category covers all surprise pictures that rely on their novelty

Good photographs seldom just happen. They have to be planned, as Ulli Michel knows only too well.

Chief photographer for Reuters in southern Africa, Michel was among the more than 2 000 foreign and local journalists who descended on Cape Town in the summer of 1990 to record the release from prison of African National Congress President Nelson Mandela.

Michel's snap of a smiling Mandela walking to freedom holding hands with his then wife Winnie among a sea of raised fists was wired around the world and appeared on the front pages of most newspapers internationally.

"It was the most important picture of my life," Michel has said. "But what lengths we had to go to."

To get the shot – one of only eight frames Michel clicked before the surging crowd blocked his view – preparations began two months earlier with a task force of eight people. They planned possible routes, chartered aircraft and booked motorcycle messengers, arranged for a temporary darkroom as well as portable phones and walkie-talkies and rented a house opposite the Mandela home in Soweto. Scaffolding was ordered to ensure better vantage points.

How much did it cost to get the picture? "What, all expenses?" he asked. "Oh, about forty thousand rand, tops. But that's what we spent for the entire Mandela coverage, not just for the one picture. I consider it cheap in comparison to what other agencies and, in particular, the TV networks spent."

Estimates for media coverage of the first 50 steps Mandela took to freedom ranged between R2 million and R8 million – that is R40 000 to R160 000 per step.

"I've never seen anything like it before in 20 years of working for the BBC," said cameraman François Marais. "It was the biggest single news event ever."

for impact. Varieties are "first ever photograph of ...", such as the earth seen from space for the first time, and "new views", such as the first photographs of an unborn baby in the mother's womb.

- **Sequences**
  As well as fulfilling a design role, a sequence of pictures that shows the progress of action may have strong editorial value.

- **Juxtaposition**
  This is an important group of image types, usually run in pairs, which work by showing relationships. These relationships often contrast or compare, for example, the lives of the rich and the poor. Often the intention is one of deliberate surprise achieved by showing relationships of which the reader may not have been aware. The following varieties are found: unconscious mimicry (similar gestures and expressions from political opponents), scale contrast (dwarfed man/mighty works), anachronism (old-fashioned remnants in a modern city) and bizarre oddities and kitsch in context.

- **Point-of-view shots**
  Generally wide-angled, these shots show a point of view of an individual or group. The person will feature in the foreground, for instance a prison yard from a tower, with a guard right next to the camera.

- **Words and numbers**
  Both of these have extra visual "weight" where they appear in the photograph and attract the viewer's eye particularly strongly. They can convey additional information, often in juxtaposition (see above).

Types of picture stories

There are surprisingly few kinds of photographic features run in magazines, newspapers and books, although the range of treatments can be very varied. Many magazines, in fact, plan to run a balanced selection in each issue of the kinds of feature that they favour.

- **Place stories**
  Stories on particular places, from Paris to Ecuador, are popular with all kinds of magazines. They provide a good variety of shots, from small features to overall views and provide considerable scope for design. *National Geographic*, for example, uses this type of story regularly, with little or no news content, but taking a broad view. Treatment may vary according to the publication, from travelogue to political tract.

- **Periodic events**
  Festivals, coronations, royal weddings have obvious – and predictable – visual interest, so the coverage can be planned and scheduled well ahead of time. In fact, some magazines are virtually obliged to provide coverage of certain events.

- **Commodity stories**
  Similar in certain respects to place stories, these provide as thorough a review as possible of products used by man. The definition of a commodity tends to be quite loose, and could include rice, gold or integrated circuits.
- **"State-of-the-art" update**
  A special version of the commodity story, this type of story often has a scientific, "high-tech" bias, dealing with a topic or field where there is rapid development, such as cosmology or lasers.
- **Discovery**
  Sometimes related to a "state-of-the-art" update, discovery stories may deal with scientific and technical subjects, such as super-conductivity, or with discoveries in natural science, such as a newly discovered species or an archaeological discovery.
- **Social group**
  Unusual or closely knit social groups are appealing subjects, provided that the coverage has sufficient depth and intimacy. A remote tribe or religious group such as the Hassidim are typical subjects.
- **Nature**
  Specific nature stories tend to concentrate either on the species, such as lions in the Serengeti, or on a particular habitat, such as life on a coral atoll.
- **Biography**
  This may be a fairly concise story on a personality or a longer, more evocative treatment of a historical figure. The approach can vary widely from, for example, "A day in the life of ..." to "Following in the steps of ..." (Freeman, 1985).

Tips on working with photographers

- **Brief the photographer**
  If you are not taking the picture yourself, give the photographer as much information as possible about the story.

  If assignment cards are used, fill in the names of the important subjects, and suggestions for types of poses.

  Consider whether you need vertical or horizontal photos to suit the page design. It is sensible to get photographs shot in both formats. Also, do you need overall panoramic shots or close-ups?

  Do not forget to include directions – not just an address. Also give a telephone number in case the photographer gets lost or has problems getting there at all.
- **Go with the photographer, or meet him or her there, if possible.**
  Working as a team will usually improve a story because you will be seeing the action from another point of view. The photographer's questions will often help clarify the story in your own mind.

- **Be imaginative**
  If you are obliged to take yet another photograph of a cheque-giving ceremony, consider taking the photograph from a different angle or watching the recipient's face for a reaction. Avoid boring pictures of posed handshakes – grip-and-grin shots – and other visual clichés.
- **Do not interfere with the photographer**
  If you have suggestions, be tactful. Remember photographers have professional pride and are not writers' lackeys.
- **Print them all**
  Experienced house journal and newspaper editors usually choose photographs from contact sheets or proof sheets (strips of negatives laid side by side and printed on a single sheet of photographic paper). This allows them to see all the work the photographer has done. Always ask the photographer to print the full frame of the photographs and do the cropping yourself. Often photographers crop out just the extra millimetre or two you need to make the photo fit snugly into your design.

HOT TIP

Browse through international news magazines and photography books on a regular basis, keeping your eyes open for ideas you can use to make your next photograph more exciting.

You as a photographer

As a corporate journalist, more often than not you will end up being your own photographer. In this regard your success will not depend only on your technical know-how and artistic flair; to a large degree it will be determined by your ability to relate to and manage people. Bearing the following in mind will certainly be of help to you:

- The key to good subject rapport is patience and professionalism.
- Be on time every time.
- Dress properly for the occasion. If you are doing a dirty industrial shoot, jeans and a T-shirt may be fine, but they are not the right attire for photographing your board of directors or a black-tie gala affair. Always take your dress cue from the subject/s. Dress so that they will feel comfortable with you as a guest.
- When working with people always stay in control. If you have planned your picture in advance, this is relatively easy to achieve. Introduce yourself politely but firmly. Explain to your subjects what you are trying to achieve and why, and then arrange them. If you are working with a difficult or moody client, point out that you are trying to capture an image that will make him or her appear acceptable and professional to the specific target audience. You can only succeed in doing him justice if he co-operates.
- Be aware of other people's personal space. If you encroach on this without asking permission and explaining why, you are likely to end

up with an extremely tense subject. Make sure that you involve everybody present when working with a group. It takes only one bored individual to ruin an otherwise excellent shot.

EXERCISE *Briefing photographers*

Review the tips on working with photographers and develop a simple form to brief photographers. Ask your colleagues for feedback, modify and keep at hand to use when you assign a photographer, or to clarify the brief when you need to pick up a camera yourself.

Picture editing

You do not have to choose a great photograph. It will immediately stand out because, says Tony Sutton (1986:37) "it has the impact and power which come with these factors: presence, balance, composition, surprise, subtlety, movement – or uniqueness." To help you sift through the so-so pictures (i.e. the majority of pics that end up on your desk), Dr Mario Garcia of the Poynter Institute for Media Studies in the United States suggests you pay attention to the following factors:

* For futher discussion on photographic ethics, refer to Chapter 13.

- **Appropriateness**
  Ask yourself whether the picture is saying the right thing.

  It is true, a single photograph can say more than a thousand words – but make sure you choose the one that is saying the right things. Don't let your urge to be creative blur your vision of just what it is you want to accomplish with the photograph.

  On June 16, 1976, *The World* photographer Sam Nzima was sent into Soweto to cover the student uprising. He saw a lot that would have made dramatic pictures: students angrily marching, burning cars, building barricades, attacking government officials. He did not take a shot. "I did not take an earlier picture of death. I saw a lone policeman trying to run from the students. He hit a pole and fell. They slaughtered him like a goat and set him alight. I couldn't take pictures then," Nzima recalled (Tyson, 1993:110).

  When he did focus his camera, he shot six frames that included an image that, says former *Star* editor Harvey Tyson, "instantly symbolised the whole tragedy."

  "It was to my mind more powerfully emotional than all the hours of harrowing TV coverage which was run and re-run around the world for days," Tyson wrote. "It was a photograph of a tall teenage boy in overalls, a shy young girl in her trim school uniform, and of her younger brother. The body of 12-year-old Hector Peterson lies limply in the arms of the tall, urgently striding teenage stranger. Running to keep up, is the dead boy's sister, Antoinette Peterson.

In the young faces of the two is mirrored the shock and tragedy of all that happened in Soweto that day."

The impact of Nzima's shot echoes still. Hector's funeral, which thousands attended, became the focus of the people's grief and is still recalled at annual commemorations on June 16.

Few photographs you see are likely to have the same kind of impact. But, if possible, select photographs that can move your audience emotionally in some way.

- **Design possibilities**

  Photographs have to fit. If you are choosing a photograph, consider the design possibilities. Do you need to run a photograph down a single column? Or what about a close-up with impact? Select photographs that can be cropped to fit more than one shape.

- **Quality**

  Is it technically good? Avoid photographs that are too dark, too light, out of focus or grainy. Often these flaws are magnified in print. When it comes to printing pictures, bigger is better – usually, that is. So, if you have a particularly good picture, don't be afraid to use it big. Some newspapers, like *Liberation* in France, regularly run photographs up to half a tabloid-size page.

  Editors of house journals are often required to run pictures taken by amateur photographers. In that case, clever cropping and downsizing may help to disguise some of the photograph's compositional and technical flaws.

Cropping and sizing pictures

- **Cropping**

  Often the original print contains too much information, especially if it has to be made smaller to fit a layout. You want attention only on the important part of the image, so you must eliminate portions that do not suit your purposes, in other words, you have to crop the picture. There are three principles to consider when you crop:

  - A good photograph has only one subject or object of attention, only one area to which the eye is drawn to get the message.
  - Pleasing pictures tend to be composed in thirds, not halves. It is especially important not to run a strong line, like a flag pole or horizon, through the middle of a photograph.
  - Cropping should not eliminate important information. Never let the viewer suspect that something is missing.

- **Sizing**

  Even though most photographs are sized on-screen using computer design software, it is important to know how the the basis for these calculations. The are several methods to calculate how your picture will run when it is cropped and altered in size. Here are two of them:

The diagonal method

* You can begin with either the horizontal or vertical measurements. For our examples we started with horizontal measurements.

- Cover the photographs with a sheet of tracing paper and outline the area you want to use with a ruler and soft-tipped pencil.
- Now draw a diagonal line from corner to corner of the cropped section of the photograph.
- Decide how wide you want the photograph to run in the layout and, using a ruler, draw a line perpendicular to that width across to the diagonal line.
- Then draw a line at right angles and extend it to the base of the photograph. Measure that line to get the new length of the photograph.

original length 8 cm

new length 11 cm

original width 11 cm

new width 14 cm

Figure 12.4 The diagonal method

- To enlarge a photograph, extend the original diagonal line and then follow the same steps.

The formula method

It is best to do a layout by planning your photograph and editing your copy to fit, than to go about it the other way round. However, in practice you often have to plan to use your photograph in the space that is left over once the copy has been placed. When that happens, the formulae given below will be useful.

12

8   8

12

7

5   5

7

When researchers began comparing studies of the world's oldest civilisations, they discovered a fascinating thing. From the inhabitants of ancient Greece to the remote societies in Outer Mongolia, people shared the same appetite for news. "The first questions Mongols put to each other when they meet is invariably the same," an anthropologist noted in 1921. They ask: "'What's new?' And [then] each of [them] begins to pour out his whole supply of the news" (Maiskii, 1921). Even the same basic definition of what constitutes news remained constant over time. "Humans have exchanged a similar mix of news ... throughout history and across cultures," wrote media historian Mitchell Stephens (1997:27). In fact, they even looked for similar qualities in the messengers they picked to gather and deliver the news: they singled out those who could run swiftly over the next horizon, accurately gather the information, and compellingly retell it (Kovach and Rosensthiel, 2001:9).

How can these consistencies be explained? The answer, scholars have concluded, is that news fulfils a basic human instinct – the need to know what is happening beyond our own direct experience (Molotch and Lester, 1974). Being aware of events we cannot witness ourselves gives us a sense of security, control, and confidence (Kovach and Rosensthiel, 2001:9).

When the flow of news is hindered, historian Mitchell Stephens points out, "a darkness falls" and "we grow anxious. Our hut, apartment, village or city becomes a 'sorry' place" (1997:12). The world becomes, as it were, too quiet. We feel alone. South Africa's anti-apartheid hero Nelson Mandela knows that feeling all too well. For much of the 27 years he spent in jail, he and his comrades were locked up on Robben Island, cut off from the outside world. He recalled how he yearned for news during those long years behind bars. "Newspapers were more valuable to political prisoners than gold or diamonds, more hungered for than food or tobacco; they were the most precious contraband on Robben Island," he wrote in his autobiography (1994:492). "We were not allowed any news at all, and we craved it."

Stephens calls that craving "a hunger for awareness" (1997:12).

We need news to live our lives. It helps us to distinguish between threats and opportunities, enemies and friends. News helps us orientate ourselves, and it helps us connect with others. If the mass media is the system that societies generate to supply this news, then journalism is its lifeblood. That is why the character of the news and the quality of the journalism is important: they influence our thoughts, our experiences, our cultures. It certainly is a powerful position to be in. And those who want to write for the media – from inside a newsroom as a journalist, or from the outside as a publicist or source –

Figure 12.5 The formula method: reduction

To reduce a photograph

To calculate the % reduction required:

Size of layout / size of photograph x 100 = % reduction

= 5 / 8 x 100

= 63% (rounded off to the nearest full %)

To calculate how much you have to crop the width of the picture:

Size wanted / (% reduction / 100)

= 7 / (63 / 100)

= 7 / .63

= 11

Therefore, 12 cm – 11 cm = 1 cm. You will have to crop 1 cm from the width of the photograph and reduce it to 63% of its original size to make it fit the layout.

7

5   5

7

12

8   8

12

When researchers began comparing studies of the world's oldest civilisations, they discovered a fascinating thing. From the inhabitants of ancient Greece to the remote societies in Outer Mongolia, people shared the same appetite for news. "The first questions Mongols put to each other when they meet is invariably the same," an anthropologist noted in 1921. They ask: "'What's new?' And [then] each of [them] begins to pour out his whole supply of the news" (Maiskii, 1921). Even the same basic definition of what constitutes news remained constant over time. "Humans have exchanged a similar mix of news … throughout history and across cultures," wrote media historian Mitchell Stephens (1997:27). In fact, they even looked for similar qualities in the messengers they picked to gather and deliver the news: they singled out those who could run swiftly over the next horizon, accurately gather the information, and compellingly retell it (Kovach and Rosensthiel, 2001:9).

How can these consistencies be explained? The answer, scholars have concluded, is that news fulfils a basic human instinct – the need to know what is happening beyond our own direct experience (Molotch and Lester, 1974). Being aware of events we cannot witness ourselves gives us a sense of security, control, and confidence (Kovach and Rosensthiel, 2001:9).

When the flow of news is hindered, historian Mitchell Stephens points out, "a darkness falls" and "we grow anxious. Our hut, apartment, village or city becomes a 'sorry' place" (1997:12). The world becomes, as it were, too quiet. We feel alone. South Africa's anti-apartheid hero Nelson Mandela knows that feeling all too well. For much of the 27 years he spent in jail, he and his comrades were locked up on Robben Island, cut off from the outside world. He recalled how he yearned for news during those long years behind bars. "Newspapers were more valuable to political prisoners than gold or diamonds, more hungered for than food or tobacco; they were the most precious contraband on Robben Island," he wrote in his autobiography (1994:492). "We were not allowed any news at all, and we craved it."

Stephens calls that craving "a hunger for awareness" (1997:12).

We need news to live our lives. It helps us to distinguish between threats and opportunities, enemies and friends. News helps us orientate ourselves, and it helps us connect with others. If the mass media is the system that societies generate to supply this news, then journalism is its lifeblood. That is why the character of the news and the quality of the journalism is important: they influence our thoughts, our experiences, our cultures. It certainly is a powerful position to be in. And those who want to write for the media – from inside a newsroom as a journalist, or from the outside as a publicist or source – should recognise

Figure 12.6   *The formula method: enlargement*

To enlarge a photograph

To calculate the % enlargement required:

Size of layout / size of photo x 100 = % enlargement

= (12 / 7) x 100

= 171%

To calculate the required height of the photograph:

Size wanted / (% enlargement /100) = photo width

= 8 / (171 / 100)

= 8 / 1.71

= 4,68 cm

Therefore, 5 cm – 4,68 cm = 0,32 cm or 3,2 mm

You will need to crop 3 mm (round off) off the height of the photograph and enlarge it 171% of its original size to make it fit the layout.

Sending photographs to the printer

Once you have decided on the dimensions you want to use, follow these steps:

- Place a sheet of tracing paper over the photograph, sticking it to the back with tape.
- Mark the area to be used with a ruler and soft-tipped pencil.
- Write the dimensions and percentage reduction or enlargement on the back of the photograph with a wax China marker or soft-tipped pencil. Never use a felt-tip marker or pen because the ink is likely to come off, smudging other pictures, when stacked together.
- Clearly mark the photograph (A, B, C or D) and the corresponding space on the layout.
- Never use staples, pins or paperclips to attach notes to photographs.

Creating the final layout

Creating a layout is a bit like playing with Lego blocks – fitting pieces, one by one, into a single design. Doing it is not difficult, but doing it well requires thought and creativity.

Of course, instead of plastic blocks, the designer has to bear the following elements in mind:

- Stories of varying length.
- Summary blocks or "blurbs".
- Different typefaces, particularly for headlines.
- Photographs and graphics.
- Number of columns per page (the grid).
- Colour.
- Advertisements.
- White or "empty" space.
- Layout styles, for example modular or dynamic (see below).

Putting it all together

Now it is time to put it all together. My approach to design is confirmed by designer Jeff Level's observation: "The news shouldn't have to be deciphered by readers – most newspapers have a crossword puzzle for that challenge" (Level, 1992:2).

That is why I advocate simple, modular design like that followed by Cape Town's *Die Burger*, Johannesburg's *The Sowetan* and Sanlam's house journal, *Die Sanlammer*.

- Dynamic layout, on the one hand, means that each page of a publication is approached independently with no consistency of elements like column width.

- Modular layout sees every story – that means copy, headlines, photos and graphics – as a single, four-cornered module that fits into a specific page grid, with standard-sized gutters (like the lines of mortar between bricks in a wall).

These rectangles and squares can be used in a variety of configurations. The best combinations bear these points in mind:

- **Focus**
  Each page and indeed each story must have a clear focus to direct the viewer (just like articles). Because people are more attracted to visuals than to copy, pictures and graphics usually automatically become the focal points on a page.
- **Balance**
  Elements must be balanced. Take great care to ensure that headlines are appropriately sized for copy blocks. Avoid large, bold headlines on short stories and small headlines on large copy blocks.
- **Contrast**
  To avoid bland layouts, you need a measure of contrast on each page to create tension.
- **Unity**
  The elements must form a united whole. Using no more than four typefaces (one for copy and three for headlines) and consistent graphic elements contribute greatly to unity of page.
- **Clarity**
  The information must be instantly clear – remember that a page is not a crossword puzzle.

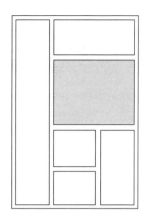

Good focus, balanced, good vertical depth and contrast

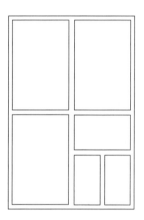

No focus, poor balance, awkward proportions

The production process

When he was at the South African headquarters of the World Wide Fund for Nature in Stellenbosch as director of communications, Bun Booyens stayed busy. Very busy. The agency produces policy documents, research reports, public awareness information, press information, campaign documents, newsletters and more. The following production guide is a modification of the guide Booyens and his staff used to make sure their projects were on track.

Step 1: Draw up a publication profile

The publication project planning guide or briefing form, as Booyens calls it, should be distributed to everybody involved in the process. "If it is not clear from the briefing form exactly what you have in mind, chances are that someone will improvise along the way – for better or worse," says Booyens. It is important that the publication profile is circulated well in advance of Step 2, the briefing meeting.

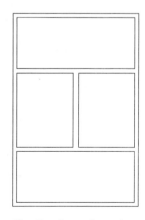

Visually uninteresting and boring

PUBLICATION PROJECT PLANNING GUIDE

1. About the publication

Name	A titlepiece (sometimes called a masthead). That is the top part of any magazine or newspaper where the name appears.
Objectives	What do you want to achieve?
Target audience	Who do you want to reach?
Format	Tabloid newspaper (A3), traditional magazine size (A4) or some other format?
Length	How many pages? Remember: most printers work in multiples of four, as pages are folded in half when bound.
Paper	Newsprint, glossy or matt? The weight and finish of the paper are two critical factors that will affect the quality of the publication – and, of course, the budget.
Illustrations	Photographs and illustrations are excellent ways to communicate visually, but they are expensive and need expertise. Consider the resources available.
Colour	A full-colour journal will be more expensive than a two-colour or black-and-white publication. But a less colourful magazine need not be of a lesser quality.
Print run	How many copies have to be printed?
Frequency	For the publication to be effective it is also important to determine at what intervals and what times during the year it should be published. This will probably be determined by your budget, but clearly the more frequent the publication, the better the communication.
Distribution	Another factor which must be considered is distribution – where and how. For example, if it is to be mailed to readers, you should choose a format that can be mailed cost effectively.
Promotion	How will the publication be promoted?
Feedback	What mechanism is in place for feedback from readers?
Online link	Corporate intranets are increasingly being used for this purpose, with Eskom's award-winning editor Annamarie Murray leading the way. Summary information from the staff newspaper is published on the company's intranet at the same time as the printed version is distributed and readers are encouraged to e-mail reactions to the editor. This is an excellent way to promote two-way communication

2. About the people

Project manager	Who is the project co-ordinator?
Writers	Who will write the articles for the magazine? Is this a staff person or freelance writer/s?
Sub-editor	Who will edit and proofread the publication?
Designer	If you don't have a staffer with the requisite skills and equipment, this will be a significant budget item.
Translators	Does the publication need to be translated? If so, by whom? What will it cost and who will proofread the final version?
Production co-ordinator	Who will oversee the production process?

Promotions	If the publication needs to be promoted, who will do it and what costs will be incurred?
Reprographics and printing	Do you have reliable suppliers of these services?
Approval	Who will sign off the project before it goes to print?
All this human infrastructure is essential to the success of the project and needs to be put in place before you proceed.	
3. About the cost	
Budget	What budget is available? Consider the items listed above: format, quantities, paper stock, typesetting, printing, in-house labour and consulting fees. Which person or section of the company should be billed?

Figure 12.7 Planning a publication step by step. While this guide is designed to assist discussions when setting up a house journal, it can be adapted for any publication, from an annual report to a brochure.

Step 2: The briefing meeting

This is the chance to get the key people involved, the project manager or editor, the sub-editor and proofreader, the writer/s, the photographer/s and illustrator/s and the design team to clarify the steps necessary to produce the publication. "Misunderstandings will disrupt the process and will almost certainly cost the project money," says Booyens.

Step 3: Establishing costs

After the briefing meeting, the design co-ordinator or production manager will need to set up a preliminary budget for the project. The following will need to be considered:

- Design
- Photograph/s and illustration/s
- Writing/editing
- Translation
- Reprographics
- Quantities
- Printing
- Distribution
- Promotion

The production manager may have to ask for several different quotes. While cost is important, it is also important to establish a relationship with suppliers of services. It is the printer and his machinery who will ultimately determine the quality of the final product.

HOT TIP

Working with a printer
Typical questions your printer will ask:
1 What method of printing (lithography, gravure, letterpress, flexography, silk screening, digital, etc.) do you want to use?
2 What material (paper, cardboard, etc.) would you require?
3 How many colours on how many pages, labels, etc.?
4 How many pages, labels, boxes, etc.?
5 What artwork (photographs, graphics, etc.) is required and how will it be supplied (slide, line drawing, etc.)?
6 What type of finishing and binding? (If it is a publication; saddle-stitch, loose pages, folds, etc.)
7 How will the job be proofed?
8 How will the product be packed (boxed, banded, shrink wrapped, etc.)?
9 How will the product be delivered?
10 What is the schedule for the supplying of material, proofing and delivery?

Choose a good, reliable printer with technology compatible with your own software. A personal visit to the selected printer is an absolute must; check with them in which format they require the publication to be when it is presented for printing.

Working with a printer geographically close to your own office is definitely a plus as minimum time will be wasted if there is a hitch (and there often is).

Step 4: Create a production schedule

Your working schedule or deadline depends on how frequently a publication appears and how long it takes to distribute the publication to all staff. In other words, if you want the magazine to appear in the first week of every month, you have to distribute it to branches (if your company is that big) the week before.

The best way to work out a schedule is to plan backwards:

- Decide when the publication must appear.
- Find out from the printer what their turnaround time is (i.e. how long it will take to print the publication once the final drafts have been given to them). Subtract the number of days from the date you want the publication to appear. This will give you the date on which you have to supply the printer with all the final copy, photographs and artwork.
- From this date, work out how many days you or the graphic designer will need to do lay-out and how many days you will need to proof the pages – subtract the number of days again from the previous date.
- Determine how long it will take to collect news, take photographs, write and edit copy and get articles approved by the original source. Subtract the number of days on the calendar. This will give you the date on which you should start working on the latest issue of your publication.
- This exercise must be repeated for every issue as there are some months with a number of public holidays.

Example:

Magazine A appears on the first Tuesday of every month. The printer has a five-day turnaround (excluding weekends). The layout artist needs

SCHEDULE FOR MAY EDITION				
Magazine A				
To appear	Final proofs to printer	Start lay-out	Proof lay-out and final corrections	Collecting news, writing, editing and approving
Tuesday, May 6	*April 23 (May 1 is a public holiday)*	*April 14 – 18*	*April 21, 22*	*April 4 – 11*

Figure 12.8 Drawing up a production schedule requires planning backwards, as this example shows. In order to get the publication to the readers on May 6, the editor will have to start working on stories from at least April 4.

five days for lay-out and you need two days to proof the pages. Collecting, writing, editing and approving of stories take another six days. (Work only with weekdays as printing over weekends will cost more.)

Step 5: Copy writing

It is important to state exactly how you want the copy supplied. For example:

- On a CD-ROM in MS Word or ASCII, with the copy unmarked. No page breaks, font instructions and layout commands on the disk.
- At least two printouts of the complete text.
- Special layout instructions must be given in red ink on the printout of the text. No instructions should be put on the disk itself.
- The copy must have been proofread.
- All copy must be checked for facts and figures.

Step 6: Copy agreement

All the key people must now see the copy. In corporate publications it is sensible to get articles approved by the original source, especially if it is a technical article, if it has a slightly controversial content or contains lots of figures. This will save you the problems and cost of having to make changes at a later stage. Clearing copy with sources in the corporate environment has the added advantage that editors build relationships of trust with their sources, who are often members of senior management, while also creating the perception that the editor is responsible.

Copy editors must now do their work. Check the content and check the style.

- *Remember: The design co-ordinator will expect one set of rewrites: make your changes to copy now, or hold your peace.*

* See Appendix C for a basic guide to style

Step 7: Illustrations and photography

"Imagery is memorable and powerful," says Booyens. "Make sure you have money in your budget for photographs and illustrations, and plan your timescale carefully to allow for artwork to be produced."

Step 8: Develop design

When the planning is complete, the budget set and the text agreed upon, the design team can settle down to the creative part of the project.

Step 9: Approve of prototype or "dummy" design

A dummy design – a prototype to show what the final product will look like – is circulated for comment and approval.

Step 10: Designer/layout artist starts work on individual pages

The copy and artwork is supplied to the designers and work on individual pages can begin. "Small editorial changes may be required to make the pages flow and to synchronise the text and the photographs," says Booyens.

Step 12: First proofs

A set of first proofs, usually printouts of the layout, are circulated. Some minor editing changes can be made, but the time for rewrites is long past. If significant changes have been made, get the approval of the author. If you tamper with the layout, it is likely to cost – time and money. Check for:
- spelling and punctuation errors
- broken type
- awkward hyphenation
- uneven line spacing
- column rules not lining up with type

Step 13: Final proofs

Circulate these to all on the list created when drawing up the publication profile. Look out for:
- incorrect orientation of photographs and artwork
- omission of lines of text or artwork
- incorrect page numbers
- continued page lines (one word on a line is called a widow or orphan)
- continuity of text

- proper credits
- if the publication has a contents page, check that page numbers in the contents correlate with the page numbers of the actual articles.

Step 14: Signing off

This is essential. The project should not go to print until it is signed off by those agreed upon in the publication profile or brief.

Step 15: Reprographics

The first stage of the printing process is to create bromides or film. This is expensive, so it is essential that it doesn't happen until everyone is satisfied. Remember repro, as this stage is called, takes time. Budget for it.

Step 16: Dyeline proofs

The production co-ordinator or designer should check dyeline proofs before print plates are made to ensure that pages are running in the correct sequence. On large print orders, printers will want to proof a job before the final print run. This is costly and time consuming, but it can save unnecessary expenses, should something go wrong.

Step 17: Printing

"Please remember that if the project is late in arriving for printing, there is precious little the printer can do to make up for lost time," says Booyens. "Machines run only so fast and once the job is printed, it must be allowed to dry before folding, stapling or binding."

Step 18: Delivery

Make sure the printer knows exactly where you want your publication delivered. Budget for long-distance delivery if necessary.

Step 19: Distribution

If the publication is to be mailed, make sure you have the envelopes and address labels prepared – and the hands to do the job. Printers are sometimes geared to do this distribution for you. If not, and you cannot do it yourself, get a professional mailing house to distribute for you. If you want to launch the publication at an event, now is the time.

Step 20: Evaluation

At the end of the process, it is important to get everyone together and evaluate the product *and* the process. This will most likely save a great deal of time and energy the second time around.

Definition

Dyeline proofs A method of proofing single colour negatives. May also be used to check multiple colour negatives for fit, etc. by making multiple exposures onto the same sheet of proofing material.

▓HO▓ LINK

For more tips on the printing process, working with type and creating websites, check out the advice offered by the communications department of the Edmonton Public School Board at: http://communications.epsb.ca/tips.shtml.

Regular research should be done amongst readers as well. Set up focus groups of readers from different strata of the company; they will guide you on reader interests and often help you realign your publication to your marketplace.

NOTE: Amongst many other accolades ,The Standard won the 2002 Best Publication Award from the South African Press Club and was a finalist in 2003.

CASE STUDY Editor Tina Heron on *The Standard*

The Standard is the Standard Bank Group's (SBG) monthly staff publication. It is a full colour, 12-page A3 publication distributed to about 40 000 Standard Bank staff in 17 sub-Saharan African countries, as well as 21 countries outside Africa including the UK, Hong Kong, the US, Russia and several in South America.

– The majority of the readers are women – about 66% make up the bank's total staff complement.
– English is the common language but for many it is a second or third language.
– Average age is 32.
– About 70% are on non-managerial level for which the educational minimum is a school-leaving certificate. The remaining 30% comprise managerial to executive level with tertiary qualifications.

How the publication fits into the organisation's strategy

The roles and objectives of *The Standard* are to:
• Facilitate understanding of issues that affect the bank and its people.
• Encourage individuals to take pride in Standard Bank and act as ambassadors of the brand.
• Promote togetherness under one brand.
• Demonstrate the various activities of the bank and its people.

Promoting the bank's core values
We do this by:
• Promoting understanding of the bank's business, strategy and the environments within which it operates.
• Highlighting the bank's achievements.
• Recognising successes of individuals.
• Celebrating the diversity of our people.
• Proactively identifying issues that affect the bank and its people.
• Interpreting for people how events or decisions affect them.
• Showing how people contribute to the business and the difference they can make.
• Demonstrating how people's actions and interactions make a difference.

The editor

My role as editor is to:

- Plan, manage and oversee the writing, design and production process of 11 publications a year.
- Ensure that the publication is produced, printed and distributed to all group staff each month (except January).
- Ensure that the publication is of high quality and keeps up with latest trends in communication and publishing.
- Ensure that the publication's overall communication is accessible to readers in terms of tone and language; is presented in a pleasing manner; and, from a visual point of view, is easy to read.
- Ensure that news content is as objective as possible, current, balanced, credible and of interest to the audience.
- Ensure that content is balanced to include a fair representation of the bank's business and community activities.
- To represent correctly the diversity of the people who make up the fabric of the bank.

Process and content

Planning

Story leads are gathered from people on all levels throughout the bank, including the communications specialists in its communication department. They are primary sources of leads and together we ensure the articles support business and communication strategies.

Copy tasting helps the editor plan each edition, determining lead stories for each page, from hard to soft news, and news on marketing to individual achievements.

The editor draws up a 12-page pencil thumbnail sketch that outlines space allocation of articles, photos and graphics required on each page. Deadlines for each page are allocated.

In consultation with the communications specialists, the editor is able to brief writers, photographers and illustrators on the objective for each topic. The editor allocates deadlines to each writer and states the number of words required. A maximum of 350/400 words for a lead article is required including sidebar/s and/or info boxes, to keep the eventual design of the article in mind.

Writers send the copy to the editor indicating the number of words written.

When pages are completed and the copy is received, the editor cuts down copy where needed, checks language tone, provides blurbs and appropriate intros, indicates any areas of concern/confusion and passes the copy onto the sub-editor.

The sub-editor cleans up the copy from a grammatical point of view, suggesting headlines and passes it back to the editor. The editor sends it to the source to ensure factual accuracy.

Production

Once completed copy, photos, graphics and/or info graphics for each page is ready, the editor briefs the designer so the production process can start. The designer will provide ideas and input on the overall look and feel of the edition.

As layout is completed on a page the editor checks for readability, balance, literals and accuracy.

Three proofreaders check for literals, copy drop-off and plain language respectively.

Once any errors have been addressed, the editor completes one final check and hands the signed-off pages to the designer to prepare for repro and printing.

Once it is printed *The Standard* is delivered by courier to South Africa and the rest of the world. Head office staff collect their copies from newsstands placed on each floor of Standard Bank Centre, Johannesburg.

Evaluating the publication

Evaluating *The Standard* in the past has been in the form of a readership survey conducted every couple of years, to determine what staff like and dislike about the publication.

In the most recent survey in 2002 it was found that staff have a very high awareness level of the publication (98%) and over 80% had read at least three editions in the three months prior to the survey.

The letters page is the most read and most credible part of the publication while CD and book competitions are a popular reason why staff read it. The majority of readers are happy with the content and balance but suggested more articles on individuals and provincial branch staff achievers.

Another way of evaluating the publication's success is the numerous awards it has received.

Conclusion

I trust this discussion has helped "word people" get a better understanding of both the importance and the process of the design and production process – and made them realise the challenge of competing for the attention of modern readers, who are products of the television age. According to US design expert, Dr Mario Garcia, American research has shown that 77 per cent of newspaper readers do not recall life without TV and 66 per cent do not recall life without colour TV (Haffajee and Stober, 1992:9).

All newspaper readers watch at least one hour of TV a day. The TV age and the pace of life have made them impatient readers, Garcia says, and today's newspapers should reflect this. "They should have the speed of television, the relaxed visuals of magazines and the directness of radio."

Understanding key terms

Bed [Zu. Ukulungela ukuphrinta / Xh. loo nto ilungele ukushicilelwa / Afr. van die steen af]: A newspaper put to *bed* is ready to be put on the presses for printing.

Break [Zu. Udaba luyaqhubeka / Xh. isithuba apho ibali lisaqhubekela phambili khona / Afr. breek]: The place where a story is continued on another column or page.

Bullets [Zu. Amachashaza / Xh. amachaphaza angqukuva / Afr. kolle]: Round dots (often in place of numbers) used to highlight one-paragraph topics or items on a list.

Edition [Zu. Udaba olusha / Xh. uhlelo / Afr. uitgawe]: Total unchanged press run; when new material is added to a new run within the day and it is so designated, this is another edition. Large papers have as many as a half dozen editions in one day.

Gravure [Zu. Indlela yokuphrinta]: A method where the printing areas are below the surface of the printing plate. Fast drying and solvent inks are poured into the printing areas so that when the paper is pressed up against the surface, the ink is absorbed by the paper.

Lift-out/pull-out [Zu. Ingxenye ephindiwe / Xh. isivakalisi okanye umhlathi ophindaphindiweyo ebalini ngeenjongo zokukwenza umboniso / Afr. uittreksel/prikkel/lokker]: Sentence or paragraph from a story repeated for display purposes.

Letterpress [Zu. Okushicilelweyo / Xh. ifoto ebonisa intloko namagxa / Afr. hoogdruk]: The face of the printed image is raised and ink is transferred onto paper or other print surfaces.

Lithographic offset [Zu. Indlela yokuphrinta / Xh. ukushicilela elilicwecwe ekukrolwe kulo oonobumba / Afr. vlakdruk]: A printing method of higher quality than letterpress in which the print and non-print areas are on the same plane of the offset plate. The plate is dampened with water in each cycle. Water repellent areas accept ink, non-print areas accept dampness, thus ink is first transferred to a rubber covered "blanket" cylinder and then to the paper. As offset plates last longer than letterpress blocks, this method is more economical.

Mug shot [Zu. Isithombe sekhanda namahlombe / Xh. ifoto ebonisa intloko namagxa / Afr. nabyskoot]: A head-and-shoulders photograph.

Pica [Zu. Ubungako bezinhlamvu / Xh. ipika / Afr.pika]: Unit of measure sometimes called an "em", which equals 12 points, or about 4 mm.

FROM THE EDITOR'S DESK

Jennie Fourie on successful corporate publications

Jennie Fourie is co-founder of the South African Publications Forum, a network of corporate publication practitioners. The main activities of the forum are an annual corporate publication competition for company newspapers, newsletters, magazines, videos and the like, as well as training and networking opportunities.

What are the most important ingredients of a successful publication?

A corporate publication is only successful if it is read by the audience for whom it is intended. A successful corporate publication includes a healthy mix of motivation and information. To be trusted as a legitimate communication tool, it should give voice to all groups in an organisation – not only be his master's voice.

What are the most common challenges for editors?

Industrial editors are sometimes in the unenviable position that they do not fit into the company structure. They should remain impartial at all times and not take sides in possible disputes between management and workers. They are often overworked and are hard pressed to meet deadlines. Communicators should, however, not be put off to enter into the field of industrial editing – it is a very rewarding career when you see that your publication does what it should be doing. It can also be a very sociable job and is perfectly suited to a curious person with a keen mind and a good nose for news.

How has the role of print publications changed in an increasingly online context?

Most companies find that a print publication can live harmoniously with an online form of communication. The online communication tool has the benefits of immediacy and brevity, but a print publication can be used to go into issues in more depth. Companies often find that employees tend to take their print corporate publications home to read at their leisure. Obviously the content should cater for this need.

How can the success of a corporate publication be measured?

There are several ways to measure the success. One is not to distribute publications to individuals, but to place them in a central point where pick-up rate can be measured. It is also possible to do formal research through questionnaires or even interviews to determine whether the publication does what it intends to do. A good question to include is whether staff would be willing to pay for the publication. If the answer is "yes", you have a winner.

What advice do you have for those who are looking to make a career in publications?

In order to be successful, you need to adhere to good journalistic practice – reading, writing accurately, understanding ethics and the like. You should also spend the minimum time in your office – what is said around the water cooler or in the tea room is what you should write about. You should also be self-confident and able to defend your stories when placed under pressure.

For details on the SA Publications Forum, see: http://www.sapublicationforum.co.za

Putting your learning to work

ACTIVITY 1 Draw up a dummy design

Create a modular design for page 3 of an A4 publication by clipping and pasting the following items from magazines or newspapers:

- one story;
- a headline, with a kicker;
- a summary or blurb;
- three photographs and captions.

Remember to draw margins and a grid on the page before pasting in the design elements.

Compare your effort with those of your classmates and discuss the focus, balance, contrast, unity and clarity of each design.

ACTIVITY 2 Telling the story with pictures

Cut three stories from a newspaper or house journal that might be improved by the use of pictures.

- Explain what type of picture you would use with each story.
- Write captions for each picture.

ACTIVITY 3 Cropping and sizing photographs

Crop and size the photograph below to fit a 3 x 3 x 3 cm space. Repeat the exercise for a horizontal space of 10 x 3 x 14 cm.

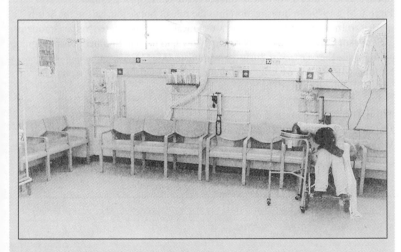

(PHOTOGRAPH BY SUE HILLYARD)

About this photo: Sue Hillyard, a photojournalist and trainer, spent two years documenting the drama at the Groote Schuur Hospital Emergency Room. This image, Sunday Night, formed part of her critically-acclaimed exhibition, The Human Touch.

HOT LINK

Need some advice on starting your own publication? Check out these two sites:

The Periodical Publishers Association (UK) offers extensive advice tailored to smaller print and online publishers starting out in the business. The information was gathered by the Independent Publishers Advisory Council (IPAC), a panel of smaller publishers with years of industry experience: http://www.ppa.co.uk/new_publishers/index.asp.

The Media Development and Diversity Agency (MDDA) of South Africa was set up by an Act of Parliament (Act 14 of 2002) to enable "historically disadvantaged communities and persons not adequately served by the media" to gain access to industry. For more about the type of help they offer, see: http://www.mdda.org.za

Bibliography

Adam, P. Stark and Garcia, M. 1990. *Eyes on the news.* St. Petersburg, FL: Poynter.

Clampitt, P.G., Crevoure, J.M. and Hartel, R.L. 1986. Exploratory research on employee publications. *Journal of Business Communication.*

Ferreira, T. and Staude, I. 1991. *Write angle; the ABC for house journals.* Johannesburg: Write Minds.

Freeman, M. 1985. *Encyclopedia of practical photography.* London: New Brighton Books.

Grunig, J.E. and Huang, Y. 2000. From organization effectiveness to relationship indicators: antecedents of relationships, public relations strategies, and public relations outcomes. In: J.A. Ledingham and S.D. Bruning, eds., *Public relations as relationship management: a relational approach to the study and practice of public relations.* Mahwah, NJ: Erlabaum.pp. 23-53.

Haffajee, F. and Stober, P. 1992. Luring those readers from TV's glitz. *Weekly Mail,* May 22–28, 1992.

Haley, A. 1992. Why type should be readable and legible. *Ragged Right,* No. 2, Summer 1992.

Hazelhurst, D. 1992. Why and how. *Rhodes University Journalism Review,* December 1992.

Heyneman, L. 1993. Layout and design workshop, a two-part series presented at the Cape Technikon, Cape Town.

Hon, L.C. & Grunig, J.E. October, 1999. Measuring relationship in public relations. Paper presented to the Institute for Public Relations, Gainesville, FL. In: Huang, Y., 2001. OPRA: A cross-cultural, multi-item scale for measuring organization-public relationships. *Journal of Public Relations Research,* 13(1), 61-90. Hillside, NJ: Lawrence Erlbaum.

Larkin, T.J. and Larkin, S. 1994. *Communicating change.* New York: McGraw-Hill.

Level, J. 1992. Notes on newstext. *Ragged Right.* No.1, Spring 1992.

Pigeon, M.J. 1979. An investigation into the role of house journals in the South African Industry and Commerce. A technical report presented to the Graduate School of Business, University of Cape Town, in partial fulfilment of the requirements for the Masters of Business Administration Degree, 1979.

Sutton, T. 1979. *Creative newspaper design.* Johannesburg, Review Press, 1986.

Sutton, T. Edwin Taylor: The man who started a graphics revolution. *Ragged Right,* No. 2, Summer 1992:5.

Tyson, H. 1993. *Editors under fire.* Sandton. S.A. Random House, 1993.

Van Bosch, P. 1997. Interview with author. Cape Town.

White, J.V. 1992. How to use design to edit newspapers. *Ragged Right,* No. 1, Spring 1992.

13

Ethics and the responsible journalist

Introduction*

Ask many journalists about ethics, and their answer is likely to be: "Huh? What's that?" But whether they acknowledge it or not, journalism is not a neutral craft, nor is it a purely technical skill. Choices confront journalists constantly, and decisions have to be made one way or another. Politicians often call for "responsible journalism", demanding that those working in media pay close regard to the ethical implications of their work. Often with good reason, journalists usually reject such admonitions as suspect interference with ulterior motives.

KEY CONCEPTS

The difference between media law and ethics; key factors that influence media freedom; dominant perspectives on ethics; common ethical issues; guidelines for ethical decision-making.

* In this chapter, I've invited four other journalists and educators to contribute: Prof Guy Berger of Rhodes University, who wrote the introduction to this chapter; the late Prof Francis Kasoma of the University of Zambia, who provided insight into Afri-ethics; Harold Gess, an award-winning photographer who contributed the discussion of ethical photojournalism; and Dr Herman Wasserman of the University of Stellenbosch, who edited a draft of this chapter and provided most useful suggestions.

Within their own ranks, however, there is certainly the need to exercise conscience. Yet, many media people react to daily choices with little conscious awareness of the diverse options available to them. They are motivated out of habit in some cases; in terms of their background and general outlook in others – and under instruction in many more.

Firstly, there is tradition. What would you do if you were a SABC radio programme host, and asked to announce not merely that Company X sponsored the programme, but that Company X, the best in town, was the sponsor? According to British convention, editorial and advertising should be clearly demarcated; far less so the more commercialised American style. In eclectic South Africa, different media opt for different mixes of these two traditions.

Secondly, in addition to tradition, all journalists operate in a professional context that sets parameters for them. There are news values and modes of writing that they conform to. There are conventions, customs and policies attached to the particular medium they are working for. Often there are explicit codes of conduct to which they subscribe, voluntarily or otherwise. By their nature as journalistic employees, they are obliged to execute these as well as other reasonable instructions from their superiors – or be prepared to quit their jobs. On the other hand, some media codes are observed mainly in the breach – and by employers as much as employees. The code of conduct of the South African Press Council bans any payments by a newspaper to a person engaged in criminal activity. When the Sunday newspaper, *Rapport*, paid racist mass murderer Barend Strydom for his story during 1993, it successfully flouted the code by arguing that Strydom was no longer engaged in crime.

Besides the codes of conduct of the Broadcasting Complaints Commission of South Africa and the Press Ombudsman, there are codes drawn up by other groups such as the Media Institute of Southern Africa and each media enterprise also often has its own code.

Journalists are not free agents in full control of their production. Many of their decisions are made for them – by traditions, by the nature of their work, by formal strictures, and by order of their employers. To operate in such a situation is, of course, an ethical choice on its own, and one that sometimes sees journalists organising to change things.

But usually, buttressed by their context, journalists do not see their every action as an ethical dilemma. And yet, each individual media worker – whether reporter, sub-editor, photographer, news editor, and so on – still often does have moments of very clear, and difficult, choices.

A sub-editor operating within the constraints of newsworthiness may nevertheless still wrestle with which story to give pride of place to, which ones to cut and how to cut them. The question of whether to push home an intrusive question to a bereaved person may trouble a reporter supposed to milk the tragedy. And should a company be given "below-the-line" or free advertising within an editorial context in cases where, often with a cynical eye to corporate image, that company does a good deed or offers a journalistic merit award? Blood-and-guts photographs may bring home to readers the horror of violent death; they may also help to sell a newspaper. But does the moral imperative really rest so easily with the commercial? There are also other, sometimes more subtle, questions (some of which we will discuss here). But whatever the scenario, no journalist, at any level in a media enterprise, is without ethical power. Even those working under the supervision of superiors who make the decisions still have the choice to refuse to obey – even if it costs them their job. However, while it is ultimately the decision of each individual to choose what they will do, there is an accumulation of experience in the collective history of journalism. It is from tapping the wisdom of others – of colleagues, traditions, codes of conduct and so on – that a journalist is empowered not merely to make a choice, but to make an informed choice.

"Journalism without a moral position is impossible. Every journalist is a moralist. It's absolutely unavoidable. A journalist is someone who looks at the world and the way it works, someone who takes a close look at things every day and reports what she sees, someone who represents the world, the event, for others. She cannot do her work without judging what she sees."
MARGUERITE DURAS,
FRENCH AUTHOR AND
FILMMAKER

Media law and ethics

In a report released to coincide with World Press Freedom Day on 3 May 2004, the group Reporters without Borders summed up the situation this way: In 2003, 42 reporters were killed and more than 120 others imprisoned. As many as 766 other reporters were arrested, at least 1 460 physically attacked or threatened, and 501 media censored. "Nearly a third of the world's people live in countries without press freedom," the report said (Veilletet, 2004). Clearly, the media freedom enshrined in the South African Constitution is rare in Africa and elsewhere. But what exactly does it mean to have a "free press"? For one thing, it does not mean the press is free from all restraints. A law merely regulates what can or can not be done or said in order to safeguard certain interests. These interests are fourfold:

- To protect journalists against abuse of authority by the state.
- To protect the state against misuse of privileges and rights by journalists.
- To protect the public against misuse of privileges and rights by journalists.
- To protect the journalist against unfair accusations and actions by the public.

Media law has an either-or approach. Either you obey the law or you do not. If you do not obey the law, there are punitive consequences or sanctions imposed by courts of law. It does not matter whether the law is reasonable or unreasonable. It also does not matter whether you know about the existence of the law or not, in line with the maxim: ignorance of the law is no defence.

A law does not say how a responsible reporter *ought* to behave; it merely states what the minimum standards of behaviour are.

When we start using words like "should" and "ought", we are talking about ethics. Ethics, based on the Greek word *ethos*, meaning character, deals with the philosophical foundations of decision-making, or choosing among the good and bad options one faces. Morality, on the other hand, comes from the Latin *mores*, and refers to the way or manner in which people behave (Black and Bryant, 1992:580). Thus morality has come to mean socially approved customs, or the practice or application of ethics. Ethical journalism, therefore, is more than just acting according to socially acceptable norms – it also means evaluating those norms critically, and thinking about what it means to be a responsible journalist.

The approach to the practice of ethical journalism varies according to the philosophical convictions of a particular journalist. Among journalists, there are situationists, antinomianists, Machiavellianists (who permit unethical behaviour at certain times provided it is done rarely and clandestinely), teleologists, deontologists, hedonists, egoists and others.

This chapter is not a complete discussion about journalism ethics. We merely attempt to place the discussion into context, by exploring freedom in the journalistic context and reviewing key philosophies from Western as well as African perspectives. Then we take a look at some common situations in which ethical decision-making comes into play, some of which have been woven into earlier chapters, e.g. news judgements, the use of obscenities and relationships with sources. Throughout, we pose many questions, but only answer some. And even so, you may not agree with our observations. Ethics seldom provides us with a clear right or wrong answer – rather, it often makes us aware of grey areas. This does not mean we can each decide what is right or wrong on an individual basis, or base our decisions on our emotions or "gut feel". This would result in *ethical relativism*, where each person in society decides for him or herself what is right or wrong without having standards commonly agreed upon.

Journalism ethics is a field of study that teaches us how to think about ethical issues in a systematic fashion, and how to engage in constructive debate about difficult judgements. It is therefore important that one develops an ethical sensitivity to recognise ethical problems that arise in our day-to-day work as journalists, and acquire the skills to reason about these issues. It is very important that journalists regularly discuss ethical matters with one another in the newsroom, at editorial meetings, in professional bodies. It is through discussion and debate, rather than through intuition or feeling, that one moves towards answers on ethical dilemmas.

Factors that influence media freedom

Clearly, freedom of expression and the media is scarce in our part of the world. But freedom is a big word. A typical dictionary defines freedom as the condition of being free from restraints by authority or external forces (such as the oppressive laws instituted by the regime of Robert Mugabe in Zimbabwe). That is only part of it; that is so-called "negative freedom". "Positive freedom," in turn, is being free to do as one wishes.

The freedom and independence of the media, wrote British media expert David Webster (1992:1), depends on three factors:

- media regulation;
- the presence of able managers and the ability to be economically viable; and
- the degree to which professionalism and responsibility are exercised.

Let us briefly examine each factor:

Media regulation

Webster suggests that beyond the commonly accepted laws to protect copyright and prohibit defamation and slander, no regulation is necessary. Not everyone agrees.

In South Africa, media workers have contended with government and other controls on the following:

- Topics which may be reported (for example, the judiciary, energy affairs and state security may not be scrutinised).
- Sources of information, like physicians, who may not be quoted by name.
- Presentation of information, like comparative advertising.
- How information is distributed (complaints abound about government's reluctance to allow more freedom of the airwaves, as well as the monopoly of the printed press by private conglomerates).
- To whom it may be distributed; literature as well as music and video material are subject to bannings and age restrictions.

These restrictions are upheld by the courts as well as by professional bodies such as the Broadcasting Complaints Commission of South Africa, the Press Ombudsman, and the Advertising Standards Authority.

One law, in particular, is still being severely contested by South African journalists: Section 205 of the Criminal Procedure Act – usually referred to simply as Section 205 – which requires journalists to reveal their sources to law enforcement officials in investigations. This, argue journalists, makes them agents for the government and, therefore, compromises their status as neutral parties – and puts their lives at risk. If gang members, for example, believe that journalists will hand over their notes and photographs to law enforcement officials, they are, at best, unlikely to speak to the journalists. The South African National Editors' Forum (Sanef) in 2003 opposed the efforts made by the Hefer Commission to subpoena the journalist Ranjeni Munusamy for this reason, saying it might cause a so-called "chilling effect" which would make sources hesitant to speak to journalists. At worst, the journalists may be harmed. That, of course, is not uncommon.

But changes have been made. The most dramatic is the move to open the airwaves, both radio and television, to private broadcasters. The licensing of community radio stations and the establishment of the Media Development and Diversity Agency were aimed at giving communities access to the media and broadening the media environment to include more non-commercial media outlets.

These and other modifications in media regulations are expected as South Africa continues to redefine itself in a post-apartheid society. That the controls will change is certain. That there always will be controls is certain, too. Whereas statutory regulations about media ownership and diversity, as well certain restrictive measures regarding media content remain, an important shift took place during the democratisation process in the 1990s.

This shift was one away from governmental censorship towards *self-regulation* of the media. This means that whereas the government used to control media content through a range of laws, it was now mostly left to the media themselves to make decisions about (un)ethical conduct by journalists. Many media institutions have their own ethical codes, but professional bodies such as the Press Ombudsman, of which most print media are voluntary members, as well as the Broadcasting Complaints Commission of South Africa (BCCSA), also set guidelines for ethical journalism. The public can lodge complaints about unethical behaviour at these bodies, who then rule on the complaint, and can fine journalists who transgress their ethical guidelines.

This is a significant shift towards professionalisation of the media industry, which hands over responsibility to journalists to regulate their own behaviour, rather than imposing legal constraints on the media. Lucas Oosthuizen (2002:138), describes the importance of self-regulation as follows: "Self-regulation is an important prerequisite for the recognition of the professional status of an occupation. Non-adherence to their own codes would therefore militate against such recognition for journalists and increase the potential for formal control. Journalism training in ethics is therefore imperative" (Oosthuizen, 2002:138).

HOT LINK

For a summary of the arguments for ensuring that sources of journalists remain confidential, see the submission by Raymond Louw, a member of the Media Freedom Sub-Committee of the SA National Editors' Forum, to the Commission of Inquiry headed by Judge Hefer into allegations made against National Director of Public Prosecutions Bulelani Ngcuka and others at: http://www.polity.org.za/pol/news/2003/?show=42585.

HOT TIP

The codes of conduct of the Press Ombudsman and the Broadcasting Complaints Commission of South Africa are included as appendices on pp. 376–382.

Definition

What does it mean to be a profession? Most answers refer to the opinions of Justice Louis Brandeis of the American Supreme Court (1914,1927), who said that a profession has a socially valuable body of knowledge; is responsible for advancing that knowledge; is responsible for transmitting that knowledge to the next generation; sets credible, useful standards, and guards and enforces those standards, OR risks its surrender to corporate or governmental control; is accountable for the conduct of its members (i.e. self-governance); values performance and service to others over personal reward.

Professionalism and responsibility

- A certified accountant who falsifies figures on a client's tax return could lose his licence.
- A doctor who gives people prescriptions for drugs they do not need could lose his licence.
- A journalist who pretends to be someone else in order to get information for a story could win a Pulitzer Prize.

In recent years, the international journalism community were shocked by unethical behaviour by journalists, such as fabricating stories (e.g. Stephen Glass of the *New Republic* and Jayson Blair of the *New York Times*) or publishing fake photographs (e.g. the British *Daily Mirror* that ran unauthenticated photographs of Iraqi prisoners being abused, forcing its editor, Piers Morgan, to resign). Not long after, a spate of revelations of plagiarism and conflicts of interests brought South African journalism in disrepute to such an extent that the South African National Editors' Forum (Sanef) in 2004 sought to "repair the reputation of the **profession**" through regional ethics workshops.

Licensing journalists as a way to ensure they keep to a mandatory code of ethics – as is the case for accountants, doctors and lawyers – has long been debated. Proponents say granting licences to journalists will ensure better qualified media workers under better control. Opponents argue that allowing only licensed journalists access to the media is a denial of free speech and will open the way for governments to revoke licenses of journalists that criticise them. Critics of the Zimbabwean government, including Sanef, say that this is what the compulsory registration of journalists with a government-appointed commission in that country amounts to.

So far, no proposal to license South African journalists has been implemented. But there have been some close calls. Like in 1981: The press should put its house in order, warned then-president P.W. Botha, nicknamed "Die Groot Krokodil" (The Big Crocodile). "If they fail to do so, the Government will take steps to do it for them" (*Equid Novi*,1981:106). In response, the South African Media Council (since 1993 the Press Council of South Africa) was established two years later. First on their agenda: "Assist all involved in the media to maintain the highest professional standards by complying with the code of conduct" (Froneman, 1993:256). The Press Ombudsman has since replaced the Press Council. According to its Constitution, it was set up by the South African National Editors Forum (**SANEF**), the Forum for Community Journalists (**FCJ**), the South African Union of Journalists (**SAUJ**), the Media Workers Association of South Africa (**MWASA**), the Newspaper Association of Southern Africa (**NASA**) and the Magazine Publishers Association of South Africa (**MPA**) to provide for "a readily accessible,

Critics of the Zimbabwean government's decision to license journalists argue that allowing only "approved" journalists access to the media is a denial of free speech and will open the way for governments to revoke licenses of journalists that criticise them.

impartial and independent complaints mechanism".

The Press Ombudsman provides an avenue for the public to air their grievances and the industry to enforce some discipline, and is therefore important. The council is an industry initiative, which consists of an equal number of journalists and public representatives. The Press Ombudsman and Appeal Panel are empowered to deal with complaints in the following ways, as set out in their Constitution:

- Dismiss the complaint.
- Reprimand a respondent adjudged to have been guilty of an infringement of the code.
- Make any supplementary or ancillary orders or directions that he/she or it may consider necessary for carrying into effect orders or directives made in terms of this clause and, more particularly, give directions as to the publication of his/her or its findings.

The Press Ombudsman also has a professional code of ethics, in which it sets out guidelines for journalists to act responsibly. Its preamble explains the basic principle underpinning the code as that "the freedom of the press is indivisible from and subject to the same rights and duties as that of the individual and rests on the public's fundamental right to be informed and freely to receive and to disseminate opinions". The preamble to the Broadcasting Complaints Commission of South Africa's (BCCSA) code is similar to that of the Press Ombudsman, as are the sanctions it can impose – with the difference that it may also impose fines of up to R30 000.

Codes of conduct can be helpful to journalists as they struggle to distinguish right from wrong. But such codes remain little more than lists of rules which are often thoughtlessly broken – unless they reflect the ethical principles of individual media workers. Media codes are only guidelines, not clear answers – journalists still need to develop skills in order to implement them in practical situations.

Able management and economic viability

Structures of ownership, whether non-profit, government, public or private, are seen to have a direct bearing upon media content.

Community-based media, such as community radio, newsletters and e-zines, are usually organised on a non-profit basis by specific interest groups, such as religious groups. Typically, such media either operate on little or no advertising and rely on donations from their audiences and other sponsors to operate.

NOT-FOR-PROFIT MEDIA ORGANISATIONS	GOVERNMENT OR STATE-OWNED MEDIA ORGANISATIONS	PUBLIC MEDIA ORGANISATIONS	PRIVATELY-OWNED MEDIA ORGANISATIONS

Figure 13.1 Media ownership typically falls into one of these categories.

Government ownership of newspapers, television and radio were – and remain – a key aspect of authoritarian societies, such as Zimbabwe, China and Cuba. By controlling the media, these regimes typically attempt to exert ideological control over their citizens by controlling the free flow of information.

There is a difference between government and state ownership. While the former means that the media are usually a mouthpiece for the political regime, the latter means that media is accountable to the public through (ideally) independently-appointed and broadly representative boards of directors. Public ownership of television and radio has long been a feature of liberal democractic systems, such as those in western Europe, and of modern democracies, such as South Africa. Publicly-owned media can be funded from taxation, a license fee, revenue generated from advertising, sponsorships and other commercial activities, such as the production and selling of content to other media organisations (Devereaux, 2003:57). Public media typically aim to cater for a wide range of audience (and some minority) interests and tastes.

HOT LINK

Heading their master's voice? Read more about Rupert Mudoch, the chairman of News Corporation, which publishes 175 titles on three continents, distributes 40 million papers a week and dominates the newspaper markets in Britain, Australia and New Zealand, in an article by Roy Greenslade published in *The Guardian* (UK) on 17 February 2003, available online at: www.guardianonline.co.uk (access is free, but registration is required).

Media may be privately owned by companies controlled by individuals, families, shareholders or holding companies. Historically, many newspapers were owned by individual entrepreneurs. But increasingly privately-owned media companies are now owned and controlled by large, often global conglomerates. And the fact is that more and more media production and distribution is controlled by a small number of privately-owned players. These organisations often have immense economic and political power. For example, in the run-up to the American-led invasion of Iraq in 2003, global media tycoon Rupert Murdoch argued strongly for the war – and perhaps that's why the 175 News Corporation editors around the world backed it, too.

A political economy perspective of the trends in media ownership, says McQuail (2002:82), notes that there is a reduction in independent media sources, concentration on the largest markets, avoidance of risks, and reduced investment in less profitable media tasks (such as investigative reporting and documentary film-making). There is much to be concerned about. "We also find neglect of smaller and poorer sections of the potential audience and often a politically unbalanced range of news media" (ibid).

Concentration and conglomeration, according to this perspective, have serious implications for media content (especially for factual genres such as news, current affairs and documentaries) and media audiences. Devereaux (2003:62) points out that:

Audiences are constructed primarily as consumers rather than citizens who have a right to be informed. Concentration and conglomeration also have implications for media workers. Casualization of media work has increased and the greater economies of scale demanded by the media oligopolies has also resulted in job losses ... if cultural production is driven predominantly by the relentless search for profit and is increasingly undertaken by media organizations that have a wide range of economic interests, then the political economy perspective would lead us to conclude that one of the first casualties tends to be media content which directly challenges the prevailing capital interest.

EXERCISE *A question of influence*

What kinds of constraints do you think exist for media professionals who work for privately-owned media organisations, given their dependence on advertising and sponsorship?

Defining key concepts of ethics

The acts of gathering and writing news are collectively referred to as news reporting or simply reporting. Journalism consists of team work, with each person in the newsroom and outside the newsroom within the media house doing their bit. But the reporter is the first point of reference with regard to the facts in the story, which have a direct bearing on how the news was collected, written and edited.

Responsible journalism is about reporters being conscious of or caring about the ethical problems that arise between them on the one hand and news sources and the general public on the other. A reporter who reports responsibly is one who cares about the effects of the news on society generally and on individuals she reports about. She is an ethical and caring journalist.

As we have seen, media ethics deals with principles, values and virtues which guide the morality of journalistic actions. Ethics deals with the philosophical foundations of decision-making, of choosing between good and bad options. Morality, on the other hand, has come to mean socially approved behaviour, or the practice of ethics.

- Principles are guidelines which serve as a compass to give direction to one's actions regarding what constitutes right or wrong, good or bad action. An example of a journalistic principle is: Journalists should report the truth.
- Values, which may be moral or non-moral, are what individuals aim at doing or achieving because these values are in line with either their or society's expectations. Values define what is good and what individuals should aim at getting or achieving. A value deriving from the

journalistic principle in the example given above might be: It is good for a reporter to report the truth.

- Virtues are the qualities of a person which help him achieve the values he has set out to achieve by following a principle. A virtue, in line with the journalistic principle and value given above, could be: A reporter cross-checks information.

Classical theories of ethics

While media ethics may be new, ethics as a philosophical discipline seems to date from the Greek philosophers around 400 BC. Well-argued classical theories of ethics, from which media ethics could partly be explained, have been put forward.

Meta-ethics or descriptive ethics

The most well-known of these are probably teleological ethics, deontological ethics and virtue ethics, all of which belong to the class of metaethics or descriptive ethics (distinguished from normative or applied ethics). Each one of these theories has its advantages and its weaknesses, and has been critiqued and developed over the years. Other ethical theories, such as an ethics of justice or feminist ethics, have also been developed, but we will concentrate on the classical theories here.

Teleological ethics

Teleological ethics focuses on the nature of the consequences of an action. Teleological ethicists consider consequences to be the sole determining factors of an action's ethicality. For the moral, rightness of an action is the good that results from it. They are in perfect agreement with the maxim: the end justifies the means. Applied to journalism, a teleologist would, for example, go ahead and report a story if its outcome would be good for the individual named in the story or society as a whole, or both. There are, of course, many varieties of teleological ethicists, ranging from those who hold that the good that results from an action must be for the self (egoists), to those who maintain that it must be for the greatest number (utilitarianists).

Deontological ethics

Deontological ethics is oblivious of the outcome of actions. What matters is the principle upon which the action is based, and not the consequences. Applied to media ethics, a deontological reporter would be one who, after holding to the principle that reporters must report the truth, goes ahead and reports the truth even if he is certain that thousands of people will die because of the story.

For a deontologist, what matters is to report the truth and not the consequences of reporting that truth. Just as for teleological ethics, there are many varieties of deontological ethics. They range from pure deontology, which rigidly ignores the outcome of the actions as long as they are based on sound principles, as in the example given above, to various types of mixed deontology in which there is some attention paid to the consequences while the focus is still on adherence to principles.

Virtue ethics

Based on the thoughts of Aristotle, this ethical theory argues that one will make the right ethical decisions if one becomes virtuous – and one becomes virtuous by doing virtuous deeds. Accordingly, this ethical theory locates the rightness of an action in the character of the person who performs that action, and assumes that one learns right from wrong through years of experience. Aristotelian theory is often used to argue that the virtuous person will be able to distinguish between two extremes, and the ethical action will therefore be the one that occupies the so-called Golden Mean between two undesirable alternatives.

Normative or applied ethics

Normative or applied ethics is based on duties which guide human action. Human beings perform actions because they feel obliged out of duty to do them. The duty may be for example to self, a professional body, an employer or a religious affiliation. A reporter may feel obliged to report the truth and, indeed, go ahead and report the truth out of self respect, or because her editor requires her to report the truth, or because she belongs to a media association or council which requires its members to report the truth, or because she is a Christian or Muslim and Christianity or Islam requires that a reporter should report the truth.

There are many varieties of normative ethics. They range from traditional legalistic ethics, which requires people to stick to what the rules say as a guide to their actions, to antinomian ethics, sometimes known as non-ethics, in which the only guide to action is what the individual person feels like doing at a particular moment.

In media ethics, an example for traditional legalistic ethics would be reporters who only follow what the media codes of ethics say as a guide to their ethical performance. They do no more and no less. If, for instance, the code of ethics says that they should report the truth and says nothing about reporting accurately, they would not bother about the accuracy in their news story because that is not specified in the code.

Reporters who follow antinomian ethics are usually not consistent. For example, they would report the truth today, if that is what they feel like doing, and report falsehood tomorrow when it suits them. Africa is full of such reporters.

An African perspective of ethics

Apart from classical paradigms of media ethics, reporters in Africa ought to pay attention to ethical foundations in African society. Journalism, apart from being a world profession whose products should be valid in any part of the world, is also rooted in the particular society which that media serves.

The tragedy facing African journalism of the 1990s and beyond, however, is that the continent's journalists have closely imitated the professional norms of the North (formerly known as the West), which they see as the epitome of good journalism. Consequently, the ethical foundations, their aims and objectives that African journalists follow have been blueprints of the media in the industrialised societies of the North. Some African journalists even claim that the Northern standards they follow are world journalism standards which every media person should observe. They refuse to listen to any suggestions that journalism can blend standard ethical requirements with African ethical roots and still maintain its global validity and appeal.

An African view of life and human nature

To understand the foundations of African ethics (Afri-ethics*), we need to start from an analysis of how an African views life and human nature.

The world of an African consists of the living and the dead (Figure 13.1). The living and the dead all share one world – the world of the living-dead or dead-living – in which they also share one life and one vital force. What the living do or do not do affects the dead, and what the dead do or do not do affects the living. The dead are not actually "dead", they merely transfer to another life – the life of the dead-living or living-dead. The living need the dead to carry out a normal and full life. The dead, in turn, need the living to enjoy their "life" to the full (hence libations and other sacrifices by the living to the dead).

What the dead do, or do not do, can have a telling effect on the living. The evil spirits (bad dead people), for example, have the power and influence to haunt those among the living against whom they have a grudge by generally making life difficult for them. The good spirits, on the other hand, have the ability and the power to protect the living from problems which come with life's vicissitudes or are deliberately planted on them by evil living people or spirits.

There are good and bad people among the living, just as there are good and bad spirits among the dead.

The living-dead are in a continuum. At one end are the very good people and at the other end are very bad people. In between are good people and bad people. Because African society is communal, there is constant interaction between the good people and the not-so-good.

* Prof Frances Kasoma, a leading media scholar, coined the phrase "Afri-ethics" and contributed to this discussion.

The aim is to have the good acts of the good people rub off on the not-so-good so that they, too, can emulate them and also become good.

The yardstick for good acts is whether or not they serve the community – the whole community consisting of the living and the dead – either as a family, a clan or the tribe (ethnic group). When acts only serve to propagate or satisfy pursuits of individuals, they are not regarded to be as good as those that serve the family, clan or tribe and may even be regarded as bad acts if they are harmful to the family, clan or tribe.

The more beneficial to a larger community the acts are, the ethically better they are. Thus, acts that only serve an individual are not as good as those that serve the whole family and, similarly, acts that only serve the family are less good compared to those that serve the clan and the tribe. Acts that are only for the good of the individual at the exclusion of the clan and the tribe may even be regarded as bad.

A noteworthy ethical point in African life is that the bad people in a community are constantly advised and counselled so that they become better members of the community. They are not simply condemned and ostracised. The counselling is usually done by elders who, because of their wide experience in life, are looked up to as being wiser than the younger members of the community. When it is elders who are going wrong and there are no peers to advise them, there is also room for young people to advise elders provided proper etiquette is followed. The need for common good for the community overshadows all acts in African society.

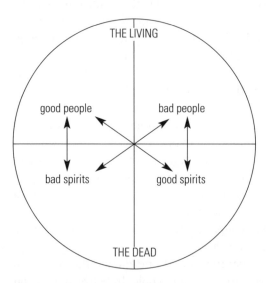

Figure 13.1 Graphic view of the foundations of Afri-ethics

There are two types of ethically bad behaviour by the living: that generated by self-will and that brought about by the influence of either bad people or bad spirits acting on the person. The living have no control over the latter type of bad behaviour and therefore cannot be blamed for it completely. The blame is heaped on bad spirits or evil people who have taken possession of, or cast a spell over the actors, and are making them behave in such a manner.

Africans, however, condemn people whose bad actions are brought about by their own free will or choice. While Africans believe that some people may be led to do bad things by bad spirits or evil people, they also believe a human being can be in full control of his or her actions, including the bad ones.

The influence of the community, particularly the family, is sometimes taken into account when apportioning blame to a person for his bad behaviour. Some personal acts are, thus, attributed to the family influence or background. Africans believe that a family with bad people usually begets ill-mannered children and that a good family begets well-behaved people. So, although an individual may be blamed for the actions arising from her own free will, Africans also look at and may blame the person's behaviour partly on the family upbringing.

Africans believe that it is unusual for a good person to come from a bad family and vice versa. The ethical responsibility of a person who hails from a bad family is, therefore, not accorded the same weight of blame as a person who comes from a good family. A person with a good family background is blamed more for the same bad act than a person from a bad family. The reverse is also true: a good act from a person who hails from a bad family is valued much more than the same good act from a person with a good family background.

Africans also recognise the influence of friends and close associates, who may not necessarily be members of the immediate extended family, on a person's behaviour. Those repeatedly caught engaged in bad behaviour are advised to change their friends and join the company of well-behaved people. If they refuse to listen, they are condemned as bad people belonging to bad company.

A similar continuum exists among the dead. There are very good spirits and merely good spirits, just as there are very bad spirits and merely bad spirits among them. The bad spirits connive with the bad people to make life difficult for both the good people and the good spirits.

There is a constant struggle between the good and the bad among the living and their counterparts among the dead. The good people and spirits try to win over the bad people on their side by showing them that it does not pay to be bad. Only when they fail to convert them, and after the bad people degenerate into irredeemable states such as witches or

> *" A horse has four legs, yet it often falls" – Zulu proverb*
> (Leslau & Leslau 1985:7)

wizards, does society give up and ostracise these very bad people from the community so that its well-being can be preserved.

The good spirits guard over and protect the good people from falling into evil ways engineered by the bad spirits. They carry out this assignment generally by protecting all the people in the family, clan and tribe. They also particularly do this to those after whom they are named or who bear their totem.

The basis of morality in African society is the fulfilment of obligations to kinspeople, both living and dead. It is believed that some of the departed and the spirits keep watch over people to make sure that they observe the moral laws and are punished when they break them.

Afri-ethics applied in the newsroom

African reporters can enrich their ethical journalism by applying some of these basics in African morality to the practice of their journalism. Moreover, the African paradigm of morality can teach world journalism the value and usefulness of enforcing ethical principles, values and virtues through the communal rather than individual approach. After all, journalism is a team or communal profession and not a profession of individuals. Unlike in other professions, journalists should sink and rise together because of what they do collectively or as individuals, or both. Even what might look like individual journalistic action has a bearing on journalists as a whole.

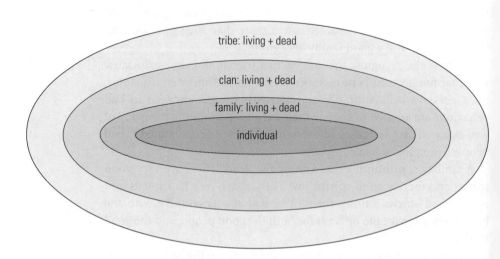

Figure 13.2 The ethical influence on an individual

Guidelines for making ethical decisions

When you've got your notebook or camera out, the source is talking and the editor waiting, it is pretty difficult to remember intricate philosophical argument. It is, quite frankly, difficult to *do* ethics. For exactly that reason, journalism professors Jay Black, Bob Steele and Ralph Barney have suggested these three principles to guide journalists as they put ethics to work (1995:17):

Seek trust and report it as fully as possible
- *Inform yourself continuously so you can inform, engage, and educate the public in clear and compelling ways on significant issues.*
- *Be honest, fair and courageous in gathering, reporting and interpreting accurate information.*
- *Give voice to the voiceless.*
- *Hold the powerful accountable.*

Act independently
- *Guard vigorously the essential stewardship that a free press plays in an open society.*
- *Seek out and disseminate competing perspectives without being unduly influenced by those who would use their power or position counter to the public interest.*
- *Remain free of associations and activities that may compromise your integrity or damage your credibility.*
- *Recognise that good ethical decisions require individual responsibility and collaborative efforts.*

Minimise harm
- *Be compassionate for those affected by your actions.*
- *Treat sources, subjects, and colleagues as human beings deserving of respect, not merely as means to your journalistic ends.*
- *Recognise that gathering and reporting information may cause harm or discomfort, but balance those negatives by choosing alternatives that maximise your goals of truth-telling.*

Ethical problems: responsible news gathering

News is gathered in three ways:
- Obtaining information from people who have witnessed it.
- Witnessing the event yourself.
- Finding news from other sources such as magazines, books, radio and television stations, newspapers, posters, banners and news releases.

Persons as sources of news

Sources speaking to a reporter do not readily give news which incriminates them or others in wrongdoing. Yet, as we saw above, much of the news which is reported is incriminating in one way or another. The fears of sources are often genuine and unless they are allayed by the reporter, few sources would be willing to give reporters information. It is an ethical principle in journalism that reporters should protect their sources. There are many ways to do this. We shall deal with only a few main ones in this chapter.

They include:

- Keeping sources confidential.
- Using formulas which make sources hard or impossible to identify.
- Not being emotionally attached to sources.
- Not using deceptive methods.
- Not invading the privacy of sources.
- Cultivating sources.
- Avoiding pack journalism or "group think".

* See discussion in Chapter 4 on developing personal sources.

Keeping sources confidential*

Generally in news reporting the identity of sources should be revealed, otherwise news consumers would not regard the news that is reported as genuine. The natural tendency of news consumers when faced with an unsourced news story, especially if the story is intriguing, is to conclude that the reporters made it up.

When reporters are interviewing sources, therefore, the assumption should be that the identity of the source should be revealed unless a special request is made by the source not to have her identity revealed. Reporters should not assume the source does not want to be named. The request itself should be mutually agreed upon by the reporter and the source, with the reporter being convinced of the need for the source to be protected. Sources may agree to be identified after being convinced by the reporter of the need to be identified.

In the event of the reporter agreeing not to reveal the source, he should not break the promise, even if it means going to jail for refusing to disclose the source to a court of law. The ethical requirement for the reporter not to name the source only applies to cases where the reporter has made this undertaking. It does not apply to any source who has not been named in a story. Thus in court a reporter can reveal the identity of a source whom he did not name in the story but with whom no undertaking or promise of confidentiality was made.

Using formulas which make sources difficult or impossible to identify

There are formulas, words and expressions that reporters use to mask the source in cases where they have promised not to identify him or her. These include:

- a source
- an informed source
- a well-informed source
- a reliable source
- a usually reliable source
- a very reliable source
- a source within
- according to an insider

Such expressions carry specific nuances of meaning and should be used only to transmit that meaning. When using these expressions reporters should also inform the reader/listener/viewer that the source requested not to be identified. Sometimes, however, instead of masking the source, such formulas actually make it easier for readers to identify the source. This is the case when a statement like "a top district government official who did not want to be named said" is used. There may be only one top government official in the district and the people reading/listening/viewing the news would immediately know who it is. Reporters should, therefore, avoid such formulas and opt for the ones which make the source they do not want to identify less easily identifiable.

When the nature of the information is such that no matter what formula is used, the source would still be identified, the reporter should spread the field of suspicion by asking other sources to confirm or corroborate the same information. In such a case, the reporter would have to attribute the information to "sources" rather than to "a source" and make identification difficult. While trying to get the same information from other sources, it is unethical for a reporter to reveal the identity of the earlier source, even when she is specifically requested to do so.

Sometimes sources in their fear not to be identified may tell a reporter that the information they are giving him is "off the record". When such a request is made, it is unethical for the reporter to insist that the information has been given to him and he should, therefore, use it at all costs. What the reporter should do is ask the source what she means by "off the record". The source may either be saying that she has merely given you background information which may not be used at all as it is given, or that you can use it but without quoting her as the source. In the latter case, you may also want to suggest to the source a formula you would want to use to mask her identity such as "a source close to the minister" and see if she agrees to its being used. "Off the record" information that is not meant to be used by the reporter at all is still useful. The reporter can use it as a tipoff to get the story from relevant sources or authorities. "Off the record" information gives the reporter the type of inside information which helps him know what questions to ask the relevant sources or authorities.

Not being emotionally attached to sources

The two extremes of emotional attachment to sources that should influence news reporting are love and hate. Both can make it difficult for a reporter to report fairly. Although there is no such thing as a completely objective news story (and objectivity should not be confused with having no viewpoint or being value-free), reporters should try as far as possible to divorce themselves from dangers that would make their reporting unduly slanted or pre-conceived.

When a reporter falls in love with a source, which does not happen every day, or when a reporter hates a source, then it is incumbent upon the reporter to desist from using the loved or hated person as a source. Here we are talking about real love and real hatred and not about anything in between. The greatest temptation for reporters not to consciously report the truth is strongest when the reporter either loves or hates the source. The ethical thing for the reporter to do is to hand over the reporting of the story involving a loved or hated source to a colleague who is less emotionally attached. The same goes for handling stories involving close relatives. They should be given to other reporters.

There is no doubt that if we love someone, they are in the best position to give us the best news tips about what is happening to them or around them. Reporters should desist from the temptation of jumping to write the stories from such tips, quoting their loved ones as anonymous sources. They should use the tips to get the story from other sources whom they could then quote.

As for hated sources, there is always the urge to take revenge or make them pay for whatever wrong they might have done to the reporter. Few reporters can resist that urge. It is, therefore, better for the reporter to keep away from the hated source. This can be done by avoiding such sources or, if assigned to cover such a source, explaining to superiors why the story should be given to a reporter who is likely to be more fair to the source.

Not using deceptive methods

Lying in order to obtain information has been used by reporters more or less successfully. This is an area where a pure deontological approach would cause ethical problems. The ethicality of lying depends on a number of factors, including:

- how big the lie is;
- how profound or important the information being sought is, in relation to the lie;
- whether all the alternatives to obtain the information have been exhausted and the lie is the only cause of action left, and the information needed is undoubtedly in the public interest;
- whether the harm arising from the lie is less serious than the harm prevented by revealing the information;
- whether the act of lying was a deliberate action by the reporter following consultations with colleagues and superiors in which the effects of the lie are weighed rather than a routine action which reflects a habit;
- when the reporter is willing to disclose to her readers/audience afterwards that deception was used to gather the information, and is able to justify the deceptive means.

Posing as someone is, indeed, an ethical problem in news gathering. In order to extract information from unsuspecting or reluctant sources it is not uncommon for reporters in Africa to pose as a plain-clothes police officer or the like. But realise that impersonating people, particularly public officers, is a crime in many countries. The question arises then whether reporters should resort to committing a crime to gather news. While deontologically it is ethically wrong for reporters to commit a crime in news gathering, a consequentialist approach would judge such actions on how serious the crime being committed is in relation to the news being obtained and how essential the news is to the people it is meant to serve.

Frances Kasoma recalls one occasion when, as a reporter for the *Times of Zambia*, he badly needed a comment from the then Minister of Home Affairs, Mr Aaron Milner. He telephoned Mr Milner's office several times and was told each time by his secretary that he was not in. He checked every possible place he could have been, including State House and his home, and was told that the minister was at his office.

Finally, he drove to Mr Milner's office. Upon entering the secretary's office he was able to hear Mr Milner talking to someone in his office. Visibly upset with him, the secretary repeated her earlier assertion that Mr Milner was not in the office. He quickly drove back to the office and telephoned Mr Milner's office once more. When the same secretary answered, he said in a deep voice: "Can I speak to Aaron?" The secretary readily said, "Hold on, sir" and put him through to Mr Milner. After getting the comment from a rather perplexed Mr Milner – who asked how

---

HOT LINK

Are there instances when it might be appropriate to use deception, misrepresentation or hidden cameras in newsgathering? Ethics coach and author Bob Steele thinks there might be – you can fulfill some stringent criteria to justify your actions. Read his argument at http://www.org/content/content_view.asp?rd=886.

"One falsehood spoils a thousand truths" – Ashanti proverb
(Leslau & Leslau 1985:7)

he had got through to him, but got no answer – Kasoma hung up. A few minutes later, the secretary telephoned and half sobbing asked him: "Why did you lie to me that you were the Minister's friend by calling him by his first name?"

"I was admittedly not on first-name terms with Mr Milner," said Kasoma, "but I laughed and hung up."

Given the circumstances, this kind of lying is typically considered permissible in news gathering. "It is what might be called resourcefulness in news gathering," says Kasoma.

Not invading the privacy of sources

The need for the free flow of information sometimes conflicts with the right of individuals to privacy. The problem is usually when public officials demand that they have as much right to privacy as any citizen. In Zambia, for example, a cabinet minister in 1996 threatened to shoot a reporter if he ever stepped in his home again to interview him on a story. What the cabinet minister forgot (or did not know) is that as a public official his claim to privacy is far less than that of a private citizen.

Nonetheless, even public officials should have some privacy. Under normal circumstances, for example, one cannot burst into a minister's bedroom to interview him.

Cultivating sources

Reporters need to cultivate sources because they are the lifeblood of their career. When sources are wronged, or believe they were wronged, the reporter should try to pacify them. When the mistake is already publicised, the reporter should make presentations to her media manager to have the mistake promptly corrected, no matter how small the mistake might be. Many a source has been known, for example, to shun a reporter who misspelt his name.

If the source is wrong in blaming the reporter or there is, in fact, no wrong done, the reporter should explain the situation to the source. For example, many news sources have been upset with a reporter for what they think is an incriminating headline. What they may not know is that the reporter has nothing to do with writing the headline of a story. That is the

---

HOT TIP

Privacy checklist

1. How important is the information I am seeking? Does the public have a right to know? A need to know? Or merely a desire to know?
2. What level of protection do individuals involved in the story deserve? How much harm might they receive? Are they involved in the news event by choice, or by happenstance?
3. How would I feel if I were being subjected to the same scrutiny?
4. Do I know the facts of the story well enough? What else do I need to know?
5. What can I do to minimise the privacy invasion and the harm? Can I broaden the focus of the story by including more "victims", thereby minimising harm to a select few? Can I postpone the story without significantly jeopardising information to the public?
6. Do I need to include other individuals in the decision-making to gain more perspective?
7. Should I be focusing more on the system failure or the big-issue picture as opposed to focusing intensely on individuals?
8. Can I clearly and fully justify my thinking and decision? To those directly affected? To the public?

(Source: Black et, al, 1995:182)

responsibility of the sub-editor who edited the story. Some explaining of this fact might help the source not to blame the reporter and thereby sour the relationship.

It is useful, however, for the beginner reporter to know that in news reporting the reporter is, sometimes, bound to step on some toes. A news reporter, by the nature of her work, is bound to displease some people while at the same time pleasing others. But there is something wrong with the reporter who is always making enemies of sources, just as there is something wrong with the reporter who always pleases his sources.

If a news source still remains displeased with the reporter even after he has tried to pacify him, it is hard luck. But the reporter should not keep away from such a source unless the source specifically wants to end the reporter-source relationship.

Gifts

What gifts a journalist may accept in good conscience is determined by company policy as well as individual ethics. In an age of professional manipulation of the press by governments, politicians and companies, there are countless freebies and other goodies offered to those in the media. Accepting a free MNet decoder and subscription may not influence a television critic's reviews of MNet programmes. But what about being wined and dined in style by those ever-so-pleasant public relations and promotional personnel? Free tickets to the theatre may be acceptable in the case of arts critics; consider, though, a big insurance company offering financial journalists a seat in their corporate box at an international rugby tournament. The crunch choice may never come – the same financial journalist may never be asked to suppress or to sauce-up a story about that company. But on other, less dramatic, issues, there is the danger of a slow disarming of journalists. A comfortable, if not cosy, culture can grow to take the place of an erstwhile scepticism and adversarial journalism. There are plane tickets, trips and junkets, the use of a car, sponsorships, and promises of exclusive stories. Lines need to be drawn, but how and where? These ethical questions need to be posed – pre-eminently by journalistic practitioners themselves in the course of their daily work.

HOT LINK

See the advice on gift giving to public relations practitioners on p.280, and the Sunday Times' policy on gifts and freebies at: http://www.sanef.org.za/ethics_codes/sunday_times/277048.htm.

Avoiding pack journalism

On September 18, 1960, the then United Nations Secretary General Dag Hammarskjold, on a peace mission to war-torn Zaire, was flying from Zaire to Ndola in Zambia. Scores of reporters, some from the international news media, were awaiting his arrival at the tiny airport.

They stood behind the fence, near the regular touch-down of the airport's only runway. After a long wait they saw a small plane land at the opposite end of the runway and stop at the airport's control tower at the other end of the airport's apron.

Through the wire fence, they saw several men alight from the plane, one of whom they took to be Hammarskjold. A car drove up to the plane and sped off with the passengers. The reporters, including some from the international news agencies, subsequently filed stories of Hammarskjold's arrival in Ndola, only to correct them later when it was established that the person the reporters had convinced themselves was Hammarskjold was in fact someone else. Hammarskjold had died in a plane crash near Ndola that same night.

This is a good example of pack journalism in which reporters agree to all report the same facts in a story so that if they are wrong, the blame would be less serious since everyone on the scene had made the same mistake.

It needs a brave, independent-minded reporter to differ from the pack since friends could label her a black sheep who is trying to be too clever. Not only does the conscientious reporter risk being ostracised from the pack of fellow reporters, but the reporter's editor is also likely to carpet her for not getting the same story as the others.

Reporters observing the news

The reliance on reporters' observations in news gathering should be handled with care. As a general rule, reporters should desist from naming themselves as the source of the news by virtue of the fact that they witnessed the event. Even when the reporter has witnessed the event, he should have the facts corroborated by other sources or responsible authorities.

If, for instance, a reporter witnesses a road accident and a person lying by the accident scene presumed dead, he should corroborate his eye-witness observations of the accident with other witnesses on the scene, whom he should then quote. He should also contact police and medical authorities to confirm other details, such as the cause of the accident and whether the person who was lying by the roadside presumed dead is actually dead.

If there are no eye witnesses, or none of the eye witnesses is willing to speak to the reporter, or when authorities are not available to confirm what the reporter observed, the reporter should always put his readers on guard by informing them that the news they are reading/listening to/viewing was as observed by "this reporter" and was neither corroborated by eye witnesses nor confirmed by authorities. This is a good precautionary measure just in case the reporter's observations were wrong, as sometimes happens.

A situation in which reporters are themselves the subject of the news is even trickier. This is the case, for instance, when a reporter is attacked by a news source or arrested by police while on duty for, for example, trespassing. The greater ethical complication arises from the fact that the reporter is, undeniably, emotionally involved in the incident and, usually and naturally, may tend to narrate the happenings in his favour while creating the impression through his reporting that he is providing an "objective" view. It is always better to assign another reporter to do the story who would then interview the parties involved, including the reporter who is in trouble. It should be made clear in the story that the reporter who is writing the story is not the same reporter who is in trouble. If the reporter who is in trouble has to write the story, again it is important that readers are told so that they know how to take the information they are being given.

Plagiarism

News, like any intellectual property, is subject to copyright regulations. It is unethical to pirate news and other information from other sources and parade it as yours. There are certain basic copyright assumptions reporters should know regardless of which of the two copyright conventions – the Berne Agreement or the Universal Copyright Convention – their country subscribes to. One of them is the understanding that in any copyright law it is the manner in which the ideas are expressed that is protected and not the ideas themselves. If, for example, a reporter gets an idea for a news story from another newspaper or a radio station and works on the story herself, there is no copyright violation even if the reporter interviews exactly the same sources as those interviewed by the reporter who wrote the original story.

If a reporter has to lift the story or information from another publication, radio, television station or a news agency report, copyright regulations require that the reporter gives credit to the owners of the story. This requirement is not only in the interest of the owners of the news story who deserve to get the credit for the story, but it is also of benefit to the reporter's media house which has lifted the story because in the event of the story proving to be inaccurate, the originators of the story, and not the media house that has lifted it, would be blamed in the first instance. This is so notwithstanding certain legal arrangements that often exist between media houses and news agencies that those who use their stories do so at their own risk, meaning they are legally liable for the stories.

Reporters whose duty it is to monitor broadcast stations should always ensure that the news they get from these stations is credited to the stations that broadcast them. It is not necessary to credit the particular reporter who filed the story, in cases where her identity is revealed in the report.

When reporters obtain certain specific information such as statistics from documents to beef up their news stories, they should always indicate where the information has been obtained, for example: "According to information just released from the Central Statistical Office, half of the country's population ...". This also serves to reassure news consumers that the information they are getting is authoritative and genuine and that the reporter has done her homework.

It is a very serious matter if reporters are caught using other people's writing for their own. In recent years several plagiarism scandals, such as the Jayson Blair case referred to above, made headlines across the world. This is journalistic dishonesty which calls for severe punishment and brings the profession into disrepute.

Withholding information

This is another difficult issue confronting journalists. In South Africa, it is not only unethical, but also illegal to identify rape victims, directly or through their families. It had been simply a convention in the USA, until the case of the 1992 William Kennedy Smith rape trial, when certain television networks presented his accuser in full face to their viewers.

There are also laws against identifying children in trouble with the law, and against identifying detainees. Yet there are also cases in which these laws are defied for reasons that may be commercial sensation in some cases, or a greater ethic in other cases. *Rapport* published the photograph of Janusz Walus before he appeared in an identity parade or was charged in court with the murder of political leader Chris Hani. In another case, *South* newspaper published a photograph of a streetchild being arrested, without any of the conventional placing of disguising stripes over the eyes, under the headline: "The Face of Fear". Both cases have ethical implications. (Here again, there are some more recent examples – perhaps the Bristol Bovey or Cynthia Vongai plagiarism scandals of 2003, Vusi Mona's conflict of interest, etc.)

And what about reporting information that could provoke a copy-cat effect? The difficulty is that copy-cat cases are often unintentional – a graphic report about child drug abuse on one paper saw shopkeepers calling to complain that some youngsters sought to emulate the problem. Similarly, publishing news about the horrific "necklace" form of murder in South Africa arguably helped to spread and

▓▒▓▒ LINK

The worst of times? *The Media* editor Kevin Bloom looks at why 2003 was described as "an annus horribilis for the South African media" and wonders aloud if it will be remembered as the year the media learned the price of not acknowledging its responsibilities. Read his piece at: http://www.themedia.co.za/article.aspx?articleid=42342&area=/media_insightco.

popularise the atrocity. Should journalists publish regardless of such issues, and if not, is there not a danger of self-censorship beginning to cloud the reporting process? Withholding information also crops up in relation to the protection of sources by journalists. Many journalists refuse to give evidence voluntarily in court cases, no matter the proceedings at stake, and many South African journalists have even refused to testify when subpoenaed to do so.

The decisions involved are often personal ones, but the general working principle is that a journalist's job is to gather and disseminate information, and that actions that may hinder this mission would be avoided. The assumption is that journalistic access and credibility require going no further than generating information; it is up to other individuals and agencies to act on it.

Collecting information can also raise tricky questions: is it ethical for a person to withhold the fact that he is a journalist? What about more extreme cases, where a journalist pretends to be a completely different person in order to get information? In a controversial case in 1992, South Africa's *Weekly Mail* newspaper (now the *Mail & Guardian*) faced a civil suit in court for allegedly having bugged the offices of former covert military operative, Staal Burger. Was the paper justified in using underhand methods to seek information about possible antisocial conspiracies?

Discrimination

Discrimination is another ethical dilemma for journalists. How relevant are characteristics like race? In road accident stories? In racially motivated assaults or terror attacks? In crime stories? Similarly, ageism can crop up as an ethical matter, in references to women as "girls", or in the general neglect of concerns of young children and the elderly. And what about gender: it seems normal to some to describe the attire of women featured in articles; to others this is a form of sexist evaluation.

Computer-assisted reporting

"I would hope that we don't let technology change principle," says Ron Meador, assistant managing editor for special projects at the Minneapolis *Star Tribune* (Steele and Cochran, 1995:12).

HOT LINK

Strip the Back Page! The South African advocacy group GenderLinks launched a "Strip the Back Page" campaign to encourage editors to stop publishing pictures of scantily-clad women, which the group considered offensive. The South African National Editors Forum (Sanef) did not endorse the campaign. You'll find the details about the campaign – and guidelines for gender sensitive reporting – at: www. http://www.genderlinks.org.za. Sanef's statement on the matter is at http://www.sanef.org.za/press_statements/307707.htm.

Some other useful guidelines are:

Reporting mental illness: http://www.nuj.org.uk/inner.php?docid=422.

Reporting on lesbians and gays: http://www.nlgja.org/pubs/toolbox_intro.htm.

Reporting on race relations: http://www.poynter.org/content/content_view.asp?id=4448.

In other words, using the computer does not alter traditional concerns about accuracy, fairness, privacy, plagiarism or other ethical issues. But the truth is, using the computer to gather and analyse information can put reporters and editors on unfamiliar territory. Some of the major concerns are:

- Reporters can break into private electronic mail boxes or data bases.
- Sources can disguise their identities online.
- Sources can deliberately place false or misleading data online.
- Electronic information and sites are often temporary, which makes them difficult to verify.

Ethical news writing

The newsroom, the place where reporters write their news stories, is not an ideal place for reflective and careful writing. There are many distractions. Reporters coming and going, some loudly discussing their stories with colleagues, others taking a story dictation from another reporter on the telephone, still others getting a story from a telephone on a poor line which forces them to shout, and so on. Under these circumstances, it is not surprising that reporters sometimes make mistakes, even with the best intentions. Some mistakes, however, arise because the reporters are too lazy to cross-check the facts and trust their memory or a single source. Other mistakes arise from the reporters' zeal to add condiment to the bare facts in the story, thus making it sound exaggerated. It is therefore also important for newsroom managers to create the environment for debate about ethical issues. Ethical journalism requires an investment of time, money and effort. News managers should guard against putting so much pressure on individual journalists that they do not have the resources or the time to make proper ethical decisions. Editors and managers should invest in ongoing career training for journalists, which should emphasise the skills needed for ethical decision-making. Moreover, journalists making ethical decisions should be rewarded, and not only journalists writing those stories that improve circulation or ratings.

The main ethical problems confronting news writers include inaccuracy, unfairness and obscenity.

HOT TIP

Checklist for online reporters
1 What are we thinking of doing? Why?
2 Who should be involved in the decision-making process?
3 What else do we need to know to make a good decision?
4 Are we doing anything in our news gathering with computers that we would not justify with other methods of reporting?
5 What alternative actions have we tried or should we consider to obtain the same information?
6 Who would benefit and who would be harmed by our actions?
7 Which actions maximise our truth-seeking and truth-telling duties and best honor the other principles related to intrusion/privacy?

(Source: Steele & Cochran, 1995:12)

Inaccuracy

African reporting leaves much to be desired in terms of accuracy. Inaccuracy means not paying meticulous attention to details. It is closely related but not equivalent to truthfulness. A story may be true but inaccurate. Numerous or big inaccuracies, however, can result in a story not being true.

An inaccurate reporter is one who simply does not care about seemingly small things such as spelling (particularly of names and places), figures, sequence of events as well as details of facts. For him it does not really matter whether the person's name is written as Kaunda or Kuanda, whether the source said she thought she would win the elections or whether she said she might win the elections, whether 12 people were killed in a riot or 13, whether the person who was lynched was a man or woman, and so on.

Sometimes inaccuracy in news writing takes the form of reporting facts or statements out of context. This often happens in paraphrasing speeches in news writing. A paragraph may be inserted in a story out of context to the extent that news consumers understand the statement in a context which the person giving the speech did not mean. A story might therefore be accurate, but without the proper context, it does not convey the truth as fully as it should.

One of the most common ways of misreporting in Africa is to put words in the mouth of the speaker. For instance, the reporter may have got a tip that Minister so-and-so would resign tomorrow. The reporter contacts the minister and puts the following question to her: "Is it true that you are going to resign tomorrow?" and the minister replies, "Yes, it is true" and says nothing further. The reporter, in writing the story, begins it with the following words: "Minister so-and-so announced yesterday that she would resign today". This is not accurate. What the minister did was to confirm her resignation in answer to a question. She did not announce her resignation. Accuracy in news writing has very often to do with the correct and effective use of words. Journalists should use their words carefully and mean what the words mean. Otherwise a situation soon arises where news consumers who are constantly subjected to careless use of words adopt the attitude not to take the words reporters use seriously and engage in guess-work regarding the meaning of the words. When this happens, reporters have failed in effectively informing the news consumers.

Unfairness

Unfairness in news writing means that the journalist does not give a hearing to all the contending sides in a story; she does not give all sides. It means not giving those being accused the right of reply in the same story or waiting to publish what they say in their defence in a subsequent issue or, worse still, never giving them a say at all.

Few people in Africa read newspapers regularly and many people, therefore, may not see the subsequent story in which the accused defends himself. The motives for political bigotry and accusing others with mischief are many and varied. Journalists are often merely used as pawns in the political chess game. By giving the accuser exclusive publicity, the press treats the accused party unfairly.

Sometimes the defence or other side of the story is included in a news story but is deliberately "lost" in the story by burying it in an inconspicuous part of the story. This is what happens when the defence is put at the tail end of the story. Because few news readers read a news story to the end, the defence often ends up not being read. That is almost as good as not including the defence in the first place. This is why some reporters prefer a complex or compound news lead (or intro) in which both the accusation and the defence are highlighted. The writer then keeps alternating, as the news unfolds, between the two positions until the end of the story. Some news editors call this style "killing the story" since the writer is giving the accusation and undoing it at the same time. Such interpretation already smacks of bias. It assumes that the accusing party is correct and the defending party is wrong. Few news stories permit reporters to have such blatant bias.

One of the best examples of news writing in which the accusation is highlighted more than the defence, is in court reporting. Although in the British and allied court system the accused is presumed innocent until proven guilty, court reporters nearly always highlight the accusation, the prosecution's case, and end up with the defence. Sometimes the defence does not come until several days, weeks and even months later, by which time the public have become fed with the prosecution's case in which the accusation is highlighted. By the time the reporters turn to the defence, the story is no longer fresh and many readers may not even bother to read what the defence is saying.

Painting a false positive picture

Unfairness does not only arise from negative bias when reporters paint a false picture of people in the news. It also happens, and often so, when reporters paint a false positive picture of people in the news. This type of unfairness is particularly prevalent among reporters writing for the government media. Reporters pick the most favourable angle to a news story. As the story is being written, unfavourable details are left out and words and expressions are used which make the people in the news look good.

A lot of government media reporting in Africa today involving the head of state and his ministers is generally of this type. Nothing ever seems to go wrong with them. Even their mistakes are blamed on someone else and not them. Reporters weave their way out of embarrassing their heroes in the news for rewards of various types which may range from promotion to in-kind rewards.

It is an interesting hobby to compare news stories about the president or government ministers covered in the leading government newspaper with the coverage of the same story in a leading outspoken independent newspaper. It is sometimes hard to believe one is reading the same story covering the same event.

While the unfairness in a negatively biased story is obvious – the person in the news is made to suffer injustice due to the journalist's reporting style – the unfairness in a positively biased news story is less obvious. Here the unfairness is not so much against the person in the news, who is usually happy that the reporter has got him off the hook, but rather against the news consumers who deserve to be told the truth but are, instead, given a false picture. It is also unfair to make a person bask in an aura of success when she does not deserve such treatment. The principle that good should be rewarded and wrong-doing punished is turned upside down.

Treating your subject fairly

Fairness in news writing also demands that people in the news not be made laughing stocks, hated or shunned because something that has happened to them for which they are not responsible. Two examples immediately come to mind: rape victims and mentally sick people.

It is unethical for a reporter to name a woman who has been raped or give any details that would make it easy for her to be identified, such as the name of her husband, residential address or work place. The trauma of being raped is bad enough for a woman without reporters making it worse by making her suffer twice by being shunned by society. In addition, the stigma of rape is greater today with the possibility of contracting HIV/Aids from the rapist.

Although the identity of a rape victim may be revealed in court, a court reporter should not include it in his news story. The same applies when police release the name of the woman: to be fair to the victim the reporter should leave it out of the story, unless the victim – or rape 'survivor', as they are often referred to in a more positive light – chooses to identify herself in an attempt to break down the stigma surrounding rape.

People living with HIV/Aids should also not be identified unless they have given their consent, and they are aware of what their consent will entail – so-called "informed consent". It is the duty of a journalist to inform news subjects fully of what the consequences will be of their agreeing to be identified.

" If your mouth turns into a knife, it will cut off your lips" – Zimbabwean proverb
(LESLAU & LESLAU 1985:48)

A similar situation arises concerning news stories about mental patients. Their identities should never be revealed, even if they are known during news gathering. Mental sickness is often a temporary state and people with mental lapses soon return to normal. It would not be fair to cause the person to be shunned by society by announcing their mental condition through the media, particularly when it is possible that they will recover.

New journalism

Fairness in news writing also means not embellishing the news story with additional, often fictitious details for the sake of making the story interesting. The art of writing a news story by using the style of fiction is known as new journalism. In some forms of new journalism, a genre that was experimented with in the sixties and seventies in the USA by figures such as Tom Wolfe and Truman Capote, dialogue may be invented, or facts postulated without being confirmed. New journalism may be all right for an audience that knows about its existence and takes it into account in the proper understanding of the story. It is, however, highly misleading to readers who may regard every word used as factually correct.

Interpretative reporting

Closely connected with new journalism as a problem in responsible news writing is interpretative reporting. In interpretative reporting the reporter goes beyond the bare facts of the story and interprets for the reader the meaning of the event or happening. Since the why and how of events are rarely addressed by news sources, the reporter hazards an explanation based on the facts available to him. This opinionated form of news writing is often condemned by critics when the opinion turns out to be wrong. Supporters of interpretative reporting, however, say it is not fair to give news consumers facts only without telling them the deeper meaning or relevance of these facts to their lives.

Critics and supporters of interpretative reporting are not agreed regarding the best type of audience for interpretative news reporting: the informed one or the less informed one. Critics say for news consumers who are barely literate, as most people are in Africa, interpretative news writing is dangerous because the people may mistake the reporter's opinions for facts. The supporters refute this position on the premise that it is precisely the barely literate people who need the meaning of news and events to be put in context and explained to them in the same news story. It is also argued that any form of reporting, also when it seems only factual, contains elements of selection, framing, and editing which comes down to intepretation on the side of the reporter.

However, both the critics and supporters of interpretative news writing agree that interpretative news writing can be dangerous when the interpretation is wrong. It is this possibility of wrong interpretation that worries media ethicists, all the more so because at the time of writing many news writers are convinced that their interpretation is correct and it is often only after the news has been published that additional facts previously unknown to the reporter emerge and put the news event in a new light.

For this reason interpretation that reflects the reporter's opinion has traditionally been kept out of news reports and reserved for the opinion columns such as news features, including editorials. However, even here unfairness can creep in when the opinion or comment is based on falsehood rather than fact and when the opinion or comment is not in the public interest.

Obscenity

Another ethical problem in news writing is the use of obscene or offensive words. Obscenity occurs in news writing when reporters use indecent or unacceptable words or expressions. What is obscene usually depends upon a particular society in a particular time and place. News should be written in a respectable manner that does not offend people's sense of good taste. (See Appendix C: Style guide, p. 390.)

Responsible photojournalism

The idea that the photographer is an objective bystander – removed from the action while recording it – is, in most cases, a myth. The choice of position from which to photograph, the choice of lens, the shutter speed, developing and printing techniques and other technical decisions will all affect the picture and, ultimately, what the photographer says to the viewer.

More importantly, the presence of the photographer on a scene will often influence what takes place there. Here's a simple test. Turn your camera on a group of people in a bar or at a football match and watch how they start playing up to (or hiding from) the camera.

There is, however, a big difference between these problems and deliberate attempts to change the action before you by setting up pictures, or manipulating them after the event.

Manipulation of photographs

Manipulation of photographs is probably the biggest ethical issue facing news photography today. Manipulation is not something new. It has existed since the earliest days of photography. However, digital technology is making it easier, quicker, more effective, and much more difficult – if not impossible – to detect.

Photographers have traditionally used darkroom techniques such as "cropping", "dodging" and "burning-in" to produce a better print of the recorded image. While this may change the technical quality and impact of the picture, it does not change the information that is recorded on the original negative.

Modern digital editing has largely replaced the darkroom, bringing an array of powerful tools to the desktop of the photographer and picture editor. It has also opened up a debate which forces us to question the whole purpose of news photographs. Some photographers and editors believe it is acceptable to manipulate an image to give it more impact, make the message clearer or make it fit a page design better. Others believe that it is acceptable to alter a photograph to recreate a scene when the photographer could not adequately capture the instant. Still others believe that any tampering with the image is unacceptable.

Some very good examples of photo manipulation have appeared as news photographs in the last few years. The following are a few of them:

- During the murder trial of former US football star OJ Simpson, *Time* magazine manipulated a picture of Simpson for use on the cover, darkening his face and altering his features slightly, producing a less sympathetic image of the man. The public became aware of the manipulation only because *Newsweek* chose to use the same photo on the cover without manipulating it.
- The British tabloid *The Sun*, seeking a sensational front page photo, removed the middle section of a photograph in order to move Prince William to a position next to a topless woman in a beach scene.
- During Nelson Mandela's first public appearance on the balcony of the Cape Town City Hall after he was elected president on May 9, 1994, he released a white dove in front of a crowd of thousands assembled on the Grand Parade. A photographer for *Die Burger*, the Cape Town daily, missed the moment, but careful picture editing brought it back down close to his hands.

The problem, as in most questions of ethics, is where to draw the line. News publications must aim at effectively informing their readers and at being as factually accurate and credible as possible. When the reader knows that some photographs may have been manipulated, *all* photographs lose credibility as recordings and hence lose their ability to inform. When the reader does not know that images have been manipulated, the publication may begin to spread lies, half-truths and factually incorrect information.

Ebbe Domisse, then editor of *Die Burger*, and the photographer Henk Blom (who says he did not know his photograph would be manipulated) both agree that the decision to lower the dove into Nelson Mandela's hands was not a good one. "I immediately put out a staff bulletin at the time, saying that we should be very cautious about this kind of thing," Domisse told a reporter (Malan, 1996:34). "I also gave instructions that whenever we change pictures, we should tell our readers that we have done it in the caption."

It may be that the only way to retain the integrity of images would be to rule that while it is acceptable to improve the technical characteristics of a photograph, it is unethical to publish as a news photograph any picture that has been altered in any way so as to convey any information different from that stored on the original negative or digital camera file. Editors should insist on this as a matter of principle.

Setting up photographs

The issue of setting up photographs is another important one. It is often difficult to detect a set-up photograph by looking at it, and many photographers have resorted to this practice as an "easy" way to get the photograph they want but cannot find naturally occurring, or to recreate a picture they have missed.

The term "set-up photographs" as used here does not include photographs that are obviously set up (the attractive woman sitting in a field of flowers, the politician grinning and shaking the hand of a sports hero, for instance). It is used to describe staged photographs that are passed off, or presented, as genuine reportage.

There are a number of cases that can be used to illustrate this. It has been the practice of some photographers to throw coins into a dustbin to encourage children to dig through the contents and then pass the photograph off as starving children looking for food. Others have encouraged children to hold automatic weapons and then used the pictures to suggest that they are combatants in a civil war situation.

There really is no valid excuse for setting up photographs. Photojournalism is about recording reality as it happens with as little intrusion by the photographer as possible. Setting up a photograph goes directly against this and can only be described as unethical. It destroys the validity of the photographer's work and the practice puts into question the credibility of other news photographers' work as well.

Privacy

The invasion of the privacy of an individual is open not only to questions of ethics, but also of law. The law tends to look at factors such as whether the picture is "in the public interest" or "shows a person in a false light". The legal establishment differentiates between private individuals and public figures when deciding on whether or not to take action and the ethical debate tends to make this separation as well.

Private individuals, with the obvious exception of those involved in criminal activities, are entitled to privacy and freedom from harassment. To give an example, the way in which the press have sometimes treated mourners at funerals, shoving them out of the way to get a better picture, or photographing them in the midst of their grief, is best described as callous and unethical. A good touchstone for how to treat private individuals is to ask how you would like to be treated in a similar situation.

From an ethical standpoint, privacy of public figures is a thorny issue. The paparazzi have made a career out of hounding public figures and this has brought the ethical debate into the public arena. Many public figures have condemned the way the press behaves, and indeed the tragic death of Princess Diana in a car accident in Paris in 1997, while being pursued at high speed by the paparazzi, has brought the debate into even sharper focus. Ironically, she was one of the most outspoken public figures with regard to the invasive and callous attitude of the press.

It would perhaps be fair to say that when such people are in a public place it is open season. But when such public figures are in a private place, they should be left alone – unless there is substantial evidence that some criminal action is taking place there.

Most public figures have used the press to build their images and careers and it is only when they are portrayed in a bad light that they suddenly cry foul. Royalty, politicians, and film and sports stars rely on a continual press to ensure that they gain and maintain a following. However, when these people have retreated into private places the ethics applied to private people should be applied.

Injury, death, and dying

Most people will not forget the photographs of Chris Hani lying in a pool of his own blood after being assassinated. Or the video footage and still photographs of Afrikaner Weerstandsbeweging (AWB) members being shot in Bophuthatswana. The shock value was enormous. However, many viewers were almost as shocked by the photographers as by the photographs themselves.

The problem in these situations is in deciding what is appropriate photographically as well as in terms of behaviour.

The Chris Hani photographs were felt by some people to be appropriate to the gravity of what had happened, while others felt the "butcher-shop" treatment of the photographs was offensive both to the viewer and Hani's many friends and family.

In the case of the AWB men, the photographs themselves were shocking, but showed a moment of human tragedy which was pivotal in

Figure 13.3 Cape Times *photographer Benny Gool captured the horrific death of gang leader Rashaad Staggie who was shot, set alight and shot again by members of People Against Gangsterism and Drugs (Pagad). Following the publication of the photographs, Gool's life was threatened and he had to go into hiding.*

changing attitudes towards the right-wing in South Africa. On the other hand, many people questioned why nobody offered assistance to the wounded men sitting next to the car. The photographers had already taken their photos, the killing of the wounded men was yet to happen, but nobody did anything.

HOT LINK

There is a time and place for gory pictures, says Anton Harber, the Caxton Professor of Journalism and Media Studies and Director of the Wits University Journalism Programme. Read his column, which first appeared in *Business Day*, at: http://www.journalism. co.za/modules.php?op=modload&name=News&file= article&sid=574.

A test for ethical photojournalism

Ethical issues touch on many aspects of the photo-journalist's or press photographer's work. A few of the more important areas have been discussed here. Debate over ethics is an important consideration for the working photographer, but the following words based on the spelling of "ethic" can assist in testing the ethics of what you are doing.

E	*Empathy*	Where appropriate, have empathy for your subject.
T	*Truth*	Are you portraying the truth?
H	*Humanity*	Does the picture de-humanise you, the viewer, or the subject?
I	*Integrity*	Will it retain your integrity and that of other photographers?
C	*Candidness*	Is it a natural, spontaneous picture?

While every situation requires careful assessment by those involved, and no value judgement is being made of the behaviour in the above incidents, it would seem that the time sometimes comes when a photographer needs to act with sensitivity to the feelings of others or must put aside her camera and offer to assist victims, however unlikeable they may or may not be.

There are obviously dilemmas involved in any such situation. Photographers are often in situations where refugees, the injured, or the victims of natural disasters are the subjects of their work. While it is obvious that photographers cannot always help, no photograph is worth a human life, neither that of the photographer nor that of her subjects. An ethical approach would probably be to render assistance where it is possible and does not endanger the life of the photographer or seriously prevent her from doing her work. A photographer is there as a photographer, not as a paramedic, but this does not excuse a brazen disregard for the wellbeing of others.

Summary

Responsible journalism and the role of the reporter

Writing for the mass media responsibly is conscientious reporting. It means putting news and information to the public and being fully prepared to take responsibility for its outcome to the media, to society, to individuals in the news and to sources who have supplied the information. It is recognising that by dealing in news and other information, journalists owe society and those they report about certain precautions, explanations and actions to undo the unjustified outcomes or possible outcomes arising from their reporting. It is the humanising of journalism, a profession whose practice is prone to being insensitive to human feelings even in cases where they should be taken into account.

If reporting is about telling people what individuals in society have done, are doing and intend to do, as well as interpreting these actions and intentions in a manner that helps society to learn from its mistakes and improve on its good deeds, then reporters should perform their chores honestly, truthfully and with integrity.

Writing for the media responsibly does not mean taking the role of politicians in preventing people from knowing the truth in order to save the necks of a few individuals in power, particularly when people need to know this truth to be liberated and empowered. Responsible journalism is not sycophantic and cowardly reportage. It is brave journalism which can and does lead reporters taking full responsibility of the consequences to themselves, to the media house and to society for what they report. A common misconception is that media ethics is about things reporters should *avoid* doing. This then results in hesitance or reluctance to report on stories that have a high impact on society or might bring about some positive changes. Media ethics is also about what journalists *should* do and not avoid. Politicians in Africa have often connected responsible journalism with reporting that promotes national unity and patriotism. What they mean is this: journalists should not report news and information that tends to create divisions in a nation, but should be partners with politicians in keeping the nation state together.

Reporting that tells people that all is well in a nation, when even the people can see that all is not well, is not responsible. Such reporting creates false security and unity in a country, which often results in greater suffering for the people. It is not the role of journalists but of politicians to worry about national unity, particularly when that unity is being built around falsity. The duty and responsibility of journalists is to build society and the nation by making people aware of what is going on around them.

This chapter has discussed responsible reporting as seen from the professional journalistic viewpoint and not as often seen by Africa's politicians, who often want reporters to report what they (politicians) want the people to know. Responsible journalism is not reporting for political expediency. It is reporting that puts the needs of society first and everything else, including the need for the media to make a profit, last. When reporters exaggerate the news by sensationalising it in order to sell their newspaper, they are being irresponsible journalists. Responsible reporting is reporting that reflects reality as it is and not as journalists and those propping them up would like it to be.

██HOT TIP

The ten "commandments"
In *Media Ethics*, Johan Retief (2002:44-45) suggests the following brief code of ethics:
Preamble: The media shall be free because the public has a right to be informed. You shall therefore:
- Be accurate both in text and context and correct mistakes promptly.
- Be truthful, only using deceptive methods in matters of public importance if there is no other way of uncovering the facts.
- Be fair, presenting all relevant facts in a balanced way.
- Be duly impartial in reporting the news and when commenting on it.
- Protect confidential sources, unless it is of overriding public interest to do otherwise.
- Be free from obligation to any interest group.
- Respect the privacy of individuals, unless it is overridden by a legitimate public interest.
- Not intrude into private grief and distress, unless such intrusion is overridden by a legitimate public interest.
- Refrain from any kind of stereotyping.
- Be socially responsible in referring to matters of indecency, obscenity, violence, brutality, blasphemy and sex.

Putting your learning to work

ACTIVITY 1 Getting to grips with classical ethical thinking

Explain, by giving examples, why responsible news gathering and news writing should be a mixture of teleological and deontological ethical approaches.

ACTIVITY 2 Afri-ethics

What can responsible journalism in Africa today learn from the foundations of African ethics?

ACTIVITY 3 Freedom of expression

When the controversial religious film by Martin Scorcese, *The Last Temptation of Christ*, was censored an hour before it was to be screened at a Johannesburg film festival, the script writer surprised many by telling the crowd: "I am not anti-censorship." Paul Schrader explained further: "I think a society at some point has a collective need and a right to say this is good or not good for society." The starting point in America, for example, is a ruling by Oliver Wendell Holmes, a chief justice of the Supreme Court, where he says you cannot yell "Fire!" in a crowded room. That is an abridgement of speech which, everyone agrees, is improper because it creates danger. "The moment you accept the Holmesian dictate, you accept that censorship has a role. The question is where culture stands and how that line is drawn and how it moves."

- Compare Schrader's statement with Section 16 of the Bill of Rights (quoted in Chapter 1, p.10) as well as Schedule 10 of the Film and Publications Act (Act 65 of 1996):

Promotion of religious hatred

1) A publication or a film which, judged within context, advocates hatred that is based on religion, and that constitutes incitement to cause harm, shall be classified as XX.
2) Clause (1) shall not apply to
   a) a bona fide scientific, documentary, dramatic, artistic, literary or religious publication or film, or any part thereof which, judged within context, is of such nature;
   b) a publication or film, which amounts to a bona fide discussion, argument or opinion on a matter pertaining to religion, belief or conscience; or
   c) a publication or film, which amounts to a bona fide discussion, argument or opinion on a matter of public interest.

▟▛▙▜ LINK

Want more background information? You will find detailed information about *The Last Temptation of Christ* in the IMDB film database at: http://www.imdb.com/title/tt0095497/. The South African Film and Publications Board's website includes an interesting section entitled *From censorship to classification: the legal history*, which is available at http://www.fpb.gov.za/documents/history.htm.

Discuss your observations with your peers and formulate a 10-point guideline for the Film and Publications Board, which is charged with observing standards in the industry.

ACTIVITY 4 How the professionals act

A World Economic Forum major global public opinion survey suggests that trust in many key institutions – including the media – has fallen to critical proportions. The 2002 Voice of the People survey of **36 000 people** in 46 countries, conducted by Gallup International and Environics International showed that in Africa 40 per cent of us have little or no trust that the media are acting in our best interest. For more details World Economic Forum survey and discussions, see: http://www.weforum.org/site/homepublic.nsf/Content/Annual+Meeting+2003%5CAnnual+Meeting+Theme%3A+Trust+and+Values.

Interview a practising journalist or public relations practitioner about the ethical performance of professionals. Ascertain the following during the interview:

- What are the major ethical problems in the field today?
- How are professionals responding?
- What major ethical challenges has your interviewee faced?
- How did the person resolve them?

Franz Krüger on making ethical decisions

Krüger has worked in print and broadcasting in South Africa, Namibia and the UK, at media groups ranging from the BBC and the London Guardian to East London's Daily Dispatch and the Windhoek Advertiser. Since 2000, he has been an independent journalist and trainer. He teaches journalism at postgraduate level at Wits University, specialising in radio, ethics and sub-editing. He edits the website www.journalism.co.za, and still serves as correspondent for Canadian, Dutch, US and British radio. He has recently completed a book on ethics entitled Black, white and grey. Krüger has a BA from UCT and an MA in journalism from City University, London.

1 The mass media, it is often said, constitute the backbone of democracy. If that's true, some critics say, the backbone isn't holding up very well. Why do you think that is?

I don't know, ask the critics. I think it's dubious to try to pass judgment on the media as a whole in this way, particularly on the basis of a metaphor that is more catchy than substantive.

But journalism clearly faces a problem of public trust. There have been too many lapses, involving everything from plagiarism – even outright fabrication – to reporters making no effort to hide the axes they grind. Unethical journalism harms both the profession and democracy itself.

2 What are the major ethical challenges journalists in our region face?

Without a doubt, journalists in Southern Africa have no greater challenge than to defend – in some cases create – a truly independent role in their various societies. In some countries, the major challenge is political, with governments and parties leaning very heavily on working journalists to tell it as they'd like it to be. Where conflict runs deep, journalists find it very hard not to choose sides.

Elsewhere, commercial pressures threaten independence. Marketers have become adept at hijacking journalism to peddle their influence. Sponsorships, free gifts and travel, threats to withhold advertising – these are just some of the many ways in which advertisers try to undermine journalistic independence. Often, media companies themselves collude in order to boost their bottom line.

Whether the pressures are political or commercial, it is critically important to recognise that they threaten journalism's credibility. Journalists answer to their audiences before anyone else. It's the only way to keep the trust of the public.

3 Describe an ethical dilemma you have confronted in your career in journalism.

As a young reporter working in Windhoek in the early 1980s, my paper sent me on a junket to the remote Kaokoveld, in the far north of Namibia. I was to accompany the Red Cross as they took food aid there for distribution to hungry people. This was the local branch of the organisation, which worked very closely with the occupying South African forces.

We flew up in an army helicopter, and landed in a dry riverbed where we were given tea and snacks as hungry people watched. Then the food was distributed by SA soldiers. Only there was nowhere near enough, and the exercise was poorly organised. As supplies dwindled, desperation grew among the hungry. There was nearly a riot.

Back in Windhoek, I needed to write up the story. But how? Some people did get food, and I had travelled as a guest of the Red Cross which made me feel a sense of obligation not to be too harsh.

In the end, I described it as I'd seen it: as a propaganda exercise, and a badly organised one at that. To its credit, the paper ran the story in full, even though it was small and quite conservative by inclination. The Red Cross was furious, and I didn't get invited on trips of this kind again.

4 Would you do the same again?

That's hard to say. I would try to avoid going on junkets of this kind now. But if I ended up with a similar conflict, I would absolutely tell the truth as I saw it.

5 Please complete the following sentence: The key to ethical decision-making is …

Thoughtful and deliberate consideration that takes into account different alternatives, interests and perspectives.

Bibliography

Black, J., Steele, B. and Barney, R. 1995. *Doing ethics in journalism*, 2nd edition. Greencastle, Indiana: Allyn & Bacon.

Black, J. and Bryant, J. 1992. *Introduction to mass communication*, 3rd edition. Dubuque, Iowa: Brown & Benchmark.

Bloom, K. 2004. Worst of times. *The Media* online, 11 January 2004. [Online] Available at http://www.themedia.co.za/article.aspx?articleid=42342&area=/media_insightco. [Accessed: 16 September 2004]

Duras, M. 1997. *Outside: selected writings*. Translated by Arthur Goldhammer. Belbrook Park, East Sussex, UK: Beacon Press.

Greenslade, R. 2003. Their master's voice. *The Guardian*. 17 February 2003 [Online] Available at: www.guardianonline.co.uk (access is free, but registration is required). [Accessed: 4 September 2004]

Kasoma, F.P. (ed). 1994. *Journalism ethics in Africa*. Nairobi, African Council for Communication Education.

Kasoma, F.P. 1994. Ethical issues in reporting politics. In Okigbo, Charles (ed), *Reporting politics and public affairs*. Nairobi. The African Council for Communication Education.

Kasoma, F.P. 1992. Media ethics or media law: the enforcement of responsible journalism in Africa. In De Beer, A.S., Steyn, E., Claassen, G.N. and Lambeth, Edmund B. 1992. *Committed journalism: an ethic for the profession*, 2nd edition. Bloomington and Indianapolis: Indiana University Press.

Leslau, C. and Leslau, W. 1985. *African proverbs*. White Plain, NJ: Peter Pauper Press.

Malan, P. 1996. The lowering of the dove. *Rhodes Journalism Review*, October 1996.

McQuail, D. 2002. *McQuail's reader in mass communication*. London: Sage.

Oosthuizen, L.M. 2002. *Media ethics in the South African context*. Lansdowne: Juta.

Retief, J. 2002. *Media Ethics*. Cape Town: Oxford University Press.

Steele, B. and Cochran, W. 1995. Computer-assisted reporting challenges traditional news-gathering safeguard. *ASNE Bulletin*, January 1995.

Veilletet, P. 2004. Annual Report 2004. [Online] Reporters without borders. Available at: http://www.rsf.org/rubrique.php3?id_rubrique=416 [Accessed: 11 July 2004]

Webster, D. Building free and independent media. San Francisco Institute for Contemporary Studies. This pamphlet is available from: ICS, 243 Kearney St, San Francisco, California 94108, USA.

▓ HOT LINK

Read an excerpt from Marguerite Duras' collected essays on journalism at: http://www.dailytimes.com.pk/default.asp?page=story_27-10-2003_pg3_8 [Accessed: 6 September 2004].

APPENDIX A

The Press Ombudsman of South Africa

To understand the ethical code of the Press Ombudsman, some background information is required. The South African Media council was established in 1983 after the media came under political pressure from the government "to get its house in order". The council had its own ethical code, but was dissolved in 1992, mainly because of its political baggage.

The South African Press Council replaced the Media Council in 1992, and also formulated its own ethical code. However, the political baggage of this new council also proved to be too heavy, and the Press Council was dissolved in 1997.

The Press Ombudsman of South Africa then replaced the South African Press Council. The first Ombudsman is Ed Linington, an ex-editor of the South African Press Association (SAPA). His office is in Johannesburg.

The establishment of the Press Ombudsman came about because the founding bodies – the South African National Editors' Forum (SANEF), the Forum of Editors of Community Newspapers (FECN), the South African Union of Journalists (SAUJ), the Media Workers Association of South Africa (MWASA), the Newspaper Association of South Africa (NASA) and Magazine Publishers Association of South Africa (MPA) – were of the conviction that the public could best be served by providing for a readily accessible, impartial, and independent complaints mechanism. They decided to set up such a mechanism in the form of a Press Ombudsman and an Appeal Panel, which would mediate, settle, and, if necessary, adjudicate complaints in accordance with a code and procedure accepted by the founding bodies.

Press Code of Professional Practice

According to the Press Ombudsman's code, the basic principle to be upheld is that the freedom of the press is indivisible from, and subject to the same rights and duties as, those of the individual, and rests on the public's fundamental right to be informed and freely to receive and to disseminate opinions. The primary purpose of gathering and distributing news and opinion is to serve society by informing citizens and enabling them to make informed judgments on the issues of the time. The freedom of the press to bring an independent scrutiny to bear on the forces that shape society is a freedom exercised on behalf of the public. The public interest is the only test that justifies departure from the highest standards of journalism and includes:

- detecting or exposing crime or serious misdemeanour;
- detecting or exposing serious antisocial conduct;
- protecting public health and safety;

- preventing the public from being misled by some statement or action of an individual or organization;
- detecting or exposing hypocrisy, falsehoods, or double standards of behaviour on the part of public figures or institutions and in public institutions.

The code is not intended to be comprehensive or all-embracing. No code can cover every contingency. The press will be judged by the code's spirit – accuracy, balance, fairness, and decency – rather than its narrow letter, in the belief that vigilant self-regulation is the hallmark of a free and independent press.

In considering complaints, the Press Ombudsman and the Appeal Panel will be guided by the following provisions, which are divided into eight main areas:

1. **Reporting of news**
   1.1 The press shall be obliged to report news truthfully, accurately, and fairly.
   1.2 News shall be presented in context and in a balanced manner, without an intentional or negligent departure from the facts, whether by:
      1.2.1 distortion, exaggeration, or misrepresentation;
      1.2.2 material omissions; or
      1.2.3 summarisation.
   1.3 Only what may be reasonably true, having regard to the sources of the news, may be presented as facts, and such facts shall be published fairly with due regard to context and importance. Where a report is not based on facts or is founded on opinions, allegation, rumour, or supposition, it shall be presented in such manner as to indicate this clearly.
   1.4 Where there is reason to doubt the accuracy of a report and it is practicable to verify the accuracy thereof, it shall be verified. Where it has not been practicable to verify the accuracy of a report, this shall be mentioned in such a report.
   1.5 A newspaper should usually seek the views of the subject of serious critical reportage in advance of publication; provided that this need not be done where the newspaper has reasonable grounds for believing that by doing so it will be prevented from publishing the report or where evidence might be destroyed or witnesses intimidated.
   1.6 A publication should make amends for publishing information or comment that is found to be harmfully inaccurate by printing, promptly and with appropriate prominence, a retraction, correction, or explanation.

1.7 Reports, photographs, or sketches relative to matters involving indecency or obscenity shall be presented with due sensitivity towards the prevailing moral climate.

1.8. The identity of rape victims and other victims of sexual violence shall not be published without the consent of the victim.

1.9 News obtained by dishonest or unfair means, or the publication of which betrays a breach of confidence, should not be published unless publication is in the public interest.

1.10 In both news and comment, the press shall exercise exceptional care and consideration in matters involving the private lives and concerns of individuals, bearing in mind that any right to privacy may be overridden by a legitimate public interest.

1.11 A newspaper has wide discretion in matters of taste but this does not justify lapses of taste so repugnant as to bring the freedom of the press into disrepute or be extremely offensive to the public.

2. **Discrimination**

2.1 The press should avoid discriminatory or denigratory references to people's race, colour, religion, religion, sexual orientation or preference, physical or mental disability or illness, or age.

2.2 The press should not refer to a person's race, colour, religion, sexual orientation, or physical or mental illness in a prejudicial or pejorative context except where it is strictly relevant to the matter reported or adds significantly to readers' understanding of that matter.

2.3 The press has the right, and indeed the duty, to report and comment on all matters of public interest. This right and duty must, however, be balanced against the obligation not to promote racial hatred or discord in such way as to create the likelihood of imminent violence.

3. **Advocacy**

A newspaper is justified in strongly advocating its own views on controversial topics provided that it treats its readers fairly by:

3.1 making fact and opinion clearly distinguishable;

3.2 not misrepresenting or suppressing relevant facts;

3.3 not distorting the facts in text or headlines.

4. **Comment**

4.1 The press shall be entitled to comment upon or criticize any actions or events of public importance provided such comments or criticisms are fairly and honestly made.

4.2 Comment by the press shall be presented in such manner that it appears clearly that it is comment, and shall be made on facts truly stated or fairly indicated or referred to.

4.3 Comment by the press shall be an honest expression of opinion, without malice or dishonest motives, and shall take account of all available facts which are material to the matter commented upon.

5. **Headlines, posters, pictures, and captions**

5.1 Headlines and captions to pictures shall give a reasonable reflection of the contents of the report or picture in question.

5.2 Posters shall not mislead the public and shall give reasonable reflection of the contents of the reports in question.

5.3 Pictures shall not misrepresent nor be manipulated to do so.

6. **Confidential sources**

A newspaper has an obligation to protect confidential sources of information.

7. **Payment for articles**

No payment shall be made for feature articles to persons engaged in crime or other notorious misbehaviour, or to convicted persons or their associates, including family, friends, neighbours, and colleagues, except where the material concerned ought to be published in the public interest and the payment is necessary for this to be done.

8. **Violence**

Due care and responsibility shall be exercised by the press with regard to the presentation of brutality, violence, and atrocities.

APPENDIX B

The Broadcasting Complaints Commission of South Africa (BCCSA)

1. **Preamble**

   The fundamental principle to uphold is that the freedom of the electronic media is indivisible from, and subject to, the same constraints as those of the individual, and rests on the individual's fundamental right to be informed and freely to receive and to disseminate opinions.

2. **Reporting of news**

   2.1 The electronic media shall be obliged to report news truthfully, accurately, and with due impartiality.

   2.2 News shall be presented in the correct context and in a balanced manner, without any intentional or negligent departure from the facts, whether by:

       2.2.1 distortion, exaggeration, or misrepresentation;

       2.2.2 material omission; or

       2.2.3 summarization.

   2.3 Only what may reasonably be true which has regard to the source of the news, may be presented as facts, and such facts shall be broadcast fairly with due regard to context and importance. Where a report is not based on facts or is founded on opinion, allegation, rumour, or supposition, it shall be presented in such manner as to indicate this clearly.

   2.4 Where there is reason to doubt the correctness of a report, and it is practicable to verify the correctness thereof, it shall be verified. Where it has not been practicable to verify the correctness of a report, this shall be mentioned in such report.

   2.5 Where it subsequently appears that a broadcast was incorrect in a material aspect, it shall be verified spontaneously and without reservation or delay. The correction shall be presented with a degree of prominence which is adequate and fair so as to attract attention readily.

   2.6 Reports, photographs, or video material relating to matters involving indecency or obscenity shall be presented with due sensitivity towards the prevailing moral climate. In particular, the electronic media shall avoid the broadcast of indecent or obscene matter.

   2.7 The identity of rape victims or other victims of sexual violence shall not be broadcast without the consent of the victim.

3. **Comment**

   3.1 The electronic media shall be entitled to comment upon or criticize any actions or events of public importance, provided such comments or criticisms are fairly and honestly made.

3.2　Comment shall be presented in such a manner that it appears clearly that it is a comment, and shall be made on fact truly stated or fairly indicated and referred to.

3.3　Comment shall be an honest expression of opinion, without malice or motives, and shall take fair and balanced account of all available facts which are material to the matter commented upon.

4.　**Elections and referenda**

4.1.　Where during an election period or referendum period a signatory grants access to its services to a political party, organization, or movement, or a candidate taking part in a national, regional, or by-election, or referendum, or has itself during an election period or referendum period criticized a political party, organization, or movement, or a candidate taking part in such an election or referendum, the signatory is under a duty to grant an opposing or criticized (as the case may be) political party, organization, or movement, or a candidate, an equal opportunity to its services to state its policy or respond to the criticism of the signatory or the political party, organization, or movement, or candidate, to whom the signatory has granted access – provided that this clause does not in any way detract from the duties which a signatory has in accordance with the other clauses of this code.

4.2　For purposes of this clause, "election period" and "referendum period" mean a period which commences when the President promulgates an election or by-election for Parliament or referendum in the Government Gazette and lapses when polling closes on the (last) election day, or referendum day, as the case may be.

5.　**Privacy**

The electronic media shall exercise exceptional care and consideration in matters involving the private lives and dignity of individuals, bearing in mind that the right to privacy and dignity may be overridden by a legitimate public interest.

6.　**Payment for information from a criminal.** No payment shall be made to persons engaged in crime or other notorious misbehaviour, or to persons who have been engaged in crime or other notorious behaviour, unless compelling societal interests indicate the contrary.

7.　**General**

7.1　The electronic media shall:

7.1.1　not present material which is indecent or obscene or

harmful or offensive to public morals, which is offensive to religious convictions or feelings of a section of the population, which is likely to harm relations between sections of the population, or is likely to prejudice the safety of the state or the public order;

7.1.2 not, without due care and sensitivity, present material which contains brutality, violence, or atrocities;

7.1.3 exercise due care and responsibility in the presentation of programmes where a large number of children are likely to be part of the audience.

7.2. **Controversial issues of public importance:**

7.2.1 In presenting a programme in which controversial issues of public importance are discussed, a broadcasting licensee shall make reasonable efforts to present fairly significant points of view either in the same programme or in a subsequent programme forming part of the same series within a reasonable period of time and in substantially the same time slot.

7.2.2 A person whose views have been criticized in a broadcasting programme on a controversial issue of public importance shall be given reasonable opportunity by the broadcasting licensee to reply to such criticism, should that person so request.

HOT LINK

The Institute for Public Relations and Communication Management Southern Africa (Prisa) says it is committed to promoting – and enforcing – ethical practices amongst its members. "The level of public support our members seek, as we serve the public good, means we have taken on a special obligation to operate ethically," says the organisation in the introduction to their declaration of professional standards. The full document is at: http://www.prisa. co.za/index.php?page–id=421&id=67.

APPENDIX C
Style guide

Why do journalists need a style guide?

The mark of successful writing isn't that it is published. It isn't even that it is read or remembered. It is that the truth that it aims to convey is understood. And when it comes to how best to tell the truth, I'm a bit old-fashioned. That is, I agree with the 19th century German philosopher Arthur Schopenhauer who said:

> Truth that is naked is the most beautiful, and the simpler its expression the deeper is the impression it makes; this is partly because it gets unobstructed hold of the hearer's mind without his being distracted by secondary thoughts, and partly because he feels that here he is not being corrupted or deceived by the arts of rhetoric, but that the whole effect is got from the thing itself (2004:1).

How do we get to tell the plain, unobstructed truth? According to George Orwell, "A scrupulous writer in every sentence that he writes, will ask himself at least four questions, thus: What am I trying to say? What word will express it? What image or idiom will make it clearer? Is this image fresh enough to have an effect? And he will probably ask himself two more: Could I put it more shortly? Have I said anything that is avoidably ugly?" (Orwell and Angus, 1968).

This style guide, then, is inspired by Schopenhauer's sentiments and informed by Orwell's observations (as well as a belief that his six elementary rules are still relevant; see Chapter 10, p. 234). The intention is not to lay down stylistic standards with moral earnestness. Instead, these guidelines should assist those who believe good writing is not merely a luxury, but an obligation. The guide is divided into two sections: in the first section clarity is given on selected points of grammar, in the second some basic guidelines for communicating in journalism are reviewed.

"One should not aim to be possible to understand, but impossible not to understand."
Marcus Fabius Quintilian, 35–95AD

"People think I can teach them style. What stuff it is. Have something to say and say it as clearly as you can. That is the only style there is."
Matthew Arnold, 1822–88

Grammar points

Abbreviations and Acronyms Abbreviations and acronyms save space in publications, but should only be used when it is certain that readers will recognise them instantly. Saving space at the expense of understanding is an intolerable offence. Remember the journalistic adage "Write for those who did not read yesterday's paper", and include full references so that new readers (such as students, the newly literate, visitors and travellers) can understand the content. Refer to individual entries for guidance on how a particular abbreviation or acronym is used. Some general guidelines are:

ADDRESSES The words *street*, *avenue* and *boulevard* can be abbreviated, but only when preceded by a street name and number: *She lives at 18 Queen St* but *she lives in Queen Street*. Spell out and capitalise *First* up till *Ninth*, but use figures together with the correct two-letter abbreviation for *10th* and above: *7 12th St, 77 51st Ave.*

CASE An acronym is an abbreviation of more than three letters that is pronounced as a word. Acronyms are written in sentence case: *University of South Africa (Unisa)*; *Opec (Organisation of Petroleum Exporting Countries)*. Abbreviations that are not pronounced as words are written in upper case (capital letters): *Young Men's Christian Association (YMCA)*.

DATES, TIMES AND NUMBERS Use the abbreviations AD, BC, am, pm, no., and abbreviate certain months (*Jan, Feb, Mar, Aug, Sept, Oct, Nov* and *Dec*) when used with the day of the month, but only if space is at a premium (in correspondence, write out months in full). These abbreviations are correct only when used with figures. Correct: *In 30 BC*; *at 10 am*; *Contestant no. 7*; *on Jan 21*. Incorrect: *Late in the pm she asked for the company's telephone no.* Correct: *Late in the afternoon she asked for the company's telephone number.*

POSITION IN A SENTENCE While the *Associated Press Stylebook and Libel Manual* recommends against placing an abbreviation or acronym in parenthesis following a full name, South African editors prefer the following style, which has the advantage of clarity: *He is a member of the South African National Defence Force (SANDF).*

PUNCTUATION Traditionally, abbreviations and acronyms were punctuated with full stops (*N.P., Prof.*). However, this has fallen away in contemporary media writing, so avoid excessive use of full stops. It is now acceptable to write *ANC, Mr, eg,* and so on. Follow this book for guidelines on when to use capital letters and full stops. For abbreviations not listed here, consult the *Oxford Advanced Learner's Dictionary* or the *South African Pocket Oxford Dictionary*.

TITLES Abbreviate the following titles when used before a full name outside of a direct quotation: *Dr, Rev, Mr, Mrs, Ms* and certain other military titles. Spell out all titles except for *Dr, Mr, Mrs* and *Ms* when used before a name in direct quotations. After a name abbreviate *junior* (jnr) or *senior* (snr) after an individual's name. Abbreviate company (Co), *corporation* (Corp), *incorporated* (Inc) and *limited* (Ltd) when used after the name of a business. See entry under "company names". When applicable, an academic degree may be abbreviated after an individual's name.

WHEN TO USE ACRONYMS Certain abbreviations and acronyms, including those of some organisations and government agencies, are widely recognised, such as *ANC, SARS, SANDF,* and so on. If the entry for such an organisation notes that an abbreviation is acceptable, it does not mean that its use should be automatic. The context should determine, for example, whether *South African Revenue Service* or *SARS* should be used.

WHEN TO USE *THE* There are no hard and fast rules about when to use the definite article before an abbreviation. This is sometimes determined by whether the abbreviation or acronym is used as an adjective or noun: *ANC members voted today*, but *the ANC won the election*. A good rule of thumb is to follow spoken usage.

Capital letters While various style guides (including this one) may provide rules explaining when to use initial capitals, these guidelines are all based on one main principle: the name of something unique always takes a capital. Here are a few general rules.

DISTINCTIONS Capitals can be useful for making distinctions: *There were no No votes in the district.*

PLACES Use initial capitals for specific geographical places, areas and countries (*Japan, Bloemfontein, Vancouver, the Grand Canyon*), as well as for broader but demarcated political or geographic areas (*Southeast Asia, the Midlands*).

However, use lower case for *east, west, north, south* except when part of an official name (*South Africa*). Use lower case if, for example, you are comparing regions within a country rather than officially recognised territories: *House prices in the northeast are rising; guerrilla activity is intensifying in the south.* Use lower case for the words *province, county, state, city,* but only when these words are not part of the formal name: *the state of Alaska, the city of Seoul, the province of Mpumalanga,* but *New York City, Northern Province.*

For street names, when referring to the plural, use lower case: *He is waiting on the corner of Longmarket and Adderley streets.*

PROPER NOUNS Words that give a name that is unique to a person or thing take initial capitals: *Port Elizabeth, Workers' Day, Nelson Mandela, Diagonal Street, Duzi*

River, Western Cape. In addition, titles that are used in place of names are capitalised: *Dear Mother, I'm writing to tell you that I'm fine*. However, one would write *Nombeko's mother*, not *Nombeko's Mother*. In this case, the writer is not using a title to replace a name, but is using *mother* to describe or identify the person.

TIMES Months and days of the week are capitalised (*January, February, Monday*, etc.) and so are special annual holidays or festivals (*Easter, Yom Kippur, Ramadan, Thanksgiving, Women's Day*, etc.). Seasons, however, do not take initial capitals: *Next summer, we are going somewhere cool*. Also use lower case for centuries: *the eighth century BC*.

TITLES Styles vary. In the bibliography sections of this book, for book titles, an initial capital has been used for the first word only. Alternatively, and in the case of films and songs titles: each word takes an initial capital, except for articles (*a, an, the*), conjunctions or prepositions of fewer than four letters, unless they are the first words: *The Man Who Fell in Love With the Moon*.

Datelines (journ.) Datelines on stories indicate the place from which a story originated, and should include a city name entirely in capitals, followed in most cases by the name of the country or region where that city is located: *DURBAN, KwaZulu-Natal*. Use the city name alone only in local press reports.

Foreign phrases While some foreign words and phrases have become part of common usage, some are used to make everyday occurrences seem less common. The advice of George Orwell is particularly relevant here: Never use a foreign phrase, a scientific word, or jargon if you can think of an everyday English equivalent.

The following is a list of some common Latin words and phrases (their exact English translations are in parentheses).

ad hoc (to this); spontaneous, without a system

ad hominem (the person); used of an argument that takes advantage of the character of the person on the other side

ad infinitum (to infinity); endlessly

ad lib. ad libitum (at pleasure); used adverbially to mean invent or extemporise

ad nauseam (to sickness); to an excessive or disgusting degree

annus mirabilis (wonderful year); used to describe a special year in which several memorable events have occurred

a priori (from what is before); deductively or from prior principle

bona fide (good faith); real and genuine

caveat emptor (let the buyer beware)

cf., confer (compare)

de facto (in point of fact)

de jure (from the law); by right, rightfully

deus ex machina (god from a machine); first used to describe a Greek theatrical convention, where a god would swing down onto the stage from a machine, solving humanly insoluble problems and resolving the action of a play. Now used to describe someone from outside a situation who comes to the rescue or puts matters right.

e.g., exempli gratia (for example)

et al., et alii (and others); used in bibliographies when citing multiple authorship to save the writer the trouble of mentioning all the names: *C.L.R. James et al.*

ex cathedra (from the chair of office); authoritatively

ex officio (by virtue of one's office); this does not mean unofficially

ex parte (from or for one side only)

habeas corpus (you must have the body); a document ordering someone held in custody to appear before a court. It places the burden of proof on those detaining the person to justify the detention and to lay a charge.

ibid., ibidem (in the same place); used in footnotes in academic works to indicate that a quotation comes from the same source previously cited.

in absentia (in the absence of)

in camera (in a room); that is, in private, not in public

in situ (in [its] original place)

inter alia/inter alios (among other things or people)

ipso facto (by that very fact); thereby

mea culpa (by my fault)

modus operandi (way of operating); usually used in military contexts

modus vivendi (way of living); a practical arrangement between those who otherwise differ

non compos mentis (not having control of the mind)

non sequitur (it does not follow); lacks logic

op. cit., opere citato (in the work cited)

passim (scattered); adverb used in indexes to indicate that an item is scattered throughout the work and there are too many instances to list them all

persona non grata (person not in favour)

post mortem (after death); used as an adjective and a noun to describe a medical examination of a dead body

prima facie (at first sight); apparent, as things seem

pro tem., pro tempore (for the moment)

P.S., post scriptum (written afterwards)

quid pro quo (something for something, or one thing for another); something in return, an equivalent

q.v., quod vide (which see); means that the reader should refer to or look up the word just mentioned

re (of thing); with regard to, in the matter of

sic (thus); used in brackets within quotations to show that the writer or speaker has either made a mistake, or is using a phrase now fallen into disuse or out of favour: *"Mrs Mundela [sic] has a house in Mozambique"* or *"The fate of the Bantu native [sic] is of relevance to all mankind [sic]."*

status quo ante (the same as before); shortened to status quo.

stet (let it stand); cancels an alteration made to a text during proofreading; dots are placed under what must remain unaltered, and stet is written in the margin.

spes bona (good hope)

sub judice (under judgement); not yet decided. In media terms, this sometimes means that a matter may not be discussed with or in the press.

versus, shortened to *v* (against); used in legal cases and sports matches.

Measurement Do not abbreviate measurements unless used with figures: *One more kilometre and you will have walked 10km.* Do not use the plural form: *kgs, kms.* Use *kg* and *km.* Whether or not there is a space between the figure and the letters: 45km, 5mm, etc. depends on house style. Note that certain measurements are not abbreviated. Below are some of the most common approximate equivalents between metric and British and American measurements.

AREA

square millimetre	sq. mm
square centimetre	sq. cm
square metre	sq. m
hectare	ha
square kilometre	sq. km

Conversions

1 square inch	= $6\frac{1}{2}$ square centimetres
$10\frac{3}{4}$ square feet	= 1 square metre
6 square yards	= 5 square metres
$2\frac{1}{2}$ acres	= 1 hectare
250 acres	= 1 square kilometre

DISTANCE

millimetre	mm
centimetre	cm
metre	m
kilometre	km

Conversions

1 inch	= 2,5 centimetres
1 foot	= 30 centimetres
	= 0,3 metres
$3\frac{1}{4}$ feet	= 1 metre
39 inches	= 1 metre
11 yards	= 10 metres
5/8 mile	= 1 kilometre

5 miles	= 8 kilometres
8 miles	= 7 nautical miles

MASS

milligram	mg
gram	g
kilogram	kg
ton	ton

Conversions

1 grain	= 65 milligrams
$15\frac{1}{2}$ grains	= 1 gram
1 ounce	= 28 grams
1 ounce troy	= 31 grams
1 pound	= 454 grams
$2\frac{1}{4}$ pounds	= 1 kilogram
2,205 pounds	= 1 ton
11 US tons	= 10 tons

POWER

Conversions

4 UK horsepower	= 3 kilowatts

SPEED

kilometre per hour	km/h
knots	write out: 30 knots

Conversions

30 miles per hour	= 48 kilometres per hour
50 miles per hour	= 80 kilometres per hour

TEMPERATURE

degrees Celsius	°C

VOLUME

Write out on first mention

litre	litre (never abbreviate)
centilitre	cl
kilolitre	kl
millilitre	ml
cubic centimetre	cc
cubic metre	cu m

Conversions

1 teaspoonful	= 5 millilitres
1 UK fluid ounce	= 28 millilitres
$1\frac{3}{4}$ UK pints	= 1 litre
5 UK pints	= 6 US liquid pints
1 UK gallon	= 4,5 litres
1 US gallon	= 3,75 litres
1 barrel (petroleum)	= 42 US gallons or = 35 UK gallons

YIELD

Conversions

1 UK ton	= 2, 5 tons per hectare
19 pounds per acre	= 10 kilograms per hectare

Names People are entitled to be known by whatever name they choose, as long as their identities are clear. When people elect to change a name by which they are known, such as Benny Alexander's transition to Khoisan X, provide both names until the new name is well-known.

Use capitals for nicknames when they refer to a specific person or thing: *the Groot Krokodil, Bugsy Malone, the Springboks, the Bermuda Triangle*.

Use quotation marks when a nickname is inserted into the identification of an individual: *Peter "Snake" Mansfield*. Always check the preference of the source.

COMPANY NAMES Include the full legal name of the company early on in the story, preferably on first reference. Consult the company itself if in doubt about a formal name. Abbreviate *Co, Cos, Ltd, Pty*, etc. if they appear at the end of the company name, but do not use a comma before the abbreviation. Write out *company, corporation*, etc. in full or abbreviate, depending on whether the word appears again in the sentence: *Megabucks Co is a large company*, but *the Lingo Company of Zimbabwe ...*

NOM DE PLUME (PL. NOMS DE PLUME) Rather use an English term: assumed name, pen name, pseudonym.

TITLES in general, use initial capitals only with formal titles used directly before an individual's name. Use lower case for titles that are not used with a person's name: *the president issued a statement, the pope visits regularly*. Use lower case for titles that are set off with commas: *the current pope, John Paul IV, does not plan to retire*. Past and acting titles: Capitalise the title before the name of person who held the position, but do not capitalise the qualifying word: *former President Nelson Mandela, acting Mayor Theresa Solomon*. Long titles: Use commas to break up long titles: *Marthinus van Schalkwyk, minister of environmental affairs and tourism.*

Nobility the following are general guidelines for referring to nobility.

BARONET, KNIGHT, DAME A *baronet* (whose title is hereditary) or *knight* (whose title dies with him) is known as *Sir*. His wife is known as *Lady*. Drop the title on second reference or, if courtesy titles are the house style, use the first name, not the last name: *Sir Winston Churchill*, then *Sir Winston* instead of *Sir Churchill*. A *dame*, equivalent to a knight, is a woman honoured in her own right. At first reference, *Dame Margaret Thatcher*, then *Thatcher* or *Dame Margaret*, not *Dame Thatcher*.

DUKE Dukes are given their full titles on first reference: *the Duke of Norfolk*. On second reference, use *Norfolk* or *the duke*. Never use *Lord Norfolk*. His wife is the *Duchess of Norfolk* or *the duchess*, never *Lady Norfolk*.

MARQUESS, MARQUIS, EARL, VISCOUNT, COUNT, BARON

Any of the holders of these titles may be referred to as *Lord* — or *Lady*—. If the formal title is used, such as *Viscount Hooray-Henry*, simply drop the title on second reference and refer to *Lord Hooray-Henry*. A baron, whether a hereditary or life peer, is always *Lord* and his wife *Lady*.

The wife of an *earl* is a *countess*, of a *viscount*, a *viscountess* and of a *marquis*, a *marchioness*.

ROYALTY House styles vary, but normally one retains the titles of rulers and their consorts at second reference: *King Hussein, Queen Beatrix, Sheik Isa* or *the king, the queen, the sheik*. Titles of other members of the royal family can be dropped on second reference: *Prince Charles*, then *the prince* or, in informal articles, *Charles*. Use Roman numerals in referring to royalty: *Elizabeth II*, not *Elizabeth the Second*.

At present, the Zulu royal family is the only monarchy that is officially recognised in South Africa, although, since the advent of democracy in 1994, other royal households have been asserting their status. Members are referred to by their full names on first reference: *King Goodwill Zweletini*. On second reference, use *the king* or *King Goodwill*, never *King Zweletini*.

Numerals A numeral is a figure, letter, word or group of words that represents a number.

For Arabic numerals, use the figures 1, 2, 3, 4, 5, 6, 7, 8, 9 and 0. Use Arabic forms unless Roman numerals are specifically required.

Roman numerals are capitalised and used for wars and to show personal sequence for people, pedigree animals and boats: *World War I, Queen Elizabeth II, Windchaser III*.

The general rule in journalism is to spell out numbers from one to nine, and to use Arabic numerals for all numbers from 10 upwards. There are exceptions, such as when a number begins a sentence.

Incorrect: *20 students earned distinctions.*

Correct: *Twenty students earned distinctions.*

However, when dealing with large numbers, try to rephrase the sentence.

Incorrect: *Five thousand seven hundred fans attended the match.*

Better: *A total of 5 700 fans attended the match.*

To avoid confusion, write out million and billion: *She earns more than R2 million a year. The company has R3 billion to invest.* Do not link the word and the figures with a hyphen unless you are using a compound adjective: *They have built a 17-million-dollar entertainment complex.*

Check whether precise figures are required; it is not always necessary to write: *Exactly 1 445 346 people visited the Victoria Falls last year.* Rather round off unwieldy figures to two decimal points, with halves rounded up: *Last year, 1,45 million tourists visited the Victoria Falls.*

COLLECTIVE NUMBERS

6   a half dozen/half a dozen
12   a/one dozen (24 is two *dozen* not two *dozens*)
20   a/one score
144 a/one gross

DATES Styles differ from newspaper to newspaper, but the generally preferred style is weekday, month, day of month, and year, with commas to separate the day of the week from the day of the month (*Monday, March 10*), as well as between the date of the month and the year (*July 7, 1976*). Remember that this differs from the date order found on forms in most bureaucratic and commercial institutions in South Africa, so never use *3/5/2005*, for example, as it is not clear whether you are referring to *March 5* or *May 3*. There is no need to write st, *nd*, *rd* or *th* after numerals in dates: *June 23, May 1* and so on are correct.

Include the year only when referring to dates other than the year in which the story is being written. Where appropriate, use the less formal *October next year* or *September last year*, rather than *October 2006* or *September 2004*.

In a daily publication, use days of the week to refer to events of that week, but use the date of the month elsewhere: *The meeting scheduled for Friday has been moved to June 23.* Avoid *The meeting was moved to Thursday, June 23, 1999*; this is overkill.

DIMENSIONS Use figures: *2-by-4 plank.*

FRACTIONS Spell out amounts less than one in stories, using hyphens between words: *two-thirds, three-quarters.* Use figures for amounts larger than one, and convert to decimals if possible: *The baby has gained 8,2 ounces.*

HYPHENS AND COMMAS WITH NUMBERS Some examples are:

Act 1, Scene 3
a 6-year-old boy
R1,02
0,6 per cent
a ratio of 2-to-1
a 3-1 score

PAGES Use figures when referring to page numbers: *p. 1, p. 213.*

SETS Use numbers in sets of numerals when some of the numbers are higher than nine: *The average increased from 8,5 to 12.*

Punctuation

APOSTROPHES Apostrophes are mainly used to indicate possession. Use the normal possessive ending *'s* after singular words or names that end in *s: the boss's car, James's keys.* Use the possessive *'s* after plurals that do not end in *s: children's home, men's ties.*

Use the apostrophe alone on possessive plurals that end in *s – Danes', bosses', workers'.*

Do not use the apostrophe when creating plurals. This includes letters and numbers: *a man in his 40s; an event in the 1990s; she got five As.*

Apostrophes can also be used in certain abbreviations, for e.g. when abbreviating calendar years: *the summer of '69.*

BRACKETS If the whole sentence is within brackets, put the full stop inside.

Square brackets should be used for interpolations in direct quotations: *"Let them [the poor] eat cake."* Using curved brackets implies that the words inside them are part of the original quotation.

COLONS Use to introduce a list or series of facts, names, and so forth, an explanation or summary, usually after an independent clause.

Use as a mark of separation when reporting time, to separate chapter and verse in Bible references, or when giving the title and subtitle of an article, book, play, etc.: *John 3:16; 8:30 am; he is the author of "International media research: a critical survey".*

While colons may be used to introduce direct quotations, reserve this for formal quotations: *He said, "Let's sing"* but *Shakespeare wrote: "To be or not to be."*

A colon can be used to lend emphasis to a point: *She cares about only one thing: fishing.*

In American usage and according to some journalistic styles, the first word after a colon takes a capital, but only if it is a complete sentence: *She agreed to the following: If they filed for divorce, he would get custody of the cat* but *There were less important things to consider too: houses, cars, furniture, savings.*

COMMAS The rules for using commas differ slightly according to who is using them, but their most important function is to clarify things for the reader. Bear in mind that few things can confuse meaning as much as an incorrectly placed comma.

In a list or series, use commas to separate the elements, but do not put a comma before the conjunction: *The flag is red, green, blue, black, white and yellow.* However, use a comma before the concluding conjunction if one of the listed elements takes a conjunction: *They like pasta, pizza, and fish and chips for dinner.*

Commas at the end of a quotation are always placed inside the quotation marks: *"We have to succeed," said the rugby coach.*

Do not include a comma if the quoted statement ends with an exclamation point or question mark: *"What time will you be finished?" she asked.*

Use a comma to indicate cents only when the figure is more than one rand (or dollar, pound, etc.) and if the rand (or other currency) sign is used: *R1,01.*

Use commas to separate a person and his or her address, unless the address is preceded by *of*: *Michael Wofford, 222 Clarkson St*, but *Michael Wofford of 222 Clarkson St.*

Do not place a comma before a verb unless it is the second of a pair of commas. Incorrect: *The man who had been shot, is recovering well.* Correct: *The man who had been shot is recovering well.*

DASHES Use dashes to set off important parenthetical information: *Supporters crowded around the prison entrance, but Rohan – whose name they were chanting – did not appear.* They can often be used where you might otherwise use parentheses or commas. Dashes can also be used for question-and-answer formats; quotation marks then fall away:

Q. – *Where were you?*
A. – *None of your business.*

FULL STOPS A quotation mark is placed outside a full stop at the end of a sentence when only a fragment or partial quotation is used. If the quotation is complete, the full stop is placed inside: *Mr Ismail said that people are "going wild". Mr Ismail said, "People are going wild."*

A full stop can also be placed inside or outside a closing parenthesis, depending on the usage. If the parenthetical phrase is a complete sentence, the full stop goes inside the parenthesis. If it is not a complete sentence, it goes outside: *Karabo took all the dogs to the kennel (except the poodle). Karabo took all the dogs to the kennel. (The cost was R147,50.)*

Use three full stops (ellipsis) to show quoted material has been left out. When a sentence ends and another sentence follows, use a closing period to indicate the full stop and a further three ones to indicate ellipsis (four periods in all): *"Going shopping … exhausts me." "Going shopping exhausts me…. But what can I do?"*

Omit full stops in headlines, subheadings, captions and letters used in a formula.

HYPHENS Hyphenate compound modifiers: *50-year-old woman, old-fashioned singer, well-known drink, so-called hero.*

Use a hyphen with prefixes to proper names: *un-Christian, pre-National Party.*

Use a hyphen when writing figures and fractions: *sixty-nine, three-quarters.*

When a hyphenated title takes an initial capital, capitalise both parts: *Deputy-Director.*

Use single and not double quotation marks in headlines: *Boesak: 'I'm innocent.'*

SEMICOLONS Use to separate lists of names and designations or similar series containing commas: *Among the delegates were Jane Keen, Women's Health Project; Yashmeen Khan, Rape Crisis; and Pumla Sibeko, Child Welfare.*

Semicolons may be used to separate the independent clauses of a compound sentence that are not joined by a coordinating conjunction: *They were young; they were happy.*

In headlines, semicolons are used instead of full stops: *Eight convicts escape; prison guard arrested.*

Communication guidelines

Active voice News is, in essence, about action. Where you can, write about people doing things, not merely being subjected to actions. Take these sentences, for example:

A meeting will be held by the city councillors next week.

The city councillors will meet next week.

The first sentence is written in the passive voice, the second in the active voice. It is simple, really, as John Allen points out (2003:17):

Active: X does Y
Passive: Y is done (by X).

Writing in the active voice helps add action to your writing. Readers prefer it and editors, usually, expect it. A good, but not foolproof, way to check for sentences that use the passive voice is to check for the word *by* – and then rewrite the sentence.

Citing sources (journ.) A basic assumption in journalism is that, unless the reporter is witness to an event or circumstance, the source of information will be cited. Reported sources are, primarily, people and documents. When quoting people directly, place their exact words in quotation marks, describe the source fully and include a form of the verb *to say*: *"I'm great," said 19-year-old Bongani Dube after winning the Mr Clifton 1999 title on Sunday.* In most instances, the neutral *said* or *says* is preferable. Avoid synonyms that may give the impression that you don't believe the speaker, such as *claimed, contended* or *maintained.*

When using a document as a source, describe the document fully (do not use the academic style of citing), name the author of the document and preferably use a form of the verb *to write*: *In a memorandum dated January 10 and addressed to all Cabinet ministers, President Thabo Mbeki wrote, "I'm looking forward to the challenges of the new year"; in his 1993 novel "Killing for comfort", crime author John Smith wrote about the best ways to hide a corpse.*

Euphemism Language used to tone down controversial, painful or graphic topics. The object is to cushion bluntness or soften harshness. There are many examples: *industrial action* instead of *strike, passed away* instead of *died, the birds and the bees* instead of *sexual reproduction.* Euphemisms have their place, and can be usefully employed when writing about inflammatory topics. However, avoid couching reports in euphemistic terms to the point of journalistic dishonesty. Certain official pronouncements, especially on warfare, can be euphemistic to a ridiculous degree.

Good/bad news (journ.) Whether news is good or bad depends on whose perspective you assume. A rise in meat prices may be bad for consumers, but good for farmers. So take care to avoid value-based descriptions, unless attributed to a source. Instead of *the good news is that interest rates will drop*, write *a drop in interest rates is good news for home-owners, but bad news for pensioners living on investments.*

Journalese Consists of jargon and clichés that are particularly loved by journalists; a hackneyed style of writing. Here are some prime examples (the preferred – and often much simpler – words are in parentheses):
amid reports that
burgeoning (growing)
constructed of (made of)
conservative estimate (low, safe)
cutback (cut)
filled to capacity (full)
give consideration to (consider)
have the effect of
hit by fears that
in a bid to hammer out an agreement
in order to (to)
in the light of (because)
lash out
left much to be desired (unsatisfactory)

left people dead/angry/hurt
length of time
looks set to
major (big, large)
massive (big)
meaningful (real, significant)
ok's, okays (approves)
parameters (limits)
probe (inquiry)
reportedly
rocked by
war-torn.
Try to avoid these and similar threadbare phrases.

Obscene words A good basic principle is to refrain from language that would make your grandmother flinch. Obscenities should be avoided, unless used in direct quotations essential to a story. Remember that quoting another person does not protect you from being charged with crimen injuria. House styles differ, but obscene words are usually indicated with either full stops or asterisks corresponding with the number of letters in the words: *f... you, f*** them.* The same method can be used when quoting extremely racist words; check your house style. As words of emphasis, expletives and obscenities quickly lose their impact and become clichés. Try to use original phrases instead.

Spelling Use South African spelling (based on British English spelling) rather than American spelling. *The guide to South African spelling* (Oxford) is a useful tool that also includes names of cities, towns and rivers.

Bibliography

Allen, J. 2003. The BBC news style guide. [Online] Available at: http://www.bbctraining.com/pdfs/newsStyleGuide.pdf [Accessed: 3 October 2004]

Black, J., Steele, B. and Barney, R. 1995. *Doing ethics in journalism*, 2nd edition. Greencastle, Indiana: Allyn & Bacon.

Orwell, S. and Angus, I. eds. 1968. *The collected essays, journalism and letters of George Orwell*, Vol. IV. London: Secker & Warburg.

Schopenhauer, A. 2004. On authorship and style. *Essays of Schopenhauer.* [Online] eBooks@Adeliade. Available at: http://etext.library.adelaide.edu.au/s/schopenhauer/arthur/essays/chapter3.html [Accessed: 03 October 2004]

▓HOT LINK

Online style and writing guides

- BBC News has an excellent, free News Style Guide for journalists: http://www.bbctraining.com/pdfs/newsStyleGuide.pdf
- *The Economist* also has an online style guide: http://www.economist.com/research/StyleGuide/index.cfm
- For online writing style, check out Wired style from *Wired* magazine: http://www.hotwired.com/hardwired/wiredstyle/.
- Strunk's The elements of style [http://www.bartleby.com/141/index.html] and other style guides and writing resources [http://dictionary.reference.com/writing/] can be found at dictionary.com http://dictionary.reference.com/.
- Consult a range of grammar guides at a Web of Online Dictionaries: http://www.yourdictionary.com/grammars.html.
- For an extensive, free and multilingual encyclopaedia (there are Afrikaans entries and space for Xhosa and Zulu ones, too), see Wikipedia at: http://www.wikipedia.org

Index